# Assault Brigade
## THE 18TH AUSTRALIAN INFANTRY BRIGADE IN WORLD WAR II

The Australian Army served in numerous theatres and campaigns throughout World War II, earning distinction and at times facing significant challenges. During the Pacific War, the infantry brigade, as an intermediate formation commanding multiple infantry battalions and numerous attached units, was key in Australian efforts to secure victory.

The 18th Infantry Brigade participated in a variety of combat operations with a range of allies allowing it rare experience among Australian units. Its involvement in operations from Europe to the Middle East and onto the Pacific ensured that it was one of the most modern brigades at the close of the war. In *Assault Brigade*, Matthew E. Miller examines the challenges and development of the Australian Army's 18th Infantry Brigade throughout World War II. He follows the brigade from its inception, initial training and development, to its evolution as a combined amphibious formation. He also investigates a series of campaigns fought across the South West Pacific Area, highlighting lessons learnt and adaptations implemented as a result of each battle.

Written by a Senior Historian with over 30 years of active and reserve service, *Assault Brigade* is essential reading for those interested in Australia's military history.

**Matthew E. Miller** is a Senior Historian at the United States Special Operations Command at MacDill Air Force Base, Florida and is responsible for managing the battlefield historical collection across the enterprise. He has over 30 years of active and reserve service in the United States military and holds degrees from the University of California San Diego, the London School of Economics and a PhD in History from the University of New South Wales, Canberra at the Australian Defence Force Academy.

# OTHER TITLES IN THE AUSTRALIAN ARMY HISTORY SERIES

Series editor: Peter Stanley

A full list of titles in the series can be found at the end of the book.

Cambridge University Press acknowledges the Australian Aboriginal and Torres Strait Islander peoples of this nation. We acknowledge the traditional custodians of the lands on which our company is located and where we conduct our business. We pay our respects to ancestors and Elders, past and present. Cambridge University Press is committed to honouring Australian Aboriginal and Torres Strait Islander peoples' unique cultural and spiritual relationships to the land, waters and seas and their rich contribution to society.

# ASSAULT BRIGADE

THE 18TH AUSTRALIAN INFANTRY
BRIGADE IN WORLD WAR II

MATTHEW E. MILLER

# CAMBRIDGE UNIVERSITY PRESS

Shaftesbury Road, Cambridge CB2 8EA, United Kingdom

One Liberty Plaza, 20th Floor, New York, NY 10006, USA

477 Williamstown Road, Port Melbourne, VIC 3207, Australia

314–321, 3rd Floor, Plot 3, Splendor Forum, Jasola District Centre, New Delhi – 110025, India

103 Penang Road, #05–06/07, Visioncrest Commercial, Singapore 238467

Cambridge University Press is part of Cambridge University Press & Assessment, a department of the University of Cambridge.

We share the University's mission to contribute to society through the pursuit of education, learning and research at the highest international levels of excellence.

www.cambridge.org
Information on this title: www.cambridge.org/9781009431811

© Matthew E. Miller 2024

This publication is copyright. Subject to statutory exception and to the provisions of relevant collective licensing agreements, no reproduction of any part may take place without the written permission of Cambridge University Press & Assessment.

First published 2024

Cover designed by Anne-Marie Reeves

A catalogue record for this publication is available from the British Library

A catalogue record for this book is available from the National Library of Australia

ISBN 978-1-009-43181-1 Hardback

**Reproduction and communication for educational purposes**
The Australian *Copyright Act 1968* (the Act) allows a maximum of one chapter or 10% of the pages of this work, whichever is the greater, to be reproduced and/or communicated by any educational institution for its educational purposes provided that the educational institution (or the body that administers it) has given a remuneration notice to Copyright Agency Limited (CAL) under the Act.

For details of the CAL licence for educational institutions contact:

Copyright Agency Limited
Level 12, 66 Goulburn Street
Sydney NSW 2000
Telephone: (02) 9394 7600
Facsimile: (02) 9394 7601
E-mail: memberservices@copyright.com.au

**Reproduction and communication for other purposes**
Except as permitted under the Act (for example a fair dealing for the purposes of study, research, criticism or review) no part of this publication may be reproduced, stored in a retrieval system, communicated or transmitted in any form or by any means without prior written permission. All inquiries should be made to the publisher at the address above.

Cambridge University Press & Assessment has no responsibility for the persistence or accuracy of URLs for external or third-party internet websites referred to in this publication and does not guarantee that any content on such websites is, or will remain, accurate or appropriate.

The views expressed in this book are those of the author and not necessarily those of the Australian Army or the Department of Defence. The Commonwealth of Australia will not be legally responsible in contract, tort or otherwise for any statement made in this book.

For my wife, Michelle.

# Contents

| | |
|---|---|
| Figures and maps | viii |
| Preface | xi |
| Acknowledgements | xiii |
| Abbreviations | xiv |
| Map legend | xvi |
| Introduction | 1 |
| 1 An introduction to the brigade | 6 |
| 2 The long road to the SWPA | 28 |
| 3 The Battle of Milne Bay | 48 |
| 4 The Battle of Buna | 68 |
| 5 Rebuilding the 18th Infantry Brigade | 96 |
| 6 The Battle of Shaggy Ridge | 113 |
| 7 Amphibious warfare doctrine | 136 |
| 8 Amphibious exercises and rehearsals | 155 |
| 9 The assault brigade | 173 |
| 10 Conclusion | 203 |
| Notes | 218 |
| Bibliography | 249 |
| Index | 262 |

# Figures and Maps

## Figures

2.1 The 2/10th Infantry Battalion at Lupcombe Corner, Salisbury Plain, after being deployed to assist in the defence of England from a potential German invasion — 29

2.2 Soldiers of the 18th Infantry Brigade as they departed Mersa Matruh, Libya, to cross the desert for the assault on the Italian garrison at Giarabub — 32

2.3 The village of Giarabub with the Senoussi Mosque in the background on the day of the Italian garrison's surrender to the 18th Infantry Brigade, 21 March 1941 — 35

2.4 Troops of the 2/10th Infantry Battalion in Tobruk taking a break in the rear after their time successfully holding the line under assault by the Afrika Korps — 40

3.1 Troops walk past the two Japanese Type 95 Ha-Go light tanks used in the attack on the Allied base at Milne Bay — 54

4.1 The 18th Infantry Brigade, supported by armour, conduct the final assaults of the Buna campaign at Giropa Point — 79

4.2 Private Searle and Corporal Fletcher of the 2/12th Infantry Battalion fire on Japanese soldiers 150 yards away with a Bren Mark 1 machine gun and SMLE No. 1 MKIII rifle at Giropa Point — 81

4.3 Australian infantry and armour advance in the wake of the devastation of 18th Infantry Brigade's final assault of the Sanananda campaign in Papua — 86

4.4 General George Vasey, General Edmund Herring and Brigadier George Wootten in Papua after the hard-fought victories of the Buna and Sanananda campaigns — 92

5.1 Soldiers negotiate a river crossing with explosions all around at the Australian Training Centre (Jungle Warfare) at Canungra, Queensland 105
5.2 The 18th Brigade Intelligence Section studies maps of the area during clean-up operations in Balikpapan 109
6.1 A wounded soldier of the 2/9th Infantry Battalion is carefully carried down the ridgeline by stretcher-bearers after being injured during the reconnaissance of Japanese positions on 'Green Sniper's Pimple' 115
6.2 Troops of the 2/9th Infantry Battalion prepare for the assault on Shaggy Ridge 122
6.3 'A' Company, 2/9th Infantry Battalion, dig fighting positions high in the Finisterre Range after its assault, along with indirect fire and close air support, and drove the Japanese back to the next stronghold at Kankiryo Saddle 124
6.4 'A' Company, 2/9th Infantry Battalion occupy a knife's-edge ridge line on 23 February 1944 in preparation for the assault on Kankiryo Saddle three days later 128
7.1 Landing craft come alongside USS *Conningham* to take ashore the soldiers of the 9th Australian Division headquarters as part of Operation Postern at Lae 142
7.2 Brigadier Frederick Chilton, Commander of the 18th Infantry Brigade, at Trinity Beach, North Queensland, during the brigade's introduction to large-scale amphibious warfare training in 1944 152
8.1 Soldiers of the 2/12th Infantry Battalion assault the beach as part of the brigade's first large-scale amphibious exercise, Exercise Octopus 162
8.2 Troops of the 2/12th Infantry Battalion on Morotai staged for embarkation on the US Navy Landing Craft 171
9.1 Landing diagram with wave guide 178
9.2 Landing diagram, 18th Australian Infantry Brigade 180
9.3 Troops of the 2/10th Infantry Battalion board Landing Craft Infantry on Morotai for the last large-scale amphibious assault of World War II 188

9.4 Landing craft filled with soldiers of the 18th Infantry Brigade watch Balikpapan's oil tanks burn as they circle in preparation for the final line-up into assault waves — 190

9.5 On the crowded beachhead at Balikpapan, soldiers of the 18th Infantry Brigade coordinate with a US Army Land Vehicle – Tracked for the push inland — 192

9.6 Soldiers of the 18th Infantry Brigade on Red Beach coordinate with US Army Landing Vehicles – Tracked and the 1st Armoured Regiment for the assault on Parramatta Ridge and Hill 87 — 196

10.1 Soldiers of B Company, 2/12th Infantry Battalion pause on the high ground forward of the beachhead at Balikpapan — 212

## Maps

1.1 Italian defences at the village of Giarabub, December 1940 — 16
1.2 The assault on Giarabub, 19 March 1940 — 17
2.1 Tobruk Defence, April 1941 — 36
2.2 The Battle of the Salient, May 1941 — 38
3.1 The Battle of Milne Bay, 24 August 1942 — 52
3.2 The Battle of Milne Bay, 28 August 1942 — 58
3.3 The Battle of Milne Bay, 5 September 1942 — 61
4.1 The Battle of Buna, December 1942 – January 1943 — 69
4.2 Sanananda Campaign, January 1943 — 85
6.1 The Battle of Shaggy Ridge, January – February 1944 — 117
9.1 Amphibious landing at Balikpapan. Although landings were planned for three separate beaches, confusion led the majority of the force landing on Red Beach, July 1945 — 191

# Preface

The Australian Army has a long and admirable record in fostering serious research and publication about its history. From the outset 'Military History' was part of the formal education of staff cadets at RMC Duntroon, and for a time officers' promotion depended upon candidates being able to analyse Stonewall Jackson's Shenandoah Valley campaign in promotion exams. An understanding of the Army's history and traditions remans central to its esprit de corps in its most literal meaning, and historical study has a utility in foreseeing and fulfilling the Army's roles in an uncertain world.

Since the 1970s (as a consequence of educating officers at university level), the Army has produced several generations of educated soldiers, several of whom became historians of note. The pioneers included John Coates, Robert O'Neill, David Horner, John Blaxland, Peter Pedersen, John Mordike and Bob Hall. Their successors include Jean Bou, Bob Stevenson, Garth Pratten and Craig Stockings (either as regulars or reservists). Several of them have written books published in the Australian Army History Series. The creation of an Australian Army History Unit in the 1990s demonstrated the Army's commitment to encouraging and facilitating serious history within and about the Army.

One of the most impressive demonstrations of the Army's dedication to history has been its long association with several major publishers, and notably with Cambridge University Press. This has been a productive relationship, initially brokered by Dr Roger Lee, the long-term head of the Army History Unit, and my predecessor as General Editor, Professor David Horner. Roger's successor as head of the Army History Unit, Tim Gellel, a former member of the Australian Intelligence Corps, is continuing and indeed extending that relationship, giving the Army, and the nation that sustains it, the history they both need.

The Cambridge Australian Army History Series brings to a professional, academic and popular readership historical work of importance across the range of the Army's interests and across the span of its history.

The series seeks to publish research and writing of the highest quality relating not only to the Army's operational experience, but also to its existence as an organisation and to its contribution to the nation. It is a history to be proud of in every sense.

Dr Matt Miller's *Assault Brigade* is a product of two long-standing relationships in the study of Australian military history. The first is the commitment to military history manifested by UNSW Canberra (at the Australian Defence Force Academy, and before that at the Royal Military College, Duntroon). In addition to their own publications, many of which relate to the history of the Australian Army, its academic historians have supervised dozens of theses, many of which become the basis of books, including works in the Army History Series. *Assault Brigade* is also a product of that process, in a doctoral thesis supervised by Dr Eleanor Handcock and Professor Emeritus Peter Dennis. The other relationship this book highlights is the close association that has long existed between academic and public historians and the Australian Army History Unit. For over thirty years, historians have been integral to the unit's (and therefore largely the Army's) sustained relationship with its history. The results of that contact include a long series of conferences, at which Australian Defence Force and civilian experts met, and several series of books, each meeting the needs of various readerships, and including works in this the Army History Series. *Assault Brigade* is a fine exemplar of that productive relationship in that it explores and explains the experience of the Second AIF's 18th Brigade in the largely amphibious operations in the South-West Pacific upon which the Army's enduring expertise in littoral warfare was based. The Army naturally hopes that such an account may capture (or re-capture) useful experience and lessons. Historians merely hope to understand better the character and quality of the Australian Army in the campaigns of 1943–45, its largest operations ever. Both aims are satisfied by this book, a further demonstration of the long-standing, productive and harmonious collaboration between the Army and academic history.

Since his graduation, Dr Miller (an American by birth) has gone on to serve as an historian with the United States Army, continuing to inform its understanding and practice by doing history in the field and on the spot in recent commitments overseas, again confirming the value and utility of history to the profession of arms.

Peter Stanley, FAHA
*General Editor, Australian Army History Series*
*Hon. Prof., UNSW Canberra*

# Acknowledgements

In transitioning this work into a book, I owe a debt of gratitude to Professor Peter Stanley, General Editor, Australian Army History Series, my anonymous publisher's readers, and the staff at the Australian Army History Unit.

A special thanks is necessary for my doctoral advisors Professor Craig Stockings, Emeritus Professor Peter Dennis, and Associate Professor Eleanor Hancock. Without them this book would not have come to fruition.

# Abbreviations

| | |
|---|---|
| AACS | Australian Army Cooperation Squadron |
| AAMC | Australian Army Medical Corps |
| AAOC | Australian Army Ordnance Corps |
| AASC | Australian Army Service Corps |
| ACP | Air Controller Party |
| AIF | Australian Imperial Force |
| ALC | Australian Landing Craft |
| ALO | Air Liaison Officer |
| ALP | Air Liaison Party |
| ANGAU | Australian New Guinea Administrative Unit |
| ATI | Allied Translator and Interpreter |
| AWM | Australian War Memorial |
| BM | Brigade Major |
| CMF | Citizen Military Force |
| D | Day |
| FLEX | Fleet Training Exercise |
| FLP | Fleet Training Publication |
| FM | Field Manual |
| GHQ | General Headquarters |
| H | Hour |
| HMAS | His/Her Majesty's Australian Ship |
| HQ | Headquarters |
| LAD | Light Aid Detachment |
| LCI | Landing Craft Infantry |
| LCVP | Landing Craft Vehicle Personnel |
| LHQ | (Australian) Land Force Headquarters |
| LSI | Landing Ship Infantry |

| | |
|---|---|
| LST | Landing Ship Tank |
| LVT | Landing Vehicle Tracked |
| NCO | Non-Commission Officer |
| PE | Peace Establishment |
| PIB | Papuan Infantry Battalion |
| RAAF | Royal Australian Air Force |
| RAN | Royal Australian Navy |
| SC | Staff Captain |
| SFCP | Shore Fire Control Party |
| SNFL | Special Naval Landing Forced |
| SWPA | South West Pacific Area |
| TEWT | Training Exercise Without Troops |
| WE | War Establishment |
| WWI | World War I |
| WWII | World War II |

# Map legend

- Artillery
- Infantry
- Cavalry/Reconnaissance
- Motorised infantry
- Armoured
- Armoured transport
- Marine
- Signals
- Detachment
- Section
- Platoon
- I Company
- II Battalion
- III Regiment
- x Brigade
- xx Division
- xxx Corps
- xxxx Army
- xxxxx Army Group

- Defensive Machine Gun Placement
- Defensive Positions
- Military Land Movement
- Military Naval Movement
- Proposed Military Movement
- Military Boundary
- Perimeter Fence line
- Front Line
- Trench
- Communication Lines
- Anti-tank Trench
- Barbed Wire
- Bunker
- Tank
- Tracked APC
- Tracked APC Maintenance
- Tracked APC Medium Mortar
- Airfield
- Fuel facility
- Medical or RAP facility
- Helipad
- Ammunition facility
- Military Pier

- Friendlies and Allies
- Enemy
- Area of Occupation or Operations
- Battleground

MAP LEGEND        xvii

- City
- Farm
- North
- Track/Unsealed Road
- Road/Highway
- Airport
- Pipeline
- Highway Number
- Road Number
- Operational Rail
- Non-Operational Rail
- Under Construction Rail
- Major Port
- Minor Port
- Pier
- Bridge

- Brush
- Forest
- Jungle
- Plantation
- Grassland
- Paddy
- Marshland
- Swamp
- Coral Reef
- Sand Dune/Wadi
- Mountain Peak
- Large Body of Water
- River/Canal
- Creek

COUNTRY NAME

DISTRICT/PROVINCE NAME

City

*Water feature*

*Mountain Feature*

# Introduction

The Australian Army served in numerous theatres and campaigns throughout World War II, earning distinction and at times facing significant challenges. After Australia declared war on Germany on 3 September 1939, Australians deployed and served in combined Allied armies in Europe, North Africa, the Middle East and Asia.[1] Conversely, the Australian Army made up the bulk of Allied ground forces in the South West Pacific Area (SWPA) during the Japanese push south in the months following the attack on Pearl Harbor. After the consolidation of their initial advances, the Japanese extended their area of control and established a perimeter line of defence from the Aleutians in the north to the Gilbert and Marshalls in the south. In 1942–43, Australian troops carried the bulk of responsibility in the fight against the Imperial Japanese Army and Navy in a gruelling battle for the island of New Guinea. Thus, by 1943, the Australian Army was the most experienced Allied force in the Pacific.

The infantry brigade, as an intermediate formation commanding multiple infantry battalions and numerous attached units, was key to Australian efforts to secure victory in New Guinea and Borneo during the Pacific War. The jungles, mountains and – most important for amphibious warfare – the size of the beaches on the islands of the SWPA constrained the ability of both corps and divisions to conduct combat operations as complete formations. Nowhere in the SWPA was there terrain akin to the deserts of North Africa, which allowed for corps to manoeuvre freely, or the long, open beaches of Normandy, which enabled divisions to come ashore intact. The complex terrain of the

SWPA islands, which is sometimes constrained and at times isolated the brigades, offered these intermediate formations the opportunity to operate as a brigade.

It must be noted that this is not a traditional unit history but a history of an infantry brigade and its components, as it evolved to meet the challenges of World War II. The 18th Infantry Brigade was not unique among Australian brigades; other Australian infantry brigades had similar experiences with modernisation and the evolution of the brigade, but few, if any, had the diversity of experience in combat operations and Allied cooperation. The 18th Brigade, veterans of Tobruk in North Africa, participated in operations spanning the length of the Australian campaigns in the SWPA theatre, often operating as the 7th Division's spearhead. These circumstances of the SWPA led brigades to become more flexible and to adopt numerous combat functions previously handled at the division level. The result was an evolution of brigades into highly lethal combined arms formations.

In total, Australia met the Japanese challenge in the Pacific by raising 32 separate infantry brigades.[2] These brigades included militia and Australian Imperial Force formations that served in roles ranging from desert and jungle warfare to domestic defence against a possible Japanese invasion. The Australian brigades that fought in North Africa, for example, acted in large-scale desert warfare where the division or the corps was the key manoeuvre element, not the smaller brigade.[3]

The Japanese landed on New Guinea on 8 March 1942, threatening the isolation of Australia or, as it was initially feared, a possible invasion of the Australian homeland. However, the dense unforgiving terrain of New Guinea would prove to be 'an island too far' for the Imperial Japanese Army and Navy.[4] Poor intelligence and unrealistic expectations led the Japanese ground forces onto the Kokoda Track, arguably some of the most complex jungle and mountain terrain in the world.[5] Japanese forces on New Guinea suffered from disease, problems with mobility, and disastrously long lines of communication.[6] The Australian formations, which moved to counter the Japanese on the Kokoda Track, suffered from many of the same challenges in the Owen Stanley Range, which rises 4000 metres from the sea. In this highly constrained environment, the brigade had limited functional control of combat operations. Therefore the battle of the Kokoda Track was a battle of squads and companies as the key formations, not the infantry brigade.

In early 1943, the Australians forced the Japanese from the Kokoda Track. The Japanese endeavoured to reinforce their position on the northern coast of New Guinea in the hope that a strategic defensive ring could hold previous gains now that the goal of isolating Australia was lost. The northern coast of New Guinea, some 1600 miles long, with its complex terrain of jungles, mountains, coastal plains and harbours, made the brigade the most functional formation of manoeuvre.

The campaigns of New Guinea in 1942 and 1943 offered the first opportunity to look at the 18th Australian Infantry Brigade in the SWPA. The challenges of the campaigns in North Africa and the SWPA required Australian brigades to evolve in the areas of technology, command and administration to confront the often more experienced Japanese forces. This would become the template for both Australian and US brigades and regiments throughout the rest of the war.

The operations of the 18th Infantry Brigade offer the opportunity to examine the Australian infantry brigade and its various configurations throughout World War II. One instrumental factor in the success of any unit at any echelon of war is its commander. Early in World War II, many of the officers selected to command Australian infantry brigades had served in World War I.[7] This provided them with experience in command and organisation, but many of these experienced commanders were removed before the end of the 1942 owing to age, the challenges of jungle fighting and the complicated nature of modern warfare.

A new generation of brigade commanders emerged during the latter half of the Pacific War. Officers who led infantry brigades were challenged by the most complex form of warfare the Australian Army had ever experienced. Across the Pacific islands, such men were responsible not only for combat manoeuvre but also for the coordination of large brigade staffs, artillery, naval surface gunfire, close air support and amphibious landings in arguably the most difficult terrain of World War II.

One of the many staff functions in the infantry brigade is that of intelligence, which might have been one of the most difficult tasks in the SWPA.[8] The purpose of the brigade staff Intelligence Section is to provide the brigade commander with accurate, timely and relevant information on enemy troop strength, capabilities and potential courses of action in the commander's area of responsibility. The role of a brigade's Intelligence Section certainly evolved in areas of intelligence training, battlefield collection and intelligence-sharing with higher and subordinate commands. In addition to accurate and timely intelligence for the commander, the brigade Intelligence Section had to be able to disseminate intelligence to subordinate battalions before and during combat operations.

Infantry brigade tactics evolved significantly after the Australian divisions returned from North Africa and transitioned to jungle and amphibious warfare in the Pacific. Command and control of subordinate battalions during amphibious operations in jungles and over mountainous terrain pose significant challenges to any echelon of leadership. Leadership of subordinate combat units in complex terrain compounded by up to 300 inches of rain a year offered special challenges for the Australian Army in the SWPA.

The latter campaigns in New Guinea and the introduction of the US Army and Navy to the SWPA offered the 18th Infantry Brigade new technological advances in naval surface gunfire and close air support not available or practical for brigades in North Africa and on the Kokoda Track. This offered new challenges for the brigade commander and staff to coordinate not only brigade artillery but also naval gunfire and close air support. In the Borneo campaign, during the landing at the port city of Balikpapan, for example, naval gunfire and air support were used to facilitate the assault brigade's movement ashore. In battles at Shaggy Ridge, the 18th had the combined benefit of artillery and close air support in their efforts to dislodge mountaintop Japanese defensive positions.

In the period 1942–45, the Australian infantry brigade became a key formation responsible for the execution of amphibious warfare in the Australian areas of responsibility. Despite the infantry brigade's role in amphibious operations, often considered one of the most complex endeavours in 20th-century warfare, the Australian brigade's familiarity with and expertise in this method of fighting has not been examined in significant depth. Amphibious landings enabled the Australian Army to avoid long and difficult ground marches across jungle islands.[9] Such marches exposed troops to fatigue, disease and the enemy while the commander attempted to manoeuvre the brigade into positions of tactical and logistical advantage against Japanese formations.

The 18th Infantry Brigade conducted several amphibious operations in the SWPA. These included the first offensive amphibious raid since Gallipoli with a company-reinforced landing on Normanby Island, another amphibious raid of battalion strength on Goodenough Island, and finally a brigade-reinforced amphibious assault on Balikpapan.

In World War I, the British transitioned to the triangular division reducing the division from four to three brigades, while Australian divisions were established as triangle divisions. Subsequently, in World War II, the British and Australians further reduced the size of the brigade from four to three battalions. Conversely, the US Army did not transition from square division until it was on the precipice of World War II. After that transition, US divisions consisted of brigades of three regiments. In comparison, the US brigade was roughly the size of an Australian division, with each organic US regiment similar in size to an Australian infantry brigade.

The role of the brigade in the SWPA is important to understanding the Australian Army's contributions to World War II. By moving beyond the question of what the 18th Australian Infantry Brigade did in the SWPA and into an examination of how the brigade was structured and functioned, and how it applied operational art, there can be a more accurate investigation of the brigade's contributions to the victory over Japan. This book captures the experiences and lessons learnt from a classic intermediate military formation thrust into the enormous learning curve of modern warfare.

CHAPTER 1

# AN INTRODUCTION TO THE BRIGADE

> In order to take on the Japanese Army, with any hope of success, forces must be trained up to high standards of toughness, fighting efficiency, adaptability, discipline and morale.
> 
> 18th Australian Infantry Brigade, Intelligence Summary[1]

Throughout the course of the Pacific War, Australian infantry brigades faced monumental challenges in the SWPA, not only from the terrain and from the enemy but also owing to a rapid evolution of tactics and technologies within these intermediate formations. With time and experience, brigades evolved from rudimentary beginnings into expeditionary forces, incorporating hitherto unfamiliar attached elements, support arms and modes of transportation, all while fighting their way across the SWPA. The Australian infantry brigades adapted from formations established on World War I doctrinal, operational and tactical principles into those using more 'modern' organisational techniques and structures. Such an analysis must include a brief examination of the state of these formations at the onset of the war in terms of historical legacies, 'orders of battle' and to a limited degree the raw material in terms of manpower represented by Australian brigades at this early stage. One particularly important aspect of this analysis is the key transition of several formations between 1942 and 1945 from 'standard' Australian infantry brigades to 'Infantry Brigade Groups (Jungle)' and finally to 'Infantry Brigade Groups (Jungle)' designated as amphibious 'Assault Brigades'.[2]

## The Origins of the Brigade

Japanese army and naval forces demonstrated a high level of proficiency in expeditionary warfare during their rapid expansion across the SWPA from late 1941. The Australian Army, which had been starved of resources during the interwar period, had a strong tradition and philosophy of citizen soldiery fitting into larger allied organisations as required. Its youth, its hollowness and ageing officer corps placed it in a particularly weak position in 1939 for independent, expeditionary operations. There was history to such weakness. For example, John Moremon noted that 'in August 1914, Australia possessed no military organisation larger than a brigade and when its offer to raise and equip a division was accepted by Britain, the dominion had to create this force from scratch'.[3] From this point, the Australian Army only had 25 years of division-level experience before the onset of World War II. Moreover, it was once more a shallow type of peacetime experience.

The part-time officers and men of the interwar Citizen Military Forces may have been ordered to form brigades and divisions, but they certainly never trained as such, even in terms of realistic staff duties, let alone in an operational context. When the 18th Australian Infantry Brigade was raised as part of the 6th Infantry Division in October 1939, it was one of the first three brigades of a second Australian Imperial Force (AIF). Sergeant Owen Curtis, a soldier of the 18th Australian Infantry Brigade who had volunteered at the start of the war and would earn a commission at Buna, commented: 'It was amazing the number of returned men, 1914–1918 war that went away with us.'[4]

In 1939, the average age of an Australian infantry battalion commander was 51, an age many considered too advanced for the rigours of infantry combat. Nevertheless, seniority and longevity led much of the interwar promotion cycle in the Australian Army.[5] Moreover, senior 2nd AIF officers had considerable influence in promotions: they stuck with men they knew and rewarded old militia connections and friendships. During the interwar period, the regular promotion cycle was officers moving up one position after another until they reached brigade major, an officer who served as the operations officer and supervised the brigade intelligence officer and Intelligence Section. A successful tour as brigade major could lead to a future battalion command. This practice and the ages it tended to engender among CMF commanding officers was at odds with a general belief in both the Australian and United States armies: officers over 50 years old could not handle the rigours of leading line combat units.⁶ Subsequently, when experiences of battle began to affirm such concerns, both armies actively looked to retire these ageing officers thereby making room for a younger generation.⁷ As the war progressed, promotions for brigade in combat were based on combat proficiency (and often disease-related vacancies), not longevity. One Australian officer in the 18th Brigade recalled after the war an incident in which his company commander was injured during combat. As the senior lieutenant, he took command and led the company through the fight. 'I got through it without being wounded myself,' he recalled, 'so I just kept the company and the next thing I knew I was promoted to captain.'⁸

Garth Pratten argues that the strength of the Australian CMF in the 1930s was in part largely due to the service of World War I veteran officers and non-commissioned officers who had stayed in the force during the interwar period.⁹ This is true in the sense that it maintained the day-to-day organisation and institutional memory of the army. Few of these leaders, however, would prove capable of adapting to the highly complex nature of war in the SWPA. Indeed, most would not maintain their position long enough to have the opportunity. Senior Allied leadership in both the Australian and United States armies shared the same perspective on ageing veterans serving in combat infantry units, and active efforts were made to remove them from leadership positions. General George C. Marshall, US Army Chief of Staff, estimated that he forced out some 600 officers for issues including age before the United States entered World War II.¹⁰ Another common and problematic aspect of interwar service was the lack of career mobility. In the 2/12th Infantry Battalion, for example, some former CMF soldiers had been privates for almost a decade. This was another shared issue between Australian brigades and US regiments, especially those drawn from a 'reserve' status.¹¹

To shift the perspective from manpower to the organisational structure, in the interwar period, both Australia and the United States experienced similar reorganisations of their respective armies. The rapidly evolving field of combined arms operations, which focused on the integration of supporting fire and air support in infantry manoeuvre, was a priority.¹² During this period, however, the Australian Army fell behind other Allied forces with poorly funded and very limited technological advancement. Subsequently, Australian infantry brigades would be forced to pass through two major periods of change on the eve of and during World War II. First was the reorganisation of the infantry brigade to a modern motorised formation.¹³ Second was the integration of infantry, armour and artillery in close cooperation – for the Australians, a practice that was first tested in North Africa at the Battle of Bardia.[14]

In 1938, in response to growing global instability, Major General Ernest Squires, a former British officer and inspector general of the Australian Army, released a report on the Australian Army's 'readiness' to undertake significant military operations.[15] The report identified serious shortcomings and made numerous recommendations, including increasing the size, funding and training of the force as a whole. Thus, and in the context of a rapidly deteriorating international strategic circumstance, the Australian Government doubled the Australian Imperial Force's budget and size of the militia.[16] However, expansion, in and of itself, was not transformative. The actual transformation of the Australian Army would largely happen in the combat experiences and lessons learnt by the infantry brigades that faced the Japanese in the SWPA.

## Training and mobilisation 1939–41

Later chapters will examine the development and application of advanced infantry and expeditionary capabilities of the Australian infantry brigades from 1942 to 1945. However, to conduct such an analysis, it is important to review the baseline capabilities and training (or lack of training) of the Australian infantry brigade at the point of initial mobilisation before the deployment to North Africa and New Guinea. An examination of the 18th Infantry Brigade's initial training and the training that followed its return from North Africa demonstrates a focus on the immediate task at hand: the defence of the continent against a Japanese invasion.

The 18th Infantry Brigade 'stood up' with the activation of the Second Australian Imperial Force on 13 October 1939. Training was a challenge from the outset, with a lack of proper equipment, stores of the wrong equipment, and doctrine written for another war. On 24 January 1940, the brigade published its second (and first substantive) training memorandum. The document focused heavily on training for company movement based on the World War I experience of its veterans. It stressed a number of standard skills, such as patrolling and defensive positions. It also included instructions for maintaining horses and for conducting 'trench raids'.[17] Ironically, while outwardly anachronistic by focusing on combat experiences from past wars rather than the one at hand, many of the individual soldier skills, such as use of gas masks, digging fighting positions, defence against Armoured Fighting Vehicles (AFV), and even classic trench warfare, would later prove useful. This was also in spite of the fact that a jungle war in New Guinea could not be further from the Western Front of World War I.[18] Training for 'trench raid', for example, would seem impractical until faced with the complex trench fortifications of the Japanese in late 1942 at Buna.[19]

The new recruits and ageing veterans who formed the 18th Infantry Brigade (with considerably fewer former CMF personnel than Army authorities had hoped) that was deployed to Britain and North Africa in January 1941 had all experienced different basic and unit training during their mobilisation in Australia. This is due to the Australian Army's policy of permitting local training units to provide basic training for new recruits.[20] This was a practice that later would be found insufficient for modern war.[21] The 18th Australian Brigade, for example, was activated as part of the 6th Australian Division on 13 October 1939 and consisted of soldiers from Queensland. Its sister brigades within the 6th Division were drawn in the same manner. The 17th Brigade was raised from Victoria and the 16th Brigade from New South Wales.[22] With no standardised army-wide basic training program, this meant that troops were competent or incompetent on the basis of their brigade's training program.[23] As the war progressed, losses to disease and combat forced the infantry brigade to take in replacements. Poorly trained replacements, who arrived at the front lines during the early campaigns of New Guinea in 1943, resulted in the demand from battlefield commanders for standardised basic training centrally supervised by Land Headquarters back in Australia.[24] As the 18th Infantry Brigade would learn after the Buna campaign, combat formations did not have the time to retrain soldiers in basic skills at the unit level.

In early 1943, complaints from the commanders in New Guinea resulted in an Australian Army review of basic training units across the country, something that would be essential for standardisation of specialty training.[25] The review revealed that very few officers or non-commissioned officers then serving within training units had any experience in modern combat tactics or jungle warfare.[26] Army authorities decided on two courses of action. First, in November 1943, all recruit training was consolidated at the Australian Recruit Training Centre at Cowra, New South Wales, to ensure a standard level of basic training across the force. For the first time, this consolidation also allowed the army to provide all service members a central aptitude test and assignment to service branches on the basis of their ability.[27] Second, the army ordered deployed combat units to send experienced officers and non-commissioned officers back to Australia to serve as instructors.[28] As one would expect, the second initiative was less successful owing to the reluctance of brigade and battalion commanders to reassign their best officers and non-commissioned officers during a campaign. The Directorate of Military Training noted that the difficulty of acquiring experienced and competent combat instructors was not solved until the drawdown in overall army numbers in 1945, which resulted in a surplus of returning officers and non-commissioned officers.[29]

When the 18th Australian Infantry Brigade arrived in North Africa, it began another phase of reorganisation. Australian infantry brigades reduced the number of subordinate battalions respectively from four to three with the loss of 864 authorised positions.[30] The artillery realignment consisted of a move from 'three brigades of four batteries, each with four guns, to three regiments of two batteries each of twelve guns'.[31] Unlike the infantry brigade who lost guns, the overall number of guns within the division was not therefore reduced. This change in doctrine came from an interwar belief of most modern armies that in the mobile context of a modern war, an infantry commander could effectively manage only three subordinate elements at any given echelon.

## Australian Army 'Jungle' Units

The Australian Army's effort to adapt infantry formations to the complex jungle environment represents one of the most significant challenges to infantry organisations in World War II. The lessons learnt in the first jungle campaigns of 1942, although costly, established new tactical and operational requirements for Allied formations that would become jungle doctrine. An analysis of the after-action reports of the 18th Infantry Brigade in the early engagement of Milne Bay reveal this brigade's significant contribution to the development of jungle infantry tactics. It is also clear that Allied generalship in both the Australian and US armies made assumptions about jungle warfare that would prove disastrous for the 18th Infantry Brigade in the hard-won victory at Buna and Sanananda. The value of the 18th Infantry Brigade's contribution to the development of new tactics and doctrine would shine in the striking victories on Shaggy Ridge in 1944 and its amphibious assault on Balikpapan in 1945.

In 1942, Australian Land Force Headquarters initiated the development of jungle divisions. The need for formations capable of operating in jungle terrain was forgone; however, the force structure of these divisions was destined to change with each lesson learnt. A major transition of division organisational structures was a challenge, given that just a year earlier the same divisions underwent a modernisation along the British division's highly motorised model. Infantry manoeuvre in North Africa was generally mobile, and the majority of the training and exercises at the brigade and division level were for a motorised defence or assault.[32] The influence of the British model and North African combat was apparent in the Australian Army's training requirements even after the recall of all but the 9th Division from North Africa in February 1942 to face the Japanese threat.[33]

The Australian Army's first foray into the jungle was the hard-fought campaign over the Kokoda Track, which established a baseline for operations in the mountains and jungles of New Guinea. However, it was the 18th Infantry Brigade's after-action reports of the Battle of Milne Bay and the Buna campaign that helped advance the army's long, convoluted path to jungle divisions and subsequently jungle brigades. LHQ decided to reorganise the 5th, 6th, 7th and 11th Divisions into jungle divisions in late 1942 on the basis of these early experiences in New Guinea.[34] First, however, the army needed to draft new 'establishments' for the jungle division. Such establishments outlined in specific terms the authorised personnel and equipment of a given unit or formation during peacetime or war. Before mobilisation, Australian units under Peace Establishments were considerably smaller and less well equipped than that of a unit in 1943 under War Establishments. On 13 February 1943, jungle establishments were published for the Australian Army.

The implementation of the 'jungle division' was based on three principles established by LHQ. First, the new divisions would need to be able to add and subtract non-organic or Allied units quickly with limited integration time. The second principle was 'all units, subunits, transportation and equipment which are not essential for general operations in jungle conditions [were to be] eliminated from the jungle organisation'.[35] The third principle was the consolidation of transport and support elements at a division level. Restructured in early 1943, these selected units were now officially jungle divisions. However, the effort to develop the perfect combination of personnel and equipment would continue for the duration of World War II.

## First principle: flexible grouping

The infantry's inability to manoeuvre in jungle terrain with heavy equipment was key to the first jungle reorganisation; however, theatre mobility was equally, if not more, important in subsequent reviews. The SWPA required intermediate Allied combat formations to be able to move quickly, not only in dense jungle but also by sea and air with effective combat power. On 22 October 1942, the 18th Infantry Brigade conducted a battalion-size amphibious landing on Goodenough Island with just a few days notice.[36] On 2 October 1942, the 2/10th Battalion of the 18th Brigade was the first Australian infantry battalion wholly airlifted into a combat zone ready to fight on the airstrip if necessary.[37] These early, high-mobility combat operations, both of which will be discussed in later chapters, demonstrated that a brigade's ability to move rapidly in theatre would be equally important to its ability to move in dense terrain.[38]

## Second principle: elimination of non-essentials

Following the Buna campaign, which ran from 16 November 1942 to 22 January 1943, an Australian Army committee of officers and non-commissioned officers reviewed the weapons and equipment table of the Australian infantry jungle division. Its recommendations included the elimination of infantry motorised transportation and all equipment that was not man-portable.[39] This problematic recommendation, like many other ill-advised suggestions, was not practical outside the Kokoda Track experience. An infantry brigade could not conduct offensive actions in the jungle only with what it could carry on its back or in a cart. In particular, this recommendation resulted in the stripping of an organic brigade's lift capacity. 'The peculiar condition of the theatre of operations,' LHQ concluded, 'necessitates transport being withdrawn from all units. Sufficient transport for divisional operations in the jungle areas will be held in a divisional pool and re-allocated to units in accordance with availability in forward areas.'[40] First, LHQ approved a flat 25 per cent reduction in mechanical transport.[41] Following the initial reduction of the weapons and equipment tables, the jungle reorganisation plan then moved Bren Carriers, trucks and other motorised equipment to a division motor pool for use when the terrain permitted.[42] Such consolidation was, however, a reduction, and the divisions lost a total of 67 drivers and mechanics in the jungle reorganisation.[43] This resulted in a large division motor pool with limited staffing. With combat loss and maintenance issues, this invariably left the three subordinate infantry brigades competing for limited division resources.

The 7th Australian Infantry Division, which was ordered to complete its jungle reorganisation no later than 7 April 1943, expressed 'difficulties' with the across-the-board 25 per cent reduction and the consolidation of vehicles. The 25 per cent reduction left each brigade with a lift capacity of 162 tons, when a brigade's lift requirement was 387 tons.[44] If forward deployed in complex terrain, such as a jungle or mountainous environment, the demand for heavy vehicles and motor transport was light and manageable. However, the jungle division's consolidated motor pool had a severely limited ability to support rear areas, and even the administrative transport needs of the brigades in their movement from base camps to ranges, assault courses, or in logistical tasks such as rations trucks and ammunition. This significant shortcoming was noted in one review of the jungle scales on 13 February 1943. 'The division in assembly area prior to active jungle operations', the report noted, had only 'a proportion of transport ... for normal and administrative purposes and training'.[45] The 7th Division requested all AIF divisions have two sets of weapons and equipment tables, one for jungle warfare and one for the rear area – a plan that would be adopted later in the war.[46]

The reorganisation of the division transport also overlooked the transportation support element or 'vehicle workshop' of the infantry brigades. The initial jungle scale previously discussed reduced the brigade transportation assets by a quarter and consolidated many of the other vehicles at the divisional level. There was a failure, however, to restructure the brigade vehicle workshops concurrently. The tropical scales issued in 1943 left each of the battalion workshops intact, leaving the brigade to carry an exorbitant amount of maintenance equipment for vehicles they did not possess. As with many of the recommendations and developments in the jungle formations, improvements came from the lower echelon. In April 1944, the brigades requested the reduction to one workshop per infantry brigade, relieving the brigade of 7 tons of excess equipment and increasing the formation's ability to deploy quicker and lighter.[47]

There were also personnel implications of the jungle restructure with the infantry brigades. Concurrently with organisational transformation, a personnel issue to be resolved 'prior to future deployments' was the 'disposal of non-AIF personnel'.[48] First Australian Army had published a memorandum in March 1943 to 'direct that all units allotted to the force for combined operations will consist entirely of AIF personnel'.[49] This was not a large task, yet it was one that took up administrative time and energy. The 7th Australian Division, for example, had only 12 CMF personnel, yet all were required to be redesignated as AIF.[50] Another jungle transition-related personnel issue was deactivation of the division and brigade defensive and employment platoons in June 1943. These were largely legacy units of World War I, tasked with the physical protection of headquarters and the organisation and construction of field fortifications and trench networks. The Australian Army's efforts to embrace manoeuvre in the SWPA made these units obsolete.

As a consequence of the restructures, the infantry brigades also had to manage a surplus of non-commissioned officers and warrant officers from units and subunits disbanded. The divisions and brigade handled this largely by stopping promotions in high-density or obsolete enlisted occupational specialties and transferring the personnel to unit vacancies elsewhere in the brigade. Surplus non-commissioned officers and warrant officers in the brigade were absorbed into one of the various training positions or held as overstrength until vacant positions could be identified elsewhere in the AIF. The jungle reorganisation also displaced many junior and inexperienced enlisted soldiers who were 'consolidated' at a division overstrength unit until they could be retested and assigned to new occupational specialties.[51]

## THIRD PRINCIPLE: CONSOLIDATION AT THE DIVISION LEVEL

The jungle reorganisation was not simply the act of discarding what could not be taken into a jungle environment. First and arguably foremost, it was a consolidation of support elements at higher echelons. The major reorganisation occurred at the division level in the creation of a consolidated motor pool and field artillery regiment. The lower echelons, to lesser degrees, experienced similar reorganisation. For example, machine-gun squads at the company level were reorganised into machine-gun platoons at the battalion level. The initial substance of the transition to tropical or jungle scales was the realisation or belief that many of the vehicles and heavy support weapons simply could not be employed effectively in jungle terrain. However, as previously mentioned, the transition was never as simple as leaving things that were too heavy behind, and recommendations and reconfigurations were constant.

One of the first restructuring challenges at the brigade level was the elimination of anti-aircraft and carrier platoons. As a counter-balance, the battalions gained Vickers Machine Gun Platoons, which would prove essential in the close-quarter engagements with the Japanese army.[52] Each of these machine-gun platoons represented a consolidation at the battalion level composed of one officer and 31 other ranks divided into four machine-gun teams.[53] The light anti-aircraft capability with the division and brigade was eliminated on the premise that the Japanese

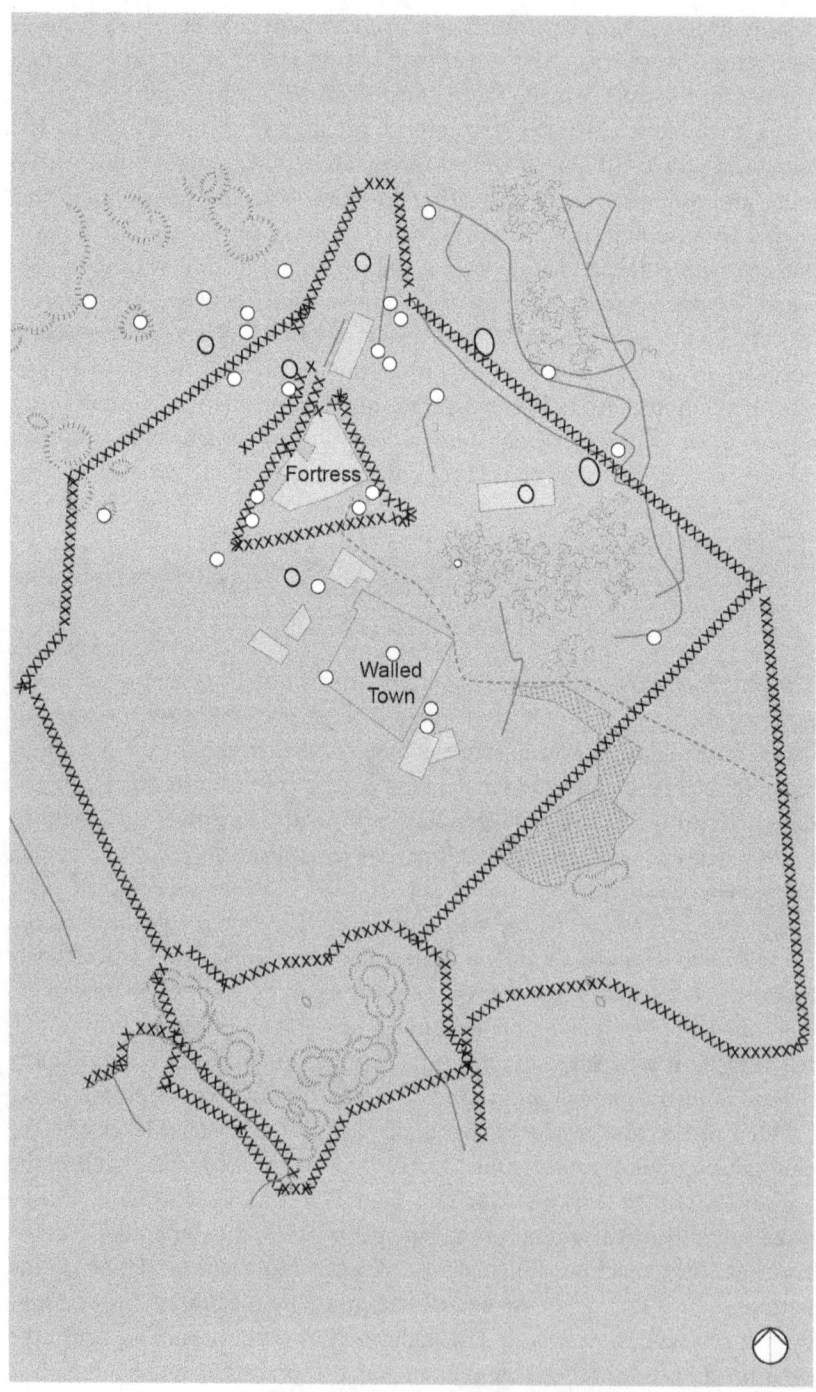

Map 1.1 Italian defences at the village of Giarabub, December 1940

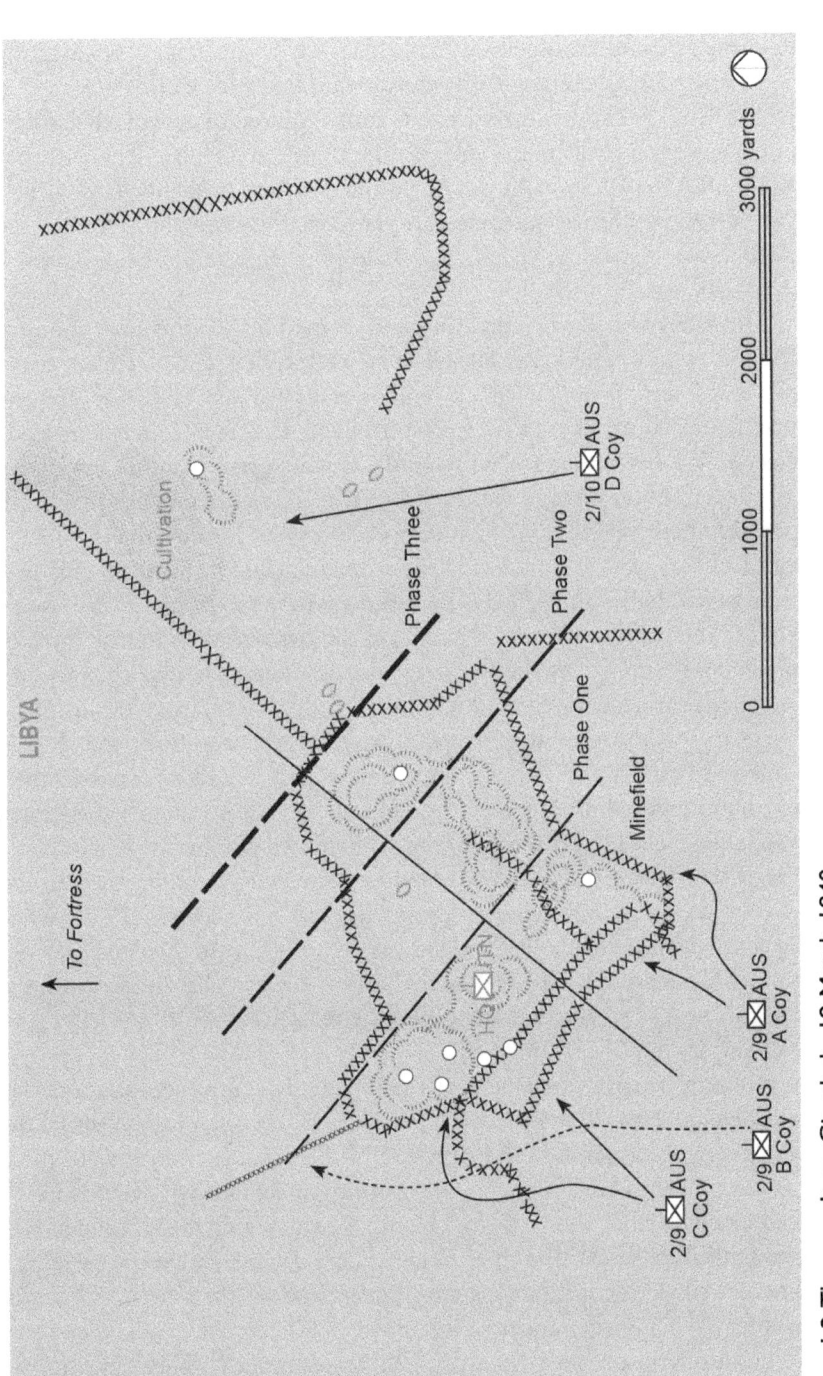

Map 1.2 The assault on Giarabub, 19 March 1940

would not be able to attack infantry effectively in the jungle with aviation assets and that Allied jungle divisions would likely have air superiority in the SWPA.[54] Additionally, battalions were required to provide one officer and 15 other ranks to the divisional carrier companies. These carrier companies would soon be found redundant and disbanded as well.[55] The newly established machine-gun platoons absorbed and retrained the balance of personnel from the battalion carrier and anti-aircraft platoons.[56]

The transition to a 'jungle brigade' came late for the 18th Infantry Brigade, which had primarily engaged in training and exercises for a motorised anti-armour defence until the day of embarkation for the defence of Milne Bay on 5 August 1942.[57] The 18th Infantry Brigade effectively fought its first SWPA battle at Milne Bay without any jungle training. Captain George Suthers from the 2/12th Battalion noted in an interview that 'we knew we didn't have the faintest idea what it [i.e. jungle warfare] was going to be like' before deployment.[58] However, this first campaign in New Guinea led to recommendations to its higher headquarters for the new jungle scales based on the early trial-and-error form of jungle combat. One of the first recommendations was that carriers and stretcher-bearers who carried wounded troops away from the front be rearmed with Owen guns instead of rifles. In addition, the poorly equipped battalion 'pioneer' companies, which would later prove their worth in jungle combat, were rearmed with the same weapons as infantry companies since the Japanese regularly attempted to infiltrate rear areas.[59] The 18th Infantry Brigade's War Diary acknowledged that its own efforts to conduct the jungle reorganisations began on 14 March 1943, while elements of the brigade were still at sea returning from the campaigns of Buna and Sanananda. By 27 March 1943 at Ravenshoe, Queensland, the combat-weary brigade had completed the reorganisation to the new tropical warfare establishment.[60]

Another important element of the jungle division reorganisation was the consolidation of divisional field artillery. As noted, at the onset of the war, the AIF reorganised the structure of the brigade from four to three battalions. This further jungle reorganisation included a restructure of field artillery from four brigades of three batteries to three regiments of two batteries each.[61] The three field artillery regiments were reorganised into one single regiment at the division level under the new jungle establishment.[62] The commander of this single field regiment would also serve as the artillery adviser to the division commander.[63] This reduction in field artillery available to a jungle division by some two-thirds would present significant challenges, in particular (as will be discussed in later chapters) when the Australian infantry confronted well-established Japanese fortifications in the jungle. The consolidation of artillery left the brigades with the same problems experienced with the establishment of a consolidated division motor pool: brigade commanders would be forced to compete for the limited field artillery available at the division.

In March 1944, the 7th Australian Division recommended a revision to the jungle division, requesting an increase in field artillery from one back-up to two regiments, and one survey battery.[64] In complex terrain, a single field artillery regiment simply could not support two manoeuvre brigades during an offensive action. Additionally, if the third reserve brigade was committed, it was highly probable that terrain and logistics in such areas as the Ramu Valley would restrict the ability to shift fire in support of that reserve. The losses suffered by the infantry in early SWPA campaigns, with shocking casualty rates of more than 80 per cent against fortified Japanese positions, resulted in sharp demands for increased artillery.[65] The role of field artillery within the Australian Army in close terrain, which was once thought by both senior Australian and US general officers to be of little use in the jungle, grew at the behest of the infantry brigade commanders, who increasingly embraced a modern version of combined arms manoeuvre. In 1943, Land Forces Headquarters in Australia assessed that 'It may be suggested that the number of guns (artillery) employed in some of the island campaigns was excessive but the fact remains that the operations were successful and that casualties were few.'[66]

The jungle realignment was not solely focused on equipment or capability. There were overall reductions in personnel strength as well, with the standard Australian infantry battalion losing one officer and 105 other ranks, resulting in a battalion of 34 officers and 769 other ranks for a total of 803 personnel. This was down from the pre-jungle, standard battalion of 35 officers and 875 other ranks.[67] In April 1943, the 18th Brigade established Warrant Officer Class 1 positions at the company level, removing the old Warrant Officer Class 2 sergeant major position.[68] This warrant officer position was consistent with the previous duties of the sergeant major to include maintenance of the rear area, administration, reserve and working parties. It is likely that the impetus of this change was battles like Buna, where the battalion and brigade rear areas were far from the front, vulnerable to infiltration, and in need of skilled management.

As discussed, not all the recommendations for changes to the jungle division weapons, equipment and staffing were positive or practical. One recommendation 'strongly' recommended the addition of pigeon-handlers to the jungle division headquarters. The suggestion cited the apparent successes of using pigeons in the New Guinea campaigns in 1942. More than two years had since passed without successful pigeon communications.[69] Indeed, since 1943, the deployment of modern wired and wireless communications radios had made the pigeon a less practical option for operations in the SWPA. None of the combat after-action reports of the Australian infantry brigades from 1943 to 1945 recommended an increase in the use of pigeons.

In March 1944, a year after the initial implementation of the jungle divisions, a review of formation was ordered. The conference on the status of jungle formations took place at LHQ in Australia on 18 April 1944.[70] The outcome of this conference included a review of the brigade establishments offering refinements that would consolidate the Australian Infantry Brigade (Jungle) as the smallest combined arms force in the SWPA. Although the majority of adjustments and consolidation would happen at the division level, these changes consolidated the infantry brigade as the smallest combined-arms manoeuvre formation in the SWPA. The 'jungle scales' consolidation of heavy equipment and vehicles at the division inadvertently relegated the division to almost rear-echelon support base status for the manoeuvre brigades because the division was now too 'heavy' for combat manoeuvre in dense jungles and mountains.

As noted earlier, a limited comparison of the US regiments is necessary for the analysis of the Australian brigade. The relationship with the US Army and the extensive use of artillery and close air support in coordination with infantry influenced the Australian jungle formations. The importance of effective combined arms support was embraced by the 18th Infantry Brigade, which had already established forward observer training down to the line company in 1943.[71] A year later in 1944, LHQ recognised the value of forward observer training in the infantry – a skill previously the purview of the artillery officer. The LHQ jungle formation conference observed: 'Operations have shown the value of infantry officers in forward positions being able to call for and direct artillery fires. It is suggested that all officers, company commander and below, be trained in elementary observation and control of fire.'[72] By necessity, the infantry brigades had already recommended or implemented training in other non-traditional skills, such as intelligence, photo interpretation and close air support, long before they were mandated in formal LHQ training memoranda.[73]

The April 1944 LHQ conference also adjusted the firepower available to formations in the SWPA. First, the jungle division's armoured force was doubled by adding a second tank regiment. This was a significant adjustment since generals – Australian and US – had hitherto assigned little value to the tank in the jungle and hence made less than optimal use of it.[74] A US observer in the Buna campaign noted that there was 'no infantry–artillery or infantry–tank team' in the SWPA, with each of the manoeuvre elements operating independently against the same objective.[75] In terms of artillery, at Buna, the infantry battalions were forced to use their anti-tank guns in a dual support role against fortifications since the artillery was with the division on the other side of the mountains.[76] Early LHQ planners had all but eliminated field artillery regiments on the basis of their estimation of mountain terrain in the Kokoda campaign. Conversely, the campaigns of New Guinea required field artillery in the jungle as a necessity in breaching Japanese field fortifications. The 1944 conference accepted the ground commander's recommendations to increase the field artillery regiments to two per division, doubling support to the infantry brigades.[77]

The conference also reinstated a cavalry capability within the AIF jungle divisions with the addition of a cavalry regiment with three squadrons in each jungle division.[78] Early in the New Guinea campaigns, cavalry units were at a loss for a mission, having been set up in 1940 to serve as mechanised reconnaissance units in North Africa and the Middle East.[79] In January 1943, the 2/7th Cavalry Regiment was a highly mechanised unit on a jungle island. Subsequently, this regiment was stripped of its Bren Carriers and sent to the Sanananda area as reinforcements attached to the 18th Infantry Brigade. As a cavalry element without vehicles, the unit was used as a quasi-infantry formation in the reserve, or as a holding force for areas taken by the infantry battalions.[80] Following Sanananda, the divisional cavalry regiments were reorganised as 'independent companies' and then later 'commando squadrons', to provide ground reconnaissance for infantry brigade groups throughout the rest of the Pacific War.[81] Likewise, the demand for pioneer units in the jungle and amphibious environment resulted in an LHQ conference decision that jungle divisions would have a pioneer battalion attached instead of pioneers consolidated at the corps level.[82]

By 1944, 18th Brigade had completed numerous combat tours, concluded an initial and subsequent jungle reorganisation and reached the final force structure that would take it through the rest of the war: the Infantry Brigade Group (Jungle). The brigade consisted of three infantry (rifle) battalions: the 2/9th, 2/10th and 2/12th. These subordinate battalions were key to the brigade's ability to conduct combat manoeuvre against the Japanese. The subordinate battalions were each organised in a flat five-company structure with a headquarters company and four rifle companies designated A, B, C and D.[83]

The brigade was commanded by a brigadier and was managed by the brigade staff consisting of the brigade major who served as the operations officer and supervised the brigade intelligence officer and Intelligence Section. The staff captain was administratively responsible for all additional Staff Section chiefs. The Staff Section chiefs included the brigade Australian Army Service Corps officer, who managed supply, transportation and a light aid section for vehicle maintenance; the Australian Army Ordnance Corps warrant officer responsible for the Ordnance Detachment; the Australian Army Medical Corps officer and field ambulance company; the signal corps officer and Signal Section; the three chaplains; and the officer designated 'staff officer native labour' who rounded out staff functions at the brigade headquarters.[84]

Additionally, the brigade had several organic combat and support units, which included a light aid detachment, a protection company, a postal detachment, a field cash office, the field artillery battery and a company of field engineers.[85] Under the 1944 jungle warfare establishments, the designation as a 'brigade group' and 'jungle' denoted that the brigade had assumed control of non-organic attached units. A machine-gun battalion, a commando squadron, a divisional carrier company, a light anti-aircraft battery, additional artillery and a company from a Papuan Infantry Battalion were common additions for a forward deployed infantry brigade group.[86]

As previously discussed, the SWPA offered two major environmental challenges: the jungle and the sea. While developing jungle divisions and brigades, the Australian Army had to plan and train simultaneously for amphibious warfare. As the campaigns in the SWPA became increasingly amphibious, Australian brigades selected for amphibious operations embraced new doctrine and tactics, largely supported by the US Navy. The Australian Army would build a close relationship with the US Navy's 7th Amphibious Force, which began as a piecemeal fleet assigned to support General Douglas MacArthur's early campaigns in the SWPA. By the end of the New Guinea campaign, which concluded with the amphibious landing on the Indonesian island of Morotai, the US Navy's 7th Amphibious Force had moved 1520 miles, conducted 13 major amphibious landings, and successfully landed approximately 200 000 Australian and US soldiers.[87]

On 1 July 1945, the 18th Australian Infantry Brigade Group (Jungle) was designated the assault brigade for the amphibious assault on

Balikpapan, code-named Operation Oboe II. As the assault brigade for this operation, the 18th Infantry Brigade Group would become one of the most complex brigade formations of the Australian Army in World War II. As with all amphibious warfare, the 18th Brigade would be required to travel by sea to an objective and launch an assault on an enemy shore from the sea.[88] The scope of the assault brigade's responsibility and capabilities were staggering. For example, when the 18th Australian Infantry Brigade Group spearheaded the amphibious landing at Balikpapan in July 1945, the amphibious task force comprised more than 200 ships. The success of the entire task force rested, at least in the initial phase, solely on the ability of the assault brigade to land, seize and secure the beachhead for the division landing.

The notion of an assault brigade was not, however, a standing formation in the AIF. Rather, 'assault' was a doctrinal term used by Allied infantry formations at any echelon to designate the spearhead of an amphibious landing.[89] The term 'assault' was also used to define the equipment scales and attachments for a formation in an amphibious landing. An example of an assault brigade would be an Australian infantry brigade group with command over Australian, US and other Allied attachments such as naval gunfire liaisons, air liaison teams, and beach groups or battalions, configured on assault (amphibious) scales, and designated as the breach element of an amphibious landing.

The idea of the assault brigade, with its size and complexity, demonstrates some of the largest challenges faced by the Australian Army in the SWPA. Training an infantry formation for amphibious warfare is a large, difficult undertaking even for longstanding experienced units. The assault brigade needed not only to achieve a high level of infantry and amphibious proficiency but also to integrate a multitude of attached units, which often arrived with deficiencies in combat skills and amphibious training.[90] To appreciate fully the challenge of the assault brigade, it must be recognised that the brigade might have command over five or more attached battalions of various functions and possibly a dozen separate companies and detachments.[91] The integration of these attachments in training, exercises and effective staff planning was the key to success or failure by the 18th Australian Infantry Brigade Group in the amphibious assault at Balikpapan.

The amphibious successes of the SWPA did not come easily to any of the Australian infantry formations. Amphibious doctrine had been largely ignored by the Australian Army following its experience at Gallipoli in 1915, which became a national day of remembrance, not a case study for future war. Conversely, the US Army and Marine Corps had studied and conducted numerous exercises based on the Gallipoli campaign throughout the interwar period. These created volumes of lessons learnt, recommendations and new doctrine, which became the foundation of the Allied amphibious campaigns of the SWPA. Australian amphibious warfare doctrine of World War II, on the other hand, evolved slowly from an amalgamation of training orders, memos and combat experience in the SWPA.

Largely due to the US control of amphibious training in the SWPA and the preponderance of the US Navy 7th Amphibious Force, which was predominantly American, the Australian Army was not deeply involved in the development of amphibious warfare doctrine even after the Pacific War began. The Australian Army's first modern amphibious or expeditionary warfare manual was a publication entitled *Combined Operations: Planning on the Brigade and Unit Levels with Special Reference to Landing Tables and Tonnage Tables*. This collection of training orders, instructions, and weapons and equipment tables, bound together under a single title, was the Australian equivalent to the US Army *Field Manual 31-5 Landing Operations on Hostile Shores* of 1941. For example, Australian documents within this collection included single-subject documents, such as the 1st Australian Corps Training Instruction Number 10, which offered notes on brigade staff planning for amphibious operations and emphasised the importance of designating the assault brigade early to ensure that the planning for the brigade and attachments was conducted on proper 'assault', 'light (jungle)' or 'normal' scales.[92] In spite of the lack of participation in the development of amphibious doctrine, the 18th Brigade staff became highly skilled amphibious planners due to the brigade's combat experience, extremely short amphibious planning timelines, and the need to compensate for planning failures at the division level.

The US and British armies used a similar amphibious terminology. The US Army *Field Manual 31-5 Landing Operations on Hostile Shores* employed the term 'assault combat teams' as the designation for the landing element that would conduct the breach of the beachhead when the force could not be landed in its entirety. The designation of the assault element was essential and needed to be determined early to ensure proper planning and combat embarkation.[93] The British *Combined Operations Staff Notebook 1945* used the terms 'assault brigade' and 'assault brigade group' in much the same way as the Australians and Americans used 'Assault Formations, which are tactically organised and equipped to carry out the initial attack on an enemy coast'.

The Australian Army first used the term 'assault brigade' in reference to the Infantry Brigade Group in 1944 with the 1st Australian Corps Training Instruction Number 6. This instruction outlined the 6th Australian Infantry Division's amphibious landing exercises at San Remo Beach and used the term 'assault brigade group' for the lead infantry brigade(s) of the exercise.[94] The 18th Australian Infantry Brigade referred to itself as the 'assault brigade' numerous times with some pride in its after-action review of the landing at Balikpapan.[95]

The designation as an 'assault brigade' represented a significant increase in responsibility for the commanders and staffs. As the assault brigade staff, they assumed responsibility for the development of amphibious load and landing plans, coordinated combined arms support, and individual combat manoeuvre onto objectives at the brigade and battalion levels.[96] Indirect fire represents an excellent example of this increase in both responsibility and capability. In the early campaigns of New Guinea, the Australian battalion commanders had to rely on a division or brigade artillery officer, in competition with other battalions, for the limited artillery support available. By comparison, when the 18th Infantry Brigade Group landed at Balikpapan as the amphibious task force's assault brigade, each of the three battalion commanders, in addition to his assigned field artillery, had his own dedicated US destroyer assigned for naval gunfire support.[97]

In terms of structure as well, the designation of the 18th Australian Infantry Brigade Group as the 'assault brigade' for the amphibious assault on Balikpapan deserves careful examination. The brigade headquarters was expanded to meet the task of amphibious staff planning, as well as the ground campaign that would follow a successful landing. This headquarters now had the following units under its direct command: 2/9th, 2/10th and 2/12th Infantry Battalions; 1st Squadron, 1st Armed Regiment (less two troops); 2/4th Field Company; 18th Brigade Signal Section; one detachment of 2/42nd Cipher Section; 6th Platoon, Bravo Company; 2/1st GD Regiment; one section of the 2/47th Light Aid Detachment (Type J) and one detachment of the 2/54th Light Aid Detachment (Type G); Field Support Section; an Allied Translator and Interpreter (ATIS) Detachment; a detachment of the 2/2nd Anti-Tank Regiment; one company from the 2/1st Machine Gun Battalion; and the 2/8th Transport Platoon.[98]

As addressed in detail in later chapters, the wide assortment of attached units offered manoeuvre options to the 18th Australian Infantry Brigade Group for the amphibious assault on Balikpapan. The brigade and battalion staffs integrated attached units into the brigade landing tables, ship assignments and movement ashore, all of which had to be facilitated by the subordinate infantry battalions. For Operation Oboe II, these attached units included: detachments from 2nd Operations Report Team; the Directorate of Public Affairs; 4th Armoured Brigade Reconnaissance Squadron; 2/25th Field PK Company; 1st Armoured Regiment Signal Troop; 2nd Engineer Signal Section; 2/125th Brigade Workshop; 1st Regimental Workshop; 209 Light Aid Detachment (Type H) and Bravo Signal Section (7th Division); the 2/5th Field Ambulance (with Surgical Team); one section of the 2/6th Dental Unit; one section of the 7th Division Protection Company; the 7th Field Military History Section LHQ; elements of A Troop, 1st Naval Bombardment Group; the 5th Air Support Party; the 5th, 6th and 7th Air Liaison Parties; and elements of the US Army 672 and 727 Amphibious Tractor Battalions.[99]

## US Army regiments of the SWPA

The defeat of the Japanese forces in the SWPA simply required more manpower than the Australian Army could muster. The US national leadership was committed to the defence of Australia and the defeat of the Japanese in the Pacific to the extent that the US Army deployed two National Guard divisions to Australia with great haste. Unfortunately, this meant that these US Army divisions deployed without the benefit of the modern training provided to divisions assigned to Europe.[100] The US regiments, like the Australian brigades, did not have any amphibious or jungle warfare training. Additionally, the US regiments lacked the combat experience – arguably the most important factor in warfare – that Australia had gained in North Africa.

The first two American divisions that joined the Australian Army in New Guinea, the US Army 32nd and 41st National Guard Infantry Divisions, were called to federal service on 15 October 1940, more than a year before the Japanese attack on Pearl Harbor.[101] Of these, the 41st Infantry Division would be one of the first to arrive in New Guinea.[102] Many of these National Guard units would not return home until the defeat of the Japanese in 1945.

These American divisions mobilised as square divisions with four regiments. The US Army 32nd Infantry Division transitioned to the triangular model following a major series of exercises known as the Louisiana Maneuvers.[103] The 1941 Louisiana Maneuvers were the largest peacetime manoeuvres in American history.[104] The transition to the triangular division configuration resulted in the US 32nd Infantry Division deploying to Australia with three infantry regiments: the 126th, 127th and 128th.

The US 41st and 32nd Divisions arrived in Australia in September 1942.[105] The two National Guard divisions had been rushed through training and deployed in a state of readiness described by General Robert Eichelberger, the commander of US Army I Corps in Australia, as 'barely satisfactory'.[106] Yet US planners were not initially concerned with the deployment of the poorly trained 41st and 32nd Divisions because they were intended to serve in a defensive role if Japanese forces invaded Australia.[107]

For all this, the US regiments that joined the fight in the SWPA were not well prepared. Samuel Milner, author of the US Army's official history of the New Guinea campaigns, noted that the 32nd Infantry Division had been moved from training site to training site so often that it drastically cut its regiments' training schedule before deployment.[108] According to the 32nd Infantry Division's own commanding general, the division never had the opportunity to complete a systematic training program before deployment in New Guinea.[109]

Once in Australia, the US regiments were immediately ordered to increase their standard of physical fitness and infantry training, and to initiate a program of training for jungle warfare; however, the 126th and 128th Regiments of the 32nd Division were sent forward into New Guinea in November 1942 before they received any jungle training.[110] So lacking was the 32nd Division's training program that one soldier told Eichelberger that during the entire 20 months since mobilisation, they had conducted only one night training exercise.[111] Regardless of the two regiments' lack of offensive or jungle training, they were sent forward. General Edwin Harding, commander of the US Army 32nd Infantry Division, who would later be relieved of command in combat, addressed the regiments in a highly confident yet nonsensical manner calling the 126th Regiment the 'spearhead of the spearhead of the spearhead'.[112]

The designation of the Australian Infantry Brigade Group (Jungle) as an assault brigade for an amphibious assault was the pinnacle of evolution and Allied cooperation in the SWPA, where the Australian infantry brigade had proven a highly adaptive formation. In five years, it transitioned from a light infantry role focused on territorial defence to the motorised infantry of North Africa, then to its most dynamic evolution and focus of this research: an amphibious infantry brigade group (jungle). The combination of Australian combat experience, its partnership with the US Army and Navy, and the embrace of new tactics and technologies would make it possible for the 18th Australian Infantry Brigade to recover from the catastrophically costly victory at Buna and go on to striking victories at Shaggy Ridge and Balikpapan.

CHAPTER 2

# THE LONG ROAD TO THE SWPA

At the end of 1939, the newly established 18th Infantry Brigade consisted of four battalions: 2/9 Battalion, 2/20 Battalion, 2/11 Battalion and 2/12 Battalion. As part of the 9th Infantry Division, the brigade was scheduled to depart Australia in May 1940 to join the British campaigns in the Middle East. In honour of this impending deployment, the 18th Brigade participated in a parade through the streets of Sydney, minus one battalion because the 2/11 Battalion had been detached to leave early for action in the Middle East.[1] With the impending reorganisation of Australian brigades from four to three battalions, the 2/11 Battalion would not return to the 18th Brigade for the duration of the war. The 2/11 Battalion would, however, join the 19th Brigade in North Africa to participate in more than a dozen battles and campaigns across North Africa, the Middle East and the SWPA.

The 18th Brigade embarked on several ships, including the *Empress of Britain*, *Empress of Japan* and *Aquitania*, and the famed *Queen Mary*. On 5 May 1940 at 1600, the convoy set sail from Australia for its first stop in South Africa.[2] From there the convoy pushed on to Freetown, Sierra Leone, and all the while at sea, the soldiers of the 18th Brigade attended classes on land navigation and basic tactics, and attended formal courses such as armourer's school. The convoy, heading north from Sierra Leone, was joined by the cruisers *Shropshire* and *Cumberland* and the carrier *Hermes* while the soldiers on the troop carriers, including the *Queen Mary*, set up machine-gun positions to be manned 24 hours a day.

The final leg of the trip was uneventful, and the convoy arrived in the Firth of Clyde on 16 June 1940. The troops disembarked at Port Glasgow and travelled by train to a poorly prepared camp at Lopcombe Corner on the Salisbury Plain in southern England. The 18th Brigade's first experience of war and its first casualties of World War II would be in the Battle of Britain. On 20 June 1940, the 18th Brigade's first night at its new encampment, the German Luftwaffe conducted a heavy air raid on Southampton just 21 miles away. The unit diary recorded: 'The noise of this raid was distinctly heard in the camp and the glow of flames was seen, and the troops are beginning to realise that they have got at last, close to the war.'[3]

The 18th Brigade became part of the Australian Strike Force, which immediately began training for the defence of Britain from German invasion. The brigade arrived as France, Belgium, Luxembourg and the Netherlands fell to the Blitzkrieg, and England was under the constant bombardment of the Blitz. The possible invasion of England by Germany by sea and air was a grievous concern. The 18th Brigade's initial role was the defence of the Wallop and Andover aerodromes from German parachute assault. The brigade would also train as a mobile mechanised force for its secondary role of opposing a German amphibious landing.

Figure 2.1 The 2/10th Infantry Battalion at Lupcombe Corner, Salisbury Plain, after being deployed to assist in the defence of England against a potential German invasion. Troops train to fight in trenches in newly issued uniforms and equipment. (AWM P00828.002)

To increase mobility and lethality, the 18th Brigade soon received Bren carriers, cars and trucks for a rapid response to any German incursion. The individual Australian soldiers who had arrived in England wearing the same kit issued in 1908 finally received the new 1938 issue of personal web kit. The 18th Brigade, with newly equipped soldiers and vehicles, planned and conducted exercises on Salisbury Plain to adapt to its new role as a mechanised force while the Luftwaffe passed over the camp every night. By July, the brigade had increased the number of Bren carriers to 28 per battalion, which allowed it to learn and practise the basics of mechanised infantry manoeuvre.[4]

On 4 July 1940, His Majesty the King visited the camp. He inspected each of the 18th Brigade's battalions and complimented the Australians on their long voyage and efforts to assist in the defence of England. The next week, the 18th Brigade suffered its first casualties of the war when a German Dornier light bomber emerged from the clouds unexpectedly and fired 300 to 400 rounds into the camp.[5] The result was several damaged tents and the first two wounded soldiers of the war for the 18th Brigade.

In September 1940, the Germans launched the Blitz with massive nightly bombing of English cities. The 18th Brigade observed an estimated 400–500 German aircraft passing over its camp every night. The next month, the 18th Brigade was ordered to move to the Colchester Garrison in Essex in eastern England. Here the air raids continued, and the battalions witnessed the German use of the 'Molotov Breadbasket', a cluster bomb designed by the Russians that contained high explosive and incendiary charges designed to burn cities.

The month spent in Colchester Garrison would be the end of the 18th Brigade's service in England. The brigade departed by train for Glasgow and left by sea on 18 November 1940. The 18th Brigade, its commander, Brigadier Leslie Morshead, and the subordinate battalions' six months in the United Kingdom was not ill spent. They witnessed the power and limitations of air power demonstrated in the Battle of Britain. The bombardment of an enemy does not automatically induce the capitulation of that enemy or its population. The 18th Brigade would see this again in Allied efforts to use air power to force the Japanese to capitate in the islands of the SWPA.

The 18th Brigade's experience in Britain also gave it the opportunity to learn and train as a mechanised infantry formation. The 18th Brigade, raised as an underequipped light infantry formation in October 1939, now had trained and exercised in military cars, trucks and Bren carriers. The war diaries of the brigade and battalions clearly show an appreciation for the lessons learnt in mechanised manoeuvre, such as the importance of vehicle maintenance, fuel and water logistics, and the impact of terrain on vehicular manoeuvre. These lessons would be key in the 18th Brigade's next role as they faced off with Germany's Afrika Korps, led by Field Marshal Erwin Rommel.

## THE FIRST ASSAULT: NORTH AFRICA

The 18th Infantry Brigade arrived at Alexandria, Egypt, on 13 December 1940 and moved on to the Allied staging base at Ikingi Maryout, about 25 kilometres from the harbour.[6] The 18th Brigade's arrival in North Africa would bring another round of Australian Army reorganisation. The Australian Strike Force and its commander in England, Major General Henry Wynter, was to become the nucleus for the newly established 9th Australian Infantry Division in North Africa; however, Wynter was to fall ill and was replaced by the commander of the 18th Brigade, Brigadier Morshead. With Morshead as commander of the 9th Division, Brigadier George Wootten took command of the 18th Brigade on 1 February 1941.[7] Later that month, the 18th and 25th B Brigades would be transferred to the 7th Australian Infantry Division, which was set for the invasion of Lebanon and Syria.

As the 7th Division prepared for campaigns in the Middle East, the 18th Brigade was detached again and tasked with an assault against Italian forces in the Libyan desert at Giarabub. Giarabub was an oasis and the furthest south-eastern Italian frontier post near the Egyptian border. The garrison consisted of approximately 1300 Italian and 700 Libyan soldiers. The fort and town were surrounded by entrenched outposts stretching into the desert. The town itself had fortified machine-gun and artillery positions, minefields and a barbed wire perimeter. Politically, the town housed the tomb of a Muslim cleric named Sayyid Muhammad ibn Ali as-Senussi, an important figure to Bedouin communities.[8] Although the mosque that housed the tomb was not an objective of the assault, the 18th Brigade did include instructions in the operations order that they were to avoid damage to it if at all possible.[9]

The campaign began before the 18th Brigade's arrival in Egypt. On 2 December 1940, B Squadron, 6th Divisional Cavalry Regiment, was tasked with raiding the various outlying posts near Giarabub and interdicting Italian logistics. The effects of B Squadron's raids and harassment succeeded in curtailing ground resupply, which forced the garrison to rely on aerial resupply. B Squadron's direct engagements with Giarabub

Figure 2.2 Soldiers of the 18th Infantry Brigade as they departed Mersa Matruh, Libya, to cross the desert for the assault on the Italian garrison at Giarabub. (AWM 030386/03)

revealed a well-equipped and committed defender and one prisoner claimed; there was no talk of surrender in the garrison, only encouragement from their commander to fight until the end.[10]

Once tasked with the assault of Giarabub, Brigadier Wootten initially wanted to bring the entire 18th Brigade to bear on the garrison, believing that this would be an excellent opportunity to expose the whole brigade to combat. This idea was overruled by General Richard O'Connor, Commander XIII Corps, owing to a lack of vehicles for an entire brigade as well as time constraints. To add to Wootten's limitations, there would be no armour or air support for the assault on this desert fortress, and he would have just ten days to seize Giarabub and return to Alexandria.[11]

'Wootten Force' was based the 2/9th Battalion with an additional infantry company, composite machine-gun platoon and mortar platoon of 2/10th Battalion attached. The 2/12th Battalion also would contribute a composite machine-gun platoon and its protection platoon. C Battery, 4th Regiment, Royal Horse Artillery, would join the artillery already deployed, and B Cavalry Squadron would bring the artillery up to 16 guns.[12]

The 18th Brigade initially joined the cavalry units to conduct vigorous patrols around the Giarabub area. Wootten and his staff conducted several reconnaissance of the perimeter to ascertain the best course of action for the assault. These were often hampered by sandstorms that limited visibility and wreaked havoc on the weapons and vehicles.[13] On one reconnaissance mission, Italians launched mounted elements from the garrison, attempting to outflank Wootten and his staff. They succeeded only in damaging one vehicle, but they demonstrated a commitment to the defence of the garrison and a willingness to fight.[14]

On 19 March 1940, Wootten ordered the 2/9th Battalion to assault Giarabub from the southern approach. The northern approach had layered machine-gun outposts and difficult terrain that created a defence in depth. Wootten determined that casualties would be significant against the line of machine-gun nests covered by Italian artillery. The southern perimeter was lightly guarded owing to the Italians' belief that the salt marshes posed a natural line of defence. For Wootten, the southern approach allowed for troops to approach from a defilade and seize the high ground called Tamma Heights.[15]

The 2/9th Battalion's assault was to collapse the Italian perimeter down to only the garrison defences at which time a final assault would be conducted. Concern over the salt marshes on the southern approach resulted in the initial manoeuvre being conducted in daylight. Sandstorms and the salt marshes did cause significant delays; however, when at 1500 the two companies of 2/9th Battalion found the first outposts unoccupied, Wootten ordered the 2/9th Battalion to advance as fast as possible to Tamma Heights. Their speed had the Italians at a disadvantage and, with minimal opposition, Tamma Heights was seized.

The night resulted in significant confusion on the battlefield. As the portions of the perimeter had collapsed, the Australian and Italian positions became intermixed, leading to impromptu skirmishes that resulted in casualties on both sides.[16] The dawn of 20 March brought a massive sandstorm that jammed weapons and blinded the 2/9th Battalion to the extent that soldiers had to follow communications wire to move between headquarters and the forward companies.[17]

The plan was for a textbook infantry assault supported by artillery. A and C Companies of 2/9th Battalion would assault across the southern front, breaching the wire, and assault the Italian garrison while B Company enveloped from the south-west. The single company of 2/10th Battalion would serve as a reserve, and B Squadron, 6th Divisional Cavalry was to harass the Italians along the northern perimeter as a distraction.

At 0515, under a waning moon, the 2/9th Battalion assaulted with A Company on the left and C Company on the right. In an effort to manoeuvre as close to the Italian positions as possible, A Company commander Captain Robert Reidy had brought his troops to within 50 metres of the first objective: a small knoll. As the barrage began at 0515, rounds fell directly on A Company's position. Gunners of the 4th Regiment, Royal House Artillery, had not taken into consideration the effects of the sandstorm and swirling wind on artillery rounds. The result was a barrage of short rounds. 'The noise and the flashes of bursting shells, with which were intermingled the cries of suddenly startled men, and the groans of the wounded, were shockingly frightening.'[18]

The 18th Brigade's first experience with friendly fire resulted in A Company suffering 12 dead, including the commander, and 20 wounded. Despite the losses, and with reinforcement from D Company, A Company seized the Italian position. The 2/9th Battalion advance faced increased opposition from caves and fortified positions on the second knoll. The Italian used caves and various fortifications as cover from the artillery barrage and mortars. The Italians continued to return accurate fire and threw dozens of hand grenades during the Australian assault. Despite the efforts of the defenders, by 1000 hours, all resistance on the second knoll ceased. The Australians took 200 prisoners, and an estimated equal number were killed.[19]

For the final assault, A and C Companies were now joined by B Company, which met stiff resistance in its western envelopment. At 1125, the 2/9th Battalion passed through a minefield to enter the town without resistance. By now, the 6th Cavalry had moved from harassment to a penetration of the northern perimeter and seized the Italian aerodromes before Wootten ordered them hold position for fear of friendly fire in the dense sandstorm. The final Italians would not fight to the end as their commander had urged. The Australians entered the fort and raised the 2/9th Battalion's black over blue standard, ending the assault on Giarabub.

The 18th Brigade and its attachments suffered 17 killed and 77 wounded, all of these being from the 2/9th Battalion.[20] Italian casualties were considerably higher but more difficult to assess in the dense sandstorms. One officer of the 18th Brigade reported he 'counted sixteen Italian corpses on one slope, but when he returned two hours later, all but two had been completely covered'.[21] Estimates put the numbers at 250 dead, 100 wounded and 1300 prisoners.[22]

The assault on Giarabub was the 18th Brigade's first offensive action of World War II; however, this was not a revolution in modern warfare and would have looked much the same if it had been fought in 1841,

Figure 2.3 The village of Giarabub, Libya, with the Senoussi Mosque in the background on the day of the Italian garrison's surrender to the 18th Infantry Brigade, 21 March 1941. (AWM 030386/15)

a century earlier. The infantry assault was well planned and executed against a fortified garrison without the assistance of armour and air support. 'A' Company's friendly fire incident was the single brigade's largest source of casualties. The Italians put up an initial spirited defence despite their isolation and hunger, while both sides were burdened with wild fluctuations in temperature and sandstorms that limited a soldier's vision to just a few feet. The 18th Brigade conducted effective reconnaissance, coordinated artillery barrages with infantry assaults, and seized the town, incurring only limited casualties. These were foundational skills the 18th Brigade would build on as it evolved in the SWPA, but first it would transition from assaulter to defender just a few weeks later at Tobruk.

## Counterassault at Tobruk

The Afrika Korps offensive in North Africa in early 1941 had driven the majority of the British Army back to Egypt, where it planned to regroup for a future offensive. The 9th Australian Division remained to lead the defence of Tobruk, the only deep-water port in eastern Libya. For Rommel and the Afrika Korps, the port of Tobruk was essential for a

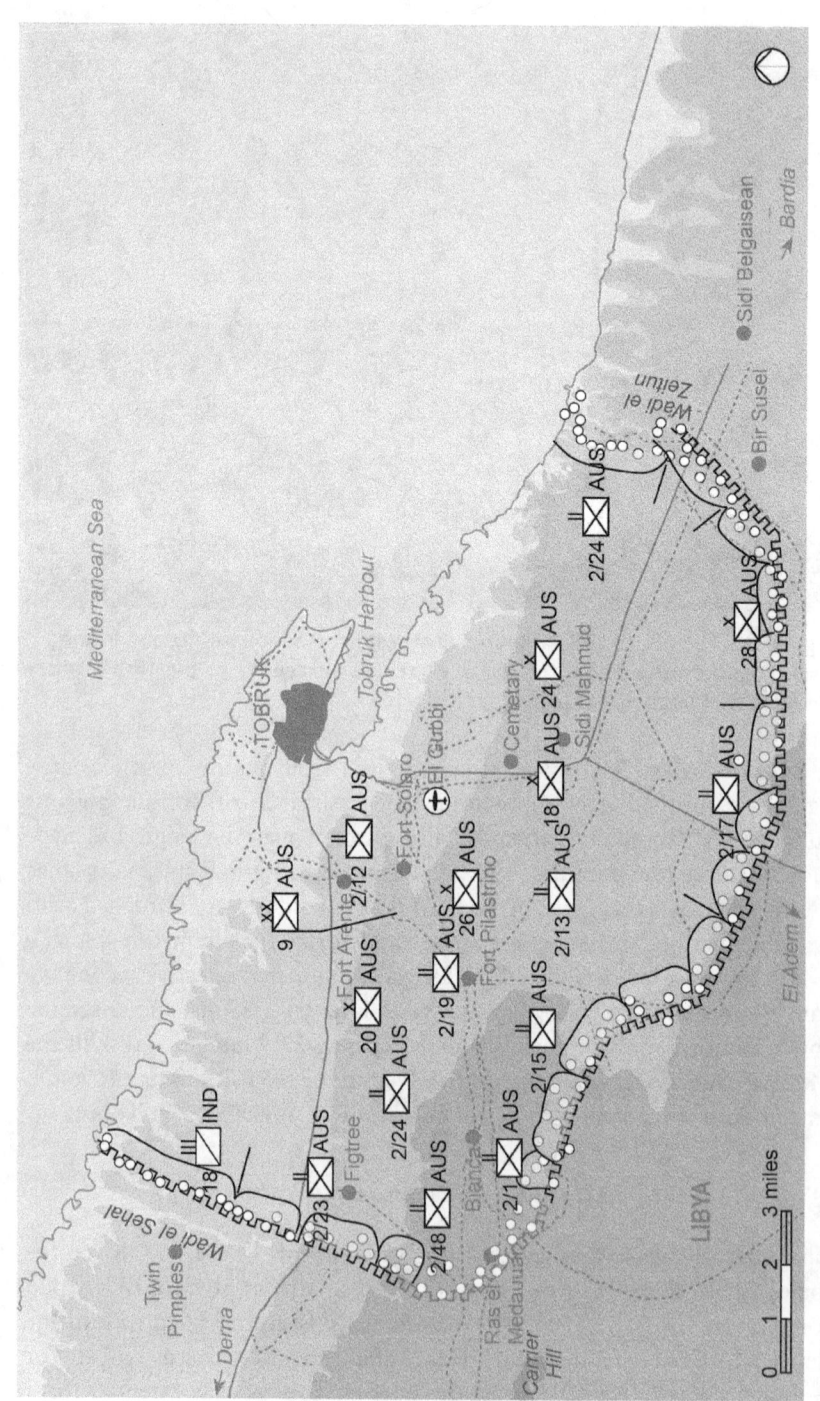

Map 2.1 Tobruk Defence, April 1941

campaign into Egypt, and Rommel decided to besiege it at the first opportunity. The 18th Brigade, newly returned from its action at Giarabub and scheduled for deployment to the Middle East, again detached from the 7th Australian Division. This time it would be to assist the 9th Division, led by the brigade's former commander General Morshead, in the defence of Tobruk.

The 18th Brigade moved by land and sea to Tobruk. Once assembled, it was assigned as the division reserve. The 18th Brigade did conduct extensive patrolling within the 30-mile perimeter of the Tobruk defences but did not see direct action against the enemy. At times, an individual battalion would backfill the line if another Australian battalion moved out to meet an Axis attack and assisted with handling of German and Italian prisoners of war after perimeter skirmishes. As the reserve, the 18th Brigade had also stood-to on several occasions for a possible counter-attack against Afrika Korps incursions but stood down as the line repulsed the German attackers on each occasion.

On 30 April 1941, the Afrika Korps launched an offensive with elements of the 15th Panzer Division, 5th Light Division and the Italian 27th Division. During the night, after some progress into the Tobruk perimeter, minefields and highly effective anti-tank guns stalled the attack. The next day, the Germans attempted to widen the breach, only to be stopped again by Australian anti-tank guns, this time supported by British tanks. The bulge or 'Salient', as the battle would come to be known, had captured several Australian positions and risked greater advance if the Afrika Korps could manage to reinforce the attack.

On the morning of 3 May 1941, Brigadier Wootten received orders to counter-attack the Germans in the Salient. Wootten was provided three options for attack by the commander of the 9th Division, General Morshead. The first was an attack against German forces from outside the perimeter. The second was an assault against the formations, armour and strongpoints in a generally south-west direction as a brigade, and the third option, 'combined attacks by a battalion, each respectively from north to south along the perimeter defences in the western portion of the enemy salient and from east to west along the perimeter defences in the southern portion of the salient'.[23] Wootten chose the third option, which he believed had the best chance of success.

The final commander's conference was held at 9th Division headquarters at 1600, at which the zero hour was changed from 1933 hours to 2045 hours to increase the likelihood of achieving surprise in the dark. The actual zero time would be pushed back again as the 2/9th Battalion

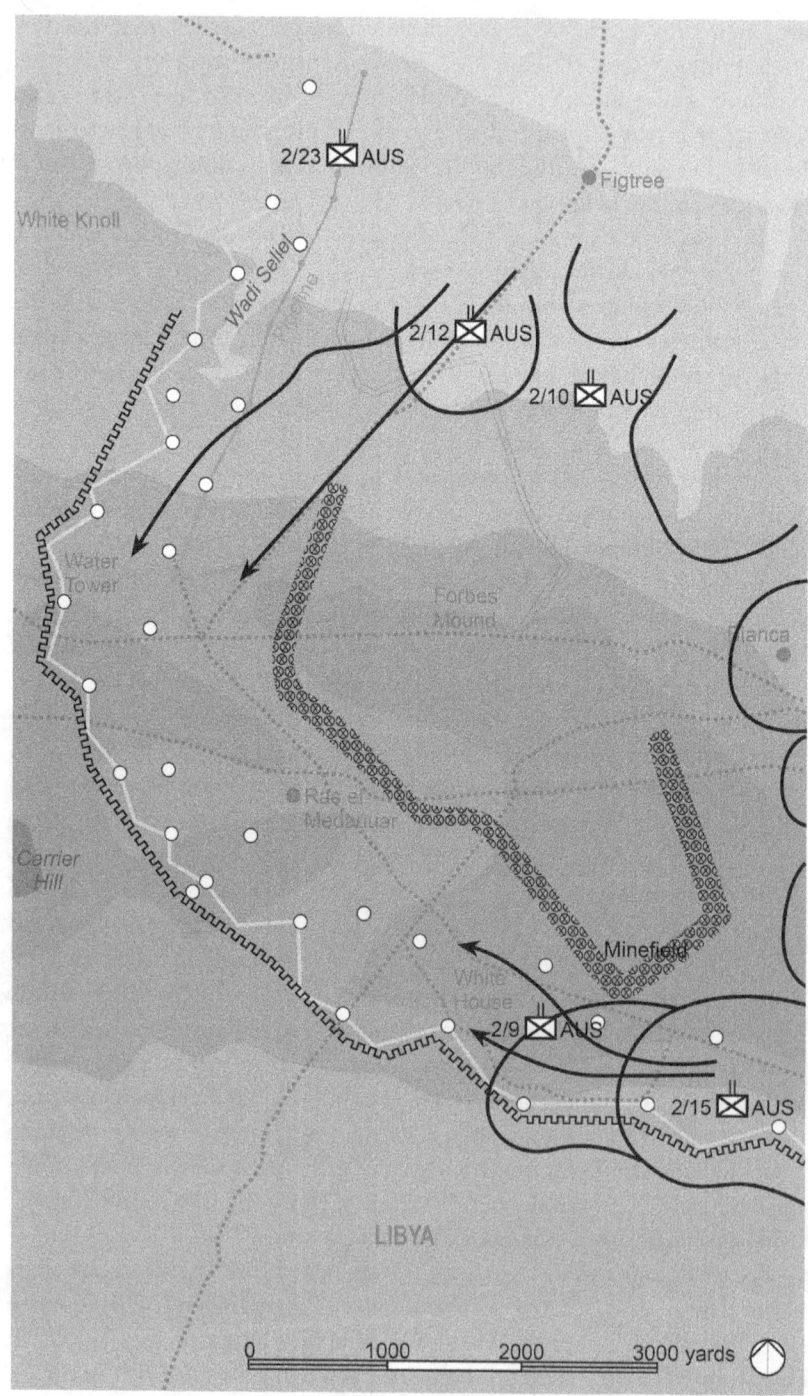

Map 2.2 The Battle of the Salient, May 1941

arrived at the departure point 35 minutes late. Wootten was able to push back the artillery schedule, but it was an indicator of challenges to come in the Salient.

The 2/9th Battalion successfully assaulted and overran the first set of enemy positions; however, a second artillery barrage began to creep along the right flank, resulting in confusion among the platoons. Although engaged with the enemy, the 2/9th Battalion failed to find its first objective: an outpost seized by the Germans on the previous day. The irregular shape of the salient line, which resulted in the confusion around the artillery barrages, and darkness led the 2/9th Battalion to attack targets of opportunity through the night, knocking out machine-gun positions and three tanks by forcibly opening the turret and dropping Mills bombs inside.

The 2/12th Battalion attacked directly into strong enemy positions. Its companies reported machine-gun fire from all sides and heavy mortars as soon as they launched their assault. Again, the irregular front line resulted in confusion with Allied and German signals. The Germans used green signal lights, which apparently called for machine guns and mortars to conduct defensive fires; however, green lights were also the 2/12th Battalion's prearranged signal to mark the forward position of Australian troops, which resulted in erratic gunfire whenever a green light was employed. The assault became so confused that Lieutenant Paul Kumnick of the 2/10th Battalion encountered about 80 soldiers from the 2/12th Battalion who 'wandered through our positions ... [T]hese troops had no idea of their whereabouts or job.'[24]

The 2/10th Battalion was assigned as the reserve and the mopping-up force to be employed at dawn. However, not long after the counterassault began, the battalion was given orders to mop up German positions along the salient. The 2/10th Battalion sent companies forward, only to be repulsed by heavy fire, and although there were some small victories against individual enemy positions, the 2/10th advance largely failed.

At 0337 and with dawn fast approaching, General Morshead asked Wootten for a decision on pressing the attack or withdrawing the 18th Brigade. Wootten recommended withdrawal while they had the benefit of darkness. During the night, the 18th Brigade had 10 killed, 121 wounded and 24 missing, while it captured a total of 23 prisoners throughout the night; and enemy casualties included 36 killed, 105 wounded and 62 missing.[25] The brigade also managed to knock out seven anti-tank guns with three small Italian tanks destroyed or damaged.[26] Regardless of enemy losses, the counterassault was still a failure.

Figure 2.4 Troops of the 2/10th Infantry Battalion in Tobruk taking a break in the rear after their time successfully holding the line under assault by the Afrika Korps. (AWM 009516)

There are several obvious concerns with the planning and execution of the 18th Brigade's counterassault in the battle of the Salient; however, all these concerns must be seen through the lens of time. The Germans and Italians had pushed far into the Salient over the previous 48 hours, and the intent of the order to counterassault was to push them back before they could reinforce: a clear priority for the defence of fortress Tobruk. However, the first concern, although not uncommon, was that the brigade commander did not appear to have been included in the initial planning. The unit diary noted that Wootten was presented with three plans of attack to choose from upon arrival at the division headquarters. This resulted in the battalions attacking simultaneously across a highly irregular perimeter and terrain, moving in near absolute darkness without prior reconnaissance. Additionally, the Royal Air Force had not been seen overhead in a month, which meant that the brigade and battalion commanders had no current aerial photographs of enemy positions.

If there was no evidence of imminent attack by the Germans, which is not present in the war diaries, this lack of intelligence of enemy strengths and locations could have been mitigated with effective ground reconnaissance of enemy positions. A delay of a few hours for reconnaissance in the afternoon and evening of 3 May would have left the battalions better prepared for a dawn counterassault on 4 May 1941.

Each of the battalion's attacks were met with an unexpectedly high volume of heavy artillery, mortar and machine-gun fire both from within the salient and from outside the Tobruk perimeter. Lack of moonlight, no rehearsals, and confused signalling further hampered locating battalion objectives in the complex terrain. To complicate matters further, the 2/9th Battalion's first two objectives were identified incorrectly on the map. The 2/9th Battalion recommended in its after-action report that less artillery focused on a specific target immediately followed by an infantry assault would be more effective than timed heavy rolling barrages, a tactic (along with ground reconnaissance) that the 18th Brigade would come to master in the SWPA.

In all, the 18th Brigade's counterassault, along with the further actions of the 9th Division, did manage to hold Tobruk against the Afrika Korps. The night of 3/4 May would be the 18th Brigade's last combat action in Tobruk. The brigade was redeployed in September of 1941 to Syria and Palestine before its return to Australia. Its experience in Britain and North Africa laid the foundations of infantry manoeuvre, close coordination of artillery, and a ground reconnaissance capability on the basis of which the brigade would become one of the most lethal formations in the SWPA.

## TRAINING FOR THE LAST FIGHT

In March 1942, the 18th Brigade had recently returned to Australia from North Africa and had published its training program in 'Training Instruction Number 23'. This was a program of basics for new and junior troops and advanced skills for officers and non-commissioned officers. The brigade's guidance to the battalions called for 46 hours of training a week over six days, with two mandatory night exercises. The basics included road marches three days a week, map-reading, message-writing, patrolling (day and night), first aid, anti-air protection, defensive positions, and anti-tank and gas training. The officers' and non-commissioned officers' training was similar with an emphasis on maps, compass-reading, report-writing, reconnaissance and the training of umpires for future force-on-force exercises.[27]

At the end of the month, 'Training Instruction Number 24' was published. This document expressed a number of concerns with the implementation of training since the return from the Middle East and the publication of 'Number 23'. 'Number 24' also expanded the guidance for road marches, pressing battalion commanders to achieve a standard of 25 miles a day for four days, and maintaining combat effectiveness on the final objective.[28] Discipline was also an area of focus, calling upon officers and non-commissioned officers to remember they were on duty 24/7 and instructing leaders to conduct administrative tasks such as inspection of soldiers' feet and equipment outside the scheduled 46 training hours.[29]

The most significant feature of 'Training Instruction Number 24' was a section entitled 'Co-operation of Infantry and Other Arms'. This represents a look at what would become the foundation of the Australian Infantry Brigade Group (Jungle). The brigade commander, Brigadier George Wootten, also expressed his intent to implement a program of affiliation with brigade units and supporting arms units.[30] The aim was to have the battalions partner with and build familiarity with armour and artillery units to support brigade infantry manoeuvres. Unfortunately, the constant relocation of the 18th Brigade between training areas in Australia and its short-notice deployment to New Guinea would limit the implementation of this forward-looking idea.

'Training Instruction Number 24' was published with two additional specialty training documents, 'Notes on Defence against Tank Attack' and 'Training in use of Assault and Recce Boats'. The guidance on defence against tank attacks instructed the battalions on what to expect when facing tanks in future campaigns.[31] The 18th Brigade had been brought back from the Middle East because of the belief that the Japanese posed a possible invasion threat to Australia.[32] It was an invasion that would never come, but the Japanese armour threat was legitimate, as the 18th Brigade would learn in Milne Bay a few months later. The second document outlined the first modern amphibious training the brigade would receive after returning to Australia. The 2/4th Field Company would conduct three hours of training evolutions twice a day for groups of 52 soldiers: two officers and 50 other ranks. Each battalion would have three days of training to include carrying boats, launching, beaching and watermanship.[33] On 16 May 1942, the 18th Infantry Brigade received an order to move to the Kilroy training area by a combination of motor and rail. This would be the brigade's third relocation in two months and would strip another five days out of the brigade training schedule.[34]

On 4 April 1942, the 18th Infantry Brigade published its first comprehensive internal document covering brigade and subordinate unit exercises in spite of the fact that the brigade had participated in numerous exercises and combat operations in North Africa. The document entitled 'Preparation of Exercises, Headquarters 18th Infantry Brigade', was important and deserves examination since the brigade would use this guidance for exercises throughout the duration of World War II. It listed four types of exercises to be conducted down to the platoon level, with the intent of standardising how subordinate elements should conduct exercises to ensure seamless integration into any formation across the brigade.[35] For example, if a company might be attached to another battalion for an exercise or operation, the standardised exercise format cut down the amount of time required for integration. Brigade and battalion exercises were intended to build upon the last exercise, with tactics exercised at the platoon, company and battalion levels contributing to brigade exercises, which would then serve as part of the division's manoeuvre capability.

The first type of exercise and logistically the simplest was the 'Training Exercise Without Troops', also called a staff exercise, in which the leadership elements conducted a walkthrough of the operation around a sand table or on a map in an effort to identify 'serious pitfalls' in the plan before an exercise or operations with troops.[36] The second was the Skeleton Exercise, which in practice was the same as a staff exercise, with the addition of representatives from various staff elements such as signals, intelligence, ordnance and supply. The last two types of exercise included the One-Sided and Two-Sided Exercises. The One-Sided Exercise included a skeleton opposition force controlled by the exercise director. This type of exercise was best used to teach basic tenets of manoeuvre such as assaults or flanking movements without follow-on actions. The final type, the Two-Sided Exercise, consisted of two or more units deployed in the field with a force-on-force engagement with the most important element being 'both commanders have freedom of action'.[37]

The 18th Brigade included a section in this document called 'Preliminary Considerations', which offered four questions for the commander and staff to consider early in exercise planning. First, ask whom you are teaching and what is the soldier's or unit's level of experience. The second question was an examination of the expected outcomes: 'What are the main lessons to be brought out?'[38] Third, the planners were encouraged to review the available pamphlets, manuals and doctrine on the task at hand. The final consideration for exercise planning was the most difficult: 'Test the soundness of your lessons by your knowledge of enemy tactics based upon experience or other acquired knowledge.'[39]

The weakness of the exercise program guidance was in the exercise outcomes. The 18th Infantry Brigade's exercise program called for an after-action conference and a consolidated report on the exercise, but it did not mandate written lessons learnt. The report only required an objective, opening narrative, situations and the exercise's timetable.[40] The lessons learnt, positive or negative, were left to the after-action conference, the minutes of which were rarely documented in the unit diary. This left units to repeat undocumented mistakes in future exercise evolutions. It also left the intuitional knowledge of a given unit's strengths and weakness to the commanders, which could be lost if the commander was relieved or killed.

On 26 May 1942, the 18th Infantry Brigade received the '7th Australian Division Operational Instruction Number 1', which outlined the planned defence for the 7th Division's area of responsibility in Australia.[41] The 7th Division records expressed a sincere fear of an impending Japanese invasion of Australia. The Australian Army had concluded that the coastal defence could not stop a Japanese landing force and that the 7th Division would be required first to withdraw and then conduct a protracted defence.[42]

On 30 May 1942, 18th Infantry Brigade initiated a piecemeal program of training and exercises directed at the defence of Australia from a Japanese amphibious invasion. The initial element of the brigade's training for a defensive role was a six-day training course called Road Blocks and Tank Stops for the pioneer platoons and six representatives from the infantry units. The instruction included lectures, demonstrations and exercises focused on stopping advancing Japanese armoured and mechanised units landing in Australia from the sea.[43]

For the next several months and up to the day it deployed forward to New Guinea, the brigade was tasked with the training to serve as a motorised defence in open terrain. The 7th Infantry Division training and exercise program was wholly defensive in nature with no provisions for confronting the Japanese on the beachhead. Additionally, the 7th Division records show no documented discussion or planning for the potential for any elements of the command to be deployed forward to New Guinea. As a direct result, none of the 7th Infantry Division's brigades received any training in jungle warfare before the 18th Infantry Brigade's combat deployment to Milne Bay in August 1942.

Three days after the publication of '7th Australian Division Operational Instruction Number 1', the brigade conducted its first staff exercise. The narrative included a warning order for the brigade that a division-sized element of Japanese troops had landed on the night of 28/29 May at Deception Bay, Queensland. The Japanese forces had broken through coastal defence and were advancing rapidly southwards along the road to Brisbane. The brigade headquarters was instructed to move immediately to Mount Archer to establish a forward brigade headquarters in support of the 7th Infantry Division's withdrawal and in preparation to serve as the division reserve.[44] The 18th Infantry Brigade, the only unit of the division to serve in Tobruk, would be left behind to fight a rearguard action against the Japanese division while the 7th Division withdrew.

In early June 1942, the 18th Infantry Brigade's subordinate battalions and companies conducted another iteration of the anti-tank pioneer course.[45] In mid-June, the brigade conducted a staff exercise called 'Murgon', focusing on the brigade commander's implementation of an 'aggressive and mobile defence'.[46] In this staff exercise, the brigade was ordered to oppose a Japanese landing force as close to the beach as possible. The staff exercise did include the production of movement and operations orders as well as a signal exercise.[47] On 2 July, the 18th Brigade commander provided feedback in the form of 'comments and suggestions' to the 7th Infantry Division regarding the Murgon staff exercise. The key points included the difference in mobility rates for tracked and wheeled vehicles, road conditions and a request for US Army-issue trousers due to dangers of poisonous plant life.[48] Strikingly, none of the after-action report comments presented to the 7th Division addressed the limited anti-armour capabilities of the infantry brigade or absence of combined arms integration. Essentially, the exercise posed a standard Australian infantry brigade against a Japanese reinforced infantry division without concern or forethought for supporting arms. The lack of an adequate after-action report from the 18th Brigade demonstrated old doctrinal thinking whereby a brigade commander would not consider air support, armour or artillery as a brigade-controlled asset.

The 7th Division did offer its subordinate brigade feedback on the various brigade and battalion training exercises conducted in June, pointing out a number of weaknesses in both essential skills and leadership.[49] It was noted that often the attack was slow owing to the leadership positioning itself at the back of the formation; literally, leading from the rear. There was also a general malaise around leadership at all levels, pointedly stating, 'Enthusiasm in men depends on enthusiasm in their leaders.'[50] Additional issues related to leadership included noise and light discipline, with soldiers openly smoking at night and unkempt uniform appearance. The 7th Division's brigades racked up an impressive list of failures, including poor map-reading, a lack of control of manoeuvre units, lack of discipline in a halt or bivouac area, poor employment of anti-tank weapons, use of passwords and sentries, and lastly, the brigade commander's use of cavalry units as bait instead of their intended role as reconnaissance units.[51]

On 22 June, the 18th Infantry Brigade decided to delay the 2/10th Battalion's training exercise by three days owing to rain, which had made some of the roads in the training area impassable to motor transport.[52] The exercise was completed from 25 to 27 June; however, the potential value of training in inclement weather – something the Australian Army would face almost daily in New Guinea – was lost to short-sightedness. Ultimately, the battalions would learn to fight in the swamps and rain on the job in New Guinea.

On 6 July 1942, the 7th Division held a staff exercise that included the 18th Infantry Brigade command staff.[53] This was a first division exercise that included the brigade command staffs and was the building block for the upcoming one-sided field exercises. The actual division exercise ran from 12 to 14 July and included the deployment and manoeuvre of the 18th, 21st and 25th Infantry Brigades of the 7th Division.[54] A clear indication of the separation of fire and manoeuvre in the Australian Army of the day was that the exercise did not include artillery. An artillery demonstration was conducted for the brigade staffs the day after the exercise concluded.[55] This was the first time the 18th Brigade had conducted manoeuvres as a brigade in the field since its return from North Africa.

The after-action conferences and reports were not favourable. The 18th Infantry Brigade's performance was conveyed in both a written after-action report and at a commander's conference with the battalion commanders and staffs. The brigade commander's conference was held on 17 July and included the tactical judgements of the written after-action report and some forward-looking observations. First, the brigade did not communicate information between echelons effectively. The battalions would also have to provide faster 'Battle Strength Updates' if the brigade was to function as a single manoeuvre force. Lastly, Wootten noted for the first time the need for expanded cipher and intelligence training across the brigade.[56]

The next day, the brigade published 'Training of Liaison Officers', which ordered each battalion to provide an officer to the brigade staff on one-week rotations to improve communications between the brigade and its subordinate battalion.[57] This problem of communication and integration of staffs within the brigade would be greatly exacerbated in the Battle of Milne Bay leading, in the long term, to significant expansion, integration and cross-training of staff functions within the brigade.

The written after-action report, entitled '18th Australian Infantry Brigade Training Memorandum Number 1', addressed several key failures.[58] First, the 18th Brigade's subordinate battalions and companies were wholly unprepared for the division exercise. There was little evidence of the basic tenets of leadership such as planning and reconnaissance. There was also a 'lack of grip' over the company leadership that resulted in Wootten adding additional company-level exercises to the battalion training schedules.[59] The brigade's driving was noted as overall 'very bad'; not a single battalion was graded as 'good'. The problem was significant enough for the brigade commander to threaten formal disciplinary action for further drive offences.[60]

'Training Memorandum Number 1' also outlined tactical problems around the employment of anti-tank weapons and, most importantly, a failure to establish a proper defence perimeter during halts and bivouacs.[61] The ineffective deployment of anti-tank weapons would prove a costly failure when the 18th Brigade engaged the Japanese for the first time at Milne Bay.

The 7th Division scheduled a second division exercise for 11–14 August 1942; however, the 18th Infantry Brigade would not get the opportunity for a second division exercise.[62] On 3 August, the brigade commander received a verbal warning order to prepare for movement. On 4 August, the 7th Division published only its fourth operational instruction since returning to Australia, which would send the 18th Brigade forward to New Guinea.[63] On 5 August, the 18th Brigade's advance party departed for Brisbane.[64]

CHAPTER | 3

# THE BATTLE OF MILNE BAY

It rains daily for nine months and then the monsoon starts.
Drea, quoting an American soldier in New Guinea[1]

The battle at Milne Bay was a confrontation of necessity between the first Australian and US combined force and the Japanese over a strategic natural harbour on the south-eastern end of the island of New Guinea. Milne Bay offered the Allies a staging base to launch operations against the Japanese SWPA headquarters at Rabaul. Conversely, Milne Bay offered the Japanese a base from which to launch operations against the Allied forward headquarters at Port Stanley, which supported the Australian troops fighting the Japanese on the Kokoda Track.

Milne Bay was a stunning natural harbour 20 miles long and 10 miles wide at widest point. The Stirling Range, with peaks reaching 4000 feet and covered by dense brush and jungle, forked to run down both sides of the massive bay. What lay between the mountains and coastline was a slim strip of flat land consisting of swamps, streams and a few rudimentary outstations. From the moment Milne Force deployed to the region it had near-constant rain and a low visibility ceiling that hampered command and control at every level. To add to these challenges the only maps of the area were field sketches conducted with compass and pace count by the 24th Field Company the month prior.[2]

The battle at Milne Bay was the first brigade-sized battle in the SWPA with the 7th Infantry Brigade (Militia) and the 18th Infantry Brigade under the Milne Bay Force. The Battle for Milne Bay would plague both sides with inaccurate intelligence, challenging terrain and terrible weather. Major General Cyril Clowes, commander of Milne Bay Force, had under his command a far stronger force than the Japanese planners expected; however, Clowes's command was plagued with daily reports of Japanese ghost forces poised to attack from every direction.[3] Through the literal and figurative fog of war, the Battle of Milne Bay exposed the early gap in the capabilities of Australian infantry brigades. Essential capabilities would be developed by the brigade and adopted by the entire Australian Army – a trend that would continue throughout the SWPA campaigns.

## OFF TO NEW GUINEA

Milne Bay would be the first test of an Australian infantry brigade in the SWPA.[4] According to US historians, the Japanese, who had just lost four aircraft carriers in the Battle of Midway, decided on a two-pronged assault on Port Moresby: one over the Kokoda Track and one around the New Guinea coast through Milne Bay.[5] However, the First Marine Division landing on Guadalcanal created two amphibious battlefronts for the Japanese to contend with simultaneously.[6] Telling of the challenges of a two-front theatre, Japanese intelligence on Milne Bay was dated and did not see Milne Bay Force move into the region. The Japanese believed the area to be an outpost defended by a few companies of Australian troops. In early 1942, this would have been accurate; however, in May 1942, based on the recommendation of General Thomas Blamey, commander of Allied Land Forces, SWPA's General MacArthur ordered the establishment of a forward air and naval base at Milne Bay.[7] MacArthur planned to use Milne Bay for bomber strikes against Rabaul and other Japanese targets without having to fly over the Owen Stanley Range, as well as a staging base for the campaign to retake the northern coast of New Guinea.[8]

In August 1942, the 18th Infantry Brigade received orders to move to the Australian coast to board ships for New Guinea. On 6 August, the brigade advanced party sailed from Brisbane.[9] The veterans of the 2/10th Battalion complained that the accommodation on their small Dutch ship was 'filthy', something inconceivable even to the infantry, who were used to dirty field conditions.[10]

The first field exercises in New Guinea quickly taught the soldiers of the 2/10th Battalion about the tropical environment, with one veteran announcing during the exercise that 'I am bravely carrying on despite heavy coconut fire'[11] – a humorous quip but a painful experience if a falling coconut hit a soldier on the head. The 2/10th soldiers quickly realised that the traditional shorts of the Australian infantry would not suffice in the jungle and that the need for American-style pants and gaiters was obvious.[12] This need had been included in previous after-action reports from training in Australia but had not yet been approved.[13]

For the 18th Infantry Brigade, the first warning of the Japanese assault on Milne Bay came from a US intelligence report that had identified 14 Japanese troopships and an additional 12 naval vessels moving down the north-east coast of New Guinea, likely headed for Milne Bay.[14] This number of ships represented two things: first, a sizeable amphibious force, which would have likely overwhelmed Milne Bay, and second, the start of Milne Force's experience with poor intelligence. The next day, another report revised the numbers to two Japanese troopships and approximately 3000 soldiers.[15] The early experience of the 18th Brigade and other Allied infantry formations in the SWPA would be plagued with inaccurate intelligence reports.

The 18th Brigade had completed its movement to Milne Bay on or about 21 August 1942, where they had joined the 7th Australian Infantry Brigade, a militia brigade, commanded by Brigadier General John Fields. On 21 August, General Clowes assumed command of Milne Bay Force. The total strength of this force at the beginning of hostilities was 9458 troops. Milne Bay Force included the 7th Infantry Brigade to include the 9, 25 and 61 Battalions, and the 18th Infantry Brigade's 2/9, 2/10 and 2/12 Battalions. Additional attached forces included the 9 Battery, 2/5 Field Regiment, 4 Battery, 101 Anti-Tank Regiment, 2/6 Heavy Anti-Aircraft Battery, 2/9 Light Anti-Aircraft Battery, two heavy Anti-Aircraft Stations, 2/4 and 24 Field Companies, and from the United States the 43 Engineer Regiment, Company E, 46 Engineer Regiment, 709 Airborne Anti-Aircraft Battery, C Battery, 104 Coastal Artillery Anti-Aircraft Battalion. The aviation component consisted of just Nos 75 and 76 Squadrons, RAAF equipped with P-40 Kittyhawks and Lockheed Hudson light bombers.[16] Clowes's only heavy weapons included a battery of 25-pounders, light and heavy Australian anti-aircraft guns at the aerodromes, 37mm anti-tank guns, and the US engineers' M2.50-calibre machine guns.[17]

Clowes was ordered to deny the enemy control of Milne Bay and to protect the three aerodromes at all costs. Only aerodrome number 1 was functional, built on the coconut plantation and only 'high ground' at the innermost section of the bay. The mud that seeped up through the grid, constructed of steel mats, made the runway slippery and dangerous.

Aerodrome nos 2 and 3 had not been completed owing to resource constraints and time.[18]

Clowes believed the Japanese task force would land on the northern shore and attempt to seize the no. 1 airstrip quickly.[19] Clowes's initial disposition of forces tasked the 7th Brigade to hold against Japanese amphibious landing from the north and south sides of the bay with 9 Battalion forward south of the plantation and 61 Battalion in the north with B Company at KB Mission, D Company more than 19 kilometres forward of no. 3 aerodrome at Ahioma. The 25 Battalion was positioned inland west of the plantation to defend against a possible Japanese airborne drop behind the Milne Bay Force headquarters. The battalions of the 18th Brigade were positioned around Clowes's headquarters as a reserve force staged to respond in any direction. All other units had been ordered to prepare defensive fortifications and defend if needed.[20]

Two Japanese task forces consisting of boats and barges departed from Rabaul and Buna in late August. On 24 August the 353 soldiers of the Sasebo 5th Special Naval Landing Force from Buna stopped on Goodenough Island to give soldiers a break from the rigors of sea travel by barge. Late in the afternoon the RAAF from Milne Bay found and destroyed the barges on the beach, thus stranding the Japanese landing force from Buna.[21] On the night of 25/26 August the Japanese task force from Rabaul landed approximately 2000 troops from the Kure 5th Special Naval Landing Force and the 10th Pioneer Unit (Naval Labour Corps).[22] Four days later a second force of 800 additional naval infantry from Rabaul landed at Milne Bay, which brought the total force to approximately 2800 Japanese troops.[23]

Although experienced in amphibious operations, the Japanese mismanaged the landing at Milne Bay. The Japanese navy shelled the beach before landing without effect. The Japanese naval gunfire was a demonstration designed to intimidate, not an attempt to engage Allied defensive positions, since the Japanese had no intelligence on the location of Allied forward outstations. Additionally, the poor weather conditions on the night of 24/25 August hampered Japanese navigation of the landing force, putting the Japanese force ashore at Lekwind, Waga Waga and Wandala. These locations were 12, 16 and 19 kilometres respectively from the intended landing site of Rabi.[24] Additionally, the Japanese landed in seven older barges, not amphibious landing craft. These older vessels in combination with inclement weather likely contributed to the vastly inaccurate beach landings.[25]

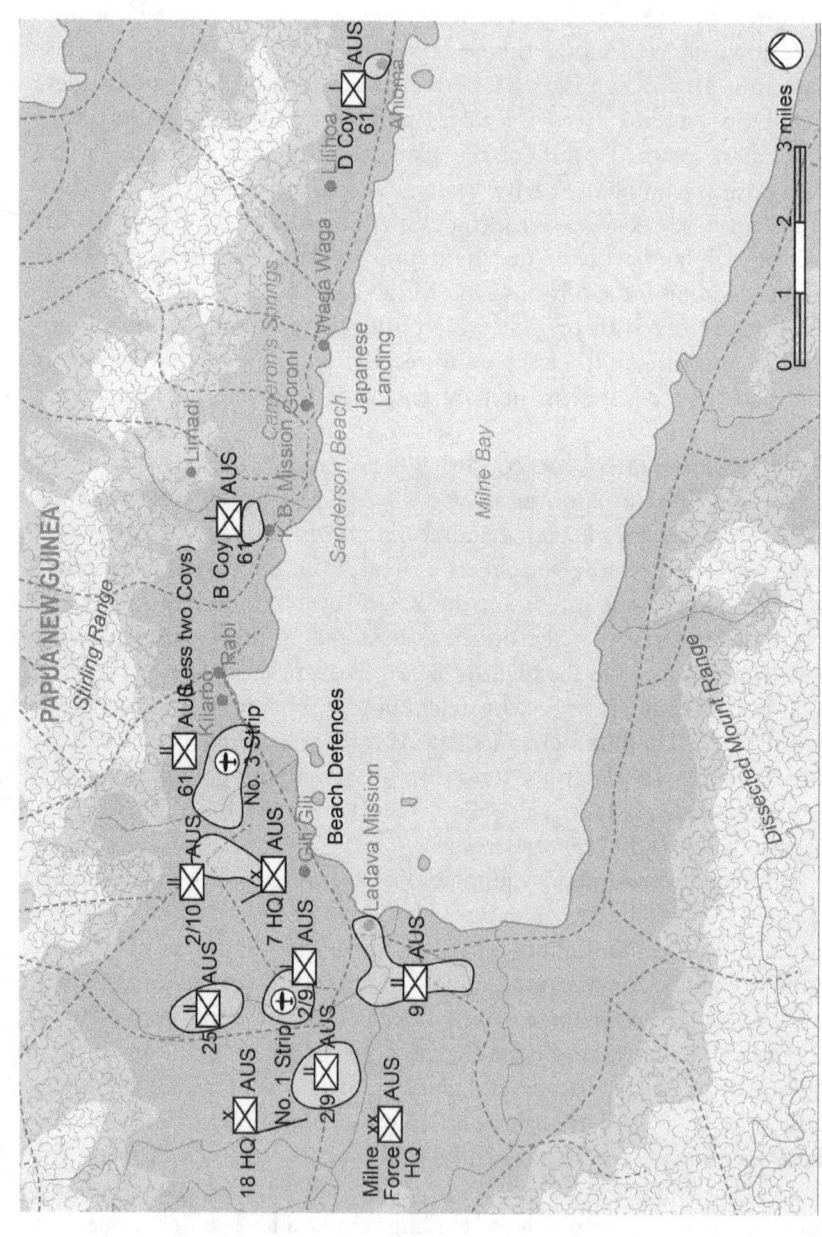

Map 3.1 The Battle of Milne Bay, 24 August 1942

Despite the missed landings, the Japanese had cut off the furthest outstation at Ahioma, near the mouth of the bay. D Company, 61 Battalion would have to conduct a hasty retrograde by two small ketches. The Japanese fired on and sank one ketch, which forced D Company ashore to conduct a dangerous march back to Milne Force through dense jungle. At KB Mission, B Company was the first to face the Japanese on land. B Company held against the Japanese advance force overnight in spite of the presence of a Japanese tank. On the morning of 26 August, B Company was reinforced with additional troops, but without effective artillery or air support it failed to advance against the Japanese force, which had also been reinforced.[26]

On 26 August a wave of intelligence reports consolidated by New Guinea Force were forwarded to Clowes's headquarters. The various reports include sightings of Japanese forces at sea and other unconfirmed Japanese landings in the bay.[27] Clowes had stated that 'the basis of the defence will be the maintenance of the offensive spirit and offensive action', but he was also committed to holding back the bulk of his force until he was confident of the primary avenue of approach of the main Japanese assault.[28]

During the day on the 26th, the RAAF was able to sink an estimated 10 Japanese barges at various landing sites, but it was not enough to deter the Japanese forces ashore from conducting aggressive reconnaissance against 61 Battalion at KB Mission.[29] Clowes believed that 5000 Japanese troops had landed, and he planned to use KB Mission as a defensive strongpoint to block the Japanese advance.[30] In reality, the Japanese had only landed between 2800 and 3000 troops and support personnel.[31]

At 0230 on 26 August, the 2/10th Battalion, under tactical control of the 7th Brigade, was ordered to advance to KB Mission, pass through the lines of 61 Battalion and conduct an afternoon attack against the Japanese advance. The 2/9th and 2/12th Battalions were designated the reserve force with Clowes's headquarters between the two battalions.[32] In practical terms, the 2/9th and 2/12th Battalions were the headquarters' defensive perimeter and not in a position from which they could have supported 2/10th Battalion. Clowes's reserve force existed in name only owing to distance and terrain. Late in the day on the 27th, the 2/10th Battalion arrived at KB Mission and set into the defensive perimeter for the night.

According to Dudley McCarthy's volume of the official history, the 7th Brigade commander Brigadier Fields ordered Lieutenant Colonel

Figure 3.1 Troops walk past the two Japanese Type 95 Ha-Go light tanks used in the attack on the Allied base at Milne Bay. (AWM 013320)

James Dobbs, the 2/Battalion commander, to deploy 2/10th Battalion as a lightly armed reconnaissance-in-force.[33] It was at this point that Dobbs decided the 2/10th Battalion would leave behind his heavy anti-tank guns to allow for rapid movement of the battalion. This was despite the 18th Brigade intelligence log notes that at 0310 on 26 August there was a 'possibility of enemy light tanks having landed'.[34]

By the evening of 27 August, the Japanese landing force, with tanks, had advanced to within striking distance of 2/10th Battalion on the perimeter of KB Mission.[35] It had been 20 hours since the first reports of tanks were conveyed to 2/10th Battalion, which still made no effort to bring up anti-tank weapons.[36] Owing to the density of terrain, Dobbs chose to move 2/10th Battalion directly up the coastal road towards the Japanese, which was also the only avenue of approach for Japanese armour, real or imagined. The Japanese landing force chose to initiate contact with 2/10th Battalion at 2100. At KB Mission perimeter, the silence was broken by one Japanese voice initiating a loud chant that lasted for one minute. This was followed by several voices in the second recitation and several hundred Japanese soldiers in the third.[37] This intimidation tactic had been described to soldiers in training briefs, but hearing the chants coming from the jungle for the first time certainly had a psychological impact.[38]

At 2115, the Japanese attacked the 2/10th Battalion's defensive line with infantry, mortars and two Type-95 light tanks in support of the infantry.[39] The Japanese tanks used bright spotlights to identify Australian positions, which were then assaulted by waves of infantry. The frontal assault that followed was described by the 2/10th Battalion's history as 'battering-ram tactics'.[40] By 2345, the defence had collapsed and 2/10th Battalion had been completely routed. The order on the line 'to split up into the jungle and reassemble at 7th Brigade' had been given.[41] Essentially, this meant every man for himself and a total collapse of the KB Mission perimeter. The troops of 2/10th Battalion were forced to retreat in small groups evading the Japanese pursuers through an unfamiliar jungle.

Captain Theo Schmedje noted in an interview that withdrawal is the 'worst bloody operation you can do everybody neglected withdrawal (in training) because you don't anticipate them'.[42] The 2/10th Battalion history does not describe the event as a rout, although it does note that some of the 2/10th elements were not accounted for until 4 September 1942.[43] The brigade intelligence officer made a note on the incident annotating in 'Intelligence Review Number 2' that 'late in the night our troops were forced to withdrawal slightly'.[44]

Later in Dobbs' narrative of the event, he would explain that his understanding of the 7th Brigade's order was to 'locate the enemy and estimate his strength'.[45] He argued that the order was a reconnaissance in strength, not an attack or an attempt to defend KB Mission, and therefore did not require anti-tank guns. This is contrary to 18th Brigade's after-action report, which states that 2/10th Battalion was ordered to engage and defeat the Japanese landing force.[46] The War Diary clearly states that all three battalions of 18th Brigade had been had advised of the presence of Japanese tanks on the battlefield. Beyond that, there was a great deal of confusion about the battle at KB Mission.[47]

In the various after-action reports, Dobbs first insisted that there was no report of tanks, then there was only one tank, and later argued he received reports that the tanks had been destroyed. In an interview in 1993, Sergeant James Wood of 2/10th Battalion when asked about the tanks said, 'Yes, yes, we'd been told they'd been knocked out.'[48] In the 2/10th Battalion after-action report, Dobbs insisted he was never informed of the possibility of Japanese armour despite brigade records to the contrary. The 18th Brigade intelligence log is intact, clearly noting the notifications of the subordinate battalions, specifically reporting at 0310 hours on 26 August 1942 that light Japanese tanks had landed at 0020 hours.[49] It is important to note that the 18th Brigade intelligence log used the phrase 'informed battalions' for normal messages but in this case used 'advised battalions' to highlight the seriousness of the report of tanks landing.[50]

The 'Report on Operations – Milne Bay, 2/10th Australian Infantry Battalion', which contains Dobbs's personal narrative on the defence of KB Mission and the assault of the Japanese tanks and infantry, makes several assertions about the night in question. First, the challenge of a long movement on unimproved roads in poor weather with heavy personal loads and little rest resulted in most troops being 'weary'.[51] Second, and shockingly, he states the unit diary notes that at 0300 hours 61st Battalion reported the destruction of two enemy tanks.[52] This is impossible to confirm since the War Diary for this date is missing from the archives. The controversy around the night of 27/28 August becomes more confused in another document, the 2/10th Battalion's 'Report on Japanese Tactics – Milne Bay', where Dobbs, as battalion commander, stated it had been previously reported by 7th Infantry Brigade that only one tank had been sighted. 'The [tank] commander was reported to have been shot and the tank to be badly bogged.'[53] There is no record in the 18th Brigade's log of this message being received or disseminated to the battalions.

Dobbs also stated that 'in view of the only tanks reported as having been landed being stated to be out of action, and bush warfare being anticipated, the unit's only anti-tank defence was 20 S.T. grenades'.[54] This implies that he received these reports before deployment of the 2/10th Battalion. The 'War Diary Notes on Milne Bay Operations 26 August – 8 September 1942' directly implicate Dobbs in the rout of the 2/10th Battalion and the failure to bring up anti-tank weapons.[55] The most surprising element of Dobbs's after-action report is the section on tactical lessons learnt from the battle. None of his lessons learnt included recommendations or comments on the absence or future use of anti-tank guns.[56]

However, the 7th Brigade's after-action report, 'Lessons from Recent Fighting', notes that each battalion had two anti-tank guns but ignored the incident by simply stating that the battalions 'had no chance of using them in these operations'.[57] Conversely, the 18th Brigade's after-action report, signed by Brigadier Wootten, concluded that the 2/10th Battalion, which had been temporarily transferred to the 7th Brigade, could have held against the Japanese if the anti-tank guns had been employed, especially in light of the anti-tank gun test conducted by 61 Battalion after the battle.[58] Although reports from the battlefield claimed the Australian anti-tank guns could not affect the Japanese tanks, the tests against the abandoned Japanese tanks found that the .55 anti-tank round 'easily penetrated the driver position ... and one bullet aimed at the turret passed completely through both sides'.[59] Irregardless of the confusion surrounding Japanese tanks and Australian anti-tank guns, 2/10th Battalion lost 43 killed and 26 wounded during its first confrontation with the Japanese KB Mission.[60]

## Holding the Line

On 27/28 August, Brigadier Field reinforced the support units at No. 3 Aerodrome with 25 and 61 Battalions. Attached was the US 709th Anti-Aircraft Battery (Airborne) and the 43rd and 96th Engineers, who held key positions in the defensive perimeter with their formidable .50-calibre machine guns.[61] This defence would force the Japanese force, fresh from its success at KB Mission, to cross the 2000-metre-long and 100-metre-wide incomplete airfield. On the night of 28 August, an assault, initiated by flares and the chants of Japanese soldiers, was launched against No. 3 Aerodrome. The frontal assault across the open terrain faced a wall of heavy machine-gun fire with disastrous results for the Japanese. Not a single Japanese soldier made it across the airfield.[62]

On 29 August Clowes received orders from GHQ in Brisbane to clear the north shore immediately. Clowes choose to deploy 2/12 Battalion to advance forward of No. 3 Aerodrome and recapture KB Mission; however, the same day Clowes received intelligence reports from GHQ of another Japanese amphibious task force near Milne Bay and decided to hold back the 2/12th.[63] There was no Japanese attack on the night of 29/30 August, and early morning patrols by 61 Battalion found that the tanks never reached the airfield. In fact, the Japanese light tanks were not light enough, and later were found abandoned in the mud along the mission road.[64] 61 Battalion also reported that there were indications the Japanese might be in the process of a withdrawal from the area.[65]

On the night of 31 August, despite 61 Battalion's reports of a Japanese withdrawal, the Japanese launched their final assault against No. 3 Aerodrome. With torrential rains and the US 96th Engineers' .50-calibre machine guns in the perimeter defence, the Japanese frontal assault again suffered catastrophic loses.[66] This would be the final Japanese offensive action in Milne Bay.

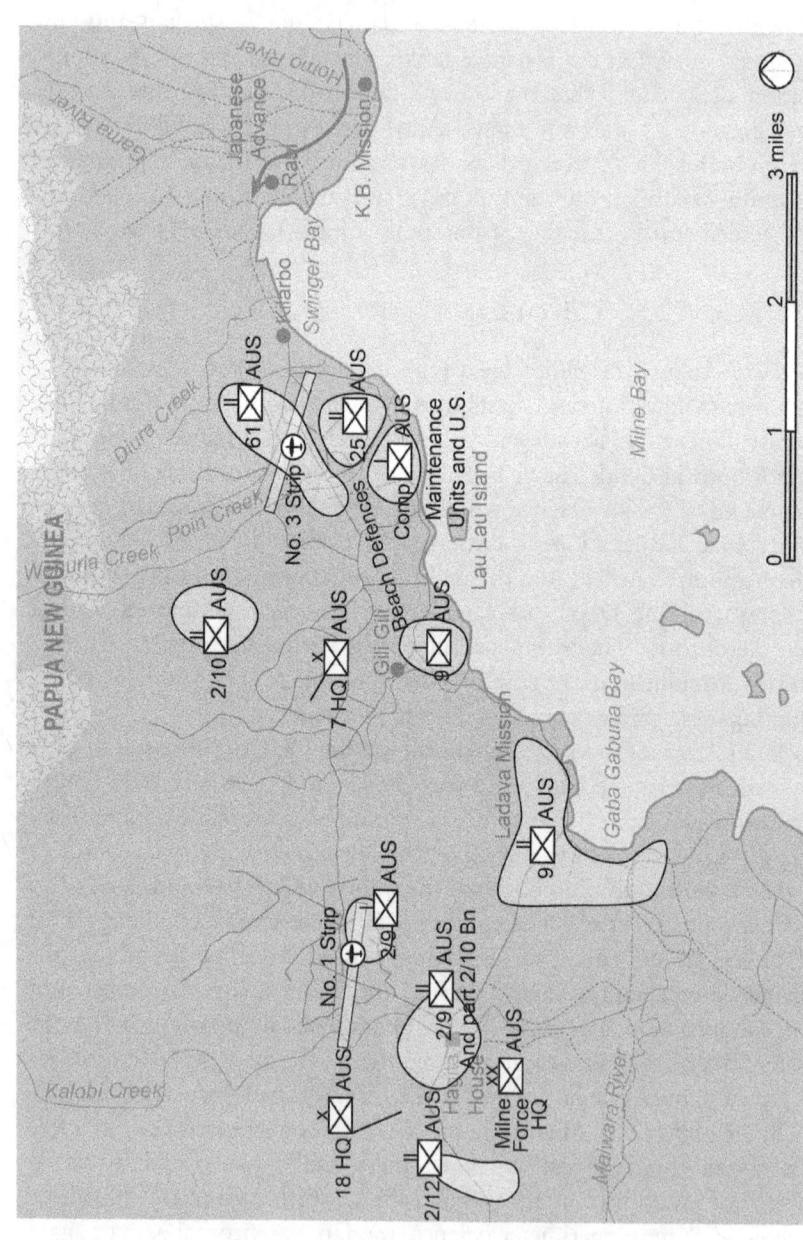

Map 3.2 The Battle of Milne Bay, 28 August 1942

Clowes's commander's conference of 31 August decided the 2/12th Battalion would finally have the opportunity to advance. The 2/12th was ordered 'to attack and destroy enemy forces on the North Shore of Milne Bay from Gili Gili to KB Mission, with a view to later mopping up the East Cape Peninsula'.[67] The order continued, 'not more than one infantry battalion will be committed without prior approval of Milne Force'.[68] This was another demonstration of Clowes's conservative employment of forces, again sending a single infantry battalion against the Japanese landing force, without giving the 7th or 18th Brigade commanders the ability to commit their reserve. Clowes was again lining up his battalions to face the Japanese one at a time.

The 2/12th Battalion advanced with several stiff engagements against pockets of Japanese troops finally to recapture KB Mission. Although the records are unclear, it is likely that it was Wootten, looking at the 2/10th Battalion's experience, who ordered A Troop, 4th Battery, 101st Anti-Tank Regiment, forward by barge to support the 2/12th.[69] On 2 September 1942, the 18th Brigade was able to begin operations as a brigade when 2/9th Battalion was given a verbal warning order to prepare to move by boat to KB Mission. This was not an attempt to envelop the enemy but a practical necessity. The rains had washed out the tracks and roads, making the sea the most practical means by which to deliver support and reserve elements. It was still an extremely dangerous manoeuvre. The three 'powered coastal luggers' suffered constant failures, and the 2/9th reported that although the luggers held only 60 soldiers, they filled them with 120 soldiers for speed of movement.[70]

On 4 September, the 2/9th Battalion launched what was the 18th Infantry Brigade's first combined arms assault of the SWPA campaign. The 2/9th advanced through the 2/12th Battalion lines with the support of the RAAF and field artillery against Japanese troops east of KB Mission. The assault was successful, and the 2/9th set up a defence perimeter while the 2/12th moved up in support. As the 2/9th Battalion stepped off on the offensive, a few of the soldiers of the 2/10th Battalion had still not made it back to Allied lines.[71] The 18th Brigade was on the offensive, but the Japanese commander, with no reinforcements or resupply, had already decided his position was untenable. On the same day, 4 September 1942, the 18th Brigade's offensive began and the Japanese started to evacuate by sea.[72]

Wootten deployed the 2/9th Battalion to pursue the Japanese retreat and the 2/12th Battalion to clear the north shore area. This clearance operation finally demonstrated the ability of the 18th Brigade to manoeuvre as a brigade formation along the coast of Milne Bay. The clean-up operations lasted for two additional weeks. The daily logs of the 18th Brigade tracked the challenges of the terrain and weather on both the 2/9th and 2/12th Battalions. The 2/9th highlighted the difficulties, reporting: '[M]en are very tired, and are cracking up. The commanding officer does not think they can go much further.'[73] The response from the 18th Brigade Headquarters and Brigadier Wootten was firm: 'No withdrawal without approval from this HQ.'[74] With the rout of the 2/10th Battalion, Wootten could not allow another withdrawal. In the end, the Japanese force had lost an estimated 600 soldiers and sailors in the operation compared to 123 Australians killed and 198 wounded. The US casualties at aerodrome no. 3 by comparison were exceptionally low, with only one killed and one wounded.

## After-action assessment

The 18th Infantry Brigade's after-action reports on the battle at Milne Bay offered several lessons learnt that would shape the future doctrine of the Australian infantry brigade in both its standard and jungle configurations. Milne Bay resulted in four key areas of development for the infantry brigade, namely combat manoeuvre, artillery, air support and intelligence.

Owen Curtis of the 2/12 Battalion described the 18th Brigade's first experience with jungle warfare in a post-war interview. Curtis noted that warfare in the desert against the Germans and Italians was a straightforward infantry action. The German army would attempt to breach the wire and assault the defence positions with basic fire and manoeuvre.[75] The jungle, mountains and rivers simply would not allow the large-scale open terrain manoeuvre seen in North Africa. The SWPA required a change in tactics for the Australian infantry.

At Milne Bay, Curtis noted that the Japanese would conduct extensive reconnaissance from the concealment of the jungle. If a unit withdrew, the Japanese would pursue to prevent its soldiers reorganising and therefore the Allied commander could not mass for a counter-attack. Curtis also offered insights into the Japanese use of intimidation in the offence, as previously noted in the 2/10th Battalion's first engagement.[76] After the Japanese reconnaissance determined the most advantageous point in the defence for an assault, they would then deploy elements to another part of the defensive line to create noise by singing or sounding horns.[77] The intent was to draw resources off the point of the line the Japanese wished to attack. If the commander on the line became unnerved or believed the

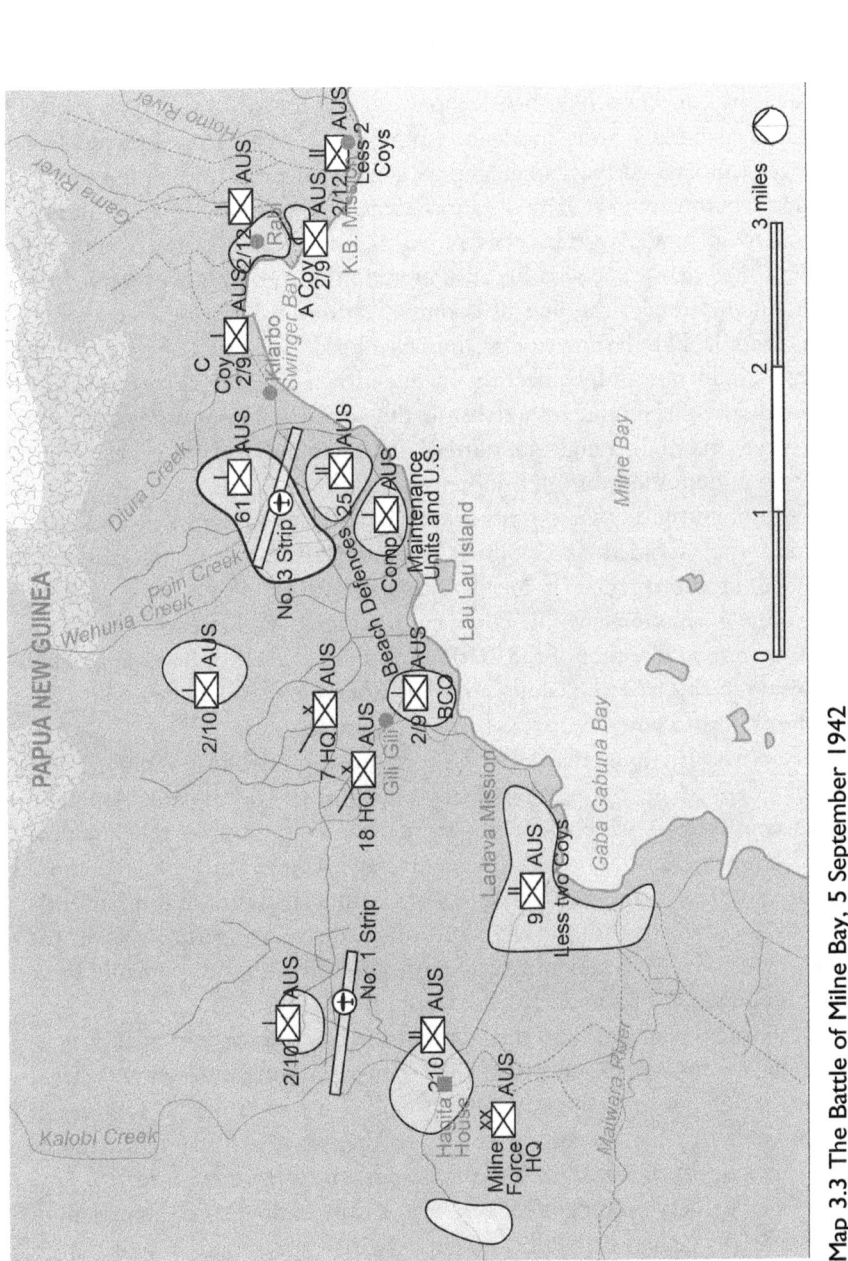

Map 3.3 The Battle of Milne Bay, 5 September 1942

Japanese deception, he might move additional troops or even crew-served weapons away from the point of the Japanese assault.

Many of the after-action reports dispel the myth of the Japanese soldier as an invincible fighter; one significant observation was the Japanese soldier's poor marksmanship skills.[78] The 18th Brigade had always emphasised marksmanship as a point of pride and as the key to combat manoeuvre in light infantry tactics. The importance of marksmanship in jungle warfare was noted not only for the effectiveness of killing the enemy but also because ammunition resupply was very difficult. In the jungle, the line of communication and logistics were often stretched. Unlike the entrenched lines of World War I or Tobruk, ammunition could not simply be run up and down the line as needed. The individual soldier, and by extension the squad, platoon and company, needed to maintain a high standard of fire discipline to avoid being caught low on ammunition during a Japanese assault.

Although the Japanese units conducted effective movement and infiltration, they avoided close combat when the Australian formations were massed in the offense. If faced with a disadvantageous position, the Japanese formations would conduct disciplined withdrawals, avoiding chaotic retreat like that of the 2/10th Battalion. The 18th Brigade quickly adapted to this by establishing a mobile reserve to counter Japanese infiltrations and to pursue Japanese troops in retreat.[79]

Reports also noted that Japanese formations tended to avoid the jungle and remained near the main roads and paths. Additionally, Japanese weapons systems were found to be inferior. For example, the Japanese 2-inch mortar was found to be ineffective and required direct hits to injure Allied soldiers.[80] The ineffectiveness of the mortar meant that it had little effect on the strength of the Australian defensive perimeters. If the Japanese mortars could not weaken a defensive line, the assault force had to attack the perimeter at full strength.

Logistical problems and the fact that the brigade was not operating as a single manoeuvre element until the Japanese landing force was in retreat make it difficult to analyse the 18th Brigade's use of artillery. However, it is possible to make some judgements on the use of artillery in the jungle and in support of the 2/9th Battalion's pursuit of Japanese forces.

Field artillery officers, who were historically in the rear or a position of observation such as on a hill, could not see their rounds fall into the jungle at Milne Bay. The jungle canopy also led the artillery officers and forward observers to recommend that in the jungle, artillery fire be directed behind the enemy and worked back towards friendly lines. One report stated:

'[T]he artillery observer needs to be within 100 yards of the enemy to be effective.'[81] Two issues were highlighted: the artillery officers could not see their target in the jungle, and the range on a map would not be accurate owing to the high jungle canopy. Rounds would hit the canopy and fall onto Allied lines when the same range and arch would have been sufficient in open terrain.

The early Milne Bay casualties included the two artillery observation officers. Their deaths were significant because their loss hampered the use of artillery and communications with the field artillery. Since infantry officers were not trained to conduct forward observation, the infantry battalions were left without supporting fire.[82] Another role of field artillery at Milne Bay was for marking Japanese formations for air support. The artillery fired smoke, which hung in the jungle canopy for longer than it would in the open, which allowed the air support to conduct more accurate fires.[83] The 18th Brigade's initial encounter with artillery in the jungle would lead to the training of each infantry officer as a forward observer in later campaigns.

Clowes's after-action reports identified specific limitations for Australian Army artillery in the jungle. He stated, 'The use of field artillery must be regarded as a special case since the observations for artillery fire is generally most difficult in jungle country.'[84] There is at least one disagreement with this perspective: Wootten, the 18th Brigade commander, who saw artillery as a necessity, repeatedly ordered 2/9th Battalion to use artillery as a first option when assaulting Japanese positions.[85]

Once the Japanese were in retreat, the 18th Brigade used its field artillery to disrupt the Japanese lines of withdrawal. This confusion allowed the Australian pursuit force, the 2/9th and 2/12th Battalions, to engage the disrupted formations, enveloping the smaller straggler elements.[86] The 2/9th Battalion noted that 'it is to be appreciated that most of the artillery ranging was done on the sea'.[87] The artillery officer would stand on the shoreline and fire a round along the beach as a method of determining distance. Then the field guns could adjust fire inland on Japanese formations. With 2/9th Battalion as the main body of the pursuit operation, Wootten repeatedly sent messages to it to use all available supporting arms. However, since Australian battalions had not trained extensively for manoeuvre supported by artillery, the 2/9th Battalion commander used artillery only when Japanese resistance was too heavy. Australian troops would pull back and provide the artillery the opportunity to soften the Japanese resistance.[88] In the end, a lack of tactics for the employment of artillery in the jungle and training for forward observation relegated artillery to an afterthought at Milne Bay.

It is also important to assess the role of air support in the destruction of Japanese forces at sea and on the ground at Milne Bay. Importantly, this support was general air support, not close air support directly controlled by ground manoeuvre elements. That would come later in the war. This was a case of available air power engaging targets of opportunity on the battlefield.

In one report, Clowes highlighted the value of collaboration with the aviation element assigned to Milne Force, but this was far from what would be needed in future brigade combat operations. Clowes stated, 'Our system of using one to three Air Liaison Officers in each squadron has definite advantage, particularly in jungle operations.'[89] These air liaison officers were not, however, forward air controllers; they were infantry and artillery officers assigned to perform three tasks. First, they were to inform the P-40 squadrons of the location and disposition of forward Allied ground formations. This helped pilots to distinguish between Allied and Japanese formations and thereby reduce friendly fire casualties. The second task was the briefing of aviation assets on known and suspected locations of Japanese troops, supply dumps and possible convoy routes. Lastly, the air liaison officers debriefed returning pilots for intelligence on Japanese formations, movements or reinforcements.[90]

None of these three tasks included the attack aviation working in direct support of the brigade or infantry battalions in attacks against Japanese positions. The ground infantry officer did not have the ability to direct air support from the front lines. Partly this was because of a lack of communications equipment, but the simple fact was that a ground infantry officer was never trained for the task. Two additional difficulties resulted from the speed of the P-40, which was not designed as a close air support platform. When on station, the aviators had to look for attempts by ground artillery units to mark Japanese targets with smoke in the jungle canopy.[91] This was dangerous for infantry units since Allied pilots could rarely see their targets under the canopy.

It did not take long after the 18th Infantry Brigade arrived at Milne Bay for the brigade staff Intelligence Section to realise that the intelligence capabilities of a brigade needed to be expanded. The task of the Intelligence Section this early in the war was like most other combat discipline: outdated and unprepared for modern warfare. Its stated task in the document 'Intelligence in the Brigade', dated 21 October 1942, included maintaining the Intelligence Diary, tracking enemy and friendly troop dispositions, and enciphering and deciphering messages.[92]

The infantry brigade and battalion headquarters at the start of the 18th Brigade's experience in the SWPA included one intelligence officer, one sergeant and an enlisted orderly or clerk.[93] It was immediately clear that this was not enough staff in a jungle environment. During the 2/9th Battalion's pursuit of the Japanese force in retreat, the intelligence officer requested that the brigade permanently assign two additional enlisted soldiers at the battalion headquarters Intelligence Section. One of these additional soldiers would serve in the headquarters section while the other served as a runner because of the havoc the rain dealt the radio equipment.[94]

One of the most frustrating challenges for the Intelligence Sections of the 18th Infantry Brigade was the failure to issue or acquire waterproof bags and other equipment. The primary equipment of the intelligence soldier in the SWPA was maps, tracing paper, notebooks, cipher sheets, handbooks and charts of enemy orders of battle, all which were highly susceptible to water damage on an island that often saw more than 200 days of rain per year.[95] Another challenge associated with water was the slow movement of runners. The combination of rain, jungle and the enemy's propensity for using snipers made it difficult to deliver intelligence or orders to manoeuvre units. In the case of the 2/10th Battalion, there was no means by which the battalion commander could request reinforcements or additional instructions before the line collapsed. In an effort to remedy these issues of communication, a 'signal and reports centre' was established in each battalion, which paired an intelligence clerk with a radio man.[96] This was a great first step in integrating intelligence functions across the brigade.

Another intelligence problem that hampered the entire theatre early in the SWPA campaigns was the lack of maps. As noted earlier, the maps the brigade did have were not military grade, and they were all made of regular paper, making them susceptible to damage in the rain. The list of intelligence recommendations from the Milne Bay operation included items simply necessary to do the job, such as increased staff numbers, waterproof maps, and cases.

The most significant recommendation was to have intelligence soldiers pushed down to the company level. The battalion Intelligence Sections noted a disconnect between the information-sharing at the battalion headquarters and company headquarters.[97] Company commanders, who did not have an Intelligence Section, often planned in a vacuum without an intelligence soldier present. Whether an omission or more likely a simple lack of intelligence personnel brigade-wide, the line infantry companies did not have internal intelligence support. None of the 18th Brigade officers was ignorant of the fact that future SWPA campaigns would include more jungles and likely amphibious warfare. This increase in personnel requested by the brigade, battalion and company Intelligence Sections would be essential to the success of Australian infantry brigades as an 'assault' Infantry Brigade Group (Jungle) later in the SWPA.

The 18th Infantry Brigade's burgeoning intelligence program did make progress during the Milne Bay operation. The after-action reports attempted to provide details on the Japanese weapons that were tested in the field.[98] The brigade was conducting basic document exploitation and weapons and technical intelligence of Japanese equipment. Annex A offers a list of all items captured, inventoried and tested. The majority were destroyed, but choice items were sent to Port Moresby and Australia for exploitation. Some of the documents captured included the Landing Order and training manuals for Japanese soldiers.

On 6 September 1942, the daily log recorded the capture of a Japanese prisoner and offered instructions for the handling of prisoners at the battalion level. Japanese 'prisoners are NOT to be questioned or shown any maps'.[99] It was the brigade commander's guidance that all prisoners immediately be moved to 18th Brigade headquarters. Intelligence is perishable and timely interrogations can change the course of a battle, but the movement of prisoners to brigade headquarters was also for the safety of the prisoners and the maintenance of the unit's integrity. The mishandling of prisoners by junior or unqualified interrogators does not reflect well on a commander, nor would any reprisals against prisoners by Australian soldiers.

The historical focus of this battle often rests with the collapse of the 2/10th Battalion when faced with Japanese infantry and tanks. Much of the criticism lies with the battalion's commander not bringing anti-tank guns to the fight, but possibly more significant was Clowes's decision to put five battalions in the defence and march out the 2/10th to confront the Japanese landing force without an effective reserve. The 2/10th Battalion history is keen to point out that they 'had the pleasure of opposing and completely obliterating' the same regiment of Japanese that fought in Milne Bay at Buna in December 1942.[100] The 2/10th Battalion might have extracted an element of revenge on the Japanese naval infantry a few months later at Buna; however, the importance of the battle was the fact that the Japanese had demonstrated the lethality of armour and infantry cooperation in the jungle. This left an impression on Australian brigade commanders and changed future training and doctrine for the rest of the war in the SWPA.

Although the battle was an Allied victory, Clowes's 'maintenance of the offensive spirit and offensive action' never came to fruition. Although Keogh, in *The South West Pacific 1942–45*, commented that 'Clowes intended to launch a strong counter stroke as soon as he was sure about the real direction of attack', it is clear that he was never able to determine the 'real direction of attack' until after the Japanese withdrawal was underway.[101] If the Japanese task force had been larger or if the Japanese commander chose to exploit the victory at KB Mission, the tactic of feeding a single infantry battalion at a time, without effective reserve, could have quickly proven disastrous for the Milne Bay defence. A combination of Clowes's conservative tactics and an unending stream of conflicting intelligence reports led to a missed opportunity to prevent the Japanese escape to Buna. The destruction of the Japanese force at Milne Bay would have reduced the devastating casualties the Allies suffered at Buna. Milne Bay represents the initial round of lessons learnt for the brigade; lessons on which the Australian Army would built the Infantry Brigade Group (Jungle).

CHAPTER 4

# THE BATTLE OF BUNA

> We often laughed when we should have cried.
>
> Allchin, *Purple and Blue*

The key battles at Buna and Sanananda fought by the 18th Infantry Brigade Group as part of Warren Force would result in its most disastrous casualties of the war. The 18th Brigade would suffer more casualties in one month than all three Australian Infantry brigades suffered in the three-month battle with the Japanese along the Kokoda Track.[1] Owen Curtis, a soldier in 2/12th Battalion, noted in five weeks of fighting in the Buna and Sanananda regions of New Guinea that the brigade would suffer a staggering 96 per cent casualty rate.[2] However, these same battles would pioneer brigade-level combined arms tactics in the jungle.

In January 1943 the Japanese strategy was to reinforce New Guinea and recapture the Solomon Islands through Rabaul. It was a costly strategy for both the Japanese and Allied armies. Allied casualties at Buna totalled 620 killed and 2065 wounded. The 18th Brigade suffered 267 killed and 1508 wounded. Conversely, it is estimated that Japanese casualties had exceeded 5000.[3] It is impossible to examine an Australian brigade at Buna and Sanananda without looking at the US regimental counterparts. The Battle of Buna was so costly in human lives that it changed the Allied leadership's understanding of the need for close cooperation of tanks and artillery at the brigade level in the SWPA.

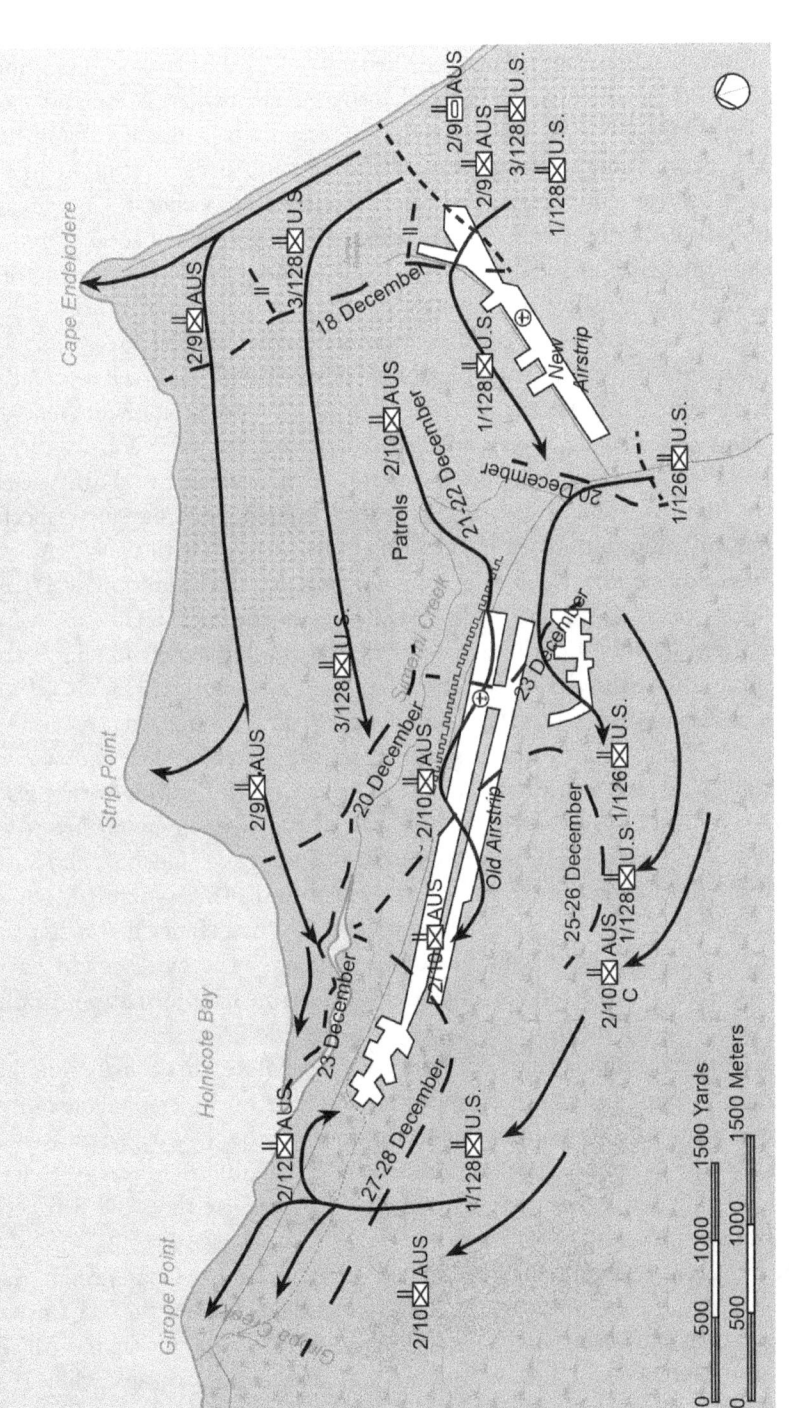

Map 4.1 The Battle of Buna, December 1942 – January 1943

The most important American general in the battles for Buna and Sanananda was Lieutenant General Robert Eichelberger, commander of the US Army, I Corps, who received the assignment after US Army VII Corps commander, Major General Robert Richardson (MacArthur's choice for the job), expressed great concern to General George C. Marshall, US Army Chief of Staff, about the possibility of serving under an Australian command.[4] Marshall understood better than anyone in the US War Department that this was an Allied war and that officers who could not function in an Allied environment would not be advanced.[5]

Eichelberger would prove his ability to work with – as well as greatly respect – his Australian counterparts; a trait his new commander General Douglas MacArthur, Supreme Allied Commander in the SWPA, did not share. Eichelberger recounted in a letter to his wife that 'shortly after I arrived in Australia, General MacArthur ordered me to pay my respects to the Australians and then have nothing further to do with them'.[6] Allied cooperation at any echelon is a significant piece of coalition warfare. In New Guinea, the US and Australian brigade and regiments were compelled by the physical environment and the Japanese to collaborate in spite of the attitudes of senior leaders such as MacArthur.

On 22 January 1943, MacArthur declared 'a striking victory' in the first campaign against the Japanese in the Pacific.[7] The victory in Guadalcanal was not declared until 9 February 1943. MacArthur also portrayed Buna as a victory of tactics and skill with minimal losses to Allied troops. The reality was entirely the opposite. Guadalcanal saw 60 000 troops committed with 1202 killed and 3070 wounded, while only 40 000 Allied troops were committed to Buna. Buna had a similar casualty rate at 620 killed and 2065 wounded.[8] The battle might have been costlier if not for the highly adaptive intermediate formations of the brigades and regiments.

The Buna campaign was declared a victory before the campaign on the island of Guadalcanal, largely to support MacArthur's personal narrative of the war, not the realities of the situation in the SWPA. To this end, MacArthur did not understand the terrain or capabilities of his National Guard units as he became increasingly frustrated by the slow progress at Buna.

Buna was tactically the opposite of Guadalcanal. At Guadalcanal, the Japanese were in the wet jungle and defending against the US forces, which held the beaches and the hard ground. At Buna, it was the Allied troops who were in the wet jungle and mangrove swamps while the Japanese held the beach and dry ground.[9] Eichelberger, who would come to command the Advanced New Guinea Force, noted in his memoirs that 'at Buna it was siege warfare'.[10] Buna and Sanananda would represent both a step back in time to siege warfare and an embrace of modern, combined arm manoeuvre. The Allied Warren and Urbana Task Forces, the first combined Australian and US task forces in the Pacific, struggled to bridge these two types of warfare against a hardened Japanese defensive line.

Another example of a senior Allied leader who early in the war did not understand the SWPA battlefields was the veteran World War I aviator, US General George Kenney, commander of the Allied Air Forces, SWPA. Kenney, an officer who had never experienced ground combat, believed that US and Australian troops stalled at Buna because they were 'lazy and complained about the rain and mud'.[11] Eichelberger would have disagreed and lamented that wounded Australian and US soldiers often died in the floods before they could be found by their units.[12] Kenney's famous adage, 'in this theatre [SWPA] artillery flies', and logistical limitations both influenced MacArthur's decision not to make armour or artillery a priority for the Buna campaign or respond to ground commanders' request for armour and artillery early in the campaign.[13] The capability to deploy close air support in close coordination with an infantry unit's manoeuvre would not come until later campaigns in the SWPA, but the need for such as relationship would be defined at the brigade level at Buna and Sanananda.

When challenged by a reporter he considered a 'callous amateur strategist' as to why the Allied force did not bypass Buna and let the Japanese 'starve and rot',[14] Eichelberger replied that the answer was in the massive size and scope of New Guinea. Geoffrey Holmes of the 2/12th Battalion noted later, 'I don't know whether you could just starve them out, or not, because the way they think, they'd stay there until there was no one left.'[15] The reality was that Allied forces did not have anywhere to bypass to that could be resupplied or reinforced from Port Moresby and Milne Bay. Additionally, the terrain and weather cannot be understated at Buna and Sanananda. Buna was a low, flat coastal area from the base of the Owen Stanley Range to the sea with dense jungles, decomposing swamps, and fields of kunai grass.[16] Land navigation was exceedingly difficult: entire companies of infantry disappeared into the deep water and overgrowth during combat operations.[17]

MacArthur and Kenney were not alone in their views on the utility of artillery and armour in jungle warfare; in fact, their perspective was textbook. The 1939 US Army *Field Manual 100-5 Operations* stated:

'Jungle warfare is characterised by close fighting. Artillery and other support weapons have only limited application.'[18] The problem was that the Operations Manual and *Field Manual 31-20 Jungle Warfare* were based the tactical understanding of jungle operations the United States had fought in Latin America against lightly armed local guerrilla movements, not against modern, highly organised and well-trained forces like the Imperial Japanese Army and Navy.[19]

The Buna campaign began with MacArthur's decision to rapidly reinforce the Australian Army in New Guinea. Major General Edwin Harding, commander of the US Army 32nd Division, recommended the 126th Infantry Regiment as the first unit to be deployed, calling them the 'best-trained and best led regiment'.[20] Subsequently, it was decided that the 126th Infantry Regiment would travel by foot over a less-travelled route of the Kapa Kapa Trail 48 kilometres from the Kokoda Track. Whether through ignorance or bravado, the decision to send the 2nd Battalion of the 126th Regiment, the top unit of the 32nd Division, over the mountains resulted in a broken command. The commanding officer succumbed to a heart attack crossing the treacherous mountains, and many of the troops fell ill or succumbed to injuries.[21] Harding's first battlefield decision would be indicative of his later judgements at Buna.

Harding's command of the 32nd Division was the first field command of his career. Having grown up and lived in Franklin, Ohio, most of his life, he would significantly underestimate both the terrain and the Japanese. He stated early in the SWPA: 'We might find it easy pickings ... may be a bum guess, but even if it proves to be incorrect, I do not think it would be too much to take Buna with the Forces we can put against it.'[22]

The 18th Brigade quickly reconsolidated and completed its after-action report, together with recommendations for the Australian LHQ after hostilities at Milne Bay subsided. The recommendations were validated by the LHQ by temporarily assigning 49 British officers to learn jungle warfare from the newly minted jungle soldiers of the 18th Brigade.[23] The British officers came from various units across India, including the Royal Berkshire Regiment, the Rajputana Rifles, the 2nd Welsh, 19th Lancers, 6th Hyderbad, Royal Armoured Cars and Indian Artillery units.[24] Although the British played only a nominal role in the SWPA, it is notable that the Australian Army's early experience in the jungle was recognised across the Allied commands in the Pacific.

The Milne Bay campaign had officially ended on 7 September 1942. Less than a month later, the 2/10th Battalion was gearing up for a first in the Australian Army: a battalion-sized combat airlift. On 5 October 1942, the 2/10th Battalion was ordered to move by air to the northern coast of New Guinea to defend against further Japanese advances out of Buna or any additional amphibious landings, although it was not defined in any of the written orders how a single infantry battalion would prevent a Japanese amphibious landing.[25]

What made this airlift significant for the Australian Army was that the 2/10th Battalion soldiers would be 'combat loaded' and ready to fight in case the Japanese attacked the airfield during the landing. Wanigela Airfield was in Allied hands, but Allied planners could not rule out the possibility that Japanese units operating in the area might attack the airfield. The combat airlift would include 80 troop lifts from Milne Bay to Wanigela Airfield on the north coast of New Guinea split among 18 available aircraft. The fear of Japanese forces or air attack at Wanigela resulted in the first lift of 18 aircraft conducting a tactical landing with aircraft spread out along the airfield. The plan included soldiers of the 2/10th Battalion disembarking the aircraft with weapons at the ready to defend the airfield from a possible Japanese attack.[26]

Again, the 18th Brigade was on untested ground from a staff planning level. Since no Australian brigade had ever conducted a combat airlift of an entire battalion, there was 'no standard payload' guide for troops, squads or companies.[27] This could result in an 'extreme possibility of overloading'.[28] Additionally, the load allowances for soldiers changed with distance of flight, fuelling facilities and type of aircraft – none of which the 18th Brigade had been required to consider before the order on 5 October.[29] After careful calculations for weight and equipment, each aircraft carried 15 soldiers with all their personal combat gear for the two-and-a-half-hour flight over the Owen Stanley Range and past the 16 000-foot snow-capped Mount Wilhelm.[30] This would have been the first time many of the soldiers had ever flown in an aircraft or seen a snow-capped mountain.

The airlift was completed successfully with no Japanese interference. Equally important, the 18th Brigade staff and subordinate 2/10th Battalion staff had been tasked with and accomplished another aspect of modern warfare, gaining valuable experience in working with army aviation as well as in staff planning for the unexpected. Rapid staff planning for an unforeseen or untested combat task would be the cornerstone of brigade-level operational art in the SWPA.

Allied aviation would become not only a key aspect of the war in the SWPA but also fundamental for brigade operations. However, at Buna it was a fledgling, amphibious support element that outpaced technology, communications and available aircraft. As much as Kenney strove to make the battles in New Guinea air-centric, it was maritime resupply that would sustain the force at Buna and Sanananda. Air planners who served on MacArthur's staff realised the limitations of air resupply only after the commitment of the Australian 7th Division and US 32nd Division to Buna. To add to the challenges, the 32nd Division's supply ships were sunk by the Japanese in mid-November, resulting in a shortage of supplies and ammunition. It was determined that if there was 'bad luck' in the form of an extended storm or low visibility over the Owen Stanley Range for more than four days, the force would deplete all food and ammunition.[31] This meant a real possibility of an Allied defeat at Buna.

On the night of 11 December 1942, the freighter *Karsik* made the first logistics run to Oro Bay to resupply Allied units at Buna. This established the route for both freighters and luggers, including the *Bath* and *Camara*, which in one night offloaded 850 tons of cargo. On 11–12 December, the maritime logistics line for the Australians outshipped the American airlift for the 32nd Division, bringing in nearly four tons of cargo to only one ton airlifted.[32] By the end of December, the 200 tons of combat supplies a day were reaching troops at Buna by sea.[33] This maritime logistics chain would supply the victory over the Japanese at Buna, who had been largely isolated from resupply.

Buna Village and Government Station was a cluster of three European-style homes and approximately 250 native huts. The strategic value of Buna was its airfields and proximity to Port Moresby at 102 miles distant and Milne Bay at 200 miles.[34] The main base of the Japanese in the SWPA was at Rabaul, 400 miles from Buna and 502 miles from Port Moresby, the Japanese objective on New Guinea. Therefore Buna would provide the ideal staging area for the assault on Milne Bay and the push to Port Moresby over the Kokoda Track. As soon as the Japanese landed the previous winter on 22 July 1942, they immediately expanded the Old Strip to 1300 by 60 metres to provide air support for an infantry push to Port Moresby.[35]

The Japanese had initially landed at Gona, north-west of Buna, and pushed to Buna the same day.[36] By the end of July, they had advanced high into the Owen Stanley Range, rapidly dismissing the limited Australian troops in the area. The Japanese quickly built fortified defences designed to canalise any Allied assault into one of four 'axes of advance' into prepared gun emplacements. First was through the swamp in front of Buna Village, while the second was across the open ground of the fork in the Soputa–Buna Track. Third was through the coconut plantation below Cape Endaiadere. The fourth and most exposed approach was across a narrow bridge that led directly into the Japanese perimeter.[37] This use of terrain, combined with a complex trench and bunker system, made the Japanese fortifications a formidable obstacle for Allied forces.

All of the 32nd Infantry Division's regiments arrived in New Guinea as 'regimental combat teams' with a variety of attached support units. However, none of the US regiments in New Guinea had ever trained as a regimental combat team. Unfortunately, these US regimental combat teams did not demonstrate anything like an understanding of operational art in regard to the 'combined arms team'. Like the Australian brigades, they were developing new tactics and capabilities in the regiments as the war progressed. Additionally, attachments assigned to US regiments in the SWPA offered little to make the regiment a more lethal combat force.

When the 127th Regiment moved forward to Buna, it had the following attachments: 3rd, 4th and 5th Portable Field Hospitals, Company B, 107th Medical Battalion, the 32nd and 37th Ordinance Detachments, and the 801st Photo Section.[38] Without armour, artillery or air force liaisons, there were plenty of attachments to treat casualties, but none to prevent them on the battlefield by more effectively defeating an enemy. In the Battle of Buna, it is clear that the officers and staff of the 32nd Division had little experience in integrated combined arms operations.

The costly battles in New Guinea hastened the US regimental combat teams' understanding of combined arms employment, which resulted in changes to subordinate attachments. By July 1943, the 127th Infantry Regiment had the following units attached: the 126th Field artillery Battalion, Company B of the 114th Engineer Battalion, a Reconnaissance Company of the 632nd Tank Destroyer Battalion, 23rd Quartermaster Detachment, the 32nd Ordnance Detachment, and the 5th, 17th and 23rd Portable Surgical Hospitals.[39] The addition of anti-tank, artillery and engineer units would greatly increase the US regimental combat team's manoeuvrability and lethality in later battles.

On 14 November 1942, New Guinea Force, commanded by Major General Edmund Herring, published the operations order for the assault on Buna.[40] The battle at Buna did not begin as a combined Allied operation, and there was little interest in cooperation between US and Australian infantry units. New Guinea Force had initially divided the Buna area of operations into two areas of operation separated by the Girua River.[41] One side was for the US 32nd Infantry Division, commanded by Harding, and the other side was for the 7th Australian Infantry Division, commanded by Major General George Vasey.[42]

The US 32nd Infantry Division's arrival was greeted by hard rains and floods, complicating its deployment in the Buna area.[43] At the same time, the Japanese reinforced Buna. Initially, the Buna garrison was approximately 1250 troops with another 800 troops nearby at Gona. On 16 November 1942, the Japanese navy landed another 1000 fresh troops and additional troops on the following nights.[44]

On 20 November 1942, the US 32nd Infantry Division met the Japanese for the first time. The assault forces included the 1st and 3rd Battalions of the 128th Infantry Regiment, with 1st Battalion of the 126th Regiment in reserve.[45] The 128th Regiment conducted a ten-minute barrage of artillery against Japanese positions. The 128th Regiment stepped off into Japanese anti-aircraft gunfire used in a direct fire role against the infantry.[46] This was a failure of the 128th Regiment to conduct adequate ground reconnaissance of Japanese positions, which could have revealed large weapons systems, such as anti-aircraft guns, and a hardened defensive line that provided cover for the initial artillery barrage.

In Harding's first action against the Japanese at Buna, he failed to order any ground reconnaissance or request aerial photographs of Japanese positions.[47] He considered his green troops to be too inexperienced in patrolling and infiltration in a jungle environment and that the casualties would outweigh the benefit.[48] When the 128th Infantry Regiment made its initial assault, both the 1st and 3rd Battalions were repelled and left confounded by the presence of fortifications. A line of well-constructed trenches and concealed machine-gun positions blunted the 128th Regiment.[49] Harding launched an infantry assault with little knowledge of where the Japanese perimeter began or ended.

The 128th Regiment had stopped and withdrawn when it encountered heavy Japanese resistance. This was not a singular incident. According to the 2/10th Battalion's own history, the US infantry officers had been taught that, if casualties became too high, the unit should halt, withdraw and use artillery to break the enemy before continuing the assault.[50] However, MacArthur and Kenney believed that artillery was of limited use in the jungle – which was supported by US Army doctrine – leaving the US regiments with an enormous problem. Since US units did not have significant artillery or tanks to support their doctrinal instructions for the use of artillery, units would simply withdraw from the attack if confronted with stiff Japanese resistance. This was the seminal problem for US infantry at Buna: dated doctrine and textbook leadership from Allied commanders. On 21 November, impatient for a victory and hundreds of miles from the front, Harding, 32nd Division commander, was sent the following message: 'Take Buna today at all cost, MacArthur.'[51] MacArthur was unaware that Harding's battle was already lost.

The 32nd Division had made a request for air support against the Japanese positions for an infantry attack on 20 November, even though Harding had little accurate information on Japanese positions. The aerial bombardment, although welcomed by the troops on the ground, was ineffective against hardened Japanese positions. In some cases, the miscommunication between the aviation units and the 32nd Division resulted in the postponement of offensive operations at Buna. The confusion between ground and air units resulted in Allied air support bombing the 1/128th Regiment on 22 November 1942.[52]

This stagnation of the 32nd Division at Buna is what would bring the Australian brigades, and specifically the 18th Brigade, to the forefront of the battle. At midnight on 29 November 1942, Eichelberger received orders from MacArthur to process immediately to Port Moresby and await orders to assume command of the 32nd Division. He took his chief of staff, six staff officers and ten enlisted men.[53] Later after the fall of Buna, Eichelberger would assume command of all troops in New Guinea north of the Owen Stanley Range.[54]

When Eichelberger arrived at Buna, he found Harding and his staff to be so far from the front that he would have had little if any communication with his own regiment during an assault on Japanese positions. This was in spite of US doctrine, which stated: '[D]uring the decisive phase of the battle the place of the commander is near the critical point of action.'[55] The US 32nd Division had suffered a failure of leadership at command level after nearly a month of failed attacks and stalemates against the Japanese front. To this point, 127th Regiment lost three regimental commanders between 11 December 1942 and 21 January 1943. Conversely, the US Colonel Clarence Tomlinson of Urbana Force asked to be relieved after three days of heavy losses to his force without advance.[56] Loss and failure of leadership, for both the US and Australians, was a significant challenge in the SWPA.

By 4 December 1942, Eichelberger had gutted the leadership of the 32nd Division, replacing them with I Corps officers he had brought from Australia. Harding was relieved and replaced by Brigadier General Albert Waldron, the division artillery officer. Colonel John Mott, commander of the 32nd Division's 'left flank force', was relieved by Colonel John Grose, the I Corps inspector general. Colonel Tracey Hale, commander of 'right flank force', was relieved by Colonel Clarence Martin, the I Corps G-3 operations officer.[57] All Eichelberger's replacements were World War I veterans and experienced infantrymen – neither of which ensured success in New Guinea.

The 32nd Division's 'left flank force' and 'right flank force', as named by Harding, had been reorganised into Urbana Force (left) and Warren Force (right). Additionally, Warren Force would become combined Australian and US forces with Eichelberger's plan for the integration of combat and jungle-experienced Australian infantry brigades into the force.

The Australian counterparts had not suffered the same failure of leadership, at least in part due to their previous combat experience. Not only had the US troops lacked training for jungle warfare but also they had not trained for static siege warfare. The 32nd Division had planned to fight in Europe – a battle in which they would rely heavily on artillery, tanks and air support on the open plains of Europe. However, owing to their rushed deployment, they had not been trained for that modern mechanised battlefield either. The technology, equipment and unit training simply had not been developed in the United States as quickly as the idea of a modern army. As one of the US Army's more experienced generals, having served with the American Expeditionary Forces in Siberia during World War I, Eichelberger had firsthand knowledge of the Japanese army. His service in Siberia left him as one of only a few US officers who was awarded the Japanese Order of Meiji, Order of the Sacred Treasure and Order of the Rising Sun. This personal knowledge of the Japanese army, along with his first-hand assessment of the battlefield, explains why Eichelberger wasted no time in the integration of Australian brigade and US regiments.

The 127th Regiment was the last regiment of the 32nd US Division to be committed to Buna on 11 December 1942. It was also the only US regiment of the 32nd Division to receive any formal training in Japanese tactics and jungle warfare; however, it was limited and not conducted until it arrived in its assembly area in Port Moresby. Soldiers were introduced to day and night patrolling in the jungle and response drills to Japanese snipers in trees.[58] The records of the 127th Regiment describe most of its early attacks against Japanese forces as 'men charging bunkers with grenades'.[59] This basic jungle training before combat did little to stem the 127th Regiment's casualties. The initial number of original soldiers totalled 2734, with only 505 soldiers still assigned on

1 February 1943. The Americans' lack of acclimatisation, training and experience took a heavy toll at Buna.

The 18th Brigade headquarters, to include Brigadier Wootten and the 2/9th Battalion, arrived by sea between 15 and 17 December with a complement of seven M-3 tanks of the 2/6th Field Armour Regiment. The need for tanks was a hard-learnt lesson from Milne Bay as well as a key element of the brigade's ability to operate as a combined arm manoeuvre force.

According to the US history of the Buna campaign, Wootten was given command of Warren Force over the American Colonel Martin because he was senior in rank.[60] On 17 December 1942, Eichelberger asked Wootten to assume command of Warren Force with orders to seize Cape Endaiadere, New and Old Strip, and Buna Government Station.[61] The 18th Brigade and Wootten had just come from a victory in Milne Bay fighting the same units in similar jungle terrain. Eichelberger chose to create combined task forces, which spread Australian combat experience and jungle knowledge across the force.

Figure 4.1 The 18th Infantry Brigade, supported by armour, conduct the final assaults of the Buna campaign at Giropa Point. Private Armitage on the far right has fixed his bayonet in expectation of the close fight to come clearing the Japanese pillboxes and trenches. (AWM 014035)

A review of the 18th Brigade's 'Operations Order Number 1', dated 17 December 1942, makes it clear that Wootten had little confidence in the 32nd Division. All the 32nd Division elements in Warren Force were relegated to supporting tasks in the operations order. The US 128th Regiment was tasked as reserve element that would occupy and hold terrain seized by the 18th Brigade.[62] On 19 December, the 1/126th and 1/128th Battalions were tasked to maintain pressure on their fronts – they were not ordered to advance. The US regiments had not had much success in the offence, but this 'pressure' would prevent the Japanese from reinforcing the units under direct assault by the 18th Brigade.[63]

The 18th Infantry Brigade Group's 'Operations Order Number 1' identified the attachments that made the 18th a brigade group: one squadron of 2/6th Armoured Regiment, one troop of 2/1st Field Regiment, one troop of 2/5th Field Regiment, one troop of 1st Mountain Battery, one detachment of 2/4th Field Engineer Company, one detachment each of 2/5th and 10th Field Ambulance, one detachment of Australian Army Service Corps and Australian Army Ordnance Corps, and lastly carriers from the 17th Infantry Brigade. The concept of 'group' or adding and subtracting attachments for specific task was the key to the Australian brigade's evolution and combat effectiveness. In addition, as part of Warren Force, the Brigade Group also listed the US Army 128th Regiment, which included the 1/126th, 1/128th and 3/128th Battalions and other enumerated US attachments.[64]

The 18th Brigade initiated an extensive reconnaissance over several days of the Buna area of operations, which determined that the Japanese had constructed a complex of bunkers that were mutually supporting and interconnected.[65] This allowed the Japanese to communicate rapidly and to facilitate the movement of reinforcements along the defensive line. It was this series of fortification against which the 32nd Infantry Division had bludgeoned itself since early November 1942.

On 18 December, the 2/9th Battalion, as the lead element of Warren Force, with M3 tanks from the 2/6th Armoured Regiment, initiated its first attack at Buna.[66] Wootten had asked the Air Corps to provide low overflights to cover the noise of the tanks, and although support was promised, it never came. One significant difference over previous assaults was the 18th Brigade's use of artillery support against registered targets identified by reconnaissance, not a traditional World War I-style scheduled 'rolling barrage'.[67] This was partly because there were not enough

Figure 4.2 Private Searle and Corporal Fletcher of the 2/12th Infantry Battalion fire on Japanese soldiers 150 yards away with a Bren Mark I machine gun and SMLE No. I MKIII rifle at Giropa Point, New Guinea. (AWM 014001)

guns or the logistical support for the ammunition requirements. However, the use of artillery against registered targets, crew-served weapons and strongpoints allowed the 2/9th Battalion to break through Japanese lines to the coast in just one hour. Eichelberger described the assault as 'gallantly and brilliantly executed'.[68]

Eichelberger had tasked the Warren Force with an assault on Durpoa Plantation, Cape Endaiadere and the New Air Strip.[69] The approach was slow, with the reserve forces 'beating the bush' to ensure the Japanese did not hide in concealed positions until the infantry passed by to attack from the rear. This was another costly lesson learnt in Milne Bay.[70]

The combined assault of tanks and infantry was a success. Eichelberger noted the 2/9th Battalion's attack 'was a spectacular and dramatic assault, and a brave one ... steady tanks and infantrymen advanced through the spare, high coconut trees, seemly impervious to the heavy opposition'.[71] However, the 2/9th Battalion was not invincible and the assault on Japanese positions without heavy artillery or air support cost the battalion 49 killed and 111 wounded in one day's action.[72] It was a major success in breaking the Japanese defensive line in the Durpoa and New Air Strip area but, more importantly, it established the precedent for infantry brigade and tank cooperation rather than as operating as separate entities on the same battlefield.

Another key to the victory of the 18th Brigade on 18 December was Wootten's order to the battalion military intelligence officers to conduct a detailed 'close reconnaissance' of Japanese positions.[73] The 32nd Division had failed to do adequate intelligence preparation of the battlefield, specifically ground reconnaissance, before their first engagement with the Japanese at Buna that quickly resulted in confusion on the battlefield. Throughout the early campaigns in New Guinea, Allied battalions and regiments found that the maps they had been issued were of no value. At Buna, they would be required to conduct their own detailed reconnaissance of each objective.[74] The development of ground reconnaissance and intelligence management at the brigade level would be a staple of infantry brigade groups for the rest of World War II.[75] The 18th Brigade's revaluation of brigade intelligence capabilities and requirements after Milne Bay contributed greatly to the victories at Buna.

The assault of 23 December 1942 would not be as successful. Five companies of the US 127th Infantry Regiment attempted an assault against another Japanese position at Buna. The 127th Regiment followed a 'rolling barrage' of artillery with infantry companies on-line – essentially, a World War I assault on an enemy defensive line. It failed to conduct a sufficient reconnaissance of the terrain between their position and the Japanese line. In correspondence to MacArthur, Eichelberger noted that the 127th Regiment advanced behind the rolling barrage; however, two of the companies became bogged down and lost the ability to communicate with the rest of the regiment.[76]

Since all companies had started on line, there was no reserve or manoeuvre company to support the one element of the 127th that managed to push through the Japanese defences. Additionally, US infantry officers were not trained to call for fire from the artillery, nor did they have an artillery forward observer. Ultimately, forward units could not exploit their advance and the entire 127th Regiment withdrew from the field. The confusion in the advance led to artillery dropping rounds onto friendly forces, the only friendly forces to overrun a Japanese position.[77] Eichelberger called the retreat the 'all-time low' of his life.[78] This assault by the 127th Regiment demonstrated the challenges of adopting new tactics during combat. The 128th Regiment, after more than a month of combat, still reverted to old tactics in spite of repeated failures.

On 25 December 1942, the 1st and 3rd Battalions, 128th Regiment and 2/10th Battalion assaulted on the Old Strip with an envelopment led by the 128th and reinforced by a company of 2/10th Battalion, while main efforts assaulted the Japanese line. It took the combined force until noon on the 28th before the Japanese fortification fell.[79] This cleared the path for the final large-scale assault of Warren Force during the Buna campaign.

On 29 December, Wootten devoted the morning to organising the combined assault force around the support of four tanks, newly arrived tanks, with seven additional tanks in reserve.[80] Wootten had been an early proponent of the integration of infantry and tanks in Australia before the deployment to New Guinea, but never had the chance to train or exercise the brigade with its armoured counterparts. The development of close cooperation of tanks and infantry would have to be worked out on the battlefield of Buna and Sanananda.

On 31 December, Warren Force finally brought all elements of a combined arms force to bear on the Japanese. Field artillery and mortars engaged Japanese positions. The 2/12th Battalion with its six tanks was able to reach the beach at 0830 on 1 January 1943. The 128th Regiment on the 2/12th Battalion's left flank had a much slower rate of advance even though it served as a guard and not the main effort. The 128th reported that the lack of tanks greatly slowed its advance.[81] This manoeuvre effectively cut the Japanese forces; however, even with the support of tanks, the 2/12th Battalion suffered 62 killed and 128 wounded.[82] The 128th Regiment did clear the southern end of the point once Warren Force assigned it a complement of eight tanks.[83] It had become clear that the cooperation of tank and infantry was essential against fortified jungle positions.

On 3 January 1943, General Blamey sent a letter of praise to Brigadier Wootten, complimenting his planning, steadiness and determination in his victory at Buna.[84] The Battle of Buna had demonstrated the flaws in outdated doctrine and changed MacArthur's belief that tanks and artillery would be impractical and impossible to manoeuvre in the jungle environment. The 18th Infantry Brigade, as part of Warren Force – one of the first two combined Australian and US ground task forces of the SWPA campaign – had demonstrated the value of combined arms and of the infantry brigade group in combat. More importantly, the 18th Brigade was developing the operational art needed to command these increasingly complex brigade formations in support of campaign objectives.

One military observer from the US War Department reported that there was no concept of an infantry–artillery or infantry–tank team among US units at Buna.[85] A second military observer noted that there were only two US-trained artillerymen in the whole of Buna.[86] This was another reflection on the SWPA Allied Headquarters misunderstanding of modern warfare in the jungle. The message back to the US War Department was clear: the key to fighting the Japanese in the Pacific was the cooperation of infantry, armour and artillery.[87]

## THE SANANANDA CAMPAIGN

Organised Japanese resistance at Buna ended on 2 January 1943, but just up the New Guinea coast the Allies had stalled at Sanananda. The decision was made to use the 18th Brigade, despite heavy losses at Buna, as a blocking force for the US offensive. By 7 January the majority of the beleaguered 18th Brigade had arrived at Sanananda. At his first staff meeting at Sanananda, Wootten discovered that the plans had changed and that his brigade would be leading the main assault against the Japanese forces.

The Advanced New Guinea Force had few maps and even less intelligence about Japanese forces at Sanananda. Eichelberger reported back to MacArthur's headquarters that he did not know whether the Japanese had one thousand or five thousand soldiers in Sanananda.[88] When Eichelberger arrived at Sanananda, he ordered all units to conduct extensive reconnaissance of the Japanese line.[89] This was a challenge in the swamp, and the 10 inches of rainfall each night made it a near-impossible task in some areas. Worse yet, during storms at Buna, soldiers sustained electrical shock by lightning strikes in the swamps.[90] The 18th Brigade Staff Intelligence Section would participate and task subordinate battalions and companies to conduct ground reconnaissance of Japanese positions. Like Milne Bay and Buna, the fledging intelligence and reconnaissance capabilities of an infantry brigade would be key in combat.

On 12 January 1943, the 18th Brigade planned a direct assault against Japanese defensive positions that would incorporate as many supporting arms as possible.[91] The 163rd US Infantry Regiment had been requested to advance on the 18th Brigade's southern flank to relieve pressure and prevent Japanese reinforcement of the defensive line. The 163rd Infantry Regiment of the 41st Infantry Division, US Army, had travelled by sea to

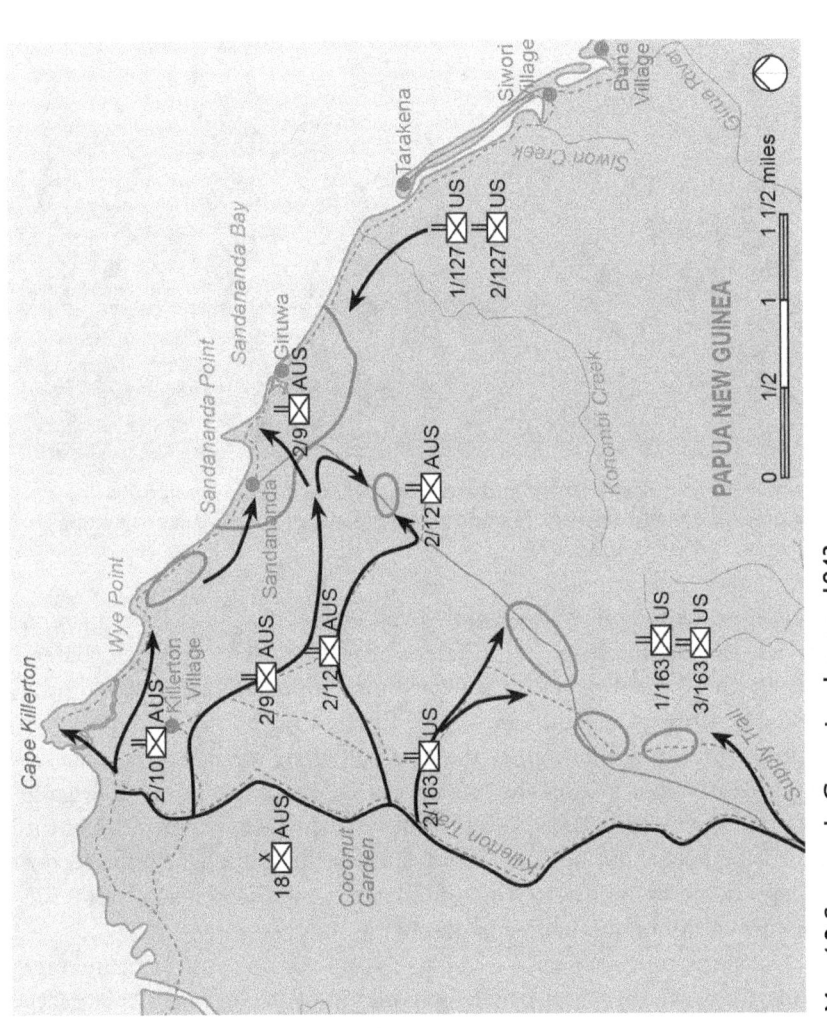

Map 4.2 Sanananda Campaign, January 1943

Figure 4.3 Australian infantry and armour advance in the wake of the devastation of 18th Infantry Brigade's final assault of the Sanananda campaign in Papua. (AWM 030258/09)

Port Moresby then flown over the Owen Stanley Range to participate in the Sanananda campaign on 27 December 1942. The 163rd Regiment was another US Army National Guard formation that had received little combined arms instruction and no jungle training before deployment.[92] Wootten intended to assault to the north all along the line to prevent the Japanese from reinforcing any one part of the line while the 18th Brigade encircled their entire force. The US Colonel Jens Doe, commander of the 163rd Regiment, did not see the advance in the same light and did not believe an attack by the 163rd would have the desired effect of relieving pressure or hold the Japanese in place.[93]

The Battle of Sanananda is relatively obscure in Australian military history; however, it was a key demonstration of the brigade's emergence as a combined arms formation in a jungle environment. The 18th Brigade would lead an attack on Japanese positions with assault elements made up of the 2/9th and 2/12th Battalions and one company from 2/10th Battalion. The assault force had three tanks from 2/6th Armour in direct support. In reserve was the rest of the 2/10th Battalion, 2/9th and 2/12th Battalion's Mortar Sections, 2/7th Cavalry Regiment, with one additional tank.[94] A significant number of artillery pieces and armour scheduled to reallocate to Sanananda never arrived owing to heavy rain. The artillery that was available was of limited use because the 18th Brigade was within 50 metres of the Japanese lines.

Again, this would be a combined operation with the US Army. Colonel Doe did not share Wootten's enthusiasm for an assault on the 12th and believed there would be unnecessarily high casualties to the 163rd Regiment. Unlike at Buna, where Wootten was the commander of Warren Force and therefore had operational control of assigned US units, at Sanananda, the relationship with the 163rd Regiment was noted as 'cooperating', not subordinate.[95]

Doe argued that his troops would be better employed in the role of cutting off Japanese supply lines.[96] At no point in the record of the conference did he articulate where these Japanese supply lines were located, but it can be assumed from his general aversion to the assault that he believed them to be behind the 18th Brigade's assault. The conference ended when Doe stated that he would not be able to attack on the 13th and probably not on the 14th, but it would be a good idea if Wootten came back the next day at 1600 to discuss the issue further.[97] The conference was recorded in a report called 'Report on the Visit to Headquarters 163rd US Regiment'.

The assault of 12 January 1943 went ahead without the participation of the 163rd Regiment. The 18th Brigade suffered 34 killed and 66 wounded in one day, and although they did not overrun the Japanese fortifications, the brutal combined arms assault did break the Japanese will to defend.[98] The force of the attack, with artillery, tanks and infantry, led the Japanese commander, Colonel Hatsuo Tsukamoto, to determine that his position was untenable. That night he gave the order to withdraw all able-bodied soldiers.[99] The 18th Brigade's assault, with infantry and armour in a mutually supported role, had forced the withdrawal of the Japanese from Sanananda. In a theatre of World War II where US and Australian historians rarely acknowledge each other, US Army official history credits the 18th Brigade's assault on Colonel Tsukamoto's position as the source of victory in Sanananda.[100]

The relationship with the 163rd Regiment would not be mended. The 163rd was relegated to flank and rear guard for the duration of the advance. The account of the battle in *With the 41st Division in the Southwest Pacific* reported the 163rd Regiment as having killed 1400 Japanese soldiers without mention of a single Australian unit in Sanananda.[101] However, in the final tally, the 163rd Regiment never participated in more than 'a long series of scattered skirmishes' on the Sanananda front.[102]

Unaware of the Japanese decision to withdraw from Sanananda, and after the 18th Brigade's assault failed to break the Japanese line, Eichelberger called a commanders' conference that included Lieutenant Colonel Reginald Pollard, senior staff officer of the 7th Division, Major General Frank Berryman, commander of the 2nd Australian Corps, and General Vasey on 13 January. Vasey described the assault against the Japanese pillboxes and bunkers as reminiscent of World War I.[103] He advocated the withdrawal of the infantry and launched a large air strike in the belief that the Japanese would flee when faced with Allied air power. Vasey's push for large-scale airstrikes is understandable considering the losses in Allied infantry units. It is still, however, one-dimensional to recommend infantry or air, but not in concert.

Over the next two days, ground reconnaissance revealed a general withdrawal of Japanese troops from the fortified positions in Sanananda. This offered Eichelberger two choices: first, consolidate and reorganise the force for a pursuit of the Japanese, or second, launch an immediate attack on the weakened Japanese lines. Eichelberger chose the latter and ordered an all-out assault against Japanese positions all along the line. It was largely up to Wootten and the 18th Brigade to organise and lead this offensive.

By 15 January 1943, the 18th Brigade had seized Sanananda and turned south to link up with Urbana Force lead by the US 127th Regiment.[104] Frank Hartley's history of the Sanananda campaign offers observation from the 2/7th Cavalry, which had preceded the 18th Brigade. The soldiers of the 2/7th Cavalry had been in a stalemate with the Japanese for several days when the 18th Brigade arrived. Hartley noted: '[W]e [2/7th] were amazed at the speed with which the [18th] brigade moved.'[105] The 2/7th Cavalry flatly stated that they were left to clean up a field of corpses behind the 18th Brigade.[106]

The costliest battles of the SWPA had finally ended with an Allied victory. Owen Curtis of the 2/12th Battalion recalled a conversation with a US Army colonel, who, after the Sanananda campaign and two weeks in the rain and swamps, said to Curtis, 'I'm not made for this kind of job. I can't do this.'[107] No one on either side of the Buna and Sanananda campaigns was made for the challenges of the jungle. The conditions in the Japanese bunker complexes in both Buna and Sanananda were horrifying at best. The battle history of the 2/10th Battalion described hospital bunkers as stacked four deep with the rotting bodies of dead Japanese soldiers and labourers. Each bunker the Allies overran revealed a combination of dead, long dead and the living who were beyond human care.[108] The battles of Buna and Sanananda were a human tragedy on all sides.

## After-action assessment

The evolution of brigade combat operations early in the SWPA can be traced by looking at the operations orders generated by Australian and US units at Sanananda. There is a considerable difference in the sophistication of the written operations orders in this theatre. A comparison of two operations orders at Sanananda, one of the US Army's 126th Regiment and the other the 18th Brigade's order from the battle of 11 January 1943, demonstrate a stark difference in the experience of the commanders and staffs.

The 18th Brigade's 'Operation Order Number 5', dated 11 January 1943, was a well-structured document, which shows the experience of Wootten and the brigade staff in regard to written orders with well-defined phases of the attack and the integration of subordinate units and supporting arms. The document demonstrates Wootten's plan for a combined arms manoeuvre supported by artillery and armour. The artillery was tasked with the engagement of registered targets in two target areas forward of the advance, as well as assigning artillery forward observers to each battalion for the assault. The armoured element provided similar guidance for the support of 2/9th and 2/12th Battalions' manoeuvre scheme. It defined the integral roles of supporting elements in infantry manoeuvre, not as a separate task but as integrated functions of the force. For example, the 2/1st Field Artillery Regiment was tasked with engaging registered targets before movement and remaining on call for targets' impeding manoeuvre as they might arise on the battlefield – not just providing a traditional 'rolling barrage' over enemy positions.

In contrast, as noted earlier, the 126th Infantry Regiment had limited training and experience in modern infantry tactics and had not trained in jungle warfare. In the 126th Regiment's Operation Order for an attack on Semimi Creek on the night of 20/21 December 1942, the document called for a ten-minute artillery barrage on the object before assault and requested the artillery remain on call in case of Japanese counter-attack. These were separate static tasks of the artillery without the flexibility required for the support of infantry manoeuvre.

The 1/126th Battalion orders for infantry manoeuvre were clearly reminiscent of textbook instructions. For example, the operations order never mentioned any combined arms manoeuvre, only specific infantry instructions. One command instructed troops to 'move 75 yards up the trail. Then the right and left flanks spread out 75 yards respectively of each side of the trail.'[109] After this advance, 'when this area has been gained the troops will dig in and hold this semi-circle formation'.[110] The instruction was textbook infantry manoeuvre in a terrain where textbook manoeuvre was simply not possible. The 1/126th Battalion's assault stalled early and retreated when engaged by the Japanese in defensive positions.[111] The fact is that Allied Headquarters in Australia deployed the 32nd and 41st Infantry Divisions to New Guinea completely unprepared for combat.

An examination of infantry tactics and manoeuvre at Buna and Sanananda highlights the limited training of Australian and US formations in New Guinea. Even captured Japanese reports assessed the Allied infantry as having 'received almost no training, even though we fire a shot they present a large portion of their body and look around. Their movements are very slow and at that rate they cannot make a night attack.'[112] On 4 January 1943, the Japanese launched one of the few attempts of a pre-emptive assault on the 32nd Division. Inexperience plagued the US National Guard soldiers who fired into the jungle at great rates of fire long before they could see the Japanese attackers. Low on ammunition, the 32nd Division withdrew in disarray into the jungle.[113]

The 18th Brigade's after-action reports noted that the Japanese defensive lines were inflexible in their tactics, which allowed Warren Force to surprise them on several occasions.[114] The utility of surprise would become a tenet of brigade operations in the SWPA. However, it is entirely possible that Japanese forces at Buna and Sanananda had suffered from exhaustion and starvation to the point where their situational awareness was collapsing.

Surprise as an element of an assault was used when enemy weaknesses, identified by photo and ground reconnaissance, were left undefended because the Japanese believed the terrain was too difficult to manoeuvre through in an assault. For example, at Buna, ground reconnaissance identified a south-west approach to the Old Strip aerodrome through tall kunai grass, deep swamp and jungle. The 18th Brigade attacked from the south-west through the swamp and jungle and quickly overran the Japanese positions.[115]

Another tactic used against Japanese defensive lines was a classic infantry tactic that would have been familiar on the Western Front of World War I: apply pressure all along the defensive line until the weak point breaks and then flood the breach. For example, on 11 January 1943, the 2/9th Battalion, which faced a strongpoint in the Japanese fortification, maintained contact and pressure even though not advancing. The 2/12th Battalion, to the 2/9th flank, had identified a weak point and applied increasing force, in cooperation with tanks, against the weak point. The pressure exerted by the 2/9th on the strongpoint prevented the Japanese from reinforcement of the line under assault by the 2/12th Battalion. Subsequently, the weak point broke within 48 hours, and 2/12th Battalion manoeuvred through the breach 'mushrooming' behind the defensive line.[116]

The 18th Brigade's after-action report also called for the reinforcement of the newly learnt jungle warfare principles, which included the use of personal camouflage, the conservation of ammunition, and noise discipline.[117] As a practical matter, stretcher barriers that carried the wounded needed to be re-armed with shorter Owen guns in the jungle. Another of the 18th Brigade's most important recommendations was to change the pioneer company's 'equipment tables' to match that of an equivalent-sized infantry unit. The pioneers' contribution to manoeuvre in the harsh terrain was of great value in the jungle environment. They operated close to the front lines and had participated in confrontations with the Japanese at Milne Bay, Buna and Sanananda. Specialty troops, like the pioneers, needed basic combat training and better weapons, especially in the poorly defined front lines of the jungle. Lastly, the 18th Brigade noted that it would be 'highly desirable' for the condiment of mustard to be added to the rations to improve the taste.[118]

The 18th Brigade Staff's Intelligence Section again demonstrated the value of increased intelligence personnel and capabilities at the brigade and battalion levels – a reinforcement of the lessons learnt at Milne Bay. At Buna and Sanananda, patrolling was the most important aspect of jungle warfare and was essential to identification of the Japanese fortifications and trenches.[119] There was clear association between reconnaissance and Allied victories. The sheer number of elements required to conduct ground reconnaissance revealed a significant shortfall in compasses and binoculars.[120] All of the equipment concerns in the after-action report of Milne Bay – waterproof materials, maps, trained intelligence specialist and so on – resurfaced, likely owing to insufficient time for the recommendations submitted in October 1942 for such to be requisitioned and deployed to New Guinea.

Every unit that served at Buna and Sanananda complained about the quantity and quality of maps. Much of New Guinea had simply never been mapped with modern equipment. As a means to augment the

Figure 4.4 General George Vasey, General Edmund Herring and Brigadier George Wootten in Papua after the hard-fought victories of the Buna and Sanananda campaigns. (AWM 014308)

inaccurate maps issued by Allied Headquarters, the 18th Brigade's Intelligence Section made great use of photo interpretation. The brigade intelligence officer praised the ability of the non-commissioned officers, trained as analysts, to interpret aerial photography with a greater degree of accuracy than the issued maps. The 18th Brigade recommended that intelligence personnel at the brigade and subordinate battalion staffs be trained in aerial photographic interpretation.[121] This would allow for rapid analysis of photos at the unit level – a great benefit given the fast pace of modern brigade combat.

The Australian and US infantry units' after-action reports rarely mention Allied air support at Buna and Sanananda. This is because close air support had not yet been developed to a point where it could be integrated into the infantry brigade's operation order. However, the diaries of captured Japanese soldiers highlight the importance of Allied air superiority at Buna and Sanananda. Allied infantry had not been able to use air support when assaulting Japanese bunkers; air power over the battlefield and the seas prevented counter-attack and, more importantly, Japanese resupply. Without logistical support, primarily food and ammunition, the Japanese could not win – it was only a matter of how difficult they could make the Allied victory. Air strikes against Japanese positions, although poorly coordinated, frustrated the defenders at Buna and Sanananda to such an extent that it was written about daily in the captured diaries of Japanese soldiers.[122]

Artillery was proven essential at Buna and Sanananda, although it was often absent or underutilised because of movement constraints imposed by the jungle, swamps and torrential rains. Additionally, artillery was not an early priority of the Allied leadership, resulting in an insufficient number of artillery units allotted to the Australian and US formations.

The 18th Brigade used the available 25-pounders in a direct fire role against Japanese pillboxes and bunkers when the terrain allowed the guns to be moved close to the front. Many of the failed assaults in Buna failed to identify or specifically target bunkers as part of the operations order. The 25-pounders, whether they penetrated the bunker or not, pinned the Japanese into bunkers long enough to facilitate infantry manoeuvre. Additionally, the 18th Brigade recommended the addition of delayed fuses for artillery used on hardened positions.[123]

There were negative reports on the use of artillery. The Japanese diaries recorded repeated occasions when sustained volumes of artillery fire, which was largely ineffective at penetrating bunkers, was used with a follow-on infantry assault.[124] The Japanese considered this a reckless tactic and wasteful use of artillery, especially since their logistics lines had become haphazard. It was not only the Japanese who had opinions about the American use of artillery. Throughout the SWPA campaigns, there would be a repeated doctrinal discussion on how much artillery was enough for a brigade. Brigade commanders on the front lines would probably have answered 'more'.

The relationship between infantry and armour in terms of jungle warfare was still in its infancy in 1942. However, there were significant advancements at Buna and Sanananda. This cooperation was in no way seamless, but it did become accepted as necessary. The 18th Brigade, as the head of Warren Force, commanded its own tanks for the first time at Buna. Despite the Allied Headquarters' resistance to the validity of armour in jungle and logistical challenges it presented, the request of infantry commanders and the failure of the 32nd Division to advance against Japanese fortifications forced a shift in rear-echelon perspectives. The tanks provided to the Buna front were slow and lightly armoured, and Japanese anti-tank systems proved effective against them in both campaigns; however, the most effective combination was the mutual cooperation of tank fire support with the tanks protected by infantry.

The concepts of integration and close cooperation between line infantry units and tank formations that Wootten had proposed in an early 1942 training document began to emerge by the time forces reached Sanananda. The basic tactics employed consisted of three tanks accompanied in the advance by an infantry element. The assault force main body would follow some 50 metres behind the forward infantry–tank team.[125] Usually, a reserve element of tanks was held back with the infantry reserve or manoeuvre element. This was the case at Sanananda, on 12 January 1942, when the 18th Brigade launched its combined arms assault against Japanese positions.[126]

Armoured units in Buna and Sanananda were often used in unconventional roles such as counter-sniper. Snipers and forward observers in high trees could stop an infantry unit's advance and prove costly in terms of casualties. Infantry units found it difficult to get close enough to engage the Japanese snipers. The addition of the tank provided the brigade or battalion commander with an option that allowed infantry units to maintain their momentum. The 18th Brigade used tanks and anti-tank guns instead of individual soldiers or squads, against trees holding snipers and forward observers whenever possible, to prevent casualties.[127] This proved a highly effective tactic that would be employed throughout the SWPA.

The official reports on the Battle of Buna called for closer coordination with tanks in future, but for all the successes, in several cases the tank crews developed an aversion to leaving their tanks, as the tank provide a sense of security. One report described them as 'cocooned' in their tanks.[128] This created leadership challenges and limited the integration of the tank crews with infantry counterparts. Additionally, tank commanders did not attend commander conferences or briefs before an assault.[129] This lack of coordination potentially resulted in unnecessary losses of tanks owing to confusion between the tank crews and infantry outside the tanks. The Japanese, on the other hand, were well versed in the use of tanks. Japanese fortifications included anti-tank mines and anti-tank guns on suspected avenues of approach.[130] Post-Buna, cooperation between infantry and tanks would need to be much closer.

## CONCLUSION

As the 32nd Infantry Division's chief of staff noted, the idea 'That the allied troops took Buna as a result of superior leadership, arms, and tactics is sheer fantasy. Attrition worked both ways, but our supply (although meager) was better than the Japanese supply as they were completely isolated. We lived the longest and therefore took our objectives.'[131] The Buna and Sanananda battles would be the 18th Infantry Brigade's most costly of World War II. The 18th Brigade reported its losses at 96 per cent between diseases and casualties by the time fighting ended in February 1943. In B Company, 2/10th Battalion, Private Wright was the only soldier to have served all the way through both Buna and Sanananda.[132] On the US side, General Eichelberger held a ceremony for the 126th Infantry Regiment after its battle in Girua, and of the 1100 soldiers who were in the regiment at the beginning of the battle, only 95 attended the ceremony.[133] As a result, formal jungle warfare training would become a requirement for all Allied formations participating in future campaigns.[134] Eichelberger noted in his memoirs that 'from Australian commanders in the field I received cooperation, sound advice, and fraternal understanding which arises from what St Paul described as the fellowship of suffering'.[135] It was this 'suffering' that forced Australian brigades and US regiments to evolve or be decimated.

The evolution of the Australian infantry brigade in late 1942 and early 1943 was one of dire necessity. The 18th Brigade's slow but steady development of an organic 'operational art' took place on the battlefield and emerged from new threats and challenges that required rapid, in-theatre solutions. Command and staff challenges such as battalion airlifts without a doctrinal precedent, new intelligence tactics, and attempts to coordinate combined arms manoeuvre at the brigade level were large steps towards the brigade as an effective combined-arms formation in the Australian Army.

CHAPTER 5

# REBUILDING THE 18TH INFANTRY BRIGADE

The 18th Australian Infantry Brigade returned from the Buna and Sanananda campaigns a victorious but physically broken force. It had suffered more than 96 per cent casualties owing to a combination of weather, terrain, disease and the enemy, and would have to reconstruct the foundations of the brigade, built around a core of experienced veterans and the assimilation of motorised troops and replacement soldiers.[1] The 18th Brigade would have to start building basic soldiering skills, the integration of jungle warfare lessons learnt, and the introduction of formal brigade leadership schools. This is also the period when the brigade undergoes a dramatic reorganisation under 7th Division's establishment as a jungle division, which was outlined in chapter 1.

The 18th Brigade returned to Australia to find the army struggling to adapt and standardise in a period of rapid technological modernisation. The brigade would have to rebuild and attempt to maintain its combined arms experience while planning for what it believed would be an amphibious operation. It would have to achieve all of this without Brigadier Wootten who, after the brigade returned to Australia, was given command of the 9th Australian Infantry Division.[2] Fortunately, the new 18th Brigade Commander, Brigadier Frederick Chilton, was a highly competent and resourceful commander, and like Wootten, he understood the potential of the brigade group as a combat formation. He would lead the 18th Brigade through the rest of World War II.

In April 1943, the 18th Brigade's 'Combat Efficiency Report' stated clearly that 'no estimate of time as to the preparedness of the Brigade can be given'.³ Essentially, it had suffered such damage that the commander and staff could not give an honest assessment of how long and how much work it would take to get the brigade back into combat. The 18th Brigade's 'Training Instruction Number 27', the first published after the return from Buna and Sanananda, addressed the challenges the unit faced during reconstitution.⁴ The instruction provided guidance on the need to begin the brigade-training program at the soldier level, building basic skills for line infantry combat. It emphasised physical training, maintenance of personal equipment, fieldworks and jungle communications. By 1943, there was little doubt the Australian brigades would be expected to participate in amphibious operations in the SWPA. Having conducted two minor amphibious operations 1942, which will be discussed in later chapters, the instruction added, 'in view of the possibility of combined operations every opportunity should be taken to teach all personnel to swim'.⁵

In the first week of May 1943, Chilton was instructed by the 7th Division to have the 18th Brigade combat-ready, with amphibious training completed in 12 weeks.⁶ To that end, Chilton and the brigade staff established an aggressive and, in practical terms, unrealistic training program intended to have the brigade combat-ready in 12 weeks to meet the division deadline.⁷ Chilton and the brigade staff underestimated a number of important challenges they would experience on the way to creating a combat-effective 18th Brigade. First, the brigade – whose ranks were decimated by disease and combat injuries – would be required to bring in large numbers of new soldiers. It would absorb the 1st, 5th and 11th Australian Motorised Regiments with the expectation that these soldiers would arrive as trained infantryman. This would not be the case, and many of the soldiers, non-commissioned officers and officers of the motorised units would require retraining in basic soldier skills. The non-commissioned officers and officers of the 18th Brigade would be required to teach old skills while they learnt a number of new skills related to combined arms operations, such as cooperation with airborne forces, close air support, and forward observer training. Lastly, the brigade was expected to do all of this while training for the most complex form of modern warfare: amphibious operations.

The first months back in Australia included recovery and ease for the 18th Brigade's soldiers. By May 1943, hundreds of soldiers of the 18th Brigade began to return from leave to begin training. The brigade held a celebration to mark three years since it first left Australia for tours in Britain and North Africa.⁸ The brigade's new commander, Chilton, used the anniversary as an occasion to connect the replacements and new recruits with the brigade's already significant combat lineage.[9]

On 5 May 1943, 'Training Instruction Number 28' was published. The first six weeks of this aggressive training cycle were intended for individual and collective training followed by six weeks of amphibious training with the intent of combating the Japanese in a 'tropical theatre of operations'.[10] Fortunately, the 18th Brigade had significant experience in jungle warfare and conducted its own jungle courses for new troops. The Australian LHQ had established a jungle training program; however, it had not yet added jungle warfare school to initial basic training.[11] As a result, troops like those of the motorised regiments had little or no jungle training when they joined the 18th Brigade.[12]

The 12-week requirement for the brigade to be combat-ready was hampered further by the 18th Brigade's reduced troop strength. The brigade would not be at full strength until 16 May 1943, so for the first 11 days of training the brigade was a skeleton force, which required the skillsets of the first week and a half-day of training to be repeated for new troops.[13] 'Training Instruction Number 28' details the brigade plan for combat in different types of warfare. The 18th Brigade's deployment to Buna and Sanananda was largely light infantry manoeuvres culminating in a combined arms siege of fixed fortifications. In an effort to maintain hard-learnt manoeuvre and siege lessons, the brigade made every effort to conduct standardised rifle and grenade ranges, collective unit training, leadership courses and individual Staff Section instruction. It also decided to limit or suspend training in areas that seemed impractical, such as gas warfare and large-scale night operations.[14] However, the brigade and its subordinate battalions were so consumed by the demands of individual and small unit collective training that some of the tactics it had pioneered, such as combined arms assaults, close air support and forward observer training for the infantry, were excluded from the first six weeks of the 12-week plan.

'Tactical Discussion Number 2' addressed the advance and first contact with the enemy. This lecture was held twice: once for the battalion and company commanders with their staff, followed by a second iteration for the officer corps of the 2/4 Field Artillery Regiment.[15] In 1942, when the 18th Brigade deployed for Milne Bay, the Australian Army had been institutionally compartmentalised on the battlefield. In other armies, most notably the German army, the practice of combined arms manoeuvre had seen great advancement with the idea of Blitzkrieg or 'lightning war', which advocated the use of combined arms to gain and maintain advantage over the enemy. The 18th Brigade, having experienced the value of artillery often 'danger close' in the jungle, began the informal training of infantry officers in forward observer techniques in 1942. Later in June 1943, Chilton ordered the brigade major and intelligence officer, along with one officer from each subordinate battalion, to participate in a 'miniature ranging' exercise with the 2/4th Field Artillery Regiment.[16] The practice of training infantry officers would eventually be embraced by the Australian Army but not before the 18th Brigade would deploy back to New Guinea.[17]

On 9 June 1943, the aforementioned 'miniature ranging' exercise was conducted with the 2/4th Field Artillery Regiment.[18] This was the first attempt of the 18th Brigade to integrate infantry and artillery cooperation since Buna and Sanananda.[19] The mini-ranging exercise did not include infantry manoeuvre, largely because the new replacements and motorised troops had very little experience in infantry manoeuvre and the possibility of accidents was high. The safety issue would have been compounded because, in all probability, the artillery troops would have been replacements as well. However, the ranging exercise did start the integration of infantry and field artillery, a key element of the brigade's manoeuvre capability.

By the end of June 1943, the 18th Infantry Brigade's combat efficiency report listed combat readiness at 44 per cent.[20] This number demonstrates clearly how unrealistic the 7th Division's expectation was of the time needed for the Brigade to reach combat readiness. An honest assessment of the first six weeks revealed the new reinforcement troops had arrived untrained and many veterans were still suffering from disease and injuries. More time and more men would be required to fill the 18th Brigade's ranks while training continued in earnest. The 18th Brigade was far from combat ready.

As previously noted, the Australian LHQ had determined the 5th and 11th Australian Motorised Regiments would be disbanded and absorbed into the subordinate battalions of the 18th Brigade.[21] On 3 July 1943, a brigade commander's conference was held to plan for the integration of these additional replacement troops. The challenge would be to absorb more potentially inexperienced and likely poorly trained soldiers while they maintained the current training plan. Chilton ordered the battalions to evaluate all reinforcements and motorised troops to identify 'those below required standards' for segregation and 'special training'.[22] This amounted to conducting basic training for replacements while attempting to train the battalions for a rapidly approaching combat deployment.[23]

The afternoon of 3 July 1943 saw the soldiers from the motorised regiments march into camp and join their respective battalions: 2/9th Battalion received 9 officers and 204 other ranks, 2/10th received 10 officers and 360 other ranks, and 2/12th 9 officers and 198 other ranks.[24] On 6 July 1943, the 1st Australian Motorised Regiment was disbanded, and its soldiers joined the brigade over four days. The 2/9th Battalion received 3 officers and 138 other ranks, 2/10th Battalion received 11 officers and 220 other ranks, and 2/12th 99 other ranks.[25] The first weekend in July included a trip to the local town of Innsifail and numerous sporting events.[26] Considered rest and recreation, the weekend's events were intended help to bond the new troops to the combat veterans of the brigade who had served in North Africa and New Guinea.

The month of July included significant administrative troop reorganisation in the 18th Brigade in addition to training and field exercises. Early in the month, the 2nd Australian Corps conducted a two-day infantry and tank cooperation demonstration in which the 18th Brigade sent 35 soldiers to observe with representation from each battalion and the Signal Section.[27] The demonstration lasted from 1100 to 1600 each day and emphasised lessons learnt in New Guinea during the Milne Bay and Buna campaigns.

Australian soldiers supported by M3 medium-sized Grant tanks conducted four separate scenarios for the observers: prepared attack, prepared attack with minefields, anti-tank defence, and haste defence.[28] Unfortunately, the demonstration largely reinforced World War I tank tactics. The 2nd Australian Corps demonstrated scenarios that consisted of tanks in support for the infantry against fixed positions, like the trench systems of the Western Front or the Japanese trench complex of Buna. What was missing was the use of tanks for the support of infantry manoeuvre against enemy manoeuvre formations similar to the Japanese use of tanks in the manoeuvre support role that routed the 2/10th Battalion in Milne Bay. Additionally, the demonstration was largely one-dimensional without the inclusion of the artillery and air support a brigade would need to face a modern enemy.

On 9 July 1943, Chilton directed the 2/9th and 2/12th Battalions to prepare for the upcoming 7th Division exercise at Mount Garnett.[29] On 11 July, the operations order for the division exercise was published and the battalions prepared to march out the next day. The exercise was made up of US troops of the 3rd Battalion and 503rd Parachute Infantry Regiment. The 18th Brigade was to serve as the 7th Australian Division's advance guard, moving forward to secure Wild River Crossing, where it would set up a defensive position.[30] It would then become the assault element for a planned attack on 14 July. However, the 18th Brigade was halted by the parachute drop of two companies of the US 3/503rd Regiment and the simultaneous attack of the 16th Australian Infantry Brigade. The 18th Brigade was prepared for its assault led by the 2/12th later the same day; however, owing to time constraints, the 7th Division ended the exercise before the attack.[31] The exercise cost the 18th Brigade valuable days of training, especially since they did not get to complete the infantry assault.

The 18th Brigade marched into the field and established a defence perimeter, where it remained for the duration of the exercise.[32] This might have been a reflection of the level of confidence the 7th Division leadership had in the 18th Brigade, which only a week earlier had absorbed more than 50 new officers and more than 1200 other ranks. The brigade's 12-week training period had been further hampered by the fact that at this point, it had conducted no collective training outside the exercise's initial road march and establishment of a defensive position.

The next division exercise, Battle-Axe, was conducted from 21 to 25 July 1943. This was the first large 'two-sided exercise' since the return from New Guinea and the influx of soldiers from three motorised regiments. On 22 July 1943, the 7th Division held an exercise conference to plan for a coordinated attack with parachute troops in a jungle environment. In attendance were the staffs of the 18th Infantry Brigade, 3rd Battalion, 503rd Parachute Infantry Regiment, 5th Army Cooperation (AC) Squadron, Royal Australian Air Force, and the assigned air liaison officers.[33] The 18th Brigade would not participate as a full brigade in the exercise. The elements that would participate included a detachment of 18th Brigade Headquarters, the 2/9th Battalion and elements from the 2/12th Battalion. This left a large portion of the brigade available for schools and individual training.

The 18th Infantry Brigade was an appropriate choice to participate in an exercise with US airborne infantry. First, it had combat experience in North Africa and New Guinea and held the distinction of being the only Australian brigade to command US infantry units in combat as part of Warren Force in Buna.[34] Second, it was the first Australian brigade to conduct the combat airlift of an infantry battalion ready to fight into a semi-permissive environment, New Guinea.[35] The staff and soldiers of the 18th Brigade would be able to contribute to the development and challenges of air load plans for infantry, disembarkation and actions in the aircraft. The need for well-developed combat airlift capability in the

SWPA was clear, although it would remain secondary to the amphibious movement of troops and logistics.

The Battle-Axe exercise was planned to assess two challenges of the upcoming Nadzab airborne operation in New Guinea and the future use of airborne forces in the SWPA.[36] The first problem was how to integrate combat parachute drops with conventional forces on the ground: essentially, how to incorporate a vertical parachute drop in conjunction with the larger scheme of combat manoeuvre. The second problem was the movement of an infantry brigade group into theatre by aircraft alone. The 2/10th Battalion had conducted a combat airlift into the Buna area of operations in 1942. However, the 2/10th Battalion moved as a light infantry battalion: basically, infantry ready to fight on the airfield, without service attachments or supporting arms. Battle-Axe was intended to further explore doctrine for an airfield seizure with parachute infantry and how to reinforce and resupply that airborne element with conventional forces.[37]

Battle-Axe had a significant impact on the 18th Brigade. It was yet another divergence from the 12-week combat readiness plan. According to the original 12-week plan in 'Training Instruction Number 28' published in May 1943, by mid-July the 18th Brigade should have been conducting amphibious warfare training and exercises. Instead, the 18th Brigade was training with a US parachute infantry regiment.[38] This was a significant change in the brigade's course, and it would certainly indicate to Chilton and the brigade staff that the next combat action either would not be an amphibious landing or would be one in which the brigade would be ill-prepared.

Battle-Axe's exercise narrative included a Japanese amphibious landing in Australia after which they suffered significant casualties and decided to form a defence perimeter. The 7th Division, with an attached US parachute infantry regiment, would move by air to seize a key airfield in Japanese-held territory. The priorities of effort were the cooperation of US paratroopers and Australian infantry, the combat airlift of infantry into an area of operations, and securing and defending a forward airfield.[39]

The concept of operations consisted of the 3/503rd Airborne Infantry Regiment conducting a combat jump onto the target airfield on the morning of 26 July 1943. After the initial seizure, the 18th Brigade's 2/9th Battalion would be landed, potentially under fire, to reinforce the paratroopers. The rest of the 18th Brigade would follow in additional airlifts. The 3/503rd would then be relieved to return to headquarters back at Cairns. Owing to a lack of aircraft, the 2/9th Battalion would be deployed on 3-ton trucks following the 3/503rd airdrop. The truck drivers were given specific instructions to disperse along the airfield exactly as the 2/9th Battalion's transport aircraft would have landed in a combat landing.[40] Although there was still no indication in brigade records, the leadership must have been aware that the 18th Brigade had been reassigned from an amphibious operation and was being considered for the follow-in force of the first Allied airborne operation of the Pacific War at Nadzab, New Guinea.

On 29 October 1943, Chilton, accompanied by members of the brigade staff, observed a US Army parachute infantry platoon conduct a live-fire exercise. The airborne platoon conducted a parachute drop followed by assault against fixed positions. The 18th Brigade staff offered several observations in a written memorandum on the exercises. First, it was noted that at the platoon level, the US and Australian armies adhered to the same basic infantry tactics. Where they differed was the US Army practice of scoring exercises. This was of great interest to the 18th Brigade staff. The airborne platoon was graded on a point system whereby points were allotted or deducted on the basis of performance. The main performance items were the overall tactical plan and control of troops on the ground, the individual movement of paratroopers, shooting accuracy, and casualties that were designated by umpires. Additionally, the United States used 'live enemies' armed with rifles and light machine guns on an adjacent range to allow for the identification of targets by sound and observation.[41]

The memorandum noted that these training techniques could be useful for brigade exercises to develop competition between the 18th Brigade's subordinate battalions. It also was considered as a means of teaching fire discipline and conservation of ammunition.[42] These were different from the US Army's plans for live fire exercises, which were largely intended to familiarise troops with gunfire before the battlefield. This live-fire finalisation as a method of instruction was a direct outcome of the Battle of Buna, where poorly trained US Army National Guard units withdrew after the first engagement of the Japanese machine guns.

Chilton and the 18th Brigade were still facing challenges at the end of July 1943. The absorption of the motorised regiments had increased manning to full strength, but the reinforcements, despite 'strenuous efforts' to bring them to up to the brigade standard, were rated only as 'fair'.[43] This required the battalions to focus considerably more time on basic infantry tactics at the expense of collective battalion training. A lack of training and exercises resulted in battalions that were not capable of participating effectively in brigade manoeuvres, let alone combined arms exercises.[44] The 18th Brigade's weapons and equipment were not much better. The brigade had reached 90 per cent of its assigned essential equipment, but a large portion was defective or unserviceable.[45] In July 1943, at the end of the 18th Brigade's training in Australia, Chilton was able to assess the brigade honestly and determined that the force needed six more weeks of training.[46]

## JUNGLE WARFARE TRAINING

Following the Buna and Sanananda campaigns, the 18th Brigade intensified its formal jungle warfare training as part of Chilton's 12-week combat readiness plan. The brigade's jungle expertise reached beyond its internal training program; its formal recommendations and lessons learnt reported to the Allied Headquarters had not fallen on deaf ears. Throughout 1943, the Australian Army sent questions to the 18th Brigade's staff or requested 18th Brigade representation at jungle warfare conferences. The brigade had also provided an instructor team to assist other units. One example was that of Captain Cecil Parbury and three enlisted soldiers of the 2/9th Battalion, who were tasked with training platoon leaders at the 2/6th Cavalry's jungle warfare course.[47]

On 26 April 1943, the brigade major, Major Oliver Jackson, was invited to the 7th Division's headquarters conference specifically to make recommendations on the Weapons and Equipment table for jungle warfare.[48] In another example, on 2 May 1943, the 7th Division requested that the 18th Brigade provide feedback on the 'suggested minimum scale of jeep transport for an infantry battalion'.[49] The 18th Brigade staff, one of the most experienced in jungle warfare, noted that the 7th Division did not provide guidance on the scope of jungle warfare. The LHQ request lacked details on the scope of operations, terrain and the condition of roads if available. The 18th Brigade provided guidance based on its experiences in Buna and Sanananda, where it was determined that five jeeps with trailers would have been sufficient for an infantry battalion. The problem with this request is it did not take into consideration the attached units of the infantry brigade group. The LHQ and 7th Division should have asked more detailed questions, including the expected number and type of attached units for a jungle deployment.

The 18th Brigade initiated a new phase of jungle training with an emphasis on the basics because of the number of fresh troops and an

Figure 5.1 Soldiers negotiate a river crossing with explosions all around at the Australian Training Centre (Jungle Warfare) at Canungra, Queensland. The 18th Brigade's early jungle combat experience in New Guinea contributed greatly to the course curriculum at Canungra. (AWM 060663A)

expectation that it would re-deploy in short order. 'Training Instruction Number 28' advised that 'in jungle warfare where a force is required to operate at great distances from its base along a single track, which is not capable of motor transport, represents the "worst case" in jungle warfare and it is therefore this type of operation [to] which our training should principally be directed'.[50] Chilton's command guidance represents the brigade's collective experience in Buna and Sanananda, where the individual soldier carried the day in assaults against Japanese positions. Hence the primacy of the individual soldier in training was always paramount. However, this also demonstrates that Chilton and brigade staff fully expected to redeploy into a resource-scarce environment without a wide array of supporting arms and technology.

Chilton and the brigade staff established five priorities for jungle training enumerated in 'Training Instruction Number 28'. The first priority was survival. Soldiers would be trained in acclimatisation, field cooking, jungle food, personal and unit hygiene, and anti-malarial techniques. Second was jungle skills such as tracking, camouflage identification, and counter-sniper tactics taught through unit-built 'sticks' lanes or the jungle assault course. Third and fourth were jungle navigation and personal camouflage. The last of the five priorities the 18th Brigade set forth for jungle training was 'patience to wait for a certain kill in ambush'.[51] This was clearly focused on junior inexperienced troops, who had in Milne Bay, Buna and Sanananda nervously engaged the Japanese before the Japanese had fully entered the 'kill zone'. These five jungle priorities were not the end-all solution to jungle warfare, and after the overwhelming losses in New Guinea, the brigade was in search of new ideas. Subordinate battalions and companies were instructed to experiment with equipment, rations, water obstacles and medical issues and to conduct the experiments in jungle or mountainous terrain if possible.[52]

It is important to note that the 18th Brigade was not the only entity deeply engaged in the challenges of jungle warfare. Advanced Land Headquarters had established the Australian Training Centre, Jungle Warfare, at Canungra, Queensland, which conducted a number of courses of instruction in jungle warfare. The most often mentioned in the 18th Brigade's unit diary was the Section Assault Course, which focused on infantry units assaulting bunkers with organic infantry weapons as part of a larger assault. This type of course would be replicated across the SWPA. There was also a Sneaker Course, which amounted to a jungle reconnaissance course that provided instruction on quiet movement in the jungle and the use of camouflage. In the Battle Course, units would observe demonstrations of tank and artillery cooperation with the infantry and participate in live-fire exercise.[53] The course, in and of itself, represents a complete reversal of the Australian and US armies' leadership's firm belief in 1942 that artillery and tanks were of little value in the SWPA.

It is in this period that the adage 'tactics in the jungle are not "black magic"' emerged. The argument was that the jungle was simply another type of terrain to be mastered and that Allied infantry tactics were sound in this environment.[54] This was essentially correct, but it was also not that simple. Soldiers' training in survival in jungle conditions, knowledge of navigation, and preventive health considerations did make infantry tactics viable, as the US and Australian armies demonstrated across the SWPA. The adage that jungle warfare was not 'black magic' was true; however, infantry tactics were in a state of evolution. The ability of a brigade commander and the staffs' ability to conduct infantry manoeuvre in close cooperation with armour, artillery and air support, later combined with amphibious warfare, might have seemed like 'black magic' to many of the infantry officers of the early 1940s. Jungle warfare's need for the cooperation of tanks, artillery and infantry in the SWPA was acknowledged in 1943 but not well developed. Additionally, infantry-directed close air support was still not discussed in the Australian doctrine of 1943.

## Establishment of Brigade Schools

The role of professional education in the soldiers and staff of the 18th Brigade expanded significantly in the period between deployments to New Guinea in 1943. Even before the leave period following Buna and Sanananda was over, the 18th Brigade had implemented additional training courses for soldiers of all ranks. These brigade schools included a specialty officer and junior non-commissioned officer course. Another special course was needed for 'motorised' non-commissioned officers to transition to infantry leaders.

The Platoon Commanders Course, the core course for junior officers, was conducted repeatedly in 1943. The senior officers in the brigade received training primarily through two methods: first, through formal Allied command and staff courses in Australia, Britain and America – the latter two requiring long travel periods and time outside the SWPA. The second, more expedient, training method was tactical discussions with division or other Allied officers, but most often with the brigade commander, Chilton. 'Tactical Discussion Number 1', conducted on 10 June 1943, included battalion and company commanders who were instructed on the Principles of War.[55] The intent of the tactical discussion was to convey knowledge to leaders in the hope that it would be passed down wherever possible within the short, 12-week training cycle.

Another of the brigade schools was the Junior Leaders Course, which provided instruction in squad- and platoon-level infantry tactics. The Junior Leaders Course conducted several iterations, with each of the 18th Brigade's subordinate battalions allotted 18 seats while the 2/5th Ambulance Section and 2/4th Field Artillery received 3 seats each.[56] It was a difficult course that ran from 0830 to 2130 and was designed for replacements and motorised soldiers, who would make up a large proportion of the junior leaders after the significant losses of Buna and Sanananda.

During this period, the 18th Brigade also conducted its Brigade Staff Course, which was focused on training brigade and battalion staff officers or potential staff officer in the 'staff duties, [broken into] duties in action, and duties out of action'.[57] The students included the intelligence and assistant intelligence officers, the quartermaster and assistant quartermaster, the adjutant and assistant adjutants, liaison officers, and junior officers assigned to brigade or battalion staffs. Notably, seats in the course were not allotted to attached units, such as 2/5th Ambulance and 2/4th Field Artillery. This would have been especially useful for the 2/4th Field Artillery, whose headquarters in the Finisterre campaign would be co-located.

A review of the course materials available in the 18th Brigade's records reveals a staff course that was comprehensive and well organised, especially for a forward-deployed unit. The course was taught by three methods: lecture, small group instruction, and group exercises. Unlike most of the internal courses conducted by the 18th Brigade, the staff course was taught in the afternoon and ran only four days a week because the brigade staff still had to run the day-to-day operations of the brigade. The course, which totalled 36 hours over two weeks, had a heavy focus on writing warning and operations orders. A review of the breadth of the 18th Brigade's service in the SWPA demonstrates the brigade staff's strength at writing operations orders, often for unexpected missions or missions with little precedent in the Australian Army.

## THE INTELLIGENCE SECTION

The role of the Australian brigade and battalion Intelligence Sections became increasingly important as the complex war in the SWPA progressed. The Australian Army considered the intelligence structure to be a stream with drops of water – information – being put into the stream at the battalion level. These drops of water would then make their way, echelon by echelon, until they reached Allied Headquarters, but that would not do much for a brigade in combat. After the return from New Guinea, and while the rest of the 18th Brigade was engaged in the aforementioned individual, collective and jungle training, the Intelligence Sections embarked on a period of professionalisation. For example, during this period the Australian Army introduced formal intelligence positions in the enlisted ranks.[58] The brigade Intelligence Section would now be made up of one intelligence officer, one intelligence sergeant, one intelligence corporal, intelligence privates and one clerk.

As noted in previous chapters, the 18th Brigade quickly realised that if a brigade group was to be capable of effective combined arms operations, it required significantly more intelligence personnel and capabilities than at any point in the history of the brigade as a formation. In order to

Figure 5.2 During World War II, the 18th Brigade Intelligence Section grew from a single intelligence officer and a clerk to a full staff of varied intelligence disciplines. Here the Intelligence Section studies maps of the area during clean-up operations in Balikpapan. (AWM 114479)

control all fire support and manoeuvre elements in combat, the brigade commander would need accurate and timely information about not only the enemy but also the terrain, weather and adjacent friendly forces. The need for accurate and timely intelligence became more important with the complexity of terrain and amphibious operations. Infantry commanders could not rely on intelligence from Allied Headquarters or infantry division Intelligence Sections because they were often too far from the front. The 18th Brigade had to be able to produce intelligence at the brigade level and during combat. To that end, the professionalisation of army intelligence was a welcome change in brigade doctrine.

The brigade and battalion Intelligence Sections were to 'receive and put together in logical order and present in a suitable form ALL available information from whatever source'.[59] The emphasis on 'ALL' or all-source intelligence, was to ensure that intelligence personnel did not exercise their own judgement on what was or was not important. Additionally, the Intelligence Sections were responsible as an 'organised system of observation of the unit area',[60] with two primary functions: the intelligence preparation of the battlespace and the enemy order of battle. The enemy order of battle, which included tracking, logging and reporting on enemy units and equipment in the area of operations, was important, and was emphasised throughout the Brigade Intelligence School.[61] Another primary task of the Intelligence Sections was ground reconnaissance. This was not intended to be a general reconnaissance section but a small element capable of conducting special reconnaissance for the battalion commander's intelligence requirements.

The roles and responsibilities of the Intelligence Section started with the leadership, namely the intelligence officer. These included the supervisor of junior personnel and the maintenance of the situation map, intelligence diary and any special maps or aerial photographs. They were also responsible for the collection and dissemination of information to the subordinate battalions. At both the brigade and battalion Intelligence Sections, there would be a new intelligence sergeant position. This enlisted sergeant would be the understudy of the intelligence officer and would manage the Intelligence Section in the intelligence officer's absence. Generally, one of the two would be always in the brigade or battalion headquarters during combat operations. The intelligence sergeant was responsible for the supervision of junior enlisted intelligence soldiers and the day-to-day operations of the Intelligence Section. These daily tasks included the maintenance of the situation map, the intelligence diary, special intelligence assessments and any special maps or aerial photos. The intelligence sergeant was also responsible for the identification and classification of enemy prisoners of war captured by the battalion or brigade.

The intelligence corporal assisted the intelligence sergeant and was his understudy in the same way the sergeant learnt and knew the job of the intelligence officer. The corporal also monitored communications, maintained the operations log and ensured that intelligence supplies were in stock. The intelligence privates would have received training in all tasks within the Intelligence Sections and assisted where necessary. The junior enlisted intelligence personnel, supervised by the intelligence sergeant, carried out numerous tasks and received specialised training. Intelligence soldiers were required to have a high level of literacy and often were promoted quickly. The intelligence soldiers drafted and maintained the intelligence products enumerated under the intelligence sergeant's responsibilities and were also trained to conduct special reconnaissance and use a variety of communication equipment.

On 1 December 1943, the 18th Brigade had established a 21-day intelligence school as part of the brigade's training programs.[62] The importance of implementing the brigade's intelligence lessons learnt is demonstrated by the number of days committed to the intelligence course. This course trained officers and enlisted personnel down to the company level on both analytic and ground reconnaissance intelligence skills. The 18th Brigade's intelligence school had room for 31 students, nine from each battalion and two for attached units. In the first iteration of the course in December 1943, the infantry battalions sent junior enlisted men to the course; the 2/4th Field Artillery Regiment and 2/5th Field Ambulance both chose to send non-commissioned officers.[63]

It was not an easy school for soldiers to complete. The brigade intelligence school results, marked confidential, often identified soldiers as 'below average' or 'not suitable for intelligence work'.[64] In each iteration of the intelligence school, many of the students were sent back to their respective rifle company. The course was taught by experienced intelligence captains, lieutenants and non-commissioned officers from the 18th Brigade and on occasion from the 7th Division. Non-commissioned officers were tasked with teaching many of the field skills such as the use of ciphers, patrolling, tracking, and communications equipment. The course culminated with a two-day field exercise after which students were required to provide a ten-minute intelligence brief "Brigade Intelligence School" \r and to complete a written exam.

In addition to the Brigade Intelligence School, intelligence officers from the 18th Brigade attended the Photographic Interpretation Course of the LHQ, School of Military Intelligence.[65] Upon return from the three-week course, the 18th Brigade, with a cadre trained in photographic interpretation, established a brigade program of instruction. On 2 July 1943, the 18th Brigade Intelligence Section initiated instructional flights intended to train all brigade and battalion staff members on photographic interpretation, which had been key in previous combat deployments owing to the poor quality of maps in the SWPA.[66] These repeated efforts by the brigade to develop internal courses and programs of instruction were paramount to the development of the highly effective intelligence capability that would emerge with the 18th Brigade's redeployment to New Guinea.

From March 1943 until August 1943, the period between the 18th Brigade's return to Australia from the campaign in Buna and Sanananda and its subsequent deployment back to New Guinea, time was spent on both the basics and the future of the brigade. The integration of the three motorised infantry regiments and the reconstitution of the force, which had suffered some of the highest casualty rates of the SWPA, challenged the veteran cadre of officers and non-commissioned officers. However, the 18th Brigade's attempt to establish combat readiness, while meeting the requirement of the 7th Division's exercise cycle and the formal training needs of the individual soldiers, was admirable. Additionally, the 18th Brigade was cognisant of its own combat lessons learnt, and its organic jungle warfare and intelligence programs were excellent examples of combat experience integrated into formal training. When the brigade again deployed to New Guinea, no one, including Chilton, could have expected that the brigade would once again be operating at the spearhead of Australian combat operations. On 2 August 1943, the 18th Infantry Brigade Group (Jungle), although still not yet combat-ready, was given 24-hours notice for movement to New Guinea.[67]

CHAPTER 6

# THE BATTLE OF SHAGGY RIDGE

The newly reorganised 18th Infantry Brigade Group (Jungle) would return to New Guinea with the 7th Infantry Division as the division's reserve force. From the reserve force to the spearhead of the Allied campaign in the Finisterre Range, the brigade would achieve a striking victory against the Japanese 78th Infantry Regiment. This was a battle that required a commander and brigade staff to manage numerous attached units, supporting arms and its own infantry formations – all while assaulting up mountainous ridgelines to fortified Japanese positions. The Finisterre campaign, specifically Operation Cutthroat, demonstrated an excellent example of an Australian infantry brigade group (jungle) in action.

## TRAINING FORWARD IN NEW GUINEA, 1943

On 3 August 1943, an advance party of officers from the 18th Infantry Brigade boarded transport headed for the Australian coast. It took eight days for the advance party to arrive in Port Moresby, New Guinea. On that same day, Chilton and the brigade staff received their first brief on Operation Exchequer, the code name for Berryman's plan to seize Lae and Nadzab, followed by the movement into the Markham Valley.[1] Soon the rest of the brigade began the move to New Guinea by motor transport, rail and finally by ship with the embarkation of the 2/9th Battalion on SS *Katoomba* and SS *Canberra* on 10 August. The last element of the brigade, the 2/12th Battalion, would not arrive in Port Moresby until 20 August 1943.[2]

On 16 September 1943, Lae, a town on the north coast of New Guinea, fell to the Allies.[3] Blamey's multiprong airborne and amphibious assault resulted in the Japanese withdrawal up the Markham and Ramu Valleys into the Finisterre Range.[4] The large-scale airborne landing of the US 503rd Parachute Infantry Regiment, with a few newly minted Australian paratroopers, seized Nadzab airfield.[5] Nadzab would become the US Fifth Air Force's primary base in New Guinea.[6] The Allied leadership did not expect Lae to fall as quickly as it had nor had they planned for a Japanese withdrawal into the Finisterre Range. As a result, the 21st and 25th Infantry Brigades of the 7th Australian Infantry Division were rushed forward to the Markham and Ramu Valleys on the north coast of New Guinea.

The 7th Division was tasked with an advance west into the Markham and Ramu Valleys to confront the Japanese in the Finisterre Range. The 18th Brigade held the role of 'reserve brigade' of the 7th Division after the 21st and 25th Brigades were sent forward. The 21st and 25th Brigades clashed repeatedly with the Japanese, but eventually stalled after several months fighting on top of ridgelines in the Finisterre Range.[7] At an SWPA Allied Commander's Conference on 30 December 1943, General Vasey, Lieutenant General Leslie Morshead (commander of New Guinea Force), Major General Edward Milford (general staff New Guinea Force) and MacArthur agreed that the 21st and 25th Brigades would need to be relieved by fresh troops.

Operation Cutthroat was planned to prevent Japanese forces in the Finisterre Range from reinforcing opposition to the US Army's amphibious landing at Saidor.[8] On 31 December 1943, the US Army 126th Infantry Regiment, which had fought with the 18th Brigade in Buna, launched Operation Michaelmas – a successful amphibious landing at on Saidor.[9] The 126th Regiment left Goodenough Island, which the 18th Brigade had seized in 1942, to land 3000 soldiers on the morning of 2 January 1944 at Saidor. The landing was successful despite the high risk in heavy rains and poor visibility.[10] This allowed for the establishment of a forward Allied airfield and port facilities from which to launch future campaigns. The secondary effect of the landing was to cut the supply lines of the Japanese 20th and 51st Infantry Divisions on the Huon Peninsula.[11] The landing, conducted in poor weather, was virtually unopposed. However, the Japanese 20th Infantry Division's 78th Infantry Regiment and Nakai Force in the Finisterre Range were within reach of

Figure 6.1 A wounded soldier of the 2/9th Infantry Battalion is carefully carried down the ridgeline by stretcher-bearers after being injured during the reconnaissance of Japanese positions on 'Green Sniper's Pimple'. (AWM 064237)

Saidor, and Allied commanders feared a counter-attack against the 126th Infantry's beachhead. Operation Cutthroat, with the 18th Brigade at the spearhead, was tasked with preventing this counter-attack.

Chilton received orders to relieve the 21st Brigade on New Year's Day, 1 January 1944.[12] The entire 18th Infantry Brigade Group (Jungle) was to be airlifted over the Owen Stanley Range to Wanigela, New Guinea, a forward staging and logistics area.[13] The airlift had 36 Dakota aircraft assigned for three days to bring in the 18th Brigade and take out the battered 21st Brigade on the Dakotas' return trip to Wanigela.[14] Each of the 18th Brigade's three infantry battalions required 48 Dakota lifts into Wanigela, with travel time at two and a half hours each way. Supporting units such as an artillery battery required 30 lifts and the engineer company 24.[15] This represented a significant increase in airlift capacity in the

New Guinea theatre since the 18th Brigade left Buna a year earlier. In Buna, General Kenney had hoped to supply Warren and Urbana Forces by air, but the lift capacity simply did not exist, and the majority of logistics had to be conducted by sea.[16] By the winter of 1943, the Allied Fifth Air Force in New Guinea could move an Australian infantry brigade group (jungle) into combat by air in just three days.

On 3 January 1944, the 18th Brigade assumed control of the Finisterre battlespace. The 2/9th Battalion took its position along the base of the famous Shaggy Ridge, while the 2/10th Battalion took the right flank across John's Knoll, with the left flank covered by the attached 2/2nd Pioneer Battalion. The 2/12th Battalion was held in the rear as the brigade reserve.[17] The 2/2nd Pioneer Battalion would prove highly valuable in the reconnaissance of ridge lines and gullies that would make Operation Cutthroat a success.[18]

The 18th Brigade would spend the first two weeks of January 1943 on acclimatisation to the weather and mountainous terrain. Chilton noted that the 21st and 25th Brigades had attempted small attacks or raids against the Japanese in the Finisterre Range only to fall back owing to lack of coordination with supporting arms and, most importantly, the lack of surprise.[19] The 21st Brigade had been tasked with assaulting and clearing Shaggy Ridge of Japanese troops, but it was never able to seize any of the three major hills along the ridge, referred to as 'pimples' by the Australians. The peaks along Shaggy Ridge were known as Green Pinnacle, the Pimple, Intermediate Snipers' Pimple, Green Sniper's Pimple and McCaughey's Knoll.[20] Corporal McLean, in an interview about the Battle of Shaggy Ridge, noted, 'If you got up on very high points you could see the coast.'[21]

The Japanese 78th Infantry Regiment had occupied and fortified a series of natural fortresses several months before the Australians entered the Finisterre Range. The Japanese had constructed wire obstacles, weapons pits, pillboxes and complex underground shelters in the months before the 18th Brigade's arrival and subsequent order to the front. These well-planned fortifications used the ridgelines and peaks to cover the obvious avenues of approach with multiple mutually supported machine-gun and mortar positions.[22] This would allow the Japanese to pour large volumes of fire on the Australian infantry as they struggled up the mountain ridgelines. The Japanese had also emplaced a significant amount of artillery fire support in the mountains to include two 75mm Type 94 field guns, two 75mm Type 41 regimental field guns, two 70mm Type 92 battalion guns, one 37mm QF gun, multiple 81mm mortars and one 20mm anti-aircraft gun.[23]

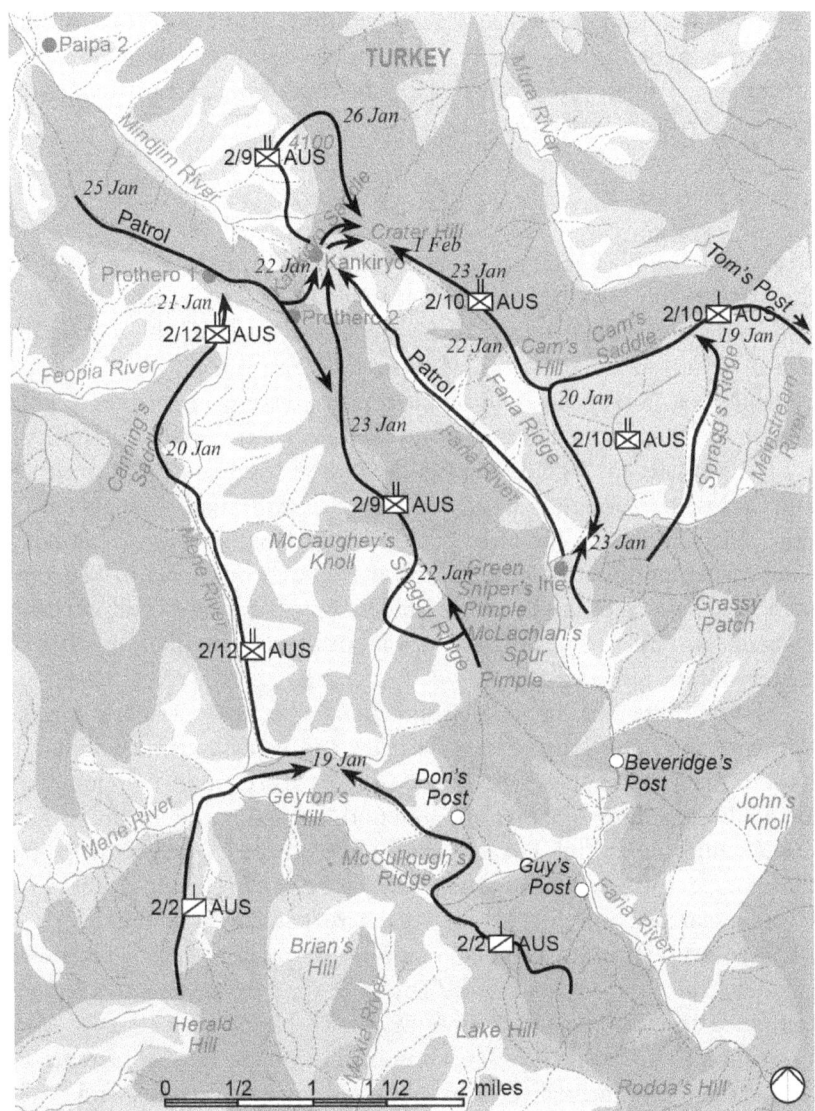

Map 6.1 The Battle of Shaggy Ridge, January – February 1944

Despite all the fortified bunkers and firepower, the Japanese would face the same problems as the Australians, primarily the resupply of ammunition for heavy weapons in inclement weather on top of a mountain. There were reports that the Japanese had maintained a 75mm round every five seconds in previous assaults with the 21st Brigade, but without steady resupply this would not be sustainable. The combination of Allied air support, artillery and weakened logistics lines would greatly reduce the Japanese artillery's effectiveness.

## THE PLAN OF ATTACK

The 7th Division's 'Operations Order Number 9' was issued by Vasey at the 18th Brigade Headquarters on 4 January 1944. The brigade's role was to hold the general line of the 21st Brigade and secure areas forward of the line to ensure that no major Japanese withdrawal took place. Vasey's guidance was fairly general; in simplest terms, the instruction was to hold the ground already held and take the high ground as logistics permitted.

The 7th Division's guidance was clear: the 18th Brigade was to patrol and raid with the intention of preventing the 78th Infantry Regiment or other elements of the Japanese 20th Infantry Division from reinforcing Saidor. Despite this formal guidance, it is clear from notes of his commander's conference in the 18th Brigade's War Diary that Chilton began planning an assault on the ridgelines immediately after the relief of the 21st and 25th Brigades.

Although the 18th Brigade Group (Jungle) was now a lighter formation with the reduction of heavy vehicles and workshops, it would still have to manage attached formations, support arms and its own infantry, all while assaulting up thin mountain ridgelines under Japanese fire. On the difficulty of the terrain, one corporal noted, '[I]t was in pretty thick jungle, and Shaggy Ridge was pretty hard to climb up, and – because it was so narrow, and the pimples were there, and they were only more or less one or two men.'[24] The planning process would require detailed use of intelligence and logistics coordination if the brigade was to conduct combined arms manoeuvre operations.

From 5 to 8 January 1943, Chilton held a commanders' conference to discuss the environmental considerations, reconnaissance needs, and available intelligence on Japanese forces in the region. Additionally, Chilton realised the need for a jeep trail to support the brigade's logistic train, which had grown accordingly with the number and size of attachments that now made up the brigade group. He immediately ordered the road be expanded and artillery stockpiles raised.[25] As Chilton and his staff assembled the attack plan, it became clear that surprise would be an 'essential factor' at all levels for the 18th Brigade in assaults against Japanese prepared fortifications, particularly if Australian casualties were to be kept to a minimum.

The attack plan of Operation Cutthroat would see several revisions. Chilton's first attack plan, drafted 9 January 1944, was straightforward: a brigade assault with supporting arms up the ridgelines.[26] The plan represented sound battlefield tactics for an infantry brigade group conducting an assault on an enemy position. However, these Japanese positions had managed successfully to defend against the 21st and 25th Brigades throughout the autumn months of 1943. The Australian brigades faced the challenge of how to employ a brigade group in a mountainous 'very dense jungle with sharp ravines and deep hollows'.[27] The terrain was so difficult to navigate that companies sometimes had to call for artillery to fire one round at registered targets to identify where they were on a map.[28]

The first weeks of January brought continued daily brigade staff planning meetings and commanders' conferences held by Chilton. The meeting and conference topics varied from ground strategy to air support coordination to general officer visits to 18th Brigade Headquarters.[29] During several of these visits, Chilton escorted VIPs to the front lines. In one case, Vasey and Morshead accompanied Chilton up a ridgeline adjacent to Shaggy Ridge in view of the natural fortress of Kankiryo.[30] Vasey and Morshead had grasped the challenges of the Finisterre Range after the 21st and 25th Brigades failed to unseat the Japanese, but Chilton took every opportunity to reinforce the difficulty to garner additional resources, such as increased air support for the assault.

As David Dexter points out in the official history, *The New Guinea Offensives*, Chilton had laid out three possible courses of action for unseating the Japanese from their dug-in mountain-top positions. The first option was a full-frontal assault along either Shaggy Ridge or Faria Ridge, and potentially both ridgelines simultaneously. The second option was a flanking manoeuvre through Cam's Saddle followed by an assault uphill onto Kankiryo. The third option was a long envelopment along Mene Ridge and through Canning's Saddle to assault the natural fortress of Prothero directly.[31] This was not an easy proposition since Prothero alone held more than 31 interconnected and reinforced pillboxes.[32]

The first option of a frontal assault along the nearly four-mile-long Shaggy Ridge presented several problems. First, a frontal assault against fortified positions offered no element of surprise, and it allowed for the Japanese to withdraw to another fortress-like feature at Kankiryo Saddle if overrun. The second option had dangerously long logistics and support lines for the assault on Kankiryo.[33] Although close air support and integrated artillery had come a long way since Buna, the coordination would likely not be good enough to ensure coverage of the slow and difficult advance, logistics and assault on Japanese fortified positions on top of Kankiryo.

Dexter observed that Chilton chose the third course of action, but this is not entirely accurate. Chilton chose a course of action that included elements of all three plans. This amounted to multiple surprise combined-arms assaults against fortified Japanese positions atop several mountainous ridgelines. Chilton's final plan would be conducted in five phases, with all three battalions on the attack and, for the first time, the coordination of field artillery and close air support would be managed jointly at brigade headquarters.

The key to Chilton's final plan for Operation Cutthroat was the day-and-a-half foot march followed by 2/12th Battalion 'creeping' up a spur running north-west to assault the Japanese stronghold at Prothero.[34] Field artillery and close air support focused on Prothero would be limited until the assault began, hoping for 'some level of surprise and shock.'[35] A diversionary assault on Cam's Hill and Cam's Saddle by the 2/10th Battalion would hopefully conceal the 2/12th Battalion's advance. The diversion was planned in the hopes of shifting the Japanese focus away from 2/12th Battalion's assault on Prothero, forcing them to commit their reserves to the wrong area, and establishing surprise for the 2/12th Battalion. Simultaneously, the 2/9th Battalion would battle its way across Shaggy Ridge to join the 2/10th and 2/12th Battalions in a full brigade assault on the final Japanese positions at Kankiryo and Crater Hill. The brigade assault, supported by field artillery and close air support, would represent the culmination of all the combat experience, exercises and training conducted by the 18th Brigade.

The staff of the 18th Brigade would play a larger role than in any previous battle, primarily in the coordination of the attachments that made up the Brigade Group. With staff meetings or commanders' conferences every day – often more than once a day – the Finisterre campaign planned evolved quickly. This was the first time the 18th Brigade had both bombers and close air support available to help facilitate infantry manoeuvre. It would also be the first time the 18th Brigade Staff had to develop and write an Air Support Plan for its operations order. The Air Support Plan was largely developed on 11 January 1944 at a planning meeting that included Lieutenant Colonel Alan Blyth, commander of the 2/4th Field Artillery Regiment, and the air liaison officers assigned to the brigade.[36] The Air Support Plan, as defined in the operations order, included different types of air missions for each of the five phases of Chilton's Operation Cutthroat.

The attachments and liaisons that supported the 18th Brigade had increased significantly since the Buna and Sanananda campaigns. At Finisterre, the attachments of the brigade group included 2/2nd Pioneer Battalion and the 7th Field Battery (A and B Troops) and 8th Field Battery (C Troop) of the 2/4th Field Artillery Regiment, which attached forward observers to each of the infantry battalions. Air support included the Royal Australian Air Force (RAAF) No. 10 Group, RAAF Kittyhawk No. 78 Squadron, Vultee Vengeance Dive Bomber No. 24 Squadron, Boomerangs and Wirraways from No. 4 Squadron RAAF, and the US Army Air Force 345th Group, called the 'Air Apaches'.[37]

## Assault preparations

As discussed in chapter 5, the 18th Infantry Brigade Group (Jungle) had quickly integrated new intelligence techniques and positions into the brigade after Buna and Sanananda. A comparison of the daily intelligence logs from the Buna and Finisterre campaigns demonstrates a stark difference in capabilities and professionalism. The Intelligence Section in Buna, understaffed and poorly equipped, was limited to basic analysis and maintenance of the intelligence log. The same brigade Intelligence Section in the Finisterre campaign included daily intelligence reports, collection tasks for subordinate and high-echelon units, and complex analyses of terrain, routes and the enemy.[38] Additionally, the Intelligence Section was now large enough to accompany units or conduct its own ground and air reconnaissance missions.

The 18th Brigade Intelligence School consumed a large number of training days for intelligence soldiers, and paid dividends in the Finisterre campaign. One of the intelligence capabilities that grew between campaigns was ground reconnaissance. The 18th Brigade Intelligence Section and the 2/2nd Pioneers initiated extensive ground patrols and route reconnaissance as soon as they relieved the 21st Brigade.[39] This allowed the battalions to identify enemy positions and register targets before conducting any assault on the Japanese fortifications.

Early in the campaign, the 18th Brigade Intelligence Section tasked 2/9th Battalion with conducting long-range reconnaissance of the battlefield with specific instructions to collect information on assault avenues of any company-sized defensive positions.[40] These missions could last as long as five days and were largely responsible for identifying approach routes for the upcoming assaults. In addition to ground reconnaissance, the brigade intelligence officer ordered aerial photography of the

Figure 6.2 Troops of the 2/9th Infantry Battalion prepare for the assault on Shaggy Ridge. In this area of the ridgeline, the forest had been obliterated by artillery and aerial bombardment during earlier fighting. (AWM 070012)

ridgelines and Japanese positions, since many of the existing maps of the area were of little use in combat operations.[41] Instead, numerous photos from these reconnaissance flights were used at all levels to develop overlays and to draft new maps, and were even used in ground navigation.[42]

The brigade Intelligence Section personnel, forward observers from the 2/4th Field Artillery and soldiers from the 2/2nd Pioneers conducted advanced reconnaissance of avenues of approach that included the time it took for soldiers to transit trails and attack routes for the close coordination of artillery fire and infantry manoeuvre. Teams were also tasked with the examination of terrain features and the hydrology of the rivers and creeks units might have to cross.[43] Forward observers and artillery officers had learnt a lot about indirect fire in jungle environments, but mountainous terrain added new challenges. This was the closest cooperation in reconnaissance the infantry, artillery and engineers had conducted to date in the SWPA. Even before the battle for the Finisterre Range, Chilton had demonstrated that his brigade group could integrate the different combat functions – artillery, air support and infantry – into the task of intelligence collection.

Another example was the primary purpose of the extensive reconnaissance effort, which was to exploit the Japanese tendency to neglect approaches where there existed natural terrain barriers they deemed impassable, as they had done both at Buna and at Sanananda.[44] The ground reconnaissance of the ridgelines and Japanese positions indicated two possible but highly precarious routes up the narrow spurs of Shaggy Ridge, and directly onto the main Japanese fortification at Prothero and McCaughey's Knoll.[45] These difficult approaches to the Japanese strongholds, identified by the aggressive use of intelligence, were quickly added to Chilton's plan for the brigade's assault on the Japanese 78th Infantry Regiment.

While the air and ground reconnaissance were going on, the 18th Brigade still needed a reliable logistics road to the front. By 16 January 1944, soldiers from the 2/2nd Pioneers, with a 70-man working party from 2/12th Battalion, had sufficiently completed a jeep track that could support an estimated 16 jeeps with trailers each day.[46] This was now the primary route for food, water and ordnance. The 18th Brigade could now move a large enough volume of materials needed to lay siege to the mountain-top fortifications. Chiton's assault plans called for significant artillery support to infantry manoeuvre. Without the jeep track, the 2/4th Field Artillery Regiment would not have been able to provide sustained fire support for the manoeuvre plan.

The final external coordination for Operation Cutthroat was the 18th Brigade staff's Air Support Plan. The learning curve was significant for a brigade staff that had not previously managed so many attached units and supporting arms. The Air Support Plan alone would require a separate daily meeting at brigade headquarters. The initial Air Support Plan, coordinated by and handed down to the brigade from the 7th Division staff, was found to be insufficient by Chilton and the brigade staff. It was determined that a significant increase in both aerial bombardment and close air support would be required to unseat the Japanese from the mountaintops. What followed was a series of Air Support Plan staff meetings of the principals, which included Chilton, the brigade major, the 7th Division Staff G1 and G3 planners, and representatives of the RAAF and the US 5th Army Air Force.[47]

Figure 6.3 'A' Company, 2/9th Infantry Battalion, dig fighting positions high in the Finisterre Range after its assault, along with indirect fire and close air support, and drove the Japanese back to the next stronghold at Kankiryo Saddle. (AWM 064260)

On 17 January 1944, the US 5th Army Air Force approved the 18th Brigade's request for an increase in both bombardment and close air support for Operation Cutthroat. The 18th Brigade War Diary described the 5th Army Air Force's response to the request for increased air support as 'Most Satisfactory'.[48] The amount of support the brigade received for Operation Cutthroat was markedly different from the support Allied leadership had provided the 18th Brigade in the Battle of Buna, where even available resources such as artillery and tanks were not sent to the front because of the Allied leadership's short-sightedness and logistical challenges. The 18th Brigade had received all the support it had asked for to carry out Operation Cutthroat – a striking difference from the Buna and Sanananda campaign, where some soldiers did not even have complete uniforms.

## The Assault on Shaggy Ridge

On 1 January 1944, Lieutenant Colonel Blyth's 2/4th Field Artillery Regiment kicked off the 18th Brigade's combat operations in the Finisterre Range with two weeks of artillery fire on Japanese positions along the ridgelines. Blyth rotated artillery batteries on and off the frontline every few days in the first weeks to build experience and not wear down any one battery. The 8th Battery served on the frontline from 1 to 10 January with limited registration fires from 1 to 6 January. From 7 to 10 January, the 8th Battery increased fires to an average of 300 rounds a day. On 11 January, the 11th Battery moved onto the front line and maintained a similar daily rate of artillery fire on the Japanese. By 18 January 1944, the 2/4th Regiment had fired a total of 3254 rounds, registering targets and engaging the Japanese.

On 18 January 1944, monsoon rains created flash floods, making the muddy ridgelines nearly impassable. The communications wire that had been laid across this difficult terrain between the spider-webbed network of the 18th Brigade Group and its numerous attachments was washed away.[49] Traversing muddy ridgelines was further complicated by the Japanese improvised explosive devices and mines along the paths blocking many of the thin avenues of approach. If the rain, mud and booby traps on the ridgelines was not challenging enough, several ridgelines had severe drops on both sides, some reported as 2000 feet.[50] The fighting on the ridgelines and jungle-filled ravines would make for fast, point-blank gunfights and 'grenade duels' with the Japanese.[51] It was clear that Operation Cutthroat would cover the full spectrum of modern war, from the bayonet to close air support.

Phase 1 of Chilton's attack plan began on 19 January 1944 with increased artillery and close air strikes against Shaggy and Sprogg's Ridges in the 2/9th and 2/10th Battalions' areas of responsibility, respectively. Shaggy Ridge was a nearly 4-mile line of intermittent Japanese defensive positions with drops of 300 to 500 feet on either side of the ridgeline.[52] Sprogg's Ridge was a shorter finger, which led to the objectives of Cam's Saddle and Cam's Hill. Phase 1 was considered complete later that day when 2/10th Battalion occupied Sprogg's Ridge.[53] The 2/4th Field Artillery Regiment's fire support plan for the 2/10th Battalion's assault included suppression of register targets, observable variations, and targets of opportunity called in by artillery forward observers and infantrymen cross-trained as observers. On the first day of Operation Cutthroat, the 2/4th Field Artillery Regiment fired more than 800 rounds from ten long- and two short-barrelled 25-pounders.[54]

Phase 1 was significant not only because of the use of combined close air support and artillery with infantry but also because it was the first time the 18th Brigade headquarters served as a combined fire control centre for an infantry assault. The 2/4th Field Artillery headquarters and air liaison elements were both co-located with the 18th Brigade headquarters. Traditionally, artillery headquarters were further from the front lines than the infantry headquarters. Co-location allowed for close coordination between the various fire support elements in relation to infantry manoeuvre. 'Operation Instruction Number 22' established further guidance for artillery and close air support to be on call for any eventuality of the 2/10th Battalion's assault.[55] If the 2/10th Battalion broke through and believed it could exploit Cam's Saddle and Cam's Hill, artillery and close air support would shift to support the battalion's manoeuvre.

On 20 January 1944, Phase 2 launched with the 2/10th Battalion's move across Cam's Saddle to seize Cam's Hill. From here, the 2/10th Battalion occupied the lower end of Faria Ridge. Faria Ridge was approximately three miles long and offered a direct route for the 2/10th Battalion to the key objectives of Crater Hill, Kankiryo and the Japanese 78th Infantry regimental headquarters less than a mile from Kankiryo. Phase 2 was completed on 22 January with the 2/10th Battalion advancing on Faria Ridge.

Phase 3 exploited the significant intelligence work of the 18th Brigade Intelligence Section and reconnaissance elements. The Japanese had again failed to secure key terrain they judged impassable. Chilton believed surprise would be the determining factor in Phase 3. On 22 January 1944, after a three-day foot march over difficult terrain, the 2/12th Battalion climbed a steep and treacherous pass and launched a surprise assault onto the mountain fortress of Prothero. The combination of surprise, artillery, close air support and an infantry assault resulted in what David Dexter described as the 'virtual annihilation' of the Japanese infantry company dug into pillboxes and field fortifications on Prothero.[56] The 2/12th Battalion seized Prothero, consolidated security and prepared for an advance south-east on Shaggy Ridge to link up with the 2/9th Battalion for an assault on Kankiryo.

At the onset of the 2/12th Battalion's assault on Prothero, Phase 4 was initiated with a 2/9th Battalion assault north-west across Shaggy Ridge. On 22 January 1944, the 2/9th Battalion assaulted a Japanese position on McCaughey's Knoll, a fortified strongpoint on a hill along Shaggy Ridge. The 2/9th Battalion's attack plan was risky in treacherous terrain. One element conducted a frontal feint directly up Shaggy Ridge towards

McCaughey's Knoll. This engagement lasted several hours, allowing the 2/9th Battalion's assault force to envelop and surprise the Japanese on McCaughey's Knoll using a spur 'up the almost precipitous slopes of Shaggy Ridge'.[57] The Japanese had constructed extensive defensive positions but had again relied on what they considered impassable terrain to stop the Australians. The avenue of approach up the spur was so steep that Australian soldiers fell to their death during the fighting. Conversely, there were reports of Japanese soldiers jumping off the other side of Shaggy Ridge to their death to avoid capture.[58] Phase 4 was over.

Phase 5 was logically contingent on the successful mission objectives of the other four phases. Phase 5 was a full brigade assault supported by a full complement of field artillery and close air support against the Japanese fortifications at Kankiryo, Crater Hill and the 78th Regimental Headquarters.[59] On 23 January 1944, the 2/9th and 2/12th Battalions jointly assaulted the Japanese who had consolidated at Kankiryo, a natural fortress reinforced with dug-in positions sometimes referred to as 'Crater Pimp'. On 26 January, the 2/9th advanced up the Faria Ridgeline to assault and seized the 78th Regimental Headquarters at an elevation of 4100 feet.

Crater Hill, the final objective of Operation Cutthroat's Phase 5, was located adjacent to Prothero and Kankiryo. It was the last heavily fortified position and last outpost of organised Japanese resistance. On 1 February 1944, all three battalions of the 18th Infantry Brigade Group assaulted Crater Hill in force with field artillery and close air support. One month after the 18th Brigade assumed command of the Finisterre campaign, the entire battlespace, including Shaggy Ridge, Prothero, Kankiryo and Crater Hill, was occupied by the 18th Brigade.[60] The brigade's assault thus far represents the pinnacle of the 18th Brigade's combined arms manoeuvre that resulted in Operation Cutthroat's striking victory.

The 18th Brigade and its relief, the 15th Militia Brigade, buried 244 Japanese soldiers in addition to numerous mass graves identified across the Finisterre Range. Chilton estimated the number of Japanese in the area at the onset of Operation Cutthroat at more than 790 soldiers. The 18th Brigade's after-action report estimated that at least 500 Japanese died in the fight on the ridge tops and in fortified positions. The 18th Brigade's actions from 19 January to 19 February 1944 not only accomplished the mission, preventing the Japanese from organising a counter-attack on the US amphibious landing at Saidor, but also ultimately destroyed the entire 78th Infantry Regiment.

Figure 6.4 'A' Company, 2/9th Infantry Battalion occupy a knife's edge ridgeline on 23 February 1944 in preparation for the assault on Kankiryo Saddle three days later. (AWM 064257)

## AFTER-ACTION ASSESSMENT

In the end, the 18th Brigade suffered 46 killed and 146 wounded in the Ramu Valley, considerably lower than Buna's casualty rate. There were environmental considerations such as disease, the strength of enemy forces and others; but the key factor was the evolution of the brigade as a combined arms force. As Chilton noted in the after-action report, it was a brigade assault; 'all three battalions were involved and the battle was planned, controlled and thought-out by the brigade headquarters'.[61]

On 2 February 1944, General Vasey arrived at 18th Brigade headquarters with Major General Ridley Pakenham-Walsh of the British Army. Over the following days Vasey, Pakenham-Walsh and Chilton visited the 18th Brigade's subordinate battalions and supporting units and even spent a night with the 2/9th Battalion in the field. On 7 February 1944, a group of officers and non-commissioned officers from the LHQ Tactical School arrived to tour the battlefield and capture lessons learnt from the 18th Brigade's victory in the Finisterre campaign.⁶² By March, the battlefield in the Finisterre Range had become a popular site. The 16th and 19th Brigade's commanders and staff as well as other groups from Allied Headquarters came for a tour or 'staff ride' of the Operation Cutthroat battlefield.⁶³

The question can be asked: what was so special about this battle that spurred so much interest? Operation Cutthroat had quickly become a case study of an infantry brigade group (jungle). There was a general recognition that the 18th Brigade had managed successfully to integrate air, fire and manoeuvre in a brigade assault. On 31 March 1944, Chilton provided a lecture for all officers in the brigade area on the lessons learnt from Operation Cutthroat. As he noted, 'It is not considered that the operation [Cutthroat] brought to light any new lessons of importance, though many lessons of previous campaigns were again emphasised.'⁶⁴ Chilton was correct in his assessment: the 18th Brigade did not launch a revolution in military affairs, nor did it employ a new super weapon, but it did demonstrate the importance of a commander and staff's ability to integrate the various element of modern warfare.

In the after-action report, Chilton identified surprise as supremely important in the defeat of the Japanese in the Finisterre campaign. He also stressed that leaders at all levels 'must become more enterprising and less conventional'.⁶⁵ This is the application of creativity, skill and experience best defined as operational art at a brigade level. What Chilton called 'enterprising and less conventional' would become the standard in brigade operations support of Allied campaigns.

One significant point of difficulty Chilton identified was the command and control of the subordinate battalions during a brigade operation. 'Further training in the technique of exercising control and command is needed. There is a tendency on the part of commanders to function individually, and to not make the proper use of the headquarters.'⁶⁶ Previously, battalion commanders had a great deal of autonomy during the actual combat action since communications were poor and warfare was less technologically complex. Often tasks were specific to the battalion, in time and space, not seen in concert with a large-scale brigade manoeuvre plan. Not just the use but also the integration of artillery and close air support as well as the potential for friendly fire made the coordination of subordinate battalions key issues in brigade operations.

In the Finisterre campaign, Chilton did not face the same resource-starved campaign his predecessor Brigadier Wootten faced a year earlier in Buna and Sanananda. Many of the uniform and waterproofing issues had greatly improved. Allied infantry communications had improved significantly since the 18th Brigade's last campaign in Buna and Sanananda. Most of the successes of the Finisterre campaign – intelligence collection, battalion manoeuvre, close air support and field artillery – all relied on communications and new radios. However, despite all the advances in communications, the weather and terrain of the SWPA took a toll on field equipment.

The new 'walkie-talkies' provided by the US Army had severe limitations once soldiers dropped below the ridgelines into the jungle ravine. For the brigades' fixed positions, such as artillery location, headquarters and observation post, the use of wire was still the most reliable form of communication in the mountains. In the end, the 18th Brigade described signal communications as 'adequate' in the Finisterre campaign.[67]

Despite the 18th Brigade's victories in the Buna and Sanananda campaigns, the infantry still only had a 'rudimentary knowledge' of the use of artillery in brigade manoeuvre in 1943.[68] The 18th Brigade implemented lessons in the methods, capabilities and limitations of field artillery that had been initiated after Buna, but there was little opportunity for live-fire training during the brigade refit in Australia. Once the 18th Brigade returned to New Guinea in late 1943, there were efforts by each battalion to sensitise the infantry to operations in close concert with artillery fire during training and battalion exercises.[69] The 18th Brigade's leadership pushed live-fire training with the understanding that, in the mountains and jungle, much of the fire support would be dangerously close.

During Operation Cutthroat, the 2/4th Field Artillery Regiment headquarters was for the first time co-located with the 18th Brigade headquarters, specifically with the brigade staff, to facilitate the need for the closest of cooperation between artillery and infantry in complex terrain.[70] Moving the field artillery headquarters forward on the battlefield to be co-located with the infantry headquarters allowed for the establishment of a 'fire control centre' with which the brigade commander and brigade staff could communicate directly. This allowed Chilton to exercise direct control of the artillery fire support during an infantry assault. The field artillery commander still commanded the artillery, but the close proximity allowed for rapid changes in fire support and split-second timing for infantry manoeuvre.[71] Chilton ordered Lieutenant Colonel Blyth's field artillery batteries to remain flexible and on-call after the initial infantry assault to support any unplanned follow-on missions or targets of opportunity. In an effort to push this level of close cooperation down to the battalions, Chilton assigned a field artillery officer to each subordinate battalion commander to serve as an adviser.[72] This field artillery officer assigned to the battalion would also coordinate forward observers at the company level. These company-level, artillery-forward observers were assigned to infantry patrols and operations whenever possible.

Chilton used artillery and close air support in dynamic ways in the Finisterre campaign. He used slow but sustained artillery fire on the Japanese positions to soften fortifications on Prothero, Kankiryo and Crater Hill.[73] The slow, deliberate use of artillery increased the infantry's chance of surprise because the Japanese became used to artillery being fired at their positions. Artillery fire was also used to bait the Japanese into returning fire, which the 18th Brigade used to identify and add targets to the brigade's list of 'registered' targets. Lastly, Chilton used artillery in support of infantry manoeuvre on the mountainous ridgelines.

The use of field artillery in Operation Cutthroat helped to demonstrate a new level of capability and coordination within the 18th Brigade. The ground and air reconnaissance, combined with increased analytical intelligence capacity, provided an accurate fire support plan to engage Japanese positions across the ridgelines. The 'fire control centre' provided a plan for each battalion assault for the 'full advantage' of all available guns.[74] The 2/4th Field Artillery planned to be able to shift fire support of each artillery battery from primary supported units to troops in contact throughout the area of operations. For example, if the 2/10th Battalion was in trouble and needed additional fire support, the 2/9th Battalion's assigned artillery battery was positioned to be able to shift fires to help the 2/10th Battalion. Additionally, in a battalion assault, Chilton could order a maximum number of guns available to suppress Japanese fortification before the infantry attack. In total, the 2/4th Field Artillery expended 15 553 high explosives, of which 3735 had delayed fuses and 658 had smoke rounds.[75] Delayed fuses, which allowed the round to penetrate earthen bunkers and field fortifications, were found to be highly effective.

An official publication of the Australian Army called *Reconquest* incorrectly describes the four-day siege of Kankiryo as an air power victory. *Reconquest* states that the 'Japanese natural fortress held off all assaults and that it was air power and artillery that ended the siege'.[76] This is an overstatement at best. As with many other battles in the Pacific, the Japanese never surrendered and rarely abandoned their positions because of bombardment: Kankiryo, Crater Hill and Prothero all had to be assaulted and held by the infantry.[77] In the end, the victory belonged to the brigade assault with the aid of close air support and artillery.

That slight aside, the use of close air support in the Finisterre campaign was enormously important for the infantry brigade group's evolution as an effective combat formation. The 18th Brigade's air support in Operation Cutthroat was used for two primary missions: heavy bombardment of Japanese fortifications, and the more dangerous close air support. Chilton used both during each of the five phases of the operation. Under these two types of mission were several tasks, including covering Japanese avenues of approach, military deception, destruction of Japanese fortifications and, lastly, close air support for the assault battalions.

Not surprisingly, as a capability, close air support was understood but almost largely ignored by the US and Australian armies before World War II, in part because of several challenges with close air support pre-1939. First was a lack of capable aircraft and radios for coordination. The second problem was the fact that the doctrine simply did not exist in the Australian or US armies. US Army *Field Manual 1-5 Employment of Aviation of the Army*, dated 15 April 1940, did not address close air support in any meaningful way.[78] Worse yet, the US Army *Field Manual 100-20 Command and Employment of Air Power* reported that close air support was the most difficult and least effective use of air power.[79]

By 1943, attitudes across Allied armies had changed. The 18th Brigade made wide use of close air support to unseat the Japanese from the mountaintop fortifications in the Finisterre campaign. Close air support in the Finisterre campaign started before the 18th Brigade took control of the battlespace, but it was the 18th Brigade who would harness its capability for infantry assaults. However, much of the bombing was still done through 'scheduled strikes' based on map locations when close air support was available.

The Air Support Plan developed by the 18th Brigade staff included an assortment of Australian and US aircraft, which admittedly experienced varied levels of success in the mountains. The Australian Army Cooperation Squadron, equipped with Boomerangs and Wirriways, was used extensively to guide in attack aircraft, such as US P-40s for close air support and aerial reconnaissance for the 18th Brigade.[80] The RAAF Vultee Vengeance – dive bombers in the Finisterre campaign – largely used 500-pound bombs with an 8- to 11-second delay in an effort to penetrate Japanese fortifications and detonate underground.[81] Unfortunately, the dive bombers were found to be of limited value due to the low cloud ceilings and the altitude at which the Vultee needed to begin its dive bombing run.[82]

The 18th Brigade reported that the close air support provided was accurate and effective against prepared Japanese defences. Forward ground reconnaissance units and troops' positions used ground panels, 2-inch smoke, and signal flares to avoid friendly fire incidents in the jungle and mountainous terrain. Although close air support was still in its infancy, ground liaisons in direct communication with Allied pilots assisted infantry units in identifying terrain features, smoke or troop panels for pilots in the air.

Operation Cutthroat was the first time the 18th Brigade was able to integrate close air support directly into its operations orders and direct the close air support from the ground. Advances in wireless communications allowed infantry commanders and forward observers to provide strike guidance directly to pilots overhead before and during ground combat. One after-action report noted that, during the assault, along 'Shaggy Ridge targets were engaged and destroyed within 100–120 yards of our forward troops'.[83]

The modernisation of the brigade Intelligence Section was one of the key factors for the 18th Brigade's victory in the Finisterre campaign. Without accurate and timely intelligence, Chilton would not have been able to surprise the enemy or employ the elements of the brigade group effectively during the assaults. Essentially, intelligence allowed Chilton and brigade staff the information needed in the right combination of resources, at the right time, to a given problem.

With each major campaign, the 18th Brigade recorded and made efforts to implement lessons learnt. In the brigade headquarters, the intelligence officer managed the parallel situation maps, gridded photos and signal diagrams to those developed in the intelligence shop. This current intelligence was essential to Chilton conducting a combined arms brigade group assault from brigade headquarters.

The successful implementation of new intelligence capability and structure was not without some notable challenges. After the Finisterre campaign, new intelligence officers would be cross-trained in the duties of the brigade staff officer.[84] Although the intelligence officer was on the brigade staff, previously he had not been cross-trained as a staff officer. During the Finisterre campaign, the intelligence officer repeatedly had to act on behalf of the brigade major assisting the commander. This left the brigade Intelligence Section to be 'run entirely by the intelligence sergeant'.[85]

The 18th Brigade's subordinate battalions had difficulty with a poor calibre of intelligence officers who were not able to perform all the battalion staff functions. This criticism was in some part unfounded. These positions were filled with junior officers new to the intelligence trade and who had probably never served on a battalion staff. Second, as noted in earlier chapters, there was no requirement, before deployment, for an intelligence officer to cross-train as a staff officer.

One major success of the 18th Brigade Intelligence Section was to emphasise small-unit clandestine ground reconnaissance over 'probing attacks' in the Finisterre Range campaign. An out-of-date maxim attributed to the Australian Army, 'you must fight to obtain information', might be redrafted 'you need information before you fight'. In one early report on intelligence collection on Shaggy Ridge, the attempts to launch 'probing attacks' proved costly in casualties without cultivating any intelligence.[86] This was due largely to the challenges of the complex terrain. Even if a probing attack did not generate casualties, it was still difficult to collect intelligence when probing uphill or over a ridge. The solution was two- or three-man reconnaissance teams, tasked by commanders or the brigade Intelligence Section, who avoided enemy contact while collecting information on Japanese positions and terrain features such as route, ridges and valleys.

The 18th Brigade Intelligence Section had invested both time and resources in training intelligence personnel to interpret photographs since the Buna and Sanananda campaign. This proved a wise investment for the Finisterre campaign. Maps of the Finisterre Range and the Markham and Ramu Valleys were not suitable for combat operations. Aerial photographs and photo-overlays became a primary task of the intelligence personnel in the brigade once deployed. One new method of intelligence collection had soldiers from the brigade Intelligence Section and forward observers aloft in surveillance aircraft while 2/4th Field Artillery fired smoke rounds onto Japanese positions.[87] The smoke would be marked onto aerial photographs, then transferred to maps and overlays sent back to brigade headquarters. These maps and aerial photographs would then be provided to long-range reconnaissance teams to confirm on the ground. These maps and aerial photographs allowed Chilton and the 18th Brigade staff to coordinate artillery and close air support throughout Operation Cutthroat.

In the after-action report of the Buna campaign, the 18th Brigade recommended an increase in the number of intelligence soldiers trained in photographic interpretation. Following the Finisterre campaign, Chilton went a step further and recommended basic photo interpretation training for all officers, including commanders, throughout the brigade.[88] Map-reading had always been an important skill for all leaders in the Australian Army. In the SWPA, aerial photographs had become just as essential to leadership, and photographic interpretation had risen to the same status as map-reading in the brigade.

The aerial photos proved so valuable to the 18th Brigade Intelligence Section that it requested the addition of trained photographers and small processing units at the brigade level.[89] The brigade repeatedly complained about the timeliness of the division photographic development shop. This resulted in a request to move capabilities down to the brigade level. In the Finisterre campaign, the photo reconnaissance mission was slow and cumbersome. The missions were flown from Port Moresby to the target of the photograph request, to shoot the photographs, then return the film to Port Moresby for development. Finally, the photographs would be flown back over the Owen Stanley Range to the unit that submitted the request. This could take several days. The 18th Brigade wanted the aviators and film developers closer to the front. This would allow the brigade Intelligence Section to conduct aerial reconnaissance and produce final intelligence products for the brigade and battalion commanders in much less time.

The brigade Intelligence Section and subordinate battalion Intelligence Sections' new organisational structures resulted in successful intelligence production throughout the campaign and made significant contributions to the defeat of the Japanese 78th Infantry Regiment. This was markedly different from the poorly trained and equipped intelligence personnel of the Buna campaign. The 18th Brigade had since dedicated time and resources to equipment and increased staffing and intelligence training. In the final analysis, the 18th Brigade Intelligence Section had not had the time or experience to mature fully as an organisation; however, the overall performance must be considered outstanding on the basis of the brigade victory and low casualty rates.

Operation Cutthroat would encapsulate numerous elements of the infantry brigades' evolving operational art: a full brigade assault with a full complement of supporting arms and close air support conducted in five phases coordinated in time and physical space to achieve a campaign objective. Most importantly, Operation Cutthroat was an operation planned and led by a brigade. In the 'Report on Operation Cutthroat', as noted earlier, Chilton was proud of the fact that this operation was conducted with the entire brigade operating as a single, well-coordinated unit.[90] Chilton and his brigade staff believed strongly that the campaign offered valuable lessons learnt for brigade operations. Operation Cutthroat showed the brigade as the key formation in the SWPA. The 18th Infantry Brigade Group (Jungle) conducted a well-coordinated operation to defeat a Japanese force, dug into mountaintop fortifications, through the coordination of supporting arms and infantry manoeuvre.

CHAPTER 7

# AMPHIBIOUS WARFARE DOCTRINE

> For almost three years, the Seventh Amphibious Force trained its personnel, fought a determined enemy, and carried Allied troops forward with accelerating pace and swelling power.
>
> Daniel Barbey[1]

Amphibious warfare, throughout military history, can be summarised in two steps: the movement of a military force by sea, and the landing of that force on the beach to seize an objective. These two steps are generally considered the most difficult and dangerous form of warfare. During World War II, US forces carried out 66 major amphibious landings.[2] A major amphibious operation is defined by two factors. In US military history, it is often noted that of the 66 amphibious landings, ten were conducted by the US Marine Corps, six were conducted by both the US Marine Corps and US Army, and 50 were conducted by the US Army.[3] Less acknowledged are the Australian Army's five major landings: Lae, Finschhafen, Tarakan, Brunei Bay and finally Balikpapan.[4]

For the Australian Army, amphibious warfare had become something of a pariah after its participation in the amphibious landings at Gallipoli in World War I. As a result, no substantive amphibious doctrinal research, training or exercises would be conducted by the Australian Army until the onset of World War II.[5] The foundations of Australian amphibious doctrine were based in the training of Australian officers and instructors in doctrine and tactics at the British Combined Training Centre in Kabrit, Egypt.[6]

However, there was still a significant interest in Britain with advancements in doctrine throughout the 1930s.[7] The British *Manual of*

*Combined Naval and Military Operations* (1913) was considered sufficient in its understanding of landing operations for Gallipoli, and later assessments blamed technological limitations in naval gunfire, air support and other issues for the battle's outcomes.[8] The challenges of Gallipoli are beyond the scope of this work; however, it is a checkpoint in both British and Australian amphibious warfare.

In 1925, the British published the *Manual of Combined Operations* with subsequent revisions and updates in 1931, 1938 and 1942.[9] They also developed a leadership-focused doctrine in *Combined Operations for Unit Commanders* in 1941.[10] Between service schools and an amalgamation of British and US doctrine, the Australian Army would have to ferret out its own doctrine as it fought its way across the SWPA.

Even then, the size and dominance of US military in the SWPA meant that Allied amphibious doctrine was heavily influenced by US amphibious doctrine. In the early 20th century, the concept of landing troops across a broad swathe of beach or beaches had been lost to history. The authors of US Army and Navy doctrine did not embrace amphibious warfare doctrine before World War I. Instead, they emphasised the tactics of small landing parties. The *US Navy Landing Force and Small Arms Instruction*, published in 1905, is one example of this focus on raiding parties. Another was the *US Army Transportation Service Regulation* of the same year, which offered no guidance on amphibious assault and advised commanders that, if the enemy could fire on the beach, it was simply better to move to another beach.[11] The US Army and Navy did not begin collaborating on amphibious doctrine until 1927 – a collaboration that would contribute greatly to the Australian-led landings in World War II.

In the SWPA, the combination of US amphibious capabilities and doctrine, matched with the Australian Infantry Brigade Group (Jungle), would result in the most powerful Australian brigade configuration in history: the Assault Brigade. Australian and US amphibious training, exercises and rehearsals culminated in the 18th Infantry Brigade Group (Jungle) reconfigured once more for its role as the 'assault brigade' or spearhead of the amphibious assault on Balikpapan.

## NORMANBY ISLAND, SEPTEMBER 1942

Although the 18th Brigade did not focus on amphibious warfare before 1944, it did conduct limited amphibious operations throughout its war in the SWPA. In March 1942 at Sandy Creek camp in South Australia, the 2/4th Field Company developed a small boat training program in which the 18th Brigade participated before its first deployment to Milne Bay, New Guinea. Two officers and 50 troops from each of the 18th Brigade's subordinate battalions learnt to carry, launch, breach and manoeuvre the boats for three days.[12] There were significant limitations. The quality of boats was poor, and the training was conducted in a calm reservoir that would have offered only the basics of watermanship.

In September 1942, during the 18th Brigade's defence of Milne Bay against a Japanese amphibious force, Brigadier Wootten tasked C Company, 2/10th Battalion, with conducting an amphibious raid onto Normanby Island.[13] Allied air power had attacked and sunk a Japanese destroyer. The survivors had occupied local villages on Normanby Island. The 2/10th Battalion was ordered to 'destroy or capture all enemy on Normanby Island'.[14] The order did not include provisions for any gunfire support from the navy, nor did it provide for any reinforcements should C Company land in the midst of strong Japanese defences.

On 20 September 1942, Wootten held a commanders' conference to discuss the amphibious operation on Normanby Island. There was some disagreement of the length of time the 2/10th Battalion troops should hold the island. The conference decided on an amphibious raid and that the troops engage the Japanese, then withdraw in short order.

Captain John Brocksopp, 2/10th Battalion, was to command all military operations while Captain Alec Marshall from the 2/9th Battalion would be assigned to HMAS *Stuart* as a liaison to the Navy. The Australian New Guinea Administrative Unit provided guides since none of the troops had ever been on Normanby Island.[15] The raid force did, however, conduct an aerial reconnaissance of the island with the RAAF 6th Squadron, which also agreed to provide air cover for the landing.[16] In 1942, because close air support had not yet matured, the loosely organised air support could provide a deterrent and, if needed, engage Japanese targets of opportunity. The 75th and 76th Squadrons also agreed to provide P-40 aircraft for security patrols while C Company was on the island and during recovery of the force.[17]

C Company embarked HMAS *Stuart* and landed on Normanby by motor launches and whalers without Japanese opposition. In his after-action report, Captain Brocksopp reported that the embarkation and landing were satisfactory and conducted on time. Upon landing at 0630, 13 Platoon moved out to the closest village while the remainder of the force conducted reconnaissance and secured the beachhead. By 0730, the rest of C Company moved out to other local villages. The headquarters element was established at Kapa Kapi village.

15 Platoon and the commando platoon moved out into the jungle after the locals informed them that 50–60 Japanese had moved out two hours earlier. By nightfall, C Company had collected seven prisoners and set up camp for the night. Between 2325 and 0150, Japanese ships patrolled the coast of Normanby Island in search of Allied troops and their survivors. The next day, C Company re-embarked on HMAS *Stuart*, halted briefly by a Japanese Type 96 fighter flying 100 feet off the ground.[18]

The Normanby expedition was a case of an inexperienced amphibious force landing without coordinated air support or naval gunfire. Brocksopp did grasp the utility of amphibious operations, arguing for a series of shore-to-shore 'aqua-hooks' to outflank the Japanese – a micro version of what would become Allied amphibious doctrine in the SWPA. The introduction of inclement weather or an unexpected Japanese force could have proved disastrous to the expedition. The ease of the Normanby operation probably led to the planning challenges faced in the 18th Brigade's next amphibious operation on Goodenough Island.

## Goodenough Island, October 1942

The 18th Brigade's second foray into amphibious warfare was Milne Force's raid on Goodenough Island.[19] On 11 September 1942, the 18th Brigade intelligence diary records a group of seven Japanese motor launches and barges landed more than a thousand troops on Goodenough Island. The report was received by a wireless unit, probably Coast Watchers, stationed on the island.[20] The barges had been en route to join the assault on Milne Bay when the RAAF forced the convoy to beach after it sank one of the barges. The RAAF subsequently destroyed the other six barges on the beach and stranded the Japanese force on the island.

The 2/12th Battalion raised Drake Force attached to Milne Force headquarters for the execution of an amphibious raid on Goodenough Island 'with a view to destroying Japanese troops on the island'.[21] Drake Force was to land two separate elements on two separate beaches at night by two navy ships. On the night of 22–23 October 1942, HMAS *Stuart* and HMAS *Arunta* landed the task force on Goodenough Island with a combination of whaling boats, ships' launches, ketches and a captured Japanese barge. This mismatched combination of unarmed landing craft could have posed grave risk to the landing force if the Japanese troops had chosen to defend the beach.

Once ashore, Drake Force headquarters was to be established on the beachhead, and two whalers and one Japanese barge would remain for the duration of the operation. The operations order called for Drake Force to land under the cover of the 8th Fighter Group, although none of the after-action accounts reported any air support during the operation. On 20 October, Milne Force published a document entitled *Possible Aerodrome Sites – Goodenough Island*.[22] It had been established that Goodenough Island would be an excellent island to support air attacks against the Japanese base at Rabaul. The island's size, at 25 miles long and 15 miles wide, could support large Allied airfields. In Dexter's account in *The New Guinea Offensives*, Drake Force was to conduct reconnaissance of potential airfields. A review of the Milne Force operations order for the Goodenough Island raid, however, shows that it did not include any instructions outside finding and destroying the enemy.[23]

On 22 October 1942, Drake Force landed at Mud Bay and Taleba Bay. The night of the amphibious landings witnessed heavy rains and significant confusion on the beach. At Mud Bay, two landing craft collided in the dark, further delaying the 2/12th Battalion's push inland. On Taleba Bay, one company of 2/12th Battalion landed from HMAS *Stuart* but met a Japanese force that had dug into very difficult terrain just forward of the beachhead. The company was in the dark, suffering from poor communications, and under fire from Japanese mortars and heavy machine guns. In 1942, close air support and naval gunfire had not yet been developed sufficiently to be used at the battalion level, especially at night or in inclement weather. Realising that the company was not in a position defend against Japanese counter-attacks, the Taleba Bay element withdrew after a brief but violent clash, re-embarked and joined the rest of Drake Force at Mud Bay.[24]

The 2/12th Battalion, without any experience in amphibious warfare, was asked to land at night from whaling boats on an unfamiliar shore against an enemy whose disposition was almost wholly unknown and without supporting arms. Drake Force fought small skirmishes with the Japanese; however, the Japanese had no interest in holding Goodenough Island and withdrew by sea on 27 October 1942. Drake Force's disorganised amphibious raid resulted in an unlikely amphibious success. However, if Japanese forces had opposed the night landing or counter-attacked the beachhead, the battle would have been an infantry force-on-force without the benefit of Allied firepower.

## OPERATION POSTERN: THE LANDING AT LAE

On 4 September 1943, Rear Admiral Daniel Barby, commander of the US Navy, Seventh Amphibious Force, and Wootten, now commander of the

9th Australian Division, conducted the first large-scale amphibious landing of the SWPA at Lae, New Guinea.[25] As it was the first major amphibious landing of an Australian brigade in World War II, examining the operation is important since its lessons learnt would directly affect future Australian landings in Borneo. In post-war correspondence, Chilton, who studied the landing before the 18th Brigade landing in Borneo in 1945, would refer to Lae as a 'rather untidy landing'.[26]

One problem with the amphibious assault at Lae was that neither the 9th Division nor the US Seventh Amphibious Force had conducted an amphibious landing in Japanese-held territory, a problem given the complexity of amphibious warfare. The 9th Division would move troops by sea to conduct an amphibious assault on two separate beaches with limited training.[27] The first planning conference was on 11 July 1943, and was attended by Admiral Barby, General Wootten and General Blamey, commander of New Guinea Force.[28] The overall concept of operations was an amphibious landing of two Australian infantry brigades with the third reserve brigade landing the following day. The plan for Operation Postern was finalised at a commanders' conference with MacArthur on 15 July 1943 at Milne Bay.[29]

Wootten, commander of the ground force, chose Red Beach near the Buso River and Yellow Beach near Malahang, well outside the range of Japanese artillery.[30] This distance would also allow for Wootten to establish his artillery quickly, which he believed essential in jungle warfare after his experience in Buna. The intent was for the artillery to be established on the banks of the Burep River before the Japanese could launch a large-scale counter-attack against the beachhead. With the legacy of Gallipoli, there was an expected caution in planning the Australian Army's first large amphibious assault of World War II. The after-action reports on the landing show that the Allies would have liked to have landed closer to Lae, but insufficient air or naval gunfire support was available to suppress Japanese artillery.[31] This was not a result of over-cautiousness; amphibious planners would assume a great deal of operational risk landing troops in range of enemy indirect fires and would do so only if it was an operational necessity.

On 1 August 1943, Wootten briefed the 20th Infantry Brigade that it would be the spearhead of the amphibious landing at Lae called Operation Postern. The general landing plan called for the 20th Brigade's subordinate battalions to fan out on the beach to block Japanese approaches and establish a perimeter. Two troops of 62nd Battery Field Artillery, one section of light anti-aircraft and one engineer detachment would also be on the initial wave. Immediately after the initial

Figure 7.1 Landing craft come alongside USS *Conningham* to take ashore the soldiers of the 9th Division headquarters as part of Operation Postern at Lae, New Guinea. The 9th Division's landing at Lae in 1943 was the Australian Army's first large-scale amphibious operation since Gallipoli in 1915. (AWM 042361)

landing of the 20th Brigade, the 26th Infantry Brigade would land pass through the beachhead and advance towards Lae.[32] The 24th Infantry Brigade would serve as the reserve force in Buna and would advance on day 3 of the operation. The 20th Brigade's war diary lists several meetings and conference in the following days, but there is no mention of an amphibious planning.[33]

On 6 August 1943, the 20th Brigade conducted its first loading exercise with a Landing Ship Infantry (LSI), a blue-water vessel capable of landing troops directly on the beachhead. The exercise resulted in significant confusion that then resulted in further planning meetings, according to the war diary.[34] Only two days later, the 20th Brigade, with its numerous attached units, attempted an amphibious landing with its poorly loaded LSIs. The 20th Brigade ran into problems from the start, the most significant of which was the inability of the infantry to disembark and unload the LSIs before the 26th Infantry arrived on the beach.[35] The poor load planning resulted in the 20th Brigade still unloading when they should have already seized the beachhead and established a perimeter. The brigade had conducted several smaller exercises throughout the month with similar results. The brigade staff was forced to hold daily load planning meetings right up until the departure for Lae.

On 20 August 1943, the 20th Brigade put to sea from Milne Bay for a full-scale amphibious landing exercise named Exercise Coconut on Normanby Island. At 0638, on 21 August, the 20th Brigade reached Red and Yellow Beaches. One battalion managed to land on Yellow Beach but immediately advanced in the wrong direction.[36] The portion of the force assigned to Red Beach completely missed its landing area and landed on Yellow Beach at H+2 hours after the first assault battalion.[37] The command and control during and after the landing was poorly executed, and the landing force never established a functional beachhead.

The after-action report on Exercise Coconut did – and rightfully so – produce a significant list of challenges for future Australian amphibious operations. First, the 20th Brigade did not have any liaisons or senior staff from the Royal Australian Navy, RAAF, US Navy or the US Army.[38] The brigade staff's planning process was done in a vacuum for an operation they had no experience in how to conduct. The 20th Brigade's subordinate units had significant problems with the embarkation process. Often, these subordinate and attached units did not know on which ship its high command was embarked. The landing instructions were complicated and often not passed down to the lowest level. For example, the reconnaissance elements of the 9th Division and RAAF both embarked on the wrong ships.[39] Even more troubling, the 2/13th Battalion commander embarked on LSI 25, only to find out later his battalion was on LSI 27.[40]

Embarkation problems plagued operation Exercise Coconut. The 20th Brigade units had no liaison with their respective ships, and no departure times had been posted. This almost resulted in units being left behind at Milne Bay. In spite of weeks of meetings by the brigade staff, most troops loaded the LSIs out of order, vehicles were not prepared for sea travel, and there were no chains to tie down vehicles on the ships.[41] Without tie downs, vehicles in the cargo space could capsize an LSI in high seas. The after-action report, probably in a face-saving effort, considered the Coconut landing a success, but this is a generous evaluation, especially for a landing on a beach without an opposition force.

On 9 August 1943, the 20th Brigade published its 'Operations Order Number 2' for Operation Postern, the amphibious landing at Lae.[42] It was a limited document because of the 20th Brigade's inexperience in amphibious warfare. The brigade had also been forced to plan without written instruction, since the 9th Division had not yet published the division operations order.[43] 'Operations Order Number 2' would have been sufficient to move troops by sea to a forward beach but was significantly lacking in any guidance for combat action on the beachhead.

The 2/13th Battalion, which would be first ashore, identified two infantry companies as the first wave on the beach. The battalion's third infantry company would land in the second wave with the brigade artillery guns. However, owing to limited space, the artillery tractors and artillery soldiers would be on the third wave. If the second or third wave became delayed or lost, the 20th Brigade would have been on the beach without heavy indirect fire support. This problem would have been compounded by the lack of air and naval gunfire support. In fact, naval gun support is not mentioned once in the 20th Brigade's operations order for Operation Postern.[44] This is more an issue of this period in the SWPA than a criticism of the 20th Brigade. In 1943, most Australian infantry brigades were still struggling with the use of artillery in manoeuvre, and now the 20th Brigade had been asked to do manoeuvre from the sea with naval gunfire support.

Operation Postern took place before the wide-scale introduction of close air support to the Australian infantry brigade. 'Operations Order Number 2' directed all air support requests to be submitted to the brigade staff at 1600 on D-Day −1, the day before the landing. At H-6 hours to H-5 hours, the Allied air forces would provide high altitude bombing of the beach, and from H-5 hours before the landing Allied aircraft would strafe the beach.[45] There was no provision for battalion commanders to coordinate close air support. In the next draft, 'Operations Order Number 4, Postern', provisions for close air support were added but only in the case of an emergency. Even then, close air support would be provided only when 20th Brigade headquarters deemed it 'practicable'.[46]

The '20th Infantry Brigade Group Operation Order Number 4, Postern', a more comprehensive document, gave a thorough explanation of the intelligence situation at Lae. However, it did not address the integration of artillery, naval gunfire or air support. The brigade's mission statement was to secure the beach and surrounding area, conduct patrols and stand by for a follow-on mission. It also detailed the attachments that made the 20th Infantry Brigade into a group. These included the 2/12th Field Artillery, one section of 2/4th Light Anti-Aircraft, 12th Light Anti-Aircraft Battery, 2/3rd Field Company, 2/8th Field Ambulance and lastly the 2/23rd Infantry Battalion of the 26th Infantry Brigade to serve as the reserve element for the landing.[47] Additionally, the US Army 532nd Engineer Boat and Shore Regiment and the 2nd Engineer Special Brigade made up much of the beach party.[48]

Air support for Operation Postern was limited to the 5th RAF and the 4th Australian Army Cooperation Squadron who were tasked with D-Day bombardment of Japanese airfields and air interdiction for the landing force if Japanese air elements attacked the convoy at sea. A second task for the 4th Australian Army Cooperation Squadron was aerial reconnaissance for the amphibious assault force as it moved off the beachhead.[49] The restriction of close air support to emergencies reflected the technology and doctrine of 1943. Close air support was a new and emergent capability with which the 20th Brigade had not trained, nor did it have air liaison officers. It also reflects the level of caution in the Allied forces and, probably more accurately, the Australian Army. This was the first large-scale Australian amphibious operation of World War II, and the possibility of Australian aircraft accidentally engaging Australian soldiers on the beach would have been of great practical and political concern.

On 31 August 1943, General Herring, on the cusp of the first Australian amphibious landing since Gallipoli, held a parade and told the troops they were lucky to have the great honour of the assault on Lae.[50] One officer noted that it was 'a rather out of place and uncomfortable glamour parade'.[51] This was at least in part because the 9th Division had been slow in its planning process and many of the exercises had gone relatively poorly. Two days later, amphibious Task Force 76, with the 20th Infantry Brigade Group, embarked on 18 LSIs and support ships put to sea for the invasion of Lae.[52]

On 4 September 1943, the amphibious assault on Lae began with the naval bombardment of the Red and Yellow Beaches. The naval gunfire support was limited to six minutes 'in order to neutralise enemy shore positions during the approach of the small craft conveying the first wave of assaulting infantry'.[53] Future planners would determine that this was vastly insufficient for an amphibious landing. The first landing craft hit the beach at 0615 without enemy action other than a single Japanese reconnaissance element, which had observed the entire landing. The 20th Brigade landed on Yellow Beach at H-Hour, roughly 30 kilometres east of Lae, and 26th Brigade landed on Red Beach near Hopoi, Allchin at H+2 without Japanese opposition.

On 5 September 1943, Wootten ordered the 26th Infantry Brigade, which landed on Red Beach, and the reserve 24th Infantry Brigade to move off the beachhead and drive towards Lae. Troops had been moved by sea and landed, and although the beachhead was a mess and the landing unopposed, the force was within striking distance of Lae. Within days, and in classic fashion, MacArthur announced that 'elements of four Japanese four divisions aggregating 20 000 at the beginning are now completely enveloped with their supply lines cut'.[54] The operative word in MacArthur's statement was 'elements' as the four divisions were not surrounded and an estimated 6000 Japanese soldiers marched out of Lae to join Japanese forces elsewhere in New Guinea.

Wootten's Lae landing was a success but not without cost. The Australian 9th Division suffered 77 killed and 397 wounded in the Lae campaign.[55] A significant 206 of these casualties occurred during the first 24 hours of a largely unopposed amphibious landing.[56] At 0700, Japanese aircraft attacked the amphibious force and caused casualties in the 2/23rd Battalion, which was the reserve element that had not disembarked. At 1630, the Japanese launched another air assault on the amphibious task force. The high initial casualty rate demonstrates the dangers and complexity of amphibious operations where 38 per cent of the total casualties were on the beach or offshore on a task force ship. Fortunately, the Japanese in the SWPA chose a strategy of not defending the beaches in favour of fighting in the complex terrain of mountains and jungles.

In *The New Guinea Offensives*, David Dexter highlights the 9th Division's accomplishment of putting 8000 soldiers, 1500 tons of stores and 20 days worth of provisions ashore in just four hours.[57] This was a significant accomplishment, but the brigades on the beachhead were extremely disorganised and largely stuck in traffic jams. Dexter then argued that it was Wootten's obsession with artillery that delayed the advance of the 26th Infantry Brigade by five days. This analysis seems to ignore the recent lesson of Buna and Sanananda where fire support was essential to overcoming Japanese fortifications. It was largely competing logistics trains and the build-up of ordnance, confounded by poor, muddy roads, that slowed the 9th Division's advance.

One significant recommendation to emerge from the Lae landing was the acknowledgement by both the 7th and 9th Division commanders that the line infantry units would require 'air liaison officers' to coordinate air support at the ground level.[58] This movement towards coordination officers for air support, naval gunfire and amphibious planning highlighted the rapid increase in the complexity of war in the SWPA. The 18th Brigade's introduction to large-scale amphibious warfare would come a year after the Lae landing.

## Brigade Amphibious Training

On 23 June 1944, in a 7th Division commanders' conference – the first since the return from the Finisterre campaign – the brigade commanders and brigade majors were provided with an outline for the future of the division as an amphibious force.[59] The subordinate brigades, to include the 18th Brigade, would begin focusing on amphibious warfare immediately. Brigadier Chilton, Major Ian Lowen (the brigade major), Lieutenant Colonel Bourne and others departed for the Amphibious Command and Staff Course in Cairns in early July 1944.[60] In October 1944, the 18th Brigade sent an original member of the brigade and leaders of the Normanby raid, Major John Brocksopp, to America to attend the US Marine Corps Staff School.[61] On 19 October 1944, the 18th Brigade began to send junior officers to the Embarkation Control Officer and Ship Adjutants course for 12 days.[62] Formal instruction for the senior officers and staff in the principles of amphibious warfare was essential if the 7th Division was to participate in upcoming Allied campaigns.

By July of 1944, the Allied amphibious warfare training program in the SWPA was a highly developed enterprise, but it began divided and poorly resourced. The HMAS *Assault* combined operations training facility at Port Stephens was one of the first amphibious warfare centres in Australia.[63] The facility was established as a Joint Overseas Operational Training School (JOOTS) in July 1942, the Australian portion being largely based on British amphibious doctrine with British instructors.[64] 'JOOTS was heavily theoretical and designed to run courses to train senior officers at the division, brigade and battalion level who would then return to their formations and units to pass on relevant information and establish amphibious warfare training programs.'[65] The other half of the base was the US Navy Advanced Landing Craft School, which became operational in December 1942. This facility spawned the first 'mobile' amphibious training teams, which deployed forward to support Australian and US infantry forces across the SWPA.

HMAS *Assault* and the US Navy Training Centre in Port Stephens, NSW, were a long way from the front lines, and in February 1943 General MacArthur turned over the entire facility to the 7th Amphibious Force for a re-evaluation.[66] On 1 October 1943, Admiral Daniel Barbey, commander 7th Amphibious Force, ordered the closure of the newly renamed Amphibious Training Centre, which took an additional 10 months to fully close.[67] With Allied advancement across the SWPA, it was determined the training needed to move closer to the front.

The US Army's basic plan for training a regimental landing team, the equivalent of the Australian Infantry Brigade Group, was – in perfect conditions – a 25-week training cycle. The 13 weeks, broken into two phases, could be conducted at the unit's home station with some soldiers being sent off to amphibious specialty schools. The first seven weeks were intended for individual training or basic soldiering skills. The next six weeks moved into collective training with company and battalion manoeuvres. In the 14th week, the Regimental Landing Team would be required to move to an amphibious training site. All further training required naval support. Weeks 14 to 19 were spent conducting three regimental field exercises. In the final four weeks, the regiment conducted training with special troops attached to it for the amphibious operation who then returned to the division for some division exercises.[68] Few units in the SWPA would have this long and comprehensive training for amphibious landings.

Two of the largest considerations for brigade amphibious operations are the combat readiness of the assault brigade and the landing site. Once the landing site has been determined, the amphibious planners must determine which additional units or attachments are needed to support the brigade. This task force or brigade group is then constrained by the size of the amphibious task force;[69] in simple terms, how many troops are needed, what support is required, and how many ships it will take to get them to the enemy's beach. Another vital consideration is the size of the shore party or 'Beach Group'. The Beach Group manages the beachhead, directs the traffic of follow-on units as each comes ashore, and organises the tons of stores and ordnance. As noted earlier, the crowded beaches of the Lae landing and its rehearsals proved one of the keys to amphibious warfare in traffic management on the beachhead.

Amphibious operations can be classified in several different ways. The first is whether the landing is Ship-to-Shore or Shore-to-Shore. The first ship-to-shore involves transporting troops and cargo by deep-water ocean-going vessels to the proximity of the landing site, then transferring assault craft before the landing. The shore-to-shore is the movement of troops and cargo directly from the friendly point of embarkation to the enemy beachhead.[70] If possible, shore-to-shore is preferred since the troops and equipment do not need to be transferred between vessels while at sea. However, there are other limitations. Shore-to-shore requires more vessels since each vessel is making only one landing.

The calibre of the brigade or attached unit can also pose significant challenges in conducting amphibious training programs. Prior unit training deficiencies, such as a lack of individual or collective basic skills, will complicate amphibious training.[71] For example, if an infantry brigade has not conducted a brigade-level field exercise or learnt to manoeuvre as a combined arms force, how can it be expected to do so while disembarking from multiple landing craft on an unfamiliar enemy beach? All these challenges are further complicated by the 10 to 20 attached units supporting the infantry brigade during the amphibious assault.

Early in World War II, the US Army determined that amphibious warfare was essential to the defeat of the Axis powers and developed a large-scale amphibious training program. The training was modular and exportable, and based largely on the work of the US Marine Corps in the 1920s and 1930s. Much of the basic training equipment could be constructed in a reasonable proximity to future amphibious operations. In the SWPA, the 7th Amphibious Force training program was established in Australia to support both US and Australian formations. The Amphibious Training Centre was designed for US infantry formations, which transferred directly to Australian brigades. The amphibious training schedule for a US regiment or Australian brigade was more than 50 hours a week, split between tactical unit training and battalion or regimental landing training.[72]

## THE BIRTH OF SWPA AMPHIBIOUS DOCTRINE

As previously mentioned, the interwar period was an era when neither the Australian nor US Army embraced amphibious warfare.[73] Conversely, the US Marine Corps, which had the primary mission of seizing and establishing forward naval bases, had spent the 1920s and 1930s conducting research, training and exercises in amphibious warfare largely based on a meticulous and 'continuous' study of Gallipoli.[74] These early amphibious warfare exercises will be discussed in chapter 8; however, it is important to note that even the famous War Plan Orange – the US war plan for confronting the Japanese in the Pacific – was largely steeped in the US Marine Corps' study of Gallipoli.[75]

The traditional philosophy on amphibious landings, represented in *Landing-Force Manual, US Navy 1927*, was to avoid heavily defended beaches, move to a lesser defended beach, and flank the objective on land.[76] Advances during World War II, such as tracked landing vehicles, close air support and effective naval gunfire, made it increasingly possible for an assault force to conduct a forced entry onto a defended beach. In 1934, the US Navy compiled the *Tentative Manual for Landing Operations*, described by US Marine General Victor Krulak as 'not too well written, it was not handsomely printed, and it was bound with shoestring, but it was there, some 127 000 words of it – more hard, doctrinal pronouncement on the seizure of an objective by amphibious assault than had ever been assembled in one place in all of history'.[77]

The treatise on amphibious warfare was subsequently repackaged and published as the *Manual for Naval Overseas Operations 1934*. After test and evaluation conducted in the Fleet Landing Exercises, the doctrine went through two more drafts before publication as *Fleet Training Publication 167: Landing Operations Doctrine, US Navy 1938*. Again, it was repackaged as US Army doctrine, *Field Manual 31-5, Landing Operations on Hostile Shores 1941*. It was this version of amphibious doctrine that would lay the foundation of amphibious operations for both Australian and US Army formations in the SWPA.

## Australian amphibious planning

On 12 October 1944, the Australian Army published the 1st Australian Corps Training Instruction Number 10 titled *Combined Operations: Planning on the Brigade and Unit Levels with Special Reference to Landing Table and Tonnage Tables*. It was a highly pragmatic collection of documents focused on providing the brigade staff with guidance for the 'scales' of an amphibious operation; that is, the configuration of attached units and equipment the brigade needs in combat operations to make up its 'group'. For example, as discussed in chapter 1, 'tropical scales' is the list of soldiers, weapons and equipment allotted to a jungle division or brigade. Common 'scales' in the Australian Army in World War II included light, normal, tropical and finally 'assault' scales.[78]

The 'assault scales' directly correspond with the designation of an 'assault brigade': the spearhead of any given amphibious landing. Another crucial planning factor for an Australian assault brigade was its tonnage tables.[79] The brigade must know how much everything weighs and how much physical space it takes up on a ship if it is to be effectively transported by sea and offloaded on a beachhead. The last component of initial planning data is the 'subunit details'. Essentially, how many additional units are attached to the brigade? What will these formations need to bring on ship? And always, how much does it weigh? All of this is needed to determine which units will embark on which ships, in what order and – equally important – how they will be disembarked on the beachhead.

In October 1944, the Australian Army decided that each Australian brigade would attend amphibious training at Trinity Beach, 12 miles north of Cairns, Queensland.[80] Although all Australian training was under the 'direction of the Amphibious Force Seventh Fleet', the training facility at Trinity Beach allowed the Australian Army to conduct training and develop doctrine for the Australian brigades.[81] The entire 7th Amphibious Force operated on US amphibious doctrine; however, the Australians had a history of British amphibious doctrine. Fortunately, the US and British amphibious doctrines were so similar that close cooperation was still possible.[82] In any case, much of the SWPA doctrine was modified to support a makeshift fleet of the 7th Amphibious Force.[83] This still allowed for the development of drills and doctrine specific to Australian infantry brigades. It is also important to note that this is another example of the importance of the brigade, which was a key formation in Australian amphibious doctrine. This focus on the brigade is what would lead to the Australian 'assault brigade'.

Doctrinally, the brigade staff planning process for amphibious operations was broken into seven steps. For the baseline analysis, these steps are listed chronologically, but in the SWPA, the brigade was often involved in several steps simultaneously. The first planning stage in Australian amphibious brigade doctrine began with the receipt of the division warning order or draft operations order. The order would be provided to the brigade Intelligence Section to begin an assessment of current intelligence on the target beach. This included all available maps, aerial photos, enemy order of battle and potentially the development of beach models.

Another initial task is the brigade staff's evaluation of the ships and landing craft allotted to the brigade group. The number of ships and crafts was based on the brigade's role in the landing. For example, a brigade scheduled to land on D+2, or the second day after the initial landing, would not need the same number of landing craft as the assault brigade since it would have fewer attached units. The brigade staff would also be assigned Royal Australian Navy and US Navy liaison officers to provide expertise in amphibious load planning. Although much of the staff planning process was managed by the Brigade Major, Amphibious Warfare, planning was a highly collaborative process.

Figure 7.2 Brigadier Frederick Chilton, Commander of the 18th Infantry Brigade, at Trinity Beach, North Queensland, during the brigade's introduction to large-scale amphibious warfare training in 1944. (AWM 067879)

The second stage of the amphibious planning effort was the initial draft of the brigade commander's concept of operations. This consisted of a discussion between the brigade commander and his staff where the division commander's intent was shared and discussed with the staff and liaisons; that is, military landing officers, naval liaisons and attachment commander, to include the beach group. The brigade commander would also consult with the staff as to the general sequence of units and equipment for the amphibious landing. The staff, liaisons and attached unit representatives were left to prepare a draft 'Distribution of Force to Ship and Craft', which provided the detailed task organisation of units, weapons systems, vehicles, stores and beach group equipment to a specific ship or landing craft.[84]

Thus far, the planning process did not differ much from that of an infantry ground manoeuvre campaign; however, stage 3 opened a bidding process for subordinate battalion and attached unit commanders. There was limited room on each ship and landing craft in the amphibious task force, and each unit needed to justify how much space it should receive.

Inevitably, some personnel, weapons and vehicles would be left behind. The brigade commander's stage 3 conference shared the initial 'Distribution of Force to Ship and Craft' with all subordinate battalion and attached unit commanders. Subordinate and attached commanders were given time, which varied based on the expected execution of the landing, to examine their own requirements and submit bids for changes to the 'Distribution of Force to Ship and Craft'. For example, if the Beach Group commander believed the Japanese air attack threat was significant, he would submit a bid for additional anti-aircraft guns on the initial landing. The entire process was a zero-sum game. If the brigade commanders accepted the Beach Group bid, something equal in size and weight had to come off the landing craft to make room for the additional anti-aircraft guns. The 'operational art' of amphibious warfare started with the planning process. The brigade commander and staff had to be able to ensure the correct combination of personnel, weapons, vehicles and supplies allocated to the correct landing wave to defeat enemy beach defences and overcome the terrain, all while focusing on the future missions inland. If the amphibious planning process was flawed, it could be disastrous on the beachhead.

Stage 4 was the reconciliation of the bid process, which could be a lengthy matter of dispute between subordinate commanders. This was also the stage where the amphibious planners outlined the individual waves of landing craft and what time they would land on the beach. In stage 5, the brigade commander returned to present the draft brigade landing plan to the division commander. The commander of the assault brigade – that is, the first brigade(s) ashore – had priority of resources, while the other brigade commander(s) and support commanders experienced a similar bid process for space on the amphibious task force.

The detailed Brigade Landing Plan was the subject of stage 6. With the division commander's feedback and approval, the assault brigade could prepare the final 'Distribution of Force to Ship and Craft' plan. Stage 6 also saw the development of the landing diagram, a visual map specifically detailed to show where personnel, weapons and equipment would be stowed on each ship. These documents became the guide for all units' embarkation at the port of departure.

In stage 7, the infantry battalion landing teams liaised with each battalion's respective ship's adjutant, a representative of the individual vessel who could assist with planning the respective battalion Landing Craft Tables.[85] For example, if 2/10th Battalion Landing Team went ashore in the LSI, then each LSI would provide a ship's adjutant. All the battalion Landing Craft Tables and ship assignments were based on the assault brigade's Landing Tables, which have been approved by division. This created problems at each echelon since the subordinate echelon was dependent on the high echelon landing tables, so that it was often the case that the units prepared landing tables in a vacuum because the higher command did not publish its tables in a timely manner.

The eighth stage was the final stage, although it was meant to be conducted concurrently with stages 6 and 7. The 'Plans for Ship and Craft Loading' was used to conduct loading of the elements on to ships and craft in an assault configuration. The difficulty of assault loading cannot be over-emphasised for both the amphibious planners and the units on the ground. Australian doctrine recommended a system of running checks, since stowage is a semi-technical process. Poor loading could result in instability at sea or, if stores or non-combat equipment were loaded after the troops, it could prevent troops from disembarking quickly and possibly result in higher casualties or loss of the landing craft. The entire landing tables planning process was designed to ensure that the assault brigade was able to disembark on the beachhead as fast and as effectively as possible, ready to fight.

The early amphibious raids of 18th Brigade on Normanby and Goodenough Islands introduced the amphibious lexicon to the common infantryman, and the Lae landing provided specific lessons for Australian brigades in an amphibious role. It would, however, be the challenging training regimen and exercise program that would prepare the 18th Brigade for the role of spearhead of the 7th Division's amphibious assault on Balikpapan.

CHAPTER 8

# AMPHIBIOUS EXERCISES AND REHEARSALS

By 1944, the 7th Division was largely focused on a future role in amphibious warfare. Each of its subordinate infantry brigades were directed to participate in training at the Amphibious Warfare Training Centre in preparation for future operations. Although the 7th Division's amphibious exercises Octopus and Seagull would be scenarios of proposed Australian participation in the liberation of the Philippines, ultimately the division would conduct two amphibious landings in an effort to defeat Japanese forces in Borneo. Chapters 8 and 9 will examine the 18th Brigade's transition to an amphibious assault brigade and the conduct of the amphibious assault at Balikpapan. In order to do so, chapter 8 will provide an analysis of the evolution of modern amphibious operation, which led to the Allied doctrine and exercise model that guided the amphibious operations in the SWPA.

In October 1944, the 18th Brigade initiated amphibious warfare training in earnest. Lieutenant Colonel Bourne, commander of the 2/12th Battalion, began to provide lectures and tabletop demonstrations of amphibious landing for all 18th Brigade officers. On 21 October, the 18th Brigade received the order to move to Trinity Beach for amphibious training.[1] Once at Trinity Beach, the brigade group began its final transition of World War II. In the months to follow, it would transition into an 'assault brigade' for the amphibious assault on Balikpapan. This transition was not solely one of increased lethality; it would also have to overcome the massive administrative challenges of amphibious warfare.

The '18th Australian Infantry Brigade Training Instruction Number 1, Planning and Amphibious Training', which established the headquarters and staff at Trinity Beach, referred to the need for a 'pool of typists' to produce the number of orders, tables and amphibious planning documents needed to conduct amphibious warfare. Each of the brigade's infantry battalions and attached units would be required to prepare staff and logistics tables for the brigade staff's amphibious planning team during each of the amphibious exercises.[2] The administrative demands of amphibious planning consumed so much time that the 18th Brigade staff would not get to participate in the brigade's first major amphibious exercise, Octopus.[3]

## A HISTORICAL LOOK AT AMPHIBIOUS EXERCISES

One of the first modern amphibious exercises that influenced the SWPA campaigns was the US Marine Corps Grand Joint Exercise of 1925. The exercise, based on a study of the Gallipoli landings of 25 April 1915, included 1727 marines from both West and East Coast Expeditionary Forces and a host of participants from Navy and Marine Corps officers' schools. The scenario had the marine force simulating a two-division landing of 42 000 men. The US Army, which like the Australian Army had little interest in amphibious warfare before World War II, played the defender with a force of 16 000 troops from active and reserve army units and the National Guard.[4] This template for amphibious warfare exercise continued for more than a decade with the US Marine Corps conducting amphibious assaults against uninterested US Army defenders.

The US Marine Corps had the primary mission of seizing advanced naval bases in support of the US Navy's mission. The US Army, like the Australian Army, was largely focused on the protection of the continental homeland, which amounted to ground defence against foreign invasion. In 1935, the US Navy established an annual Fleet Landing Exercise, which would alternate between the east and west coast. The first two Fleet Landing Exercises were largely unchanged from the previous model, with a US Marine landing force conducting an amphibious assault on an army-defended beachhead. The early Fleet Landing Exercises validated much of the work that had gone into the *1934 Tentative Manual for Landing Operations*.

Fleet Landing Exercise Number 3, in 1937, saw the first addition of a US Army formation to the amphibious landing. The US Army had determined that it would have to become an expeditionary force – the same realisation the Australian Army came to a few years later with the Japanese invasion of the SWPA. Fleet Landing Exercise 3 included a number of innovations that would be key to the development of Allied amphibious warfare doctrine. For the first time, the US Navy provided naval gunfire support and air support to the amphibious assault force.[5] Although this combined arms element consisted only of scheduled bombardments directed from the highest level, it was the first step towards an assault force, such as the 18th Brigade, possessing the capability to direct naval gunfire and close air support at the assault brigade level.

The US Army 18th Infantry Regiment and 7th Field Artillery Battalion joined Fleet Landing Exercise Number 4 in 1938. This was the largest US Army force commitment to date, with 42 officers and 547 enlisted men afloat on amphibious ships. There is no written account of the US Army's after-action in the 18th Regiment's unit archives, but the US Army did choose to opt out of the next two years of amphibious exercises. The US Navy reported that the landing force suffered significant confusion on the beach because of the use of smoke-obscured landing sites, which probably resulted in a disorganised and crowded beachhead.

Fleet Landing Exercise Number 5 and 6, in 1939 and 1940 respectively, witnessed the introduction of an experimental landing craft known as the Landing Craft Vehicle Personnel (LCVP) or Higgins boat, which outperformed all landing craft previously in use by the US Navy. The Higgins Boat was light and semi-modular, which made it easier to ship overseas.[6] The Landing Vehicle Tracked (LVT) was tested following Fleet Landing Exercise Number 6. Australian Army units would eventually conduct amphibious landing in both LCVPs and LVTs.[7] The LVTs would prove be a key element of the 18th Brigade's assault on Balikpapan.

On 23 July 1941, only two months after the US Army published its first amphibious warfare doctrine, *Field Manual 31-5: Landing Operations on Hostile Shores*, the US Army's 1st Infantry Division set out on its first divisional amphibious warfare exercise. Fleet Landing Exercise Number 7 resulted in large-scale confusion. Several of the US regimental combat teams – an equivalent formation to the Australian brigade group – were divided across the amphibious task force on different ships, counter to the new amphibious doctrine. None of the US Army regiments was able to reassemble successfully as a combat formation on the beachhead. One regimental combat team even neglected to load heavy weapons in the initial wave of the assault landing.[8] The result was a light infantry landing on a heavily defended enemy beach. By any form of evaluation, Fleet Landing Exercise Number 7 was a disaster. The challenges and failures identified in these early Fleet Landing Exercises contributed greatly to the training program of the Amphibious Training Centres of the 7th Amphibious Force in the SWPA.

## Brigade planning timetable

The Australian assault brigades would have the most difficult planning process in the division since it had to coordinate the largest number of attached units, external support and, most importantly, sustain the highest level of risk. Having examined the doctrinal process for brigade amphibious planning, it is important to review the amphibious timetable, which is a key element of successful amphibious operations. Contrary to what might be expected, the amphibious timetable is not a plan based on the date of the amphibious landing or the D-Day, as might be expected. Instead, the brigade timetable is based on the sail-away or the S-Day.

The brigade amphibious timetable is based on the day the task force puts to sea because of two important considerations. First, the specific day of the amphibious landing is never set in stone. A number of variables could move the landing forward or backward on the calendar. The second reason is more administrative: it is the last day the brigade can load personnel, weapons and equipment on ships of the task force. For these two reasons, the doctrinal amphibious planning timetable for is set at 18 days. The 18-day timetable was arbitrary, based on 18 planning steps. In the SWPA, 18 days was rare, even if the brigade had months to train for amphibious warfare. The amphibious timetable could begin only when the division warning order or operations order was issued to the brigade, which often came late and incomplete, creating a chaotic planning environment.

As noted, the process begins on S-18 when the division commander provides the brigade commander(s) with his intent to conduct an amphibious landing. This is when the division commander designates the assault brigade or brigades for the spearhead of the landing. The next day, S-17, the brigade commander issues a warning order to all subordinate commanders and the brigade Intelligence Section, which immediately begins collection and preparation of intelligence for the operation. On day S-16 the brigade commander holds the first commanders' conference and briefs the brigade staff as well as subordinate and attached commanders. After this conference, the brigade major, military landing officer and naval advisers begin the draft of 'Distribution of Force to Ships' discussed earlier in Australian amphibious doctrine. That evening, the brigade commander holds a second conference to receive the battalion commanders' comments and input on the draft plan and receives bids for space on the first waves of land ships.

Day S-15 starts with an early morning brigade commander conference at which battalion commanders submit draft outlines and tentative plans for the landing waves. This is a very short period in which to generate such complex documents, but it was necessary to get drafts completed quickly for the numerous revisions to begin. Later that day, the brigade commander meets the division commander to submit the outline plan for the assault brigade.[9] This is the first reference in Australian doctrine to the assault brigade, the key formation in an amphibious landing. This meeting allows the assault brigade commander, who is the spearhead of the landing and therefore has the priority, to request alteration to shipping, craft, support and the order of battle.

On S-14, the draft Brigade Landing Tables are issued. This provides the battalion commanders an opportunity to hold conferences with their respective battalion landing team, subordinates and attached commanders. During these conferences, each battalion commander is responsible for the establishment of the priority of combat loading for units, vehicles and weapons systems. The beach group commander conducts a similar conference to discuss which of the beach group's resources need to be ashore immediately to conduct traffic control and set up assembly areas. The Battalion Landing Tables are reconciled with the Brigade Landing Tables, and a final Brigade Landing Plan is issued on S-12. This is never the final version. Changes to the landing tables or load plans are conducted as necessary to consolidate the overall concept of operations.

The brigade conducts final checks of the landing craft tables and provides copies to division for approval on S-11. At this point, the brigade staff begins work on the essential written orders such as the operations, administrative, movement and signals orders. With the final versions of the Battalion Landing Craft Tables, Brigade Landing Tables and the operations orders completed, the brigade commander holds the final planning conference on S-10. The following day, all completed plans and tables are sent to division. From S-9 onwards to S-1, the assault brigade begins the concentration of forces at the port of embarkation and the loading of stores, vehicles and troops.[10]

## EXERCISE OCTOPUS

The timetable for amphibious planning provided in the US and Australian doctrine would become greatly accelerated for the 18th Brigade in preparation for its first large amphibious exercise. The doctrinal 18 days of amphibious planning was reduced to just seven days for Exercise Octopus. The timeline for the 7th Division's movement to the front simply did not allow for the 18-day amphibious planning cycle. The brigade arrived at Trinity Beach and received a verbal warning order from the division commander on 28 October 1944. A written order followed on 29 October, after which Chilton held the first commanders' conference with subordinate leaders. The next day, each individual battalion landing team submitted a concept of operations for Octopus. On 31 October, the 18th Brigade staff issued the draft Brigade Landing Tables, and on 1 November, subordinate units submitted changes and bids to the landing tables at the commanders' conference. On 2 and 3 November, the final Brigade Landing Tables were published, and the individual Battalion Landing Craft Table was submitted to the brigade staff as well as the beach group headquarters. The final commanders' conference was conducted on 4 November 1944.[11] For an infantry brigade with limited amphibious warfare experience, this would have been an incredibly hectic seven days.

For the individual soldier of the 18th Brigade, Exercise Octopus did not begin with landing tables but with infantry tactics, like any other operation for training in a collective amphibious task. On 3 November 1944, the 18th Brigade Headquarters, the three infantry battalions and the attached units began round-robin-style amphibious training. While amphibious operations are complex, sometimes huge in scale, and often include hundreds of ships and aircraft, fundamentally, they are about individual soldiers getting on and off boats effectively. The 18th Brigade followed the standard amphibious training template provided by the Amphibious Training Centre, while the brigade staff focused on the amphibious planning. The troops practised embarkation and debarkation on both wooden LST mock-ups and shipside. As Private Little noted in an interview, 'It [amphibious training] was entirely different. Coming down, scaling down over the side of the ships, down the cargo nets, and getting into the smaller ships. It was hard work, it was very hard work.'[12] When not training, films on amphibious warfare were shown during all meals and in the evening. Clausewitz wrote, 'War is very simple, but in war the simplest things become very difficult.'[13] To this point, all the units of the 18th Brigade repeatedly participated in formal training for wading ashore in shallow water – a simple skill made difficult by war.[14]

The first phase introduced the soldiers to the Landing Ship Infantry (LSI), the Landing Ship Tank (LST), Landing Craft Infantry (LCI) and lastly the Australian Landing Craft 40. 'The LCIs were ships designed to land on sloping beaches and disembark troops by means of two ramps on the bow, which could be quickly lowered at the tie of beaching.'[15] LCIs were 158 feet in length with a quarter inch of armour plating, a standard armament of four 20mm anti-aircraft guns and maximum speed of 15 knots and had a range of 4000 nautical miles. The LCI crew included three officers and 22 enlisted men, and the vessel had a capacity of 182 embarked troops.[16] In spite of the two ramps on the front of the LCIs, troops often trained for a ramp failure, going over the side on cargo nets.

From 5 to 10 November 1944, the brigade had the use of one LST for practice on loading and unloading vehicles, heavy mechanical equipment, and armour.[17] The infantry battalions also had use of an LST mock-up for training when the ships were unavailable. None of the loading or unloading of vehicles and equipment was conducted in low-light conditions since by this time in the war Allied Headquarters in the SWPA had largely abandoned night-time amphibious landings for safety reasons.[18] The US Marine Corps had ruled out night landings before World War II largely owing to its study and exercises based on the Gallipoli landings.[19] The challenges of a night landing would significantly increase risks to the landing force, particularly since the technology to communicate and coordinate naval gunfire and close air support during a night landing simply did not exist.

From 5 to 12 November, the brigade had use of two LSIs and four LCIs to practise landing infantry troops and inserting 1st Beach Group reconnaissance teams.[20] The individual units rotated through different stations starting with the Shipside Training Program, where troops were instructed on 'knotting, lashing, and lowering of equipment, scrambling down knots on a shipside (or mock-up) into landing craft'.[21] Troops would scale down to Australian Landing Craft 40s with all their personal equipment and with crew-served weapons such as infantry mortars and heavy machine guns. The personal equipment included a mosquito net, groundsheet, gas cape, one extra uniform, toiletries, water bottles, seven days of Atebrin and one emergency ration, all in addition to a soldier's weapon, helmet and ammunition. This training was dangerous, and safety boats were always present in case a soldier fell into the water.[22]

The 18th Infantry Brigade Group undertook amphibious warfare training with as many of its attached units as possible to ensure that non-infantry units had the same standard of training. The engineer units under the 18th Brigade attended specialised training in constructing roads on the beach, detection and demolition of obstacles and mines both in the water and on the beach, watermanship with engineer boats, and 'bridging the gap' between ships and the beach.[23] Other attachments rotated

Figure 8.1 Soldiers of the 2/12th Infantry Battalion assault the beach as part of the brigade's first large-scale amphibious exercise. Exercise Octopus, as it was called, was preparation for the brigade's expected participation in the invasion of the Philippines. (AWM 083129)

through the standard cycle of amphibious training with mock-ups, ship-side loading and unloading, and wading ashore laden with equipment. Attached formations that possessed armour, heavy weapons or heavy equipment spent the bulk of their amphibious training on the larger LSTs that would carry their equipment and vehicles to the beachhead.[24]

The Exercise Octopus scenario called for the 7th Division to seize a Japanese airfield on Unity Island. The 18th Brigade was designated the assault brigade for the amphibious assault on a Japanese garrison of 700 soldiers who were determined to repel the landing force. On the next day or D+1, the 21st Infantry Brigade Group would land on the secure beachhead, pass through the 18th Brigade's lines and seize the enemy's airfield.[25] Intelligence predicted that the Japanese would not be able to reinforce the garrison for three days. The 18th Brigade was to conduct its first amphibious landing at 0600 on Unity Beach with the support of naval gunfire and close air support.[26]

The purpose of Exercise Octopus was to introduce the 18th Brigade and individual soldiers to 'as many aspects of amphibious warfare as possible' in the shortest amount of time.[27] The training and exercise was broken into two phases. The first phase was an introduction to types of landing craft, embarkation, wading, procedures on board ship and the loading of vehicles and stores. The second phase was the actual amphibious landing against an enemy-held beach. The 1st Australian Beach

Group would serve as the cadre for the 18th Brigade's initial training in amphibious warfare, assigning instructors to each training site.[28]

Once ashore, Octopus became an exercise in infantry brigade manoeuvre. In phase 1, the 2/12th Battalion, reinforced with tanks, would capture Green Beach and destroy Japanese coastal artillery at objectives Delta and Charlie. Simultaneously, the 2/10th Battalion, also with attached tanks, would assault Red Beach and destroy coastal artillery at objectives Alpha and Bravo. In phase 2, the 2/9th Battalion, the brigade reserve force, would hold at the beachhead until called forward through 2/10th Battalion's lines to attack and capture forward objectives. Phase 3 called for an airborne landing by 2/1st Parachute Battalion and the amphibious landing of additional armour and cavalry elements.[29] The command of the landing followed the Allied doctrinal structure for amphibious landings with the navy in command of the amphibious assault until Chilton's headquarters was established ashore.[30] The shared command of amphibious assault had the secondary effect of encouraging army commanders to get ashore soon as possible.

Octopus was a large-scale exercise; however, much of the support was simulated. The US Thirteenth Air Force was tasked with the strategic bombardment of the Japanese airfields to prevent Japanese air power from attacking the landing force on the beach or the navy amphibious force offshore. The 18th Brigade's headquarters was assigned an air controller party, and each of the subordinate battalions would receive an air liaison party.[31] Highly valued air coordination elements were recommended after the confusion at Lae.[32] Additionally, the assault battalions would have a squadron of Boston aircraft on air alert from H-hour to H+3 for close air support. These Bostons were not under direct control of the battalion commanders, and each request would still have to be routed from the battalion's Air Liaison Party to the 18th Brigade's attached Air Controller Party for coordination and priority of tasking.

Octopus was the first time the 18th Brigade trained on an LSI at sea, although many other Australian brigades and US regiments had used this type of ship throughout the SWPA. The British ships *Glenearn* and *Empire Spearhead* supported the brigade's landings. On 10 November 1944, the 2/9th Battalion with 2/1st Parachute Battalion embarked on *Empire Spearhead* while 2/10th and the 18th Brigade headquarters embarked on *Glenearn*. On the morning of 13 November, the 18th Brigade landed on Unity Beach. The assault brigade was configured with 2/10th and 2/12th Battalions leading the initial landing, each with two infantry companies forward. Each battalion secured sectors of the beach and destroyed simulated Japanese coastal gun positions. Subsequently, the 2/9th Battalion (the reserve element) landed followed by the Pioneer Battalion, which was on standby to clear obstacles. At H+30 minutes, the 18th Brigade headquarters landed on the beach and by 1600, Exercise Octopus had concluded.[33] Although no record of a brigade or division after-action report exists in the unit records, on 14 November the 7th Division held an after-action conference to assess the 18th Brigade's first amphibious landing.

The 18th Brigade spent the rest of November 1944 conducting unit-level infantry training and lectures on amphibious landing like those of the US Army at Leyte.[34] Surprisingly, a large amount of instruction on amphibious warfare in the SWPA came from Allied training films that are mentioned almost daily in the unit war diaries. The 18th Brigade's next full-scale amphibious exercise would not come until March 1945.

## Operation Seagull

On 23 February 1945, the 7th Division held a planning conference for its next amphibious exercise, Operation Seagull. The entire 18th Brigade staff was in attendance, and the next day the brigade established a planning centre for Seagull.[35] The 18th Brigade staff at this point were noticing a trend in amphibious planning. The schedule would always be far shorter than doctrine prescribed. The 18th Brigade staff completed a concept of operations for Seagull in just three days. Chilton held a commanders' conference on 26 February with all infantry battalion commanders, attached unit commanders, and liaison officers.[36] On 1 March, the '18th Australian Infantry Brigade Outline Plan – Operation Seagull' was submitted to the 7th Division for approval. The brigades of the 7th Division had been provided topography, beach reports and the enemy situation. This was the largest amount of information and intelligence the 18th Brigade staff had received for any exercise to date.

The overarching scenario was based on a corps-level amphibious operation, much larger than Exercise Octopus. The scenario of Operation Seagull was for Allied forces to seize and develop forward operating bases within the Philippine archipelago. With 17 000 Japanese troops and indigenous forces conducting raid and sabotage missions against the Allied landing force, Seagull would also be the largest simulated enemy force the 18th Brigade would face.[37]

The '1st Australian Corps is to capture Morone's Island to permit its development as an advanced base and the establishment of air and naval facilities on the island'.[38] Again, the 18th Brigade would serve as one of two 'assault brigades', conducting an amphibious assault on two defended beaches with the objective of capturing Port Turan. The 18th Brigade's objectives included the destruction or capture of all Japanese coastal artillery guns and establishment of a beachhead perimeter a thousand metres inland to provide for a larger follow-on force.[39] The 21st Infantry Brigade was to assault adjacent beaches of Charlie Red and Charlie Yellow. The 1st Australian Parachute Battalion was to conduct an airborne landing on D+1 at Kenapai to secure a third beachhead for the 25th Infantry Brigade, which was the 7th Division reserve element.[40]

Operation Seagull would be the first time the 18th Brigade would employ tracked landing craft during an exercise. For Seagull, the brigade had 12 LVTs, light armoured tracked amphibious vehicles of varying configurations. The brigade's landing time drastically changed with the speed by which the infantry could move ashore. Previously, the use of landing craft such as the Higgins boat left troops at the shoreline. The front gate would open, exposing the infantry to machine gun and rifle fire from defensive positions on the beach. This left the troops to assault across the beach directly into enemy fire. The use of amphibious tracked vehicles allowed for the infantry to drive onto the beachhead while employing heavy weapons from the vehicles. This greatly improved survivability for the troops on the beach.

Chilton understood the potential of LVTs and made every effort to send as many troops as possible to LVT training. In December 1944, after Exercise Octopus, the brigade had sent 20 personnel per battalion back to Trinity Beach for instruction on the LVT with the 1st Australian Beach Group. In January 1945, the brigade sent an additional 30 personnel per battalion to include machine-gun and mortar teams to train with the LVT. Later in January, Chilton sent the entire 18th Brigade Signal Section back to Trinity Beach for LVT training.[41]

For Operation Seagull, each of the 18th Brigade's subordinate infantry battalions would be organised in an assault configuration. Each battalion commander would have an assortment of attached units. This included one company of amphibious tanks, two detachments of amphibious tractors (one of 3 heavy weapons platforms and the other 15 LVT4s), a detachment of the 18th Brigade Signal Section, one squadron of Cavalry (Commando), one battery of field artillery, a detachment of engineers, a shore fire control party and one air liaison party.[42] Later in the planning, a detachment of 2/4th Field Company and a detachment from the Engineer Special Brigade would be added to battalions.[43] The increase in attached units and capabilities required more of infantry battalion commanders and battalion staffs. That same evolution of operational art seen at the brigade commander level – the appreciation of the complex battlefield and the application of resources – was now a requirement at the battalion level.

Naval support for Operation Seagull and the 18th Brigade protected the convoys, interdicted Japanese supply lines and provided the assault brigades with naval gunfire support for the landing exercise. On D-Day, destroyers and cruisers provided scheduled beach bombardments as well as on-call fire support once ashore. The shore fire control party assigned to the 18th Brigade was a key element to the employment of this new form of fire support. Naval gunfire support has special considerations such as the range from ship and angle of the shells' approach. For the brigade and battalion commanders, the shore fire control party was essential for the effective employment of naval gunfire against Japanese positions.

Operation Seagull was so large that the 7th Division was provided with eight days of support from an escort carrier group with 128 fighter aircraft and 96 dive and torpedo bombers.[44] Land-based aircraft from adjacent islands would provide a large amount of the general air support, but close air support for the initial landing would be provided by the carrier-based aircraft. From D-Day to D+8, the escort carriers would remain on station to provide close air support and aerial reconnaissance. After D-Day+8, air support would revert to land coverage for the remainder of Operation Seagull.[45]

On 16 March 1945, the 18th Brigade approved the Battalion Landing Tables that had been produced and submitted by each subordinate infantry battalion. On 28 March, Chilton held an amphibious landing conference to brief the final operation and administrative orders for Operation Seagull. Although the 18th Brigade war diaries do not have notes on the meeting, it seems that Chilton found the brigade staff's amphibious planning unsatisfactory for the proper loading of ships; on the next day, all officers of the brigade staff were ordered to attend three days of additional landing tables training. Chilton, who had studied numerous amphibious landings including Lae, understood that the administrative task of drafting accurate landing tables was the key to combat effectiveness on the beachhead.

The 2/9th and 2/12th Battalions would serve as the assault battalions, with the 2/10th Battalion in reserve. The 2/10th Battalion (the brigade reserve force) had an identical complement of attachments to the assault battalions, with the addition of one squadron of 2/7th Cavalry (Commando) Regiment, and the remaining seven batteries of the 2/4th Field

Regiment. The 2/10th Battalion and 2/7th Cavalry each assigned a 10-man advance party to the assault battalions. The 2/10th Battalion and 2/7th Cavalry were scheduled to land at H+40 minutes.[46] The advance parties were necessary to speed the units ashore and into assembly areas where units reorganised to move off the beachhead and onto objectives inland as quickly as possible.

The attached formations provided support in a number of ways. The artillery support for the 18th Brigade's objectives in Operation Seagull would be provided by 7th Battery attached to the 2/10th Battalion landing in the second wave. The 7th Battery planned to be on the beach ready to provide artillery support for the 18th Brigade's assault on the port of Tuban at H+2. The 2/4th Field Engineer Company was tasked with clearing a path for the LVTs to advance off the beach. The 2/4th Engineers would also provide a six-man detachment to each of the assault battalions for the purpose of engineer reconnaissance and mine and obstacle clearance.[47] Without engineer support, the Japanese defenders could deny access to the landing through a combination of mines and obstacles.

Operation Seagull, the most complicated exercise the 18th Brigade had ever conducted, was largely a success. The addition of amphibious tanks, LVTs, naval gunfire and aircraft carrier support were new challenges for Chilton and his battalion commanders. The light armoured LVTs gave the infantry the ability to manoeuvre faster and with relative protection. Chilton had ordered: 'No move from the beach is authorised until ordered by brigade, NOT before H+2.'[48] Chilton's order gave the battalion commanders time to organise on the beachhead and overcome the confusion of an amphibious landing. It also prevented the assault battalions from outrunning supply lines and, more importantly, fire support.

## THE BRIGADE EMBARKS

As discussed earlier, one of the most important factors of an amphibious assault is the effective landing of infantry and support formations on the beach in such a manner that the assault force can immediately organise into combat formations, deploy fire support and engage the enemy. For this to happen, the ships and landing craft have to be combat loaded with key combat formations and with the beach coordination elements disembarking first. Chilton later noted that Balikpapan was 'the only campaign in which we had had (with very minor exceptions) everything we needed in the way of equipment and support. All previous campaigns in the

Middle East and the earlier campaigns in New Guinea had been conducted on a shoestring basis.'[49] With the 18th Brigade fully equipped and resourced, the challenge for the assault brigade was to make it all fit on the allotted ships.

The 'Embarkation Procedures on the Brigade Level – Oboe II' detailed not only the method for combat loading the 18th Brigade but also the entire assault brigade, including attached formations. Each was brought to the assembly area on Morotai, where the combat and support formations were organised into ships and landing crafts by serial groups. Each serial was then taken to the Pre-embarkation Assembly Area, where they were combat loaded on to ships and landing craft.[50] Serials assigned to LSIs and APDs were loaded by small watercraft offshore. The LSTs, LSMs and LCTs landed on the beach and loaded using the forward ramps. The 18th Brigade embarkation planners at Morotai continued to express frustration with the 7th Division, which kept making adjustments to various aspects of the embarkation effort as late as 18 June.[51]

At the time of embarkation, the 18th Brigade had deficiencies in weapons and equipment that it was informed would be waiting at Morotai. This would not be the case. The entire brigade group was at 35 per cent for machine sights, 25 per cent for compasses, 25 per cent for scout telescopes and 0 per cent of the allotted jungle sights.[52] Another important deficiency at the time of departure was ammunition. The 7th Division reported ammunition shortages across all three of its infantry brigades. One important deficiency was in 3-inch mortar ammunition. The 3-inch mortar was primarily an indirect fire weapon of the infantry that could be carried into combat. Brigadier Chilton and his battalion commanders expressed great concern that Balikpapan terrain was best suited for the 3-inch mortar. The 18th Brigade leadership had all agreed the 3-inch mortar would be one of the key organic weapon systems for the infantry on the beach.[53] Before putting to sea in Australia, the 18th Brigade had requested a full complement of 3-inch mortar rounds for the entire assault brigade plus 1000 rounds in reserve. The 18th Brigade Staff had been assured that the mortar munitions were available on Morotai. However, on 12 June 1945, the brigade found out it would not receive any additional 3-inch mortar rounds on Morotai. Chilton called the available stocks 'hopelessly inadequate' for the landing on Balikpapan.[54]

The D-Day allotment of 3-inch mortars for the Balikpapan landing worked out to 2500 rounds for the 18th Brigade, 1500 rounds for the 21st Brigade and none for the 25th Brigade – the division reserve.[55] This was a dangerously low allotment of ammunition, considering the 2500

3-inch rounds had to be distributed to the organic three infantry battalions as well as to all other attached units, such as cavalry (commando) squadrons and pioneer battalions. If the 18th Brigade's artillery or tank fire support were compromised during the landing by the state of the sea, by enemy action or other unforeseen factors, the 18th Brigade (the assault brigade) would be left with only its mortars for organic fire support.

Ordnance shortages were not the only concerns of the 18th Brigade during its two weeks on Morotai. The physical fitness of the entire 7th Division was a concern. The 18th Brigade had spent 29 days at sea on LSTs before its arrival on Morotai.[56] The short turnaround until re-embarkation for rehearsals and Oboe II was only two weeks during which there was limited time for physical fitness. At the troop level, vehicles had to be waterproofed and stores had to be identified and prepared for loading on ships. Lastly, troops at every level – brigade, battalion, company, platoon and squad – needed to be briefed on individual and unit tasks as the assault brigade for Oboe II.

On 15 June 1945, the Balikpapan sand-table was completed. This allowed commanders and leadership at each echelon to brief units on a large model of the beaches to be assaulted.[57] On 16 June 1945, the 18th Brigade's planning was largely complete, and subordinate and attached unit officers were allowed to return to their respective units.[58] The 18th Brigade staff would carry forward the amphibious planning as the 7th Division played catch-up and continued to send changes down to the brigades.

The official historian Gavin Long presented the example of the 2/10th Battalion commander, Lieutenant Colonel Thomas Daly, who briefed every member of his battalion, company by company, on the sand-table and provided insight into each phase of the operation and potential Japanese responses.[59] Unfortunately, the timeline was so condensed on Morotai that many units did not have the benefit of using the sand-table, including the 2/9th Battalion, one of the primary assault battalions. Subsequently, the sand-table was embarked on HMAS *Kanimbla* with the 2/9th Battalion on 20 June 1945.[60]

On 22 June 1945, the 18th Brigade began embarkation for the rehearsals and Oboe II, and the 2/10th and 2/12th Battalions moved to staging areas for embarkation on USS *Titania*.[61] This was the same ship that had carried the 26th Infantry Brigade Group – the assault brigade – of the Oboe I landing at Tarakan on 22 April 1945. To prevent the potential loss of two battalion headquarters and to facilitate easier command and control during the amphibious assault, the 2/10th and 2/12th Battalion headquarters were embarked on separate ships, USS *Kephart* and USS *Newman*, respectively. Both these US destroyers had been redesignated as 'High-Speed Transports' in order to support amphibious operations.

## The Morotai rehearsal

With the 18th Brigade fully embarked for Balikpapan, there was time for a final rehearsal. Morshead, concerned about a stiff Japanese defence of the beachhead, demanded a full-scale rehearsal.[62] A rehearsal differs from a training exercise in two primary ways. First, the unit is practising an actual combat mission, not a fictional scenario. Second, rehearsals are intended to include all the various units, fully staffed, which are expected to participate in the combat operation. Early in the SWPA theatre, brigades went into combat without rehearsal and sometimes without even a battle plan. In amphibious warfare, failing to conduct a rehearsal could be disastrous, considering the complexity involved in landing the infantry on a hostile foreign shore.

On 24 June 1945, the US Navy 7th Amphibious Force, Oboe II Attack Group with the 18th Brigade Group embarked as the assault brigade, conducting a full dress rehearsal for the Balikpapan landing on the island of Morotai near the Miri River. Rear Admiral Noble of the US Navy commanded the Attack Group from USS *Wasatch*. The entire task force had put to sea the day before, on 23 June, and began a simulated version of the trip to Balikpapan. The convoy passed through designated waypoints, altering formations and speed while circling Morotai. At 0230 on 2 June, they entered the approach lane to the beach.[63]

At 0505, four destroyers broke off the formation moving to pre-designated gunfire support stations with gun crews on station and ready to fire at 0615.[64] In this rehearsal, all naval gunfire was simulated between the infantry battalions and the destroyers, although all radio requests were exercised through simulated request between elements of the landing force. Each gunfire support station was a geographic space in the ocean drawn on a map for each destroyer to remain during the amphibious landing and were located far enough away from the Attack Group to allow ships and landing craft to manoeuvre, while stationed close enough to direct naval gunfire support to its assigned infantry battalion. The battalion commanders of the 18th Brigade, who were forced to plead with Allied Headquarters for small artillery pieces in Buna, each now had a US Navy destroyer dedicated to providing naval gunfire.

Figure 8.2 Troops of the 2/12th Infantry Battalion on the island of Morotai staged for embarkation on the US Navy Landing Craft – Infantry seen in the background. This was the brigade's last stop before the assault on Balikpapan. (AWM 109883)

Simultaneously, landing craft full of infantry from the 18th Brigade and its attached formations began circling outside the landing approach lanes.[65] The approach lanes each had boats or landing craft stationed at phases to provide direction and guidance as each wave of landing craft formed into assault waves. Once the controllers determined that a wave had the correct number and type of landing craft, the wave was cleared to move into its respective approach lane.

At 0651, the first wave of 37 LVTs left the assembly area, moving down its approach lane towards the beach with the Close Support Unit that consisted of eight LCI Rockets (R), six LCI Gunboats (G) and LCI

Large (L) to conduct fire runs against the beach. The fire started at 0659 with a rocket attack that lasted 10 minutes. For training purposes, each LVT Rocket fired only one rocket at the beach.[66] In an amphibious rehearsal, the coordination of manoeuvre and accurate fire was more important than demonstrating massive fire on the rehearsal beach.

The first of 17 waves of LVTs with the 18th Brigade abroad crossed the line of departure at 0752 with each of the successive waves trailing in five-minute intervals. In this rehearsal, only the first five waves of LVTs actually landed on the beachhead. The other 12 waves of LVTs, LCVPs and LCMs conducted the assembly area coordination and moved towards the beach but turned off 400 metres from the beach, then returned to their respective mothership.

The 2/10th Battalion history noted the Oboe II rehearsal had 'only a few minor hitches', although these hitches are not detailed.[67] A few minor hitches in a limited rehearsal could expand exponentially under fire from Japanese defenders. The 18th Brigade did not disembark once the task force returned to the harbour at Morotai. The opportunity for training and exercises had ended. Instead of the 7th Amphibious Force, Oboe II task force sat in the harbour for one more day before the armada of more than a hundred ships sailed for Balikpapan and the last major amphibious assault of World War II.[68]

Amphibious training and exercises had resulted in another evolution of the 18th Brigade. 18th Infantry Brigade Group (Jungle) was now an amphibious infantry brigade capable of operating in a mechanised capacity: as an assault brigade. It had already become apparent that the doctrinal solution to amphibious warfare did not keep up with the speed of amphibious warfare. The 18th Brigade's amphibious planning time for exercises and rehearsals for Balikpapan never received the recommended doctrinal 18 days of preparation time before putting an assault force to sea. The result was the commander and brigade staff planning complex operations on highly condensed timetables, with innumerable variables.

CHAPTER | 9

# THE ASSAULT BRIGADE

> The actual landing was a particularly spectacular, dramatic episode, near to 'our artist' conception of war than anything I had seen.
>
> Brigadier Chilton[1]

Balikpapan would be the last major amphibious operation of World War II. The after-action report for the amphibious operation named Oboe II repeatedly refers to the 18th Infantry Brigade – with some pride – as the 'assault brigade'. The amphibious assault of Balikpapan would represent the pinnacle of evolution in the Australian infantry brigade from a line infantry formation to an amphibious Infantry Brigade Group (Jungle). The combination of combat experience, administrative efficiency, combined arms capability and leadership would make the 18th Brigade one of the most effective formations the Australian Army fielded in World War II.

In a 1957 letter to Gavin Long, Chilton correctly noted that the significance of the landing at Balikpapan was not the ferocity of the fighting. Chilton wrote, 'from a military point of the interest of this operation is of course not so much in the details of the fighting which took place ashore, but in the nature and scale of the amphibious assault'.[2] According to the US Navy's command history of the Seventh Amphibious Force, the landing at Balikpapan was the most difficult of the entire SWPA theatre.[3] In fact, Air Vice Marshal William Bostock, who would serve as Commander of Support Aircraft for Oboe II, warned the Australian Prime Minister that the Japanese fortifications at Balikpapan could result in a

'Pacific Gallipoli'.[4] In the end, the 18th Brigade, at the forefront of the 7th Division's landing, would prove Bostock's doubts about Oboe II operation to be unfounded by carrying out a highly effective amphibious assault that would demonstrate that Bostock's gloomy comparison was completely false.

## BALIKPAPAN: INTRODUCTION

On 26 June 1945, the Amphibious Assault Force, having completed its rehearsal, departed for Balikpapan. The 7th Division embarked on the 7th Amphibious Force, Oboe II Attack Group, as more than 200 ships set sail for the three-day voyage to Balikpapan.[5] According to Gavin Long's official history of the Borneo campaigns, the initial idea behind the Oboe landings began in February 1945. The campaign plan included six amphibious landings code named Oboe I to Oboe VI.[6] Although these were division landings, Long overlooked the fact that each of the Oboe landings was to be spearheaded by Australian infantry brigade groups – the assault brigades. The designated 'assault brigade(s)' were the spearhead of the division landing force to establish an initial beachhead for the rest of the division.

Briefly, Oboe I was the amphibious assault at Tarakan led by the 26th Infantry Brigade Group of the 9th Division, which would seize oil infrastructure and airfields to support other Oboe operations. Oboe II was led by the 18th Brigade's assault of Balikpapan. Oboe III was an optional drive by a brigade of the 9th Division from Balikpapan to Banjarmasin for the purpose of seizing airfields for the Allied advance on Java. Oboe IV included the 6th and 7th Australian Divisions in the seizure and occupation of Surabaya, Batavia and Bandung, clearing all areas to the Lombok Strait. Lastly, Oboe V was capture of the remainder of the Netherlands Indies and Oboe VI clearing the remainder of Borneo.[7]

Oboe I, the amphibious assault at Tarakan, was led by the 26th Infantry Brigade Group of the 9th Division. The mission of Oboe I, according to the 9th Division's 'Operations Order 1', was to 'capture the island of Tarakan to enable the establishment and operations of naval and air units required to support OBOE TWO'.[8] Additionally, the 26th was to seize and protect the petroleum producing and processing facilities and restore the Netherlands East Indies civilian government agencies.[9]

Tarakan is an island 15 miles long and 11 miles wide at its widest point. The island has a muddy coastline, backed by mangroves and swampy flat lands. The only viable beach for a landing was heavily defended, as described by a member of the Royal Australian Air Force, James Cronk: 'That was no picnic ... they had tank traps, and sea mines on the beach, and a jetty that was loaded with explosives.'[10]

Along with the controversy over the need for the Oboe operations, Blamey publicly ridiculed Morshead's planning and execution of the landing, which was described as slow and poorly organised for the assault of Japanese strongpoints.[11] However, the landing was ultimately successful in its stated mission of capturing the port and airfield. The problems came after landing. The airfield had been severely damaged as a result of pre-landing bombardment and would not be repaired in time for the Balikpapan assault, and the 26th Brigade would spend the next weeks clearing the island of Japanese.[12]

Although the necessity of the Oboe landings was a subject of debate, that argument is beyond the scope of this book. However, one document from the papers of Lieutenant General Sir Frank Berryman, a memorandum entitled 'Oboe Two Operation: Desirability of Cancellation' by an army colonel on the general staff, went to great lengths to identify justifications for the cancellation of Oboe II. It lists the operational challenges of the operation, reports of limited air support, lack of amphibious shipping, schedules that were too demanding, and a shortage of amphibious tractors. It also states, 'The object of the present operation [Oboe II] is principally to destroy the enemy and to secure the oil facilities in the objective area. It is considered, therefore, that the operation is NOT essential for the overall defeat of the enemy.'[13] In practice, none of the outlined challenges came to fruition; the Oboe II operation received more support than any other Australian landing in the SWPA owing to MacArthur's belief that the vast petroleum reserves at Balikpapan would be necessary to sustain the invasion of the Japanese mainland.

## THE BALIKPAPAN PLAN

On 25 May 1945, the US Navy's planning team arrived on Morotai to assist the Australian 7th Division in its planning for the amphibious assault on Balikpapan. The leader of the US Navy team informed General Milford, the 7th Division commander, that he disliked the 7th Division's plan for the Oboe II more each time he reviewed it and recommended the landing location be moved further east where the navy's ships were out of the range of Japanese coast defence artillery. He went so far as to tell Milford that he thought this might prove to be the first failed amphibious assault of the SWPA.[14]

Milford disagreed with the US Navy's planning team. Clearly, both entities viewed the operation through the lens of the service experience. The US Navy's caution was a result of the sheer number of ships the US Navy had lost during the course of World War II. Second, ships are highly vulnerable in littoral waters required by amphibious assaults. Milford and other Australian infantry commanders viewed Balikpapan through the lens of New Guinea. The cost of landing in a safer location and fighting to Balikpapan would increase combat and disease-related casualties. Additionally, a successful amphibious assault on Balikpapan would be far quicker than another jungle campaign.[15] Milford prevailed; the 7th Division would conduct an assault of the Japanese at Balikpapan with the full force of the Allied air forces and naval services in support.

On 12 May 1945, at the Amphibious Training Centre in Australia, Chilton had been provided with the 7th Division's warning order and tasked the 18th Brigade as the assault brigade for the planned invasion of Balikpapan.[16] The 21st Infantry Brigade was tasked to land 2/27th Battalion with the 18th Brigade, with its other two battalions landing in later waves.

As Chilton noted in 1957, 'Balikpapan was a very strongly fortified area, stronger than any the Australians had encountered elsewhere in this war.'[17] Armed with this knowledge, Chilton took the amphibious planning process for Balikpapan especially seriously. Chilton did not brief the brigade staff until the 18th Brigade had embarked on SS *Swartenhondt* and had put to sea.[18] The silence increased operational security and provided time for Chilton to develop an 'appreciation' or concept of operations. However, by the time SS *Swartenhondt* reached Morotai, Chilton and the brigade staff had already designated the two assault battalions and one reserve battalion in a draft brigade operations order. Although Chilton did not have the 7th Division's operations order, he instructed the production of a draft brigade operations order in the correct belief that the planning time on Morotai would be extremely short.

The trip from Australia was not an easy one for the soldiers of the 18th Brigade. The LSTs were cramped, and soldiers had to sleep in tents lashed down to the deck in inclement weather. There was some concern about the fight ability of the troops after an extended amount of time on ship. However, it was not without high points for the troops, who on 10 April 1945 conducted a Shell Back Ceremony, a rite to commemorate a service member's first crossing of the equator.[19] The majority of the 2/9th, 2/10th and 2/12th Battalion staffs did not arrive on Morotai until 12 June – well into the drafting of the Battalion Landing Craft Tables.[20] As a result, the battalion commanders and battalion intelligence officer, who had been on the 18th Brigade's headquarters ship, largely completed the initial draft battalion amphibious plans without support from the rest of the battalion staff.

The 18th Brigade suffered from two challenges. First was the amphibious timetable passed down from the 7th Division, which required the 18th Brigade to complete all amphibious planning by D-10. However, Chilton and the brigade staff realised that the majority of planning to include wave diagrams would have to be completed by D-14 to meet the US Navy's planning requirements.[21] The second challenge was the problem of planning in the dark since the 7th Division staff had not yet published the division operations order for Oboe II. There were two prevalent observations of the brigade division relationship for Oboe II. In the Oboe II after-action report, the 18th Brigade would take pride that the brigade planned its own landing – it was not a 'dictated' plan from the 7th Division.[22] However, in the day-to-day war diaries, it is clear that the brigade's plan was drafted independently owing to frustration with the division's slow pace of planning.

Without timely guidance, the 18th Brigade Staff Sections had to make assumptions about the resources the brigade would receive as the assault brigade.[23] Some assumptions were common sense, such as that the US Navy would provide the amphibious assault craft. Other assumptions, such as how many assault craft would be available, were more speculative. Would the brigade air support be ground- or carrier-based? What type of naval gunfire would be available? These variables and dozens more affected all aspects of the brigade planning from embarkation to its final objective.

On 6 June 1945, the US Navy called for the final wave diagram from the 7th Division. However, the 7th Division had not yet published the Oboe II operations order. This resulted in more confusion among staff planners of the various echelons. Chilton reflected in 1957 that amphibious warfare 'was extremely difficult business and was only possible as a result of the standard of staff [18th Brigade Staff] and training in all levels of the command which had been attained after six years of war, and the flexibility this permitted'.[24]

The 7th Division published its operations order for Oboe II on 7 June 1945. The 18th Brigade staff was not much better off with the division order and expressed this in the brigade's war diaries. The 7th Division operation order was a hollow document without detailed information regarding 'units under command at landing, shipping allocation, or fire support'.[25] The 7th Division had yet to complete any of the

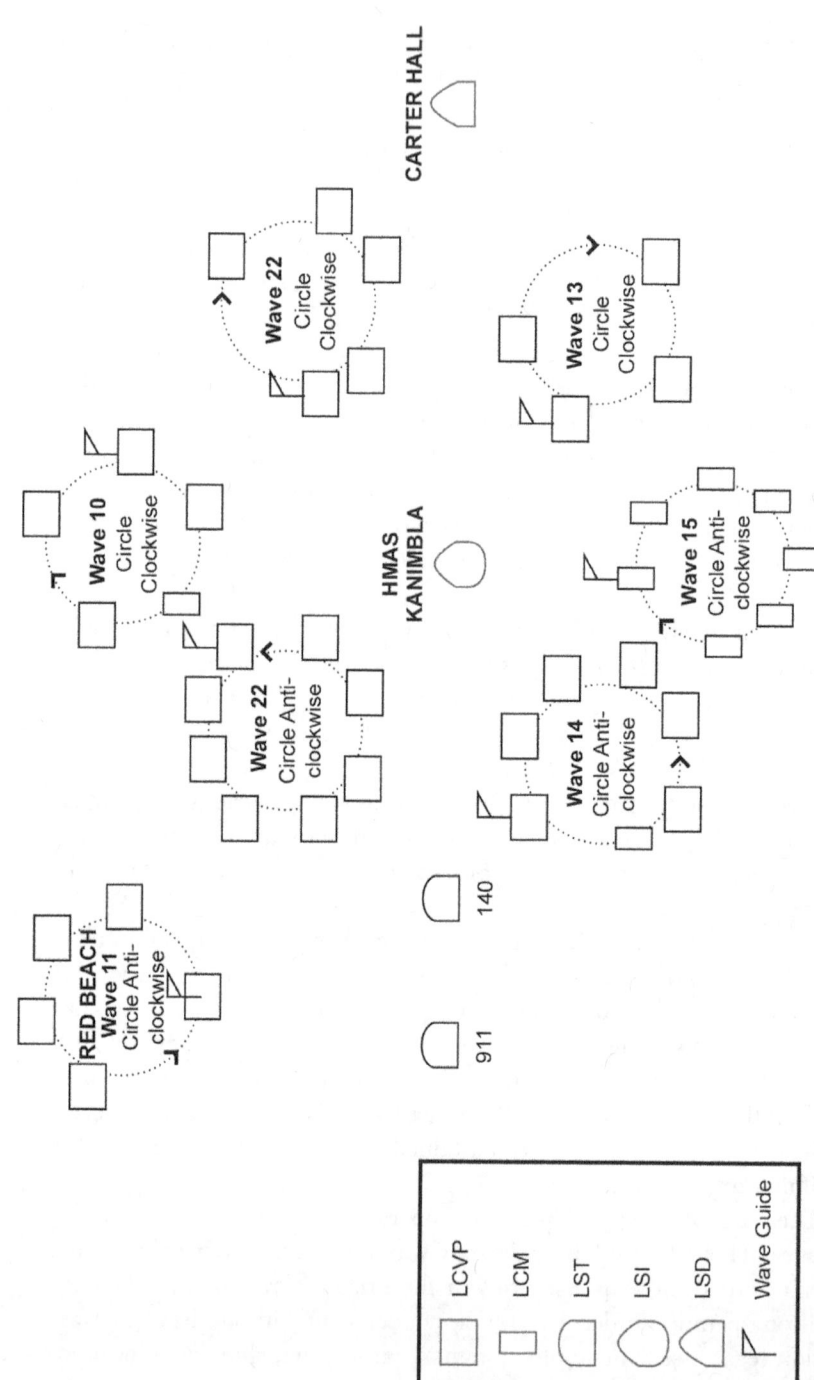

Figure 9.1 Landing diagram with wave guide

mission-essential documents such as the Landing Tables, Distribution of Force to the Convoy, and fire support plans. The 18th Brigade staff, at this point in the SWPA, had a long history of successful staff planning. Previous combat experience and recent amphibious training allowed the brigade to publish the final operations order in spite of limited guidance from the 7th Division.

Since the 7th Division had not produced a 'Distribution of Force to Ships', the 18th Brigade's wave diagram was an educated guess. A major problem arose with the US Navy's contention that the wave diagram could not be altered once submitted since changes would affect the entire amphibious landing force of more than a hundred naval vessels. The 18th Brigade, as the assault brigade, determined that its total sea lift requirements for Operation Oboe II were 5849 personnel, 219 jeeps, 193 jeep trailers, 119 2½ ton trucks, 6 miscellaneous vehicles, 34 pieces of mechanised equipment, 91 landing craft and amphibians, 32 vehicle trailers, 12 artillery guns and 1793 tons of stores.[26] This was the largest formation the 18th Brigade staff had ever managed, and the complex planning of the wave diagrams cannot be underestimated.

On 8 June 1945, Major General Milford held a commanders' conference at 7th Division headquarters. The 18th Brigade's notes of the meeting expressed concern over Chilton's desire to discuss the urgent issue of force distribution and shipping. The 7th Division insisted that only the tactical plan be discussed at the commanders' conference.[27] Without proper loading and embarkation of ships, the tactical plans ashore would suffer greatly. This reluctance to discuss and prioritise the administrative aspect of amphibious warfare at the division level seemed to derive from a lack of amphibious education or experience within the 7th Division staff. Considering that the majority of the detailed frontline staff planning in the SWPA was done at the brigade level, the planners of the 18th Brigade undoubtedly had an advantage in short-term high-intensity planning over the division staff.

Numerous drafts of the 7th Division's 'Distribution of Force to Convoys' would be produced, the final version being published on 10 June. The 18th Brigade staff immediately began drafting the brigade landing tables. On 13 June, the 7th Division issued an amended 'Distribution of Force to Convoy' for the subordinate brigades. This amended version included major changes or corrections, which further frustrated the 18th Brigade staff. The brigade had already completed the 'Distribution of Force to Convoys and the Brigade Landing Tables'. Additionally, each of the brigade's subordinate battalions had reached

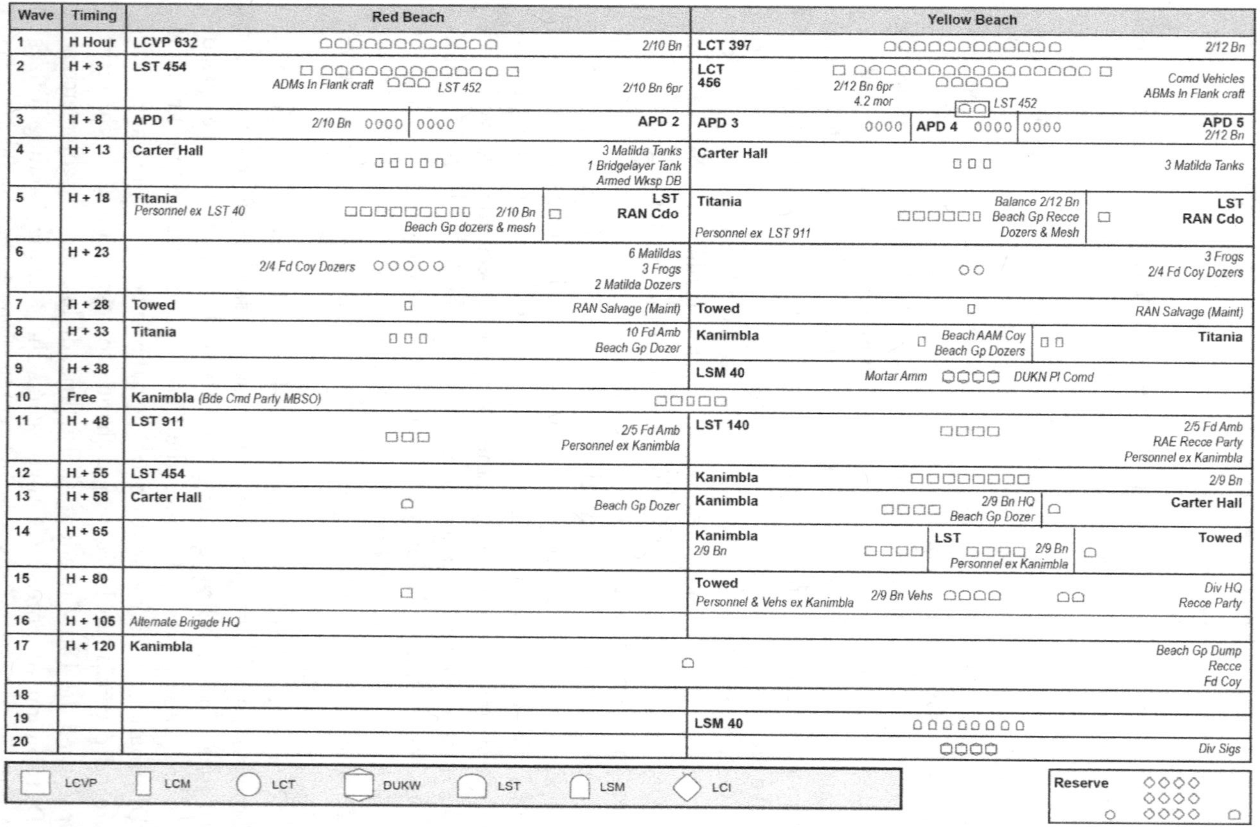

| Wave | Timing | Red Beach | | | Yellow Beach | | |
|---|---|---|---|---|---|---|---|
| 1 | H Hour | LCVP 632 | | 2/10 Bn | LCT 397 | | 2/12 Bn |
| 2 | H + 3 | LST 454 <br> ADMs In Flank craft | LST 452 | 2/10 Bn 6pr | LCT 456 <br> 2/12 Bn 6pr <br> 4.2 mor | LST 452 | Comd Vehicles <br> ABMs In Flank craft |
| 3 | H + 8 | APD 1 | 2/10 Bn | APD 2 | APD 3 | APD 4 | APD 5 <br> 2/12 Bn |
| 4 | H + 13 | Carter Hall | | 3 Malilda Tanks <br> 1 Bridgelayer Tank <br> Armed Wasp DB | Carter Hall | | 3 Malilda Tanks |
| 5 | H + 18 | Titania <br> Personnel ex LST 40 | 2/10 Bn <br> Beach Gp dozers & mesh | LST <br> RAN Cdo | Titania <br> Personnel ex LST 911 | Balance 2/12 Bn <br> Beach Gp Recce <br> Dozers & Mesh | LST <br> RAN Cdo |
| 6 | H + 23 | | 2/4 Fd Coy Dozers | 6 Malildas <br> 3 Frogs <br> 2 Matilda Dozers | | | 3 Frogs <br> 2/4 Fd Coy Dozers |
| 7 | H + 28 | Towed | | RAN Salvage (Maint) | Towed | | RAN Salvage (Maint) |
| 8 | H + 33 | Titania | | 10 Fd Amb <br> Beach Gp Dozer | Kanimbla | Beach AAM Coy <br> Beach Gp Dozers | Titania |
| 9 | H + 38 | | | | LSM 40 | Mortar Amm | DUKN Pl Comd |
| 10 | Free | Kanimbla (Bde Cmd Party MBSO) | | | | | |
| 11 | H + 48 | LST 911 | | 25 Fd Amb <br> Personnel ex Kanimbla | LST 140 | | 25 Fd Amb <br> RAE Recce Party <br> Personnel ex Kanimbla |
| 12 | H + 55 | LST 454 | | | Kanimbla | | 2/9 Bn |
| 13 | H + 58 | Carter Hall | | Beach Gp Dozer | Kanimbla | 2/9 Bn HQ <br> Beach Gp Dozer | Carter Hall |
| 14 | H + 65 | | | | Kanimbla <br> 2/9 Bn | LST | 2/9 Bn <br> Personnel ex Kanimbla | Towed |
| 15 | H + 80 | | | | Towed <br> Personnel & Vehs ex Kanimbla | 2/9 Bn Vehs | Div HQ <br> Recce Party |
| 16 | H + 105 | Alternate Brigade HQ | | | | | |
| 17 | H + 120 | Kanimbla | | | | | Beach Gp Dump <br> Recce <br> Fd Coy |
| 18 | | | | | | | |
| 19 | | | | | LSM 40 | | Div Sigs |
| 20 | | | | | | | |

Reserve

LCVP  LCM  LCT  DUKW  LST  LSM  LCI

Figure 9.2 Landing diagram, 18th Australian Infantry Brigade. Issued with 18 INF BDE Operation Order OBOE II.

'advanced stage' in planning Battalion Landing Craft Tables. All of these plans would have to be redrafted on the basis of the 7th Division's amended order. The 18th Brigade's records express a thinly veiled disdain for the ability of the 7th Division's staff.[28] The 7th Division's failure to conduct proper amphibious planning or provide detailed information to the subordinate brigades resulted in 'a complete reversal of [amphibious] planning'.[29]

For Operation Oboe II, the 18th Infantry Brigade Intelligence Section received significant intelligence support from higher headquarters. As noted by Private Raymond Baldwin, '[W]e had aerial photographs, every man knew where just about where he would go and what his task would be.'[30] The 1st Australian Corps provided the 18th Brigade with the best and most accurate intelligence it had seen in any of its previous campaigns. During the build-up for Balikpapan, the 1st Australian Corps compiled and provided the 18th Brigade Intelligence Section with a Japanese order of battle with a reasonably accurate estimate of enemy troops. The numbers of Japanese forces in previous campaigns had either been wildly underestimated or significantly overestimated. Additionally, the Allied Geographic Section provided topographical studies and local handbooks on the people and tribes who lived in the area. Lastly, the Allied Translator and Interpreter Section assigned translators and interpreters to the 18th Brigade to provide the language skills needed to assess and react quickly to intelligence on the battlefield.[31]

The 18th Brigade, out of necessity, had developed a highly capable Intelligence Section at the brigade and battalion headquarters during the war in the SWPA. In the planning of the amphibious assault on Balikpapan, the brigade Intelligence Section was a primary element of success. The war diaries of the 18th Brigade rarely mention traditional intelligence functions not related to amphibious warfare. The fact was that challenges of brigade-level intelligence tasks, which the 18th Brigade had to detail carefully in earlier campaigns, had become standard. The 18th Brigade Intelligence Section had moved from basic intelligence tasks in Buna to integrated intelligence support for an amphibious assault on a foreign shore.

## AMPHIBIOUS PLANNING

The US Army Amphibian Tractor Battalions assigned to the 7th Division each joined its respective Australian brigade on Morotai. Each of the tractor battalions integrated its operations officers into the supported

Australian brigade staff's amphibious planning team.[32] The tractor battalion commanders each began to attend 7th Division commanders' conferences.[33] The war journals of the amphibian units do not mention any direct amphibious planning integration or liaison with the division staff planners, which may account for some of the confusion and inefficiency in the amphibious planning efforts of the 7th Division.

The 18th Brigade staff's primary planning team for Balikpapan included the brigade commander, Brigadier Chilton; the brigade major, Major George Suthers; the assistant brigade major, Major Alec Marshall; the intelligence officer, Captain Connolly; the signal officer, Lieutenant Norman Brooks; the staff captain, Captain Cecil Parbury (responsible for administration, movement and personnel); and the brigade service corps officer, Captain Hilary Kelly (responsible for supplies and ordnance).[34] The 18th Brigade Intelligence Section established an intelligence centre containing maps, aerial photographs, topographic surveys and intelligence reports.[35] Unlike previous operations where intelligence was scarce and needed to be developed independently at the brigade staff level, Oboe II was flush with information for the Intelligence Section to provide the amphibious planners.

In addition to the primary brigade staff, the brigade's amphibious planning team included representatives from attached formations, who would play a key role in the amphibious assault. This wider group included the 2/9th, 2/10th and 2/12th Battalions' commanders and intelligence officers; the 1st Australian Armoured Regiment executive officer; the 2/4th Field Artillery Regiment commander, Lieutenant Colonel Blyth; the 2/2nd Australian Tank Attack Artillery Battery commander, Major Andrew Helgeson; the 2/4th Field Company commander, Major Raymond Taylor; the 2/1st Australian Machine Gun Battalion adjutant Captain Leslie Peters; the 2/5th Field Ambulance executive officer, Major Norman Pullen; and finally the 1st Australian Military Landing Group, military landing officer, Major Ernest Phillipson.[36] The last member of the planning team, Major Phillipson, was a liaison officer trained in amphibious planning, who was assigned to assist in the development of the 'Distribution of Force to Ship' and the actual embarkation of the amphibious assault brigade for Balikpapan.

## THE OPERATION ORDER

As in previous chapters, it is of great value to examine closely the 18th Brigade's operations order. Chilton emphasised this point himself in his notes to Gavin Long in 1957:

The complexity and detail of an operation of this nature is of course fairly apparent and is well illustrated in both the Australian and USN operations orders and reports. Every man, every piece of equipment, ammunition, stores, food, etc, has to be embarked or loaded in the appropriate vessel in such a way as to permit it being landed at the right spot and in the right sequence, for example stores, etc required early in the landing must be loaded and stowed last.[37]

This would be the 18th Brigade's largest administrative task of the war where the pool of typists was a key staff planning asset.

According to the '18th Australian Infantry Brigade Operation Order – Oboe II', the overarching mission was: 'The 7th Australian Division is to land on ABLE sector and capture the area Balikpapan to enable the establishment of air and naval facilities and to conserve the petroleum installations therein.'[38] The assault force was given specific instructions not to destroy any civil infrastructure: 'pumping stations, machinery, power stations, transformers, petroleum, and harbour facilities are to be kept intact'.[39] This was in keeping with the stated Allied overarching mission to secure Balikpapan's oil reserves for the invasion of the Japanese home islands.

Under this grand mission statement of the 7th Division, the 18th Brigade was at H-Hour on D-Day to land on Yellow and Red Beaches, secure a beachhead, and seize Parramatta Ridge and Hill 87 'at the earliest possible moment after H-Hour'.[40] Follow-on instructions included 'dominate Balikpapan', 'destroy enemy in the town' and 'free harbour for use at an early stage'.[41] As the assault brigade and first ashore, the 18th Brigade would need to transition quickly from an amphibious landing force into an infantry manoeuvre force to achieve the objectives inland.

In addition to protecting the physical infrastructure, there were also instructions for discipline for the behaviour of troops in regard to the local 'Mohammedans'. Unless required by combat operations, villages were off limits, and theft, looting or pillaging was strictly forbidden. All interactions were to be 'friendly but not familiar'.[42] This principle of not straining local relations came from two Allied perspectives. First, the inhabitants were considered citizens of Dutch Borneo and the Dutch wished to re-establish this relationship; and the second perspective was the issue of petroleum. If the Allies intended to use Balikpapan as a major source of oil for the invasion of the Japanese mainland, then friendly relations with the locals would be necessary for oil production.

Japan's ground force was estimated at 3900 combat troops, with 1500 reinforcements some 60 miles away at Samarinda. Additionally, there were an estimated 4500 forced labourers from Formosa and the Netherlands East Indies who could be impressed into manning Japanese fighting positions.[43] Two of the Japanese formations known to be present were the 22nd Naval Base Force and 454th Battalion.[44] There was also the possibility that units that withdrew from Tarakan after Oboe I might have been en route to join the Balikpapan defences.

The 7th Amphibious Force's Amphibious Group Eight of more than a hundred ships had several key responsibilities in Oboe II. These included the transportation and protection of the 7th Division from Morotai to Balikpapan. Second, it was responsible for the bombardment of the beaches and the interception of any Japanese reinforcement of Balikpapan from the sea. In direct support of the assault brigade, the amphibious task force were responsible for clearance of underwater obstacles before H-Hour, D-Day. Lastly, it was to provide direct naval gunfire support to each of the assault brigades' individual infantry battalions once ashore.

This last task of the Amphibious Task Force is significant in the evolution in fire support for the Australian infantry brigade. Combined arms support was one of the key elements that made the assault brigade the most powerful configuration of the Australian infantry brigade in the SWPA. The Australians first had the general support of naval gunfire in 1941 at the Battle of Bardia from both the Royal Navy and Royal Australian Navy.[45] In this assault brigade configuration, each of the infantry battalions – the 2/10th and 2/12th – would be directly supported by a US Navy destroyer, USS *Cleveland*, USS *Denver* and USS *Conway* in support of the brigade headquarters. The 2/9th Battalion in the reserve did not receive a dedicated destroyer at the onset of the operation.[46] This was a significant addition to the brigade's capabilities and challenges. In Balikpapan, a battalion commander would have indirect fire support not just from organic artillery but also close air support and dedicated naval gunfire – an enormous leap forward from Buna, where infantry soldiers had been forced to drag wooden-wheeled artillery into battle.

In June 1945, General Kenney presented MacArthur with an intelligence estimate of 18 Japanese coast defence guns and more than a hundred pieces of artillery in the Balikpapan area. He argued that these guns could be disastrous on the beachhead and received authorisation to expand the RAAF air operation to include US Army and naval aviation support.[47] Subsequently, the bombardment of the Balikpapan beachhead and rear areas would be the largest of the SWPA theatre. Private Baldwin described the bombardment in an interview in 1990: '[T]he whole beach area of Balikpapan and back in the hills a bit just erupted with shells and bomb explosions.'[48]

Japan's air power in the region was a threat to the Balikpapan landing. It was estimated that Japan had 87 aircraft in Sumatra, 68 in Malaya, 52 in Burma and Thailand, and 74 in French Indochina. In spite of available aircraft, the 18th Brigade had little expectation that Japan would commit a large air contingent to oppose the landing.[49] Chilton's belief that a Japanese air onslaught was unlikely allowed him to deprioritise anti-aircraft guns in the landing force, which opened space in the first and second waves of landing craft for additional infantry, mortars and artillery.

The 18th Brigade operation order for Balikpapan detailed air support for the amphibious landing and the brigade's follow-on objectives. The 18th Brigade would receive the largest volume of air support, potentially larger than any other brigade had seen in the SWPA. The 5th Air Support Party (ASP) had attached to the 18th Brigade headquarters to coordinate all requests for air support from infantry battalions, pioneers and commandos. Each of the infantry brigades would be assigned one of the 5th ASP's smaller elements, called an air liaison. The air liaison parties served in the same capacity for air support as forward observers did for artillery. These air liaison parties would advise the battalion commanders on the available air assets and the air assets best suited for a given target. The request was then sent to the 5th ASP at 18th Brigade headquarters for deconfliction and tasking. The 2/9th, 2/10th and 2/12th Battalions were supported by the 5th, 6th and 7th Air Liaison Party, respectively.[50] As noted early, this provided the brigade and battalion commanders additional fire support options based on the type of target.

Another element of fire support was that the 2/2nd Anti-Tank Attack Regiment would be largely assigned to 18th Brigade headquarters; however, guns could be pushed forward to assault units, as necessary. The 2/10th and 2/12th Battalions' second landing waves both had an element of 2/2nd Anti-Tank assigned, as noted earlier. These elements consisted of one 6-pound anti-tank gun for use against Japanese snipers and strongpoints. It is also important to note that the 4.2-inch mortars would be assigned to the 2/2nd Anti-Tank Regiment and had become more important with the lack of 3-inch mortar rounds. The 4.2-inch mortar would come ashore with the second wave, with four mortars on Red and Yellow Beaches. The operations order noted that the 4.2-inch mortars would be operational at H-hour+4 minutes.[51] This was 56 minutes faster than the first artillery pieces were scheduled to begin firing.

The 2/4th Field Artillery Regiment and the 2/2nd Anti-Tank Attack Regiment were to become operational at the earliest possible time to support the assault force. The 2/4th Field Artillery had an aggressive timeline for Oboe II. At H+60 minutes, the first troop was to have established firing positions on the beachhead and be able to support fire support missions. At H+90 minutes another battery would be operational, at H+120 minutes two more batteries, and the entire regiment firing by H+200 minutes.[52] This was contingent on numerous factors, including beach clearance, well-organised landings and lastly – and most importantly – the Japanese response to the landing.

Another new weapons system for the 18th Brigade was the integration of flamethrowers. The Oboe II Operation Order included the M2–2 flamethrower as an organic battalion weapons system – the same role as mortars or machine guns. Captain Howard Flaherty, a chemical officer from the 7th Division, was assigned to 18th Brigade headquarters as a technical adviser on what was called 'flame warfare'. The 2/10th and 2/12th Assault Battalions received six M2–2 Flamethrowers and associated equipment for the refuelling and recharging of tanks.[53] The flamethrower was not new to the war, but this was the first opportunity for the 18th Brigade to employ the system in combat. The flamethrower was highly effective for clearing tunnels and caves of enemy personnel.

A significant technological evolution for the assault brigade was the amphibian tractor. The key to an amphibious assault is movement onto the beach as quickly and safely as possible. This led to the development of a number of tracked amphibious vehicle variants. The vehicle chosen by Allied forces was the Landing Vehicles Tracked (LVT). LVTs brought troops to shore like Higgins boats, but then, whenever possible, drove over the beach and discharged troops forward of the water line – a great advantage over heavily laden troops slogging across an open sandy beach under enemy fire.

The 18th Brigade's operations order outlined the LVT support from the US Army 672nd Amphibian Tractor Battalion, commanded by Lieutenant Colonel Joseph Gibbs, reinforced with the 727th Amphibian Tractor Battalion. The 2/10th and 2/12th Battalions would come ashore in two assault waves on Red and Yellow Beaches, respectively. The first assault wave for each infantry battalion would be supported by two platoons of 12 LVTs, and the second waves were supported by one platoon with 11 LVTs. In the 2/10th and 2/12th Battalions' second wave, four of the LVTs in the second assault wave would carry one battery of 2/4th Field Artillery and 2/2nd Anti-Tank Attack Regiment.[54]

Although all amphibian units in Oboe II were US Army formations, the armour was Australian. The 1st Australian Armoured Regiment and 2/1st Armoured Brigade Reconnaissance Squadron would provide direct support for the two assault battalions on Red and Yellow Beaches. The 2/12th Battalion had one troop of B Squadron, 1st Armoured Regiment, two Matilda Frog tanks (modified to incorporate a flamethrower), and one Matilda dozer tank from 2/1st Reconnaissance Squadron. The 2/10th Battalion had another troop of B Squadron, 1st Armoured Regiment, with four Matilda Frogs, one Matilda dozer tank, and one Covenanter bridge-laying tank from 1st Reconnaissance Squadron.[55] The addition of tanks, and especially the amphibians as light armoured personnel carriers, effectively made the assault brigade a mechanised force.

The attached 2/1st Pioneer Battalion had numerous tasks in concert with the 2nd Amphibious Beach Group. The beachhead had to be both cleared of obstacles with demolitions, then swept for mines and booby traps placed by the Japanese defenders. They were also responsible for the extremely important task of clearing rally points for each respective assault battalion.[56] Once ashore and consolidated, the infantry battalions would move inland to assault and secure objectives. The Pioneers would also have to clear and mark manoeuvre routes off the beach quickly so the assault battalion could maintain the attack. The 2/1st Pioneers would also be on standby for any road or bridge repair along the avenues of approach to the landing objectives.

The 18th Brigade's plan for Operation Oboe II was outlined in four phases. In Phase 1, 2/10th and 2/12th Battalions were to land on Yellow and Red Beaches at Balikpapan and exploit the beachhead. Each assault battalion would land at H-Hour, with two companies in LVTs, and secure predetermined rally points for the consolidation of all attachment units. The 18th Brigade commander and brigade staff would be embarked in a landing craft near the navy control boats, which directed and coordinated the landing waves. The operations order called for the beach to be held, and Chilton's brigade headquarters landed at H+34 minutes on Yellow Beach.[57]

In Phase 2, the 2/12th Battalion was to expand the beachhead perimeter. Phase 3 had the 2/10th Battalion assaulting Hill 87 and advancing across the high ground of Parramatta Ridge. The assault plan called for one company of 2/10th Battalion to attack Hill 87 and Parramatta with a troop of 4.2-inch mortars in support. The 2/12th Battalion was to provide a base of fire with machine guns and 3-inch mortars against the north slope of Parramatta to prevent a Japanese counter-attack. In Phase 4, the reserve 2/9th Battalion was to land at Yellow Beach at H+40 minutes prepared to relieve or reinforce anywhere the assault brigade required.[58]

Naval gunfire support for Oboe II was included in Annex D of the 18th Brigade operation order. As the assault brigade, the 18th Brigade would receive the largest fire support package it had seen during the entirety of World War II. As noted earlier, each of the assault battalions would have a US destroyer assigned for naval gunfire support in its area of operations, and as impressive as this was, it was only a small portion of the naval gunfire plan. The overarching naval support plan called for beach bombardment to begin 20 days before D-Day. All Allied naval fire would be managed by one Fire Control Party Afloat until the assault brigade's command element landed on Yellow Beach, at which point naval gunfire support was to be turned over to the Shore Fire Control Party.[59] Transition of control of naval guns from the Naval Task Force to the 7th Division ashore coincided with overall transition of command from the US Navy to the Australian Army. It is important to note that only in amphibious warfare does command transfer between services – and in this case nations – during the peak of combat operations.

Ships allocated to the direct support of the assault brigade's initial landing included 5 light cruisers, 16 destroyers, 10 Landing Support Craft – Large (LSC), 8 Landing Craft Infantry – Rocket (LCI) and

Figure 9.3 After the complex process of amphibious planning for Operation Oboe II, the assault on Balikpapan, troops of the 2/10th Battalion board Landing Craft Infantry on Morotai for the last large-scale amphibious assault of World War II. (AWM 109931)

6 LCI – Gunboat. The fire support for D-Day at Balikpapan was allocated by ship. For D-Day bombardment, the cruisers were allotted 600 six-inch high explosives, 600 five-inch anti-aircraft common, 40 five-inch white phosphorus and 50 five-inch illumination rounds. Each cruiser was required to maintain additional allotments for on-call fire missions from the troop on the beach. For on-call fire missions, each cruiser maintained 400 six-inch HE, 500 five-inch AAC, 60 five-inch WP and 70 five-inch illumination rounds.[60]

The LSC and LCI ships operated far forward of the amphibious task force, either in line with the assault brigade landing waves or making runs at the beaches in front of the landing force. The ten LCSs (L) each carried 120 rockets, and the eight LCIs (R) each carried 550 rockets. The LCI (G) serves as in-close fire support roll for amphibious landings. With two 40mm guns, six 50-calibre machine guns and ten Mark-7 rocket launchers, the LCI (G) was capable of providing suppressive fire on the beach in support of the landing if requested.[61] All of the close fire support would help ensure that the assault brigade was protected in the shallows where it was most vulnerable to Japanese fires.

The '18th Australian Infantry Brigade Administrative Order Oboe II' detailed everything from the personal load of an infantryman in the initial waves to the how and where to refill the newly issued flamethrowers. The personal load of soldiers was still largely on the jungle scale outlined for Australian jungle divisions. Anti-malarial stores, insect repellent and daily rations were still key to soldiers surviving in a jungle environment. However, unlike the early days of the New Guinea campaigns, this administrative order noted that luxury items such as chocolate, breadmaking ingredients, paper and cigarettes would be available at D+2.[62]

## PRE-LANDING OPERATIONS

The pre-landing air bombardment would be one of the largest of the SWPA amphibious operations. A focused 40 minutes of aerial bombardment included ten B-24 Liberators. The B-24 Liberator squadrons came from the US Fifth Air Force, US Thirteenth Air Force and Australian 1st Tactical Air Force. The pre-landing bombardment was organised in three waves. The first wave was 24 Liberators from the US Thirteenth Air Force, which dropped 50 tons of ordnance on Japanese fortifications. The second wave came from the 1st Tactical Air Force, which included the RAAF No. 21 Squadron, No. 23 Squadron and No. 24 Squadron, with a total of 20 Liberators dropping another 50 tons of ordnance from 6800–8000 feet

Figure 9.4 Landing craft filled with soldiers of the 18th Brigade watch Balikpapan's oil tanks burn as they circle in preparation for the final line-up into assault waves. (AWM 128759)

of altitude. The last wave approached simultaneously with the 18th Brigade's approach from the sea. This included 38 Liberators from the Fifth Air Force, which dropped 70 tons of ordnance on Japanese targets further inland, and B-25 Mitchells, which flew low and produced a smokescreen over the assault brigade's first waves of landing craft.[63]

As mentioned earlier during the planning discussion with the US Navy, Yellow and Red Beaches at Balikpapan offered the strongest Japanese coastal defence in the SWPA. The Japanese had created a number of offshore obstacles the amphibious force would have to address before the assault brigade could make its landing. In the landing area, an underwater phalanx of sorts was created by pile-driving rows of coconut trees into the seabed and binding it with barbed wire. All the mine-sweeping operations and beach clearance would have to be completed within the range of Japanese coastal guns, which also put amphibious support ships further out to sea.[64]

This heavy use of Japanese amphibious mines required 16 days of mine clearance in shallow waters by Allied mine-sweepers, all while the Japanese fired artillery and mortars into the sea.[65] The extensive beach clearance operations required air diversion for the amphibious reconnaissance of beach landing sites. From 27 to 29 June 1945, between 0810 and 1000, RAAF aircraft conducted high-altitude bombardments of Japanese positions

THE ASSAULT BRIGADE    191

in Balikpapan. The RAAF was instructed to ensure that no ordnance was dropped within 120 metres of the waterline.[66] This was to ensure that no explosions occurred in the water that would seriously injury combat swimmers or on the beach where reconnaissance personnel might come ashore.

## THE LAST AMPHIBIOUS LANDING

At 0430, 1 July 1945, Operation Oboe II began with the transfer of the 18th Infantry Brigade Group into landing craft.[67] The operation was dangerous as the LSTs were overloaded, carrying 450–550 troops each, and in a medium sea state, where the troops had to go over the sides of the ships onto pontoon platforms.[68] This dangerous transfer with combat-laden troops went smoothly and was credited to the extensive and repetitive training evolutions repeatedly over the previous year.

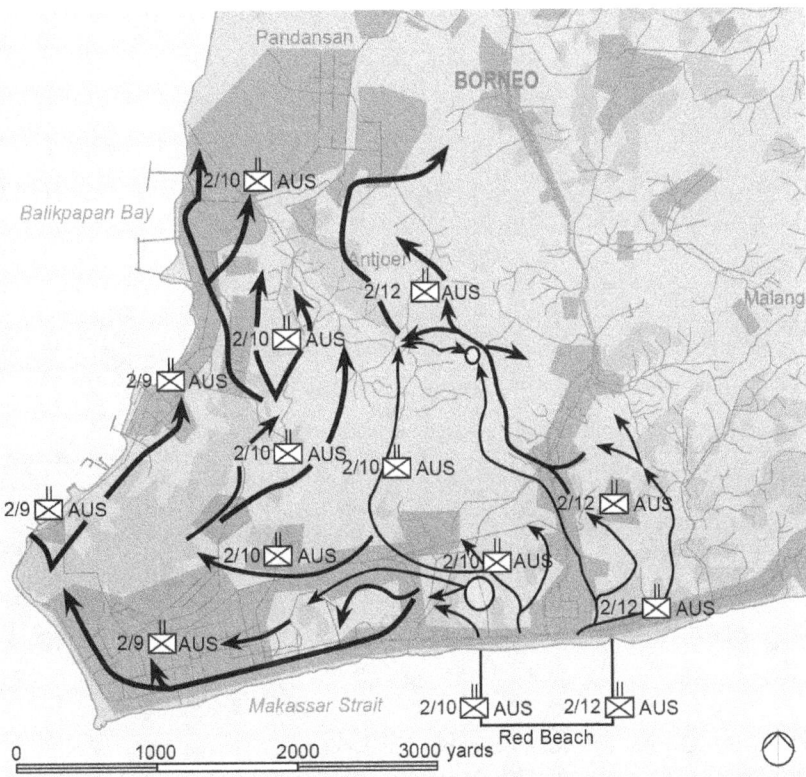

Map 9.1 Amphibious landing at Balikpapan. Although landings were planned for three separate beaches, confusion led the majority of the force landing on Red Beach, July 1945

In spite of accurate intelligence and modern landing vehicles, there was confusion in the landing. Poor dissemination of information and unsubstantiated rumour resulted in a belief among some amphibian units that portions of Yellow and Red Beaches had not been cleared by the underwater demolition teams.[69] As a result, the 2/12th Battalion landed on Red Beach and elements of 2/10th Battalion landed far left of Red Beach. The lone 2/27th Battalion of the 21st Brigade also landed on Yellow Beach instead of Green Beach, which further complicated the 18th Brigade's landing. This led to an overcrowded beachhead and vehicular traffic jams, which resulted in a need for more reorganisation in the battalion rally areas. A more dangerous outcome resulted when elements of the 2/12th Battalion, believing they were on Yellow Beach, quickly advanced towards their objectives inland. This resulted in units being cut off from the rest of the landing force for 36 hours.[70] The 2nd Beach Group had ongoing organisational problems. As the responsible party for the beachhead, it failed to inform the amphibious task force of the missed landings. This resulted in

Figure 9.5 On the crowded beachhead at Balikpapan, where many of the Australian tanks became stuck or suffered mechanical failure, soldiers of the 18th Brigade coordinate with a US Army Land Vehicle – Tracked (LVT) for the push inland. (AWM 110328A)

several subsequent waves following the first wave onto the wrong beach, thereby compounding confusion and traffic problems.

Once the beachhead congestion was untangled, the 18th Brigade was able to move out as a manoeuvre brigade largely following the operations order as written. The 2/9th Battalion, the brigade reserve, landed later than originally scheduled but unchallenged. This was another point of great risk in Oboe II. With success of the initial landings and the 2/9th Battalion essentially stuck out at sea, the vast expenditure of naval and aerial bombardment of the Japanese coastal guns and artillery proved a worthwhile investment. The delayed landing waves would have to circle in the amphibious assembly area until the beachhead was clear. If the Japanese guns were still active, the reserve force would have been forced further out to sea or continue to circle under Japanese fire without recourse. As a result, the brigade reserve would have a much longer response time and casualties if called on to support the assault battalions.

One of the most important doctrinal considerations for Oboe II was the inclusion of 'consideration ... in the tactical planning to the possibility of displaced landings' in the amphibious planning.[71] The confusion on the beachhead should be noted as a great point of success for 18th Brigade. The Oboe II landing plan was well drafted, but when the landing diverted from the plan, combat-experienced leadership that had been developed at the brigade level took over. At this point, leaders at all levels of the brigade took control under fire and returned a disorganised assault force to a manoeuvre brigade. The 18th Brigade, in its after-action report, credited junior officers and NCOs as the key to regaining the initiative at Balikpapan.[72]

The hydrographic reports provided by Allied amphibious reconnaissance units to the 18th Brigade proved to be accurate during the landing. The two landing sites, Yellow and Red Beaches, were both ideal for tracked landing craft and tanks. The coast was a shallow dead coral base, and the beach was hard-packed sand with the occasional coral boulder.[73] This was a significant help to the Beach Group and assault battalions in reorganising the beachhead after the confusion and traffic jams of the initial landings. The freedom of movement allowed by the hard-packed beach, and the absence of jungle, swamp or mangroves seen at other landing sites, greatly limited any potential for a Japanese counter-attack during the disoriented landing.

The Royal Australian Engineers of the 2/4th Field Company, which supported 18th Brigade, and the 2/9th Field Company, which was divided among armoured elements, all performed extremely well despite the beachhead traffic jam and heavy Japanese machine-gun and mortar fire. In the first waves, engineers discovered extensive 'wired' minefields on the landing sites. The minefields were never detonated by the Japanese, probably owing to the damage caused to the command wire firing systems by naval gunfire and aerial bombardments.[74] Yet again large-scale bombardment, criticised as excessive, proved invaluable. The confusion and congestion on the beach could have been disastrous if the Japanese had been able to 'command' detonate minefields underneath the landing force.

The decisive element of the amphibious assault at Balikpapan was the seizure of the high ground on Hill 87 and Parramatta. Once the 18th Brigade held these objectives, the success of the landing was ensured. Chilton wrote in his notes on the official history that 'Parramatta Ridge dominated the entire landing beach area and in fact was the dominating feature in the Balikpapan area – it was tactically key to that area'.[75] The 2/10th Battalion called for suppressive naval gunfire to support the assault; however, the destroyer assigned to the battalion (USS *Cleveland*) had been tasked elsewhere and was unable to provide fire support. Another destroyer had been assigned to 2/10th Battalion, but it had not registered targets ashore and was unable to provide support.[76] Additionally, the artillery and tanks were stuck in the confusion at the beach, which left the 2/10th Battalion with the decision to wait for support or attack. The 2/10th Battalion pushed the attack, against heavy Japanese resistance, support by 4.2-inch mortars and a machine-gun platoon.[77]

To clear the Japanese troops from trenches, tunnels and bunkers of Hill 87 and Parramatta employed all aspects of the assault brigade's resources: assault troops, with engineer support employing WP grenades, flame-throwers and, later in the battle, tanks. Chilton later referred to the seizure of Parramatta as 'the dash of 2/10th Battalion' because of the speed of combat manoeuvre. He noted in the after-action report that the high standard of training led to the successful capture of Parramatta. He believed that, without this high level of training, the casualty rates would have been significantly greater.[78] This was a key moment of the assault brigade: it had come ashore, rapidly overcome and adapted to the confusion of amphibious warfare, and finally manoeuvred to and seized its objective.

## After-action assessment

The after-action report for Oboe II prematurely stated that 'it is not considered that any new lessons arose out of the operation [Oboe II]'.[79] This statement was short-sighted because it was drafted so soon after the completion of Oboe II. Simply because the amphibious assault was successful and casualties were low – 18 soldiers killed and 70 wounded on the first day – did not mean that there were not new lessons to learn. Conversely, the Japanese defenders would lose 482 killed, with another estimated 150 killed and only 3 prisoners of war.[80] Chilton assessed the low causalities in the initial landing to leaders at all levels, who took the initiative when problems arose, and often solved these challenges through the brigade's wide assortment of supporting capabilities and the non-traditional use of amphibious vehicles.

The battle of Balikpapan was not an easy battle. The Japanese had extensive fortifications, tunnels and well-organised fields of fire on the beaches. In the urban areas, the fighting was often house to house and extremely dangerous. The fighting in the region would continue beyond the scope of this examination of the amphibious landing until the end of the war. By the end of the war, the Australians would lose 229 killed and 634 wounded in follow-on operations in the area.

Once ashore, the 18th Brigade did not make significant use of naval gunfire against Japanese fortifications. This was probably a result of the infantry battalion's inexperience with naval gunfire or as a result of positive experiences with close air support in previous battles such as Shaggy Ridge. However, all reports on the limited use of naval gunfire described it as 'quickly and accurately produced and was most effective'.[81] One highly valuable form of naval gunfire was the 5-inch star clusters. The landing force requested a significant volume of star clusters each night through D+3 to detect Japanese infiltrators.[82] The Japanese defeat on the beachhead did not prevent displaced Japanese forces from infiltrating the Allied lines and placing mines and booby traps. There were even personal reports from Australian soldiers who found booby traps that had been placed in the corpses of Japanese soldiers who had been killed in earlier night fighting.[83]

The air support provided to the 18th Brigade was significant but went largely unused. The 18th Brigade staff reported that owing to the 'fluid nature of operations' during the first three days of Oboe II, only one close air support mission was requested.[84] This ill-fated air strike was carried out by a US Navy escort carrier aircraft, which engaged the 2/10th Battalion in the only friendly fire incident of Oboe II. The 18th Brigade after-action report stated, 'the fault was entirely due to the lack of training and discipline on the part of the pilots concerned'.[85] Although this statement about the experience of the pilots was accurate, fault would also lie with the tasking authority, which will be discussed later. Aside from this incident, all other coordination with air assets worked well, and attached air liaison parties at the battalions and ASP at the brigade headquarters were highly valued members of the combined arms force.

## Armour on the Beach

Although the 1st Armoured Regiment tanks were split between the assault battalions, the landing confusion resulted in all tanks coming ashore on Red Beach. The landing of tanks was successful; however, when tanks moved off the beach, the terrain changed. The soil was of a 'boggy nature' and hampered movement significantly.[86] Additionally, movement on the beachhead was sufficient for heavy vehicles; however, just inland, the Japanese constructed a 14-foot wide anti-tank ditch to stop or slow the advance of the amphibious tanks and LVTs. There was also some concern that the Japanese would try to use the oil faculties as a defensive tactic by pumping oil into trenches or onto the beachhead and setting it ablaze. If the Japanese had pumped oil into the tank trench that spanned Red Beach, it could have slowed or stopped the Allied advance, which was already struggling with a congested beachhead. Even without a deliberate flooding by the Japanese, one soldier noted, 'The beaches were covered in

Figure 9.6 Soldiers of the 18th Brigade on Red Beach coordinate with US Army Landing Vehicles – Tracked and the 1st Armoured Regiment for the assault on Parramatta Ridge and Hill 87. (AWM 128754)

oil – even the water – if you went into the sea you would come out with a film of oil all over you because where they'd blown the refineries.'[87] Ultimately, none of the tanks assigned to Yellow Beach were able to link up with the 2/12th Battalion. The 2/12th Battalion captured all its objectives without the support of tanks.

The 2/10th Battalion, which had all the tanks on Red Beach, still had challenges with armour support. One troop of Frogs arrived near the end of the 2/10th Battalion's successful assault on Hill 87. The tank support for the 2/10th Battalion assault on Parramatta was initially of great value against Japanese fortifications early in the assault. However, as the 2/10th Battalion advanced, two of the tanks became stuck and two more had mechanical failures.

Once the 2/9th Battalion was ashore, it pushed out to its objectives in the Santosa–Klandasan area. Chilton retasked a Frog tank to support the 2/9th Battalion, which, as reserve, had far fewer attachments than the assault battalions. This was one example of close cooperation of infantry and armour that the 18th Brigade had developed over its time in the SWPA. The infantry could manoeuvre and identify hidden entrances of Japanese bunkers and tunnels, then direct the Frog, armed with a flamethrower, onto the target. The Frogs, protected by the infantry, provided one or two blasts into each bunker or cave. Units reported that the fires in the tunnels often lasted two hours. As the 2/9th Battalion's after-action report noted, 'if properly handled it is a definite battle winner'.[88]

The previously noted short planning and training time for Oboe II did affect some of the 18th Brigade's usual combined arms training. For Oboe II, the brigade spent a great deal of time training for amphibious warfare and became proficient in both planning and executing amphibious operations. However, the time dedicated to amphibious warfare took time from more traditional infantry manoeuvre training with armoured units. In point of fact, the 18th Brigade and the 1st Australian Armoured Regiment had not trained together before landing on Balikpapan.[89] The high level of skill in combined arms operations in both brigade and battalion staffs help to mitigate problems, but the after-action reports clearly demonstrate a preference for the US amphibian units the battalions had trained with at Morotai before Oboe II.

The US Army's 672nd Amphibious Tractor Battalion was an unanticipated success story of Oboe II. The 672nd Tractor Battalion was assigned to support the 18th Brigade with 51 load-carrying LVTs. Unlike the 1st Armoured Regiment, the 672nd Tractor Battalion was integrated in the 18th Brigade early in training, planning and rehearsals for Oboe II. The

672nd Tractor Battalion commander and staff participated in all aspects of the planning process and made their LVTs and soldiers available to train with the 18th Brigade at every opportunity. Its primary task was the landing of the assault battalions in the first two waves and the rapid build-up of ordnance, weapons, water and other mission-essential equipment for the assault brigade's push inland.[90]

Nowhere in the 18th Brigade operations order was there guidance for the use of LVTs as mechanised infantry support vehicles once ashore in Oboe II. However, once ashore, the LVTs and crews were called to serve in that role. The unloading of jeeps and tanks proved difficult because of the congestion and the challenging terrain beyond the beachhead. In order to maintain the speed of the advance and prevent the Japanese from counter-attacking the confused beachhead, Chilton ordered the LVTs forward in a direct infantry support role bringing mortars, ordnance and water to the front lines.

Even with limited armaments and light armour, the LVTs proved 'invaluable' to the assault battalions. The after-action report recorded one incident where an LVT was responsible for neutralising a Japanese machine-gun team in a fortified position, and in another incident, one hauled artillery inland when difficult terrain stopped the trucks. In the end, the US Army LVTs received considerable praise from Chilton: 'Throughout the planning and operations the commander and personnel of the 672nd Tractor battalion were most cooperative and anxious to assist. Crews handled their vehicles aggressively and well.'[91]

Engineer officers' involvement in the amphibious planning team contributed greatly to the major task of beach clearance. The beach had been heavily mined, yet clearance was quick, efficient and – most importantly – completed without engineer casualties. The engineer demolition teams attached to both the infantry and armour formations successfully destroyed numerous tunnels, bunkers and caves, often under fire and with the Japanese still inside. According to Gavin Long's official history, the engineer units destroyed more than 110 Japanese tunnels and fortifications, in addition to the more than 8000 mines and booby traps – a task that began at the water's edge and lasted long after combat operations ceased.[92]

## Indirect fire

Artillery proved to be problematic and forced the assault battalions to adjust how and what fire support it had once ashore. The confusion on the beachhead prevented the 2/4th Field Artillery Regiment from meeting any of its timeline requirements listed in the operations order. The first guns were not up until H+2, and the entire 2/4th Regiment would not be available until after the 2/10th Battalion completed its assault on Hill 87 and Parramatta.[93] Once the 2/4th Field Artillery was able to consolidate and establish 18th Brigade's fire control centre, the follow-on missions processed smoothly, although the bulk of the fighting had already ceased.

The 2/2nd Anti-Tank Regiment was even less effective than the field artillery. Six anti-tank guns came ashore with the assault force but saw little employment. Once on the beach, the guns were not able to keep up with the infantry on the varied terrain of Balikpapan. In the end, Chilton recommended to the Australian Army to keep anti-tank guns but only for use in open terrain or in an ambush from concealment.[94] For Chilton to relegate the anti-tank guns to a static role in an age of manoeuvre warfare was a pointed critique of a gun system that had outlived its usefulness to an infantry brigade.

The 4.2-inch mortar became the unlikely key indirect fire-support weapon of Oboe II. As noted previously, the 3-inch mortars had limited supply of ammunition and the field artillery units had trouble establishing firing points on the beach. As a result, the 4.2-inch mortar became the primary fire-support element for the assault battalions. The initial 7th Division draft plan called for two troops of 4.2-inch mortars, each of four guns, from 5th Battery, 2/2nd Anti-Tank Regiment.[95] However, this required the 18th Brigade to request fire support from the 4.2-inch mortar troops through the 7th Division, which would be slow and not directly coordinated by the brigade fire support centre, which had grown highly capable of using indirect fire in close support of the infantry. Chilton pushed for two changes in the fire support plan. First, he assigned one troop to each of the assault battalions, and second, he requested the 5th Battery headquarters be moved to the 18th Brigade headquarters. This would allow him to integrate the 4.2-inch mortars into the fire support centre it had used so successfully on Shaggy Ridge.

All the 4.2-inch mortars landed in the second wave of LVTs at H+3 minutes with the primary task of providing fire support for the assault battalions until the field artillery was established. Even though all the 4.2-inch mortars landed on the same beach instead of one mortar troop on each beach, the mortars quickly began to register targets at H+18 minutes and engaged the first Japanese positions at H+43 minutes. In part, the 4.2-inch mortars were able to engage quickly because of the integration and being co-located with the 18th Brigade fire support centre.

The 4.2-inch mortars offer an excellent example of how successful the 18th Brigade's amphibious planning was conducted. The 4.2-inch mortars landed with only 33 rounds per gun owing to the limited space on the LVTs and the belief that the field artillery would be operational at H+60 minutes. By design, the initial waves of an amphibious landing came ashore with limited supplies and ordnance. Each successive wave was planned to bring ashore ordnance and stores for the assault formations in the initial waves. By the time the 4.2-inch mortars had registered Japanese targets, in minutes each gun would have been nearly out of ammunition. However, the success of follow-on waves brought 300 rounds abroad DUKs at H+25 minutes and more than a thousand rounds at H+45 minutes.[96]

This example of the highly effective amphibious planning process and execution at the brigade level allowed for the 2/10th Battalion assault of Hill 87 and Parramatta to succeed without artillery and naval gunfire. The 4.2-inch mortars provided a large volume of high explosives to suppress the Japanese dug in on Hill 87 and an effective smokescreen for the 2/10th Battalion's assault.[97] The amphibious load plan, which emphasised rapid resupply, allowed the 4.2-inch mortar to succeed in the role of primary infantry fire support element. In the end, the 5th Mortar Battery fired more than 1500 rounds on D-Day with more than 200 in close support of the infantry.[98]

## Air support

The commander of the Naval Amphibious Group Eight noted in his report that although the use of naval and air bombardment of Balikpapan during Oboe II might have seemed 'excessive' in comparison with the other amphibious operations in the SWPA, the battle damage assessment of Japanese fortifications revealed that a more limited assault would have been 'insufficient'.[99] In spite of 20 days of naval gunfire and air bombardment, the 18th Brigade was still engaged by Japanese artillery, mortars and infantry forces.[100] The Japanese could not be bombed into submission: at the core of the evolution of the Australian infantry brigade was the belief that the infantry would have to take the ground.

Air support was an important aspect of Operation Oboe II. The bombardment of Japanese positions at Balikpapan began a full 20 days before D-Day.[101] In addition to the attacks on fortifications, the bombardment was also intended to prevent the Japanese coastal defence guns from firing on the minesweepers – a tactic that largely worked. Minesweepers were effective in the most heavily mined waters in the SWPA.

The largest disappointment of Oboe II was an incident of friendly fire involving the 2/10th Battalion. At 1600 on D-Day, the 2/10th Battalion had seized Parramatta Ridge at 1415 and set in to defend it against a Japanese counter-attack. The 2/9th Battalion, which had come ashore and advanced towards the harbour, hoped to manoeuvre quickly to get into a position to seize the harbour and town simultaneously. The 2/9th Battalion's air liaison party called for close air support to suppress heavy fire from fortified positions, a tactic that had proven highly effective on Shaggy Ridge. A navy dive bomber, neither designed nor trained for close support, was tasked with the request. The dive bomber's ordinance landed directly on the 2/9th Battalion position. Miraculously, only one soldier was seriously wounded.[102] Chilton commented in notes he provided the official historian in 1957 that 'it was a bitter experience for me to watch from a nearby hill, powerless to intervene, and even more bitter for the 2/10th battalion'.[103] Chilton noted his frustration because the entire point of adding air liaison officers and an Air Control Element at the division was to prevent friendly fire casualties.

The 2/9th Battalion, engaged with Japanese forces, requested close air support through its air liaison officer to the Air Control Element afloat. Gary Waters, former RAAF air commodore, notes that Air Vice Marshal William Bostock, RAAF, argued against using US Navy dive bombers.[104] However, Waters does not source this statement, and Bostock was the Commander, Support Aircraft Afloat on USS *Wasatch*. Waters's paper holds US Vice Admiral Daniel Barbey, commander of the 7th Amphibious Force, or Rear-Admiral Albert Nobles, commander of the naval attack group, at fault for the friendly fire incident, since these two US admirals were the only officers who could overrule the commander of air operations, Bostock. Most interesting is whether the incident would have happened if overall command for air support had already moved ashore.

Milford, the 7th Division commander, came ashore with MacArthur at 1300 to tour the beachhead.[105] Amphibious doctrine and the Oboe operation order required the rapid overall transfer from the naval task force commander to the ground manoeuvre commander – in this case Milford. Waters notes that on 1 July 1945 at 1900, command was transferred ashore to the commander of the 7th Division. The friendly fire incident with 2/10th Battalion took place at 1600. Had the 7th Division headquarters been established earlier, the Australian Army would have been the tasking authority for the 2/9th Battalion's close air support request. This is important because before the 7th Division's establishment of air control ashore, the request went directly from the assault battalion's air liaison party to brigade headquarters ASP, who sent the request to Commander Support Aircraft Afloat. Once 7th Division headquarters was established ashore, the division air officer becomes the Commander, Support Aircraft Ashore. This key element of amphibious doctrine would have had the 2/9th Battalion request the decision made by the army ashore and not the navy afloat. It is unlikely that any army air control element would have requested or tasked a navy dive-bomber with close air support for the 2/9th Battalion. This incident demonstrates the complexity of command and control in amphibious warfare.

The 18th Infantry Brigade Group (Jungle) landed at Balikpapan as an amphibious force with mechanised support, which was able to quickly overwhelm the Japanese with the expertise it had gained over years of combat. The brigade's after-action reports credited three main factors for its success: combat experience, the development of amphibious warfare doctrine and, most importantly, delegation of critical decisions to the brigade level. These factors made the brigade skilled in the 'mechanics of planning',[106] even when the 'extremely short' planning cycle diverted the amphibious planning process from the prescribed norm in Australian doctrine.[107]

Chilton noted in a letter to Long: 'On looking back, I think another point and one that can be looked at is the high standard of professional competence and training the AIF had now attained. I do not think, for example, it would have been possible for us to have carried out an operation of this complexity in our earlier years.'[108] Chilton was of course speaking of the evolution in doctrine, technology and the level of operational art the AIF had achieved during the campaigns of the SWPA.

General Milford's 7th Division headquarters would be established by 1900 hours that evening. By that time, Brigadier Chilton, commanding the most effective infantry brigade group in Australian history, had secured the 7th Division's victory. With limited support from tanks and none from artillery, Chilton had broken out of the beachhead and seized the high ground by employing resources available: LVTs and mortars. It was through this last amphibious assault of World War II that the Australian infantry brigade consolidated its role as the key manoeuvre formation of the Australian Army in the SWPA.

CHAPTER 10

# CONCLUSION

After close examination of the Allied campaigns of the SWPA, the importance of the Australian infantry brigade as a key combat formation is without question. An examination of the infantry brigade group (jungle) as an intermediate formation commanding infantry battalions and numerous attached units demonstrates the role of an infantry brigade as crucial to the victories in New Guinea and Borneo. The complex terrain of the SWPA islands, which sometimes constrained and at times isolated the brigades, offered these formations the opportunity to evolve.

The Australian Army raised a total of 32 infantry brigades before and during World War II.[1] Only a few would remain after 1945. The least fortunate – the 22nd and 27th Brigades – were 'surrendered' in the Japanese conquest of Malaysia in 1942. The 10th, 31st and 32nd Brigades (Militia) were disbanded in 1942; the 14th, 28th and 30th Brigades (Militia) were disbanded in 1943; and the 9th and 12th Brigades were disbanded in 1944. Some were deactivated because of a reduced need for homeland defence, and others had their troops redistributed as replacements for casualties. The rest of the Australian infantry brigades would be completely disbanded or reorganised into post-war formations in 1945–46. Of the 32 Australian infantry brigades fielded in World War II, none conducted a comprehensive examination of their experience at war.

This history of the 18th Brigade, conducted almost 80 years after the end of World War II, focuses on the significant contributions to the development of Australian jungle warfare, amphibious warfare, combined arms integration and the introduction of a brigade-level operational art. Several other Australian infantry brigades (and US regiments) experienced varying degrees of success in modernisation and had diverse experiences in the SWPA that offer future researchers a great opportunity for expanding the body of research on this period of military history.

The 18th Brigade proved an excellent choice for the study of the Australian infantry brigade. Although other Australian infantry brigades had similar experiences with modernisation and the evolution of the brigade, few, if any, had the diversity of combat operations and Allied cooperation. The 18th Brigade participated in operations spanning the length of the Australian campaigns in the SWPA theatre, often operating as the 7th Division's spearhead, which allowed for continuity in the study of the evolution of the Australian brigade in the Pacific War. These circumstances of the SWPA led to the brigade commander and staff becoming more flexible and adopting numerous combat functions previously handled at the divisional level. The result was an evolution of brigades into highly lethal combined arms formations.

## TRAINING FOR WAR

The Australian infantry brigade faced major challenges from both the enemy and the terrain in the SWPA. To conquer both, the AIF and – at each echelon – corps, division and brigade adapted training models with guidance from high headquarters and through initiative on the battlefield. How did the brigade train for the complex warfare of the SWPA? The answer is that the brigade trained hard and often, and incorporated new technology and tactics, whenever possible.

On 24 January 1940, the brigade published its second (and first substantive) training memorandum. The document focused heavily on training for company movement based on the World War I experience of its veterans. It stressed a number of standard skills, such as patrolling and defensive positions. It also included instructions for maintaining horses and for conducting trench raids.[2] The 18th Brigade shed much of the outdated training when it deployed to North Africa. Battles such as Bardia and Tobruk introduced the AIF to modern warfare, and the army performed well. However, the SWPA would require a new training model where classic infantry tactics were adapted to jungle and amphibious warfare.

At the onset of World War II, the Australian battalions managed regional basic training programs that varied in quality and content.

It was not until 1943 that army authorities decided all recruit training needed to be consolidated to ensure a standard level of basic training across the force. At the Australian Recruit Training Centre at Cowra, NSW, this consolidation also allowed the army for the first time to provide all service members with a central aptitude test and assignment to service branches on the basis of ability.[3] The outcome was a better soldier with standardised infantry training. This allowed the 18th Brigade to spend far less training time on basic individual soldier skills and more time on specific skills, like jungle warfare or intelligence, and on collective unit training and exercises.

Jungle warfare training began as unit-level training for forward deployed units by necessity. In August 1942, the 18th Brigade was sent to Milne Bay, both unequipped and untrained for jungle warfare. The result was the rout of the 2/10th Battalion at the hands of Japanese infantry and light tanks. The 18th Brigade had begun jungle training as soon as it arrived at Milne Bay on the basis of reports from other brigades' experiences in Malaysia and on the Kokoda Track. The combat experience in Milne Bay, both good and bad, and the training the followed, resulted in the 18th Brigade's highly effective performance in the difficult Buna and Sanananda campaigns. In Buna, the brigade employed classic infantry manoeuvre at the brigade level, with a burgeoning effort to coordinate supporting arms during assaults against Japanese fortifications.

The successes were based on the integration of jungle training and classic infantry tactics that would have been familiar on the Western Front of World War I. For example, on 31 December, Warren Force led by the 18th Brigade finally brought the developing concept of a combined arms manoeuvre brigade to bear on the Japanese. The 18th Brigade's infantry battalions attacked, supported by field artillery, mortars and armour, and worked in concert against engaged Japanese positions. At dawn on New Year's Day 1943, the 2/12th Battalion broke through the Japanese perimeter to reach the ocean. The 18th Brigade advanced through the breach and rapidly overran the Japanese. Examples like this established adaptability in training and planning as a core competency in brigade leadership and, equally important, the brigade staff. Although the Australian brigades and US regiments suffered the highest casualty rates of the SWPA theatre at Buna and Sanananda, the experience also validated the model of intermediate formations by demonstrating a rudimentary integration of artillery, armour and intelligence at the brigade level.

The 18th Brigade returned from the Buna and Sanananda campaigns in New Guinea a victorious but physically broken force. Again, it would return to training for infantry basics and jungle warfare during its transition, along with the 7th Division, in formal 'jungle' formations. The 'Jungle' division and, by expansion, the jungle brigade were intended to be lighter formations in which 'all units, subunits, transportation and equipment which are not essential for general operations in jungle conditions [were to be] eliminated from the jungle organisation'.[4] The 18th Brigade had suffered more than 96 per cent casualties to a combination of weather, terrain, disease and the enemy.[5] So broken was the force that in April 1943, the 18th Brigade's 'Combat Efficiency Report' stated clearly 'no estimate of time as to the preparedness of the Brigade can be given'.[6] However, the post-Buna era of rebuilding clearly demonstrated the ability of a brigade to assess its lessons learnt and changes in technology and to build a new training program to ensure it could deploy again quickly.

Part of the rebuilding of ranks was the challenges faced as the brigade absorbed large numbers of new soldiers. The 18th Brigade had in short order absorbed the soldiers of 1st, 5th and 11th Australian Motorized Regiments, the majority of whom lacked basic infantry skills and jungle warfare training. To bring all the soldiers to the same level in an army that still had no standardised basic training, the brigade implemented the standard regulation infantry training, but it also established a significant number of internal brigade schools. One of these was the brigade's Jungle Warfare Course, which became so recognised that other units of the Australian Army early in the SWPA reached out to the 18th Brigade for jungle warfare knowledge. Throughout 1943, the Australian and US armies sent questions to the 18th Brigade's staff or requested 18th Brigade representation at jungle warfare conferences in a theatre-wide acknowledgement of the unit's accomplishments as a brigade.

The 18th Brigade's jungle expertise reached beyond its internal training program; its formal recommendations and lessons learnt reported to the Allied Headquarters had not fallen on deaf ears. The most often mentioned in the 18th Brigade's unit diary was the Section Assault Course, which focused on infantry units assaulting jungle bunkers with organic infantry weapons as part of a larger assault. This type of course would be replicated across the SWPA. There was also a Sneaker Course, which amounted to a jungle reconnaissance course that provided instruction on quiet movement in the jungle and the use of camouflage.

There were other examples of brigade-level schools such as the Battle Course, where units would observe demonstrations of tanks and artillery cooperation with the infantry and participate in live fire exercises.[7] A Platoon Commanders Course, the core course for junior officers, was conducted repeatedly in 1943. These organic brigade schools matured with the brigade training program and, in efforts to maintain hard-learnt lessons, the 18th Brigade made every effort to conduct standardised rifle and grenade ranges, collective unit training, leadership courses and individual Staff Section instruction.[8] As the war in the SWPA progressed, the brigade combined training guidance from high headquarters with newest battlefield lessons learnt to maintain a highly effective fighting force.

## THE BRIGADE AND INTELLIGENCE

To meet the challenges and complexity of war in the SWPA, the brigade Intelligence Sections from 1942 to 1945 increased in both size and capability. The infantry brigade headquarters at the start of the 18th Brigade's experience in the SWPA included one intelligence officer, one sergeant and an enlisted orderly or clerk.[9] The complexity of the battlefield and the front lines' distance from higher headquarters forced brigades and battalions to produce intelligence at the unit level. As the war in the SWPA progressed, the intelligence capability at every echelon grew dramatically. By the time the Australian Army was planning for the amphibious landing at Balikpapan, the amount of intelligence available to the brigade was voluminous. For the brigade Intelligence Section, the key was in the expanded number of trained intelligence soldiers, the integration of intelligence from higher and lower echelon units, and new collection capabilities.

One of the most significant intelligence evolutions to brigade capability was to have intelligence soldiers pushed down all the way to the company level. The battalion Intelligence Sections noted a disconnect between the information-sharing at the brigade, battalion, headquarters and company headquarters.[10] Company commanders, who did not have an Intelligence Section, often planned in a vacuum without an intelligence soldier present. The addition of company-level intelligence soldiers allowed for continuity in information-sharing throughout the brigade. The accurate and timely sharing of information throughout the brigade would help prevent confusion such as the 2/10th Battalion experienced at Milne Bay, where some units thought the Japanese tanks had been knocked out, some thought the tanks were advancing, and yet others believed no tanks had landed.

As with infantry, artillery or tank skills, intelligence required a significant amount of training. Intelligence training became something the brigades invested in heavily. On 1 December 1943, the 18th Brigade had established a 21-day Intelligence School as part of the brigade's training programs.[11] The importance of implementing the brigade's intelligence lessons learnt is demonstrated by the number of days committed to the intelligence school. This course trained officers and enlisted personnel, down to the company level, on both analytic and ground reconnaissance skills. The course culminated with a two-day field exercise after which students were required to provide a ten-minute intelligence brief and complete a written exam.[12] Brigade commanders understood, after the initial lack of intelligence on enemy troop strength and locations in Buna and Sanananda, that the brigade would have to assume more responsibility for intelligence functions if it was to defeat the Japanese in the SWPA.

The 18th Brigade Intelligence Section had also invested additional time and resources in training intelligence personnel to interpret photographs since the Buna and Sanananda campaign. This proved a wise investment for the Finisterre campaign. Maps of the Finisterre Range and the Markham and Ramu Valleys were not suitable for combat operations. Aerial photographs and photo-overlays became a primary task of the brigade's intelligence personnel once deployed. The brigade Intelligence Section, which had spent much time and effort since Buna expanding and acquiring new intelligence skills, became a key factor in the victory at Shaggy Ridge. The brigade Intelligence Section and newly expanded battalion Intelligence Sections drafted activity reports and analysis on all aspects of the Japanese defences on Shaggy Ridge. Much of this was accomplished by ground reconnaissance, which helped identify routes used by the infantry to launch surprise attacks on the mountaintop fortifications.

Throughout the Finistrerre campaign and the amphibious assault on Balikpapan in Borneo, the 18th Brigade Intelligence Section continued to expand the ability to integrate higher and lower intelligence, collect battlefield intelligence and integrate that information across the force. At 0430, 1 July 1945, as the 18th Brigade boarded landing craft for the amphibious assault on Balikpapan, the AIF intelligence capabilities and that of the brigade Intelligence Section had matured to a point where a nearly complete picture of Japanese force was available to the soldiers on the ground.

## COMBINED ARMS SUPPORT

For the Australian brigade on the forward edge of the battlefield, often in close proximity to the enemy, it would become essential to integrate and manage its own fire support. As the campaign in New Guinea progressed, the sheer amount and type of firepower in the SWPA led all levels of the AIF down to the brigade to re-evaluate fire support integration. Artillery, tanks, close air support and naval gunfire would all become integral partners of the infantry. The key to meeting this challenge at the brigade level, the 18th Brigade, was the introduction of a fire support centre within the brigade to work with attachments and liaisons to coordinate artillery, close air support and naval gunfire – all of which were traditionally managed by attached unit headquarters.

For the Australian brigade, including the 18th Brigade, the close cooperation of infantry, armour, artillery and naval gunfire would start in North Africa and the Middle East. The Battle of Bardia witnessed the cooperation of artillery, tanks and even limited naval gunfire in support of Australian formations.[13] Still, it was hardly integrated. That would require improvements in communications, indirect fire weapons systems and an agreement on a central point of coordination. For the brigade, it was the fire support centre.

The integration started out rough for Australian brigades; in Milne Bay, the artillery forward observers were killed in the early fighting, which left the infantry without the ability to call accurate fire. The 18th Brigade and others decided early in the SWPA that infantry officers must be cross-trained in forward observer skills, not only to conduct indirect fire in support of manoeuvre but also to prevent fratricide. In Milne Bay and Buna, fire support was hampered by jungle terrain, logistics and leadership. In both Buna and Sanananda, the 18th Brigade used the available 25-pounders and tanks in a direct fire role against Japanese pillboxes and bunkers when the terrain allowed the guns to be moved close to the front. This use was effective at breaching the Japanese perimeter, but still lacked a real integration of the force.

Shaggy Ridge was significant not only because of the 18th Brigade's use of combined close air support and artillery with infantry but also because it was the first time the 18th Brigade headquarters served as a combined fire control centre for a brigade infantry assault. The 2/4th Field Artillery headquarters and air liaison elements were both co-located with the 18th Brigade headquarters. Traditionally, artillery headquarters were further back with the division headquarters, but advances in manoeuvre doctrine, communications and observation techniques allowed Chilton to exercise direct control of the artillery and close air support during an infantry assault. The fire control centre at Shaggy Ridge provided a plan for each battalion assault for the 'full advantage' of all available guns.[14]

The 2/4th Field Artillery planned to be able to shift fire support of each artillery battery from primary supported units to troops in contact throughout the area of operations. This close coordination made it possible for artillery to fire in close concert with infantry manoeuvre and allow close air support to have 'engaged and destroyed (targets) within 100–120 yards of our forward troops'.[15]

By the time the 18th Brigade landed on the beachhead at Balikpapan, its ability to integrate effective fire at the fire control centre, down to the battalions and companies, had been developed to a highly effective level. The sheer scope of available fire to include carrier-based close air support, naval gunfire from US destroyers, and organic artillery and tanks all amounted to overwhelming force on the beach. It was the long years of training, exercises and combat experience that allowed the 18th Brigade to shift immediately from the bogged-down tank and artillery support to the coordination of 4.2-inch mortars and LVTs for fire support.

## Amphibious warfare

Amphibious warfare is a complex and dangerous endeavour for any combat formation. The question of how the brigade commander and staff completed the complex task of planning, training, exercising and conducting amphibious warfare deserves a high level of attention. In the SWPA, Australian infantry brigades played a significant role often as the spearhead of division amphibious landings and assaults. By 1944, the Australian Army, including the 18th Brigade, had modernised infantry training in close cooperation with artillery, tanks and close air support, and had put this training and tactics to the test in North Africa and campaigns across New Guinea. It was all this previous training and combat experience that formed the baseline on which the 18th Brigade embraced amphibious warfare. Key was the implementation of amphibious training, exercises and rehearsals that resulted in the final evolution of the Australian brigade; the 18th Infantry Brigade Group (Jungle) as an amphibious infantry brigade: the Assault Brigade.

The SWPA was an amphibious theatre of war – a fact the Australian Army embraced despite its chequered amphibious legacy. At Lae, New Guinea, the Australians' first large-scale landing since Gallipoli, the 9th Division suffered 547 casualties, 206 of which occurred during the first 24 hours of the 20th Brigade's largely unopposed amphibious landing.[16] The high initial casualty rate demonstrates the dangers and complexity of amphibious operations where 38 per cent of the total casualties were on the beach or offshore on task force ships in what Chilton later called a 'rather untidy landing'.[17] The 20th Brigade's last training exercise for the landing at Lae was mired in confusion, poor amphibious planning and inefficient loading of ships.[18] The 20th Brigade was not prepared for Lae, not because of a failure of the 20th Brigade but as a consequence of a lack of a well-developed amphibious training program for brigades.

This would not be the case for the 18th Brigade, which on 20 October 1944 received the order to move to Trinity Beach for amphibious training.[19] At Trinity Beach, the 18th Brigade began its final transition of the war. This transition was not solely one of increased lethality; it also had to learn to overcome the massive administrative challenges of amphibious warfare. This was achieved through a wide breadth of training not only for the troops going over the side of a ship onto a landing craft but also equally important training for the leadership and staff. The brigade spent countless hours learning how to load plan the brigade's troops and equipment on landing ships. The Australian assault brigades had to master this incredibly difficult planning process since it had to coordinate the largest number of attached units and external support and, most importantly, to sustain the highest level of risk on the beachhead.

On 1 July 1945, the 18th Australian Infantry Brigade Group (Jungle) was designated the assault brigade for the amphibious assault on Balikpapan, Borneo, code-named Operation Oboe II. With the formal training for soldiers and units of the brigade, the 18th Brigade participated in two major amphibious exercises (Seagull and Octopus) that helped to improve efficiency in correctly loading equipment and units onto the ships for disembarkation on the beachhead. The last major piece of the 18th Brigade's preparation for Balikpapan was a full rehearsal – a key aspect of preparation for amphibious warfare the 20th Brigade did not have the benefit of before Lae. Morshead, concerned with a stiff Japanese defence of the beachhead, demanded a full-scale rehearsal.[20] The rehearsal for Oboe II was largely successful and was the final test of the brigade leadership, staff and coordination of attached units before the assault at Balikpapan.

At 0430 on 1 July 1945, Operation Oboe II began with the transfer of the 18th Brigade into landing craft.[21] In spite of 20 days of naval gunfire and air bombardment, the landing force was still engaged by Japanese artillery, mortars and infantry forces.[22] The 18th Brigade was to land on Yellow and Red Beaches, secure a beachhead, and seize Parramatta Ridge and Hill 87 'at the earliest possible moment after H-Hour'.[23] As Chilton

Figure 10.1 Soldiers of B Company, 2/12th Infantry Battalion pause on the high ground forward of the beachhead at Balikpapan. On one knee in the foreground a radio operator coordinates for support before the advance. (AWM 111183)

wrote in his notes on the official history, 'Parramatta Ridge dominated the entire landing beach area and in fact was the dominating feature in the Balikpapan area – it was tactically key to that area.'

Clausewitz's 'fog of war' would serve as the test of the 18th Brigade on the beachhead. Despite countless hours of planning and training, the rows of amphibious landing craft experienced confusion and miscommunications leading to waves of landing craft coming ashore on the wrong beaches. The fog of war, which was ever-present in amphibious operations, resulted in traffic jams on Red Beach and the separation of units, equipment and ammunition. The beach congestion, compounded with terrain, had left the assault brigade without armour or artillery for the push to seize Parramatta. Leadership at platoon, company and battalion levels, who were trained to take the initiative and were experienced in the integration of fire support, reorganised around the LVTs and 4.2-inch mortars to move off the beach and assault Parramatta Ridge.

Chilton later referred to the seizure of Parramatta as 'the dash of 2/10th Battalion' because of the speed of the attack – a lesson carried forward from the battalion's battles in Buna and Sanananda and highlighted at Shaggy Ridge. Chilton believed that without this high level of training, the casualty rates would have been significantly higher.[24] In the after-action reports on Operation Oboe II, the 18th Brigade – with some pride – repeatedly refers to itself as the 'assault brigade'.[25]

## THE BRIGADE COMMANDER

This work does not endeavour to be a biography of brigade commanders but rather a focused examination of the role of the brigade commander as a leader and how the role relates to the functions of the brigade and brigade staff during combat. An Australian brigade commander led the smallest combined arms formation in the army in 1942–45. As discussed throughout, the brigade commanders of SWPA had to lead not only the brigade's three battalions but also all the varied attachments during a period of great change in intermediate formations. Brigade commanders in the SWPA met these challenges through ownership of many coordination and integration tasks, previously the sole purview of the division, such as supporting fires, intelligence and amphibious planning.

Brigade leadership in the SWPA was as much about sustaining the force in the jungles as it was leading soldiers in combat. The Allied formation entered New Guinea with limited knowledge of the difficulty that this terrain would pose to the individual soldier. As knowledge and experience grew, commanders endeavoured to educate and lead the force in this difficult environment. One American commented in Buna that they defeated the Japanese because they survived in the jungle longer. This was obviously not a practical future strategy in the SWPA. Chilton, who considered the jungle a 'worst case' environment, made sustainment of the force an essential task with established of five priorities for jungle warfare enumerated in 'Training Instruction Number 28'. The first priority was survival. In addition to jungle combat skills, soldiers would be trained in acclimatisation, field cooking, jungle food, personal and unit hygiene, and anti-malarial techniques.[26]

This role of the brigade commander as responsible for the sustainment of the force paralleled the commander's role in equipping the force. There is a certain level of constraint on a brigade commander's ability to equip the force and, as outlined in this study, equipping the force often is dictated by higher headquarters in the form of scales such as light, jungle or assault. To complicate matters, equipping the force in SWPA was often hampered by logistics more than anything else; however, where possible, it is the brigade commander's job to advocate for the brigade with the division and higher echelons. In the case of Buna, Wootten and other commanders had to fight for additional armour and artillery when senior leaders questioned their utility in the jungle.[27] Later, Chilton would fight the 7th Division for an improved air support plan when he felt the resources offered for the assault on Shaggy Ridge were insufficient.[28] This would happen again in the planning for the assault on Balikpapan when Chilton had to request repeatedly that the 4.2-inch mortars be pushed down from the 7th Division and integrated into the 18th Brigade fire support centre.[29] The 7th Division relented on both accounts.[30] This role of the brigade commander as advocate paid off in each case, and was key on the beachhead at Balikpapan where the 4.2-inch mortar played a pivotal role in the rapid Allied victory.

Wootten and Chilton understood that for senior leadership, the division and corps command and staff schools were largely sufficient. However, in the SWPA, leadership needed to be pushed down to the lowest level. Both brigade commanders took the time between combat operations to establish leadership courses for officers and non-commissioned officers at the platoon, company and battalion levels. Equally important, the brigade recognised the increasing demands on brigade staff and established staff courses to improve staff functions such as intelligence and planning. The result was the 18th Brigade's establishment of its Brigade Staff Course, which was focused on training brigade and battalion staff officers or potential staff officer in the 'staff duties, [broken into] duties in action, and duties out of action'.[31]

Professional development was an opportunity for brigade commanders to personally lead tactical discussions with battalion commanders and staff.[32] In one example on 10 June 1943, Chilton conducted a tactical discussion on the Principles of War for battalion and company commanders.[33] This offered the brigade commander the opportunity to share knowledge and discuss possible combat scenarios with subordinate commanders. It also allowed Wootten and Chilton to assess the knowledge and future potential of subordinates outside field exercises for higher command or staff positions.

In addition to formal written orders, commanders at all echelons used commanders' conferences to coordinate the staff functions of the unit, subordinate commander guidance and the integration of new concepts. One example was the period between 5 and 8 January 1943: as the 18th Brigade prepared for the assault on Shaggy Ridge, Chilton held numerous commanders' conferences to discuss environmental considerations, reconnaissance needs and available intelligence on Japanese forces in the region. Additionally, Chilton used these conferences to assess or brainstorm unique issues like the need for the construction of a jeep trail to support the brigade's logistic train, which had grown accordingly with the number and size of attachments that now made up the brigade group.[34] The combination of formal orders and commanders' conferences allowed Chilton to flush out alternative battle plans for Operation Cutthroat.

All these exercises in leadership led to a battle plan for Operation Cutthroat that would result in a successful brigade assault with a full complement of supporting arms and close air support conducted in five phases coordinated in time and physical space. Most importantly, Operation Cutthroat was an operation planned and led by a brigade headquarters. Chilton and his brigade staff believed strongly that the campaign offered valuable lessons learnt for future brigade operation.

Another often less acknowledged aspect of brigade command was the increased reliance on the brigade staff, as it played a larger role in each battle of the SWPA primarily in the coordination of the attachments, fire support and logistics that made up the brigade group. In the planning and execution of Oboe II, Chilton relied heavily on the brigade staff, and again it proved both highly adaptable and capable. After endless hours of amphibious planning, commanders' conferences and liaison work with the US Navy, the assault brigade's amphibious load plan emphasised not only the rapid offloading of combat forces but also an effective phase or wave-based resupply on the beach.

The brigade staff's detailed amphibious planning established the order of loading and offloading the assault force on the beachhead that was essential for the 18th Brigade's rapid victory. In this example, owing to the delay of artillery and armour, the 4.2-inch mortars were able to provide sufficient indirect fire support because the second and third waves of landing craft resupplied the 4.2-inch mortars before the limited supply on the first wave was depleted. In the end, and largely owing to effective amphibious planning, the 5th Mortar Battery fired more than 1500 rounds on D-Day, including more than 200 in close support of the infantry.[35] This was as much a success of the soldiers of the mortar units on the beach as it was the brigade staff's amphibious planning.

The 18th Brigade's commanders in the SWPA demonstrated that the brigade was capable of planning complex operations on highly condensed timetables with multiple variables. The 18th Brigade commanders had to demonstrate a clear appreciation of both administration and combat manoeuvre if a unit was to be effective in the SWPA. The leadership responsibilities of Wootten and Chilton as brigade commanders in the SWPA were not unique to the 18th Brigade. Many examined here are classic principles of military leadership. However, it is unique in military history that brigade commanders had to lead in an era of enormous change on such a difficult battlefield as the SWPA.

The formal surrender of imperial Japan took place on the battleship USS *Missouri* on 2 September 1945, although major combat operations had ceased on 15 August 1945 with the announcement of Japan's surrender. However, demobilisation had begun before the 7th Division landed on the shores of Balikpapan. By April 1945, the Australian Government decided that 50 000 men should be released from the army and air force by the end of the year. The War Cabinet, overruling proposals put forward by the army, established a policy which allowed that 'all members of the army and air forces with operational service overseas and who had over five years' war service are to be given the option to taking their discharge'.[36] On 21 July 1945, the 'Release of Personnel with Five Years' War Service' sent home the longest-serving members of the Australia Army. Subsequently, the autumn of 1945 saw the 18th Brigade rosters dwindle quickly.

With the August 1945 announcement, the 18th Brigade held an *ad hoc* parade, and Chilton thanked all the troops for their service but warned them that there was work to be done in the rounding up of Japanese prisoners and management of the camps before the brigade would return to Australia.[37] As the duties in Balikpapan became more routine, some soldiers of the brigade went on to serve in the newly formed 34th Australian Infantry Brigade with the Australian Occupation Force on the Japanese mainland.[38] In the end, most went home to Australia.

From September to December 1945, the 18th Brigade saw many of its supporting units that made up the 'Group', such as pioneers and artillery, stripped away and deactivated. In October, a small ceremony was held after which Brigadier Chilton, the brigade's longest serving commander, 'marched out' to serve as commander of the Makassar Force in South

Sulaesi. A month later, on 3 November, the entire 18th Infantry Brigade Group (Jungle) was declared redundant. December saw the individual battalions of the 18th Brigade conduct their final ceremonies with drummers and buglers playing 'retreat' on the piece of ground where they had fought the last battle of World War II.[39] Its War Diary ended abruptly on the day of its deactivation, 3 January 1946, without ceremony.

The combination of Australian combat experience, the embrace of new tactics, doctrine and technologies made it possible for the 18th Australian Infantry Brigade (Jungle) to win striking victories in the SWPA. The Australian infantry brigade group (jungle) reached its apogee with the designation of amphibious assault brigade. The infantry brigade had demonstrated that it was a highly adaptive formation capable of close cooperation with the US Army and Navy in complex operations such as the amphibious assault on Balikpapan. In five years, the brigade transitioned from a light infantry focused on territorial defence to the motorised infantry of North Africa, then to its most dynamic evolution and the focus of this research: an amphibious infantry brigade group (jungle). The 18th Brigade's combat experience, administrative efficiency, combined arms capability and leadership made it the most lethal and effective intermediate formation the Australian Army fielded in World War II.

# NOTES

## Introduction

1 The terms 'joint' and 'combined' are often a cause of confusion in Allied military literature. The Arcadia Conference of 1941 established the formal definition of terms 'joint' and 'combined' operations. Before the conference, the British and, by extension, Australian armed forces used the term 'joint' to describe multinational operations. Following the conference, the term 'joint' was defined as operations that included two or more services from one country. 'Combined' operations were defined as plans or operations of two or more countries. *Proceedings of the American–British Joint Chiefs of Staff,* held in Washington, DC on Twelve Occasions between 24 December 1941 and 14 January 1942.
2 The 33rd and 34th Australian Infantry Brigades were formed after the Japanese surrender to serve as occupation forces in the Dutch East Indies and Japan respectively.
3 For more information on the Australian Army in the Middle East and North Africa, see: C. Stockings, *The Battle of Bardia*, Big Sky Publishing, Sydney, 2015; B. Perrett, *Armour in Battle: Wavell's Offensive*, Ian Allan, London, 1979; G. Wahlert, *The Western Desert Campaign 1940–41*, Big Sky Publishing, Sydney, 2016; I. Chapman, *Iven G. Mackay: Citizen and Soldier*, Melway Publishing, Melbourne, 1975; J. Grey, *Australian Brass: The Career of Lieutenant General Sir Horace Robertson*, Cambridge University Press, Melbourne, 1992; H. Gullet, *Not as a Duty Only: An Infantryman's War*, Melbourne University Press, Carlton, 1976.
4 G.H. Johnson, *The Toughest Fighting in the World: The Australian and American Campaign for New Guinea in World War II*, Westholme Publishing, Yardley, PA, 2011 [1943].
5 P. Williams, *The Kokoda Campaign 1942: Myth and Reality*, Cambridge University Press, Melbourne, 2012; P. Brune, *A Bastard of a Place: The Australians in Papua*, Allen & Unwin, St Leonards, NSW, 2005; P. Dornan, *The Silent Men: Syria to Kokoda and on to Gona*, Allen & Unwin, St Leonards, NSW, 1999; P. Lindsay, *The Spirit of Kokoda: Then and Now*, Hardie Grant Books, South Yarra, 2002.
6 For a work on the Kokoda campaign from the Japanese perspective see: C. Collie and H. Marutani, *The Path of Infinite Sorrow: The Japanese on the Kokoda Track*, Allen & Unwin, Sydney, 2012.

7 Pratten, *Battalion Commanders*, p. 31.
8 Numerous types of intelligence would become available in the SWPA theatre to include, but not limited to, aerial photography, strategic and amphibious reconnaissance, and signals and cryptologic intelligence.
9 Ship-to-shore operations are the 'planning and execution of the movement of troops from the beginning of their debarkation from transports until they are landed on the beach', usually over great distances. US Navy, *FTP 211: Ship to Shore Movement, General Instructions*, US Government Printing Office, 1943. Shore-to-shore operations are defined as the use of landing craft or amphibians to transfer cargo and troops from one beach terminal to another along the same coastline or adjacent island. US Army, *FM 55-50: Army Water Transport Operations*, Department of the Army, Washington, DC, 1993.

## Chapter 1: An introduction to the brigade

1 '18th Australian Infantry Brigade, Intelligence Summary Number 118, Appendix III, 27 April 1942', March–April, AWM 52 8/2/18.
2 The US Army doctrine used the term 'team', as in the phrase 'regimental combat team', in the same way the Australian infantry used the term 'group', as in the 'infantry brigade group', to signify that the organic infantry organisation has attachments.
3 J. Moremon, 'A triumph of improvisation: Australian Army operational logistics and the campaign in Papua, July 1942 to January 1943', PhD thesis, University of New South Wales, 2000, p. 45.
4 Interview, O. Curtis, 2/12th Battalion, Keith Murdoch Sound Archive, Australian War Memorial, Archive Number S541, p. 1.
5 Pratten, *Battalion Commanders*, p. 33.
6 Ibid., pp. 30–1.
7 T. Ricks, *The Generals: American Military Command from World War II to Today*, Penguin Books, New York, 2013, p. 33.
8 Interview, Curtis, p. 14.
9 Pratten, *Battalion Commanders*, p. 31.
10 Ricks, *The Generals*, p. 33.
11 Interview, Curtis, p. 14.
12 J. Grey, *The Australian Army*, Vol. I, *The Australian Centenary History of Defence*, Oxford University Press, Melbourne, 2001, pp. 160–91.
13 P. Dennis & J. Grey (eds), *The Foundations of Victory: The Pacific War 1943–1944*, The 2003 Chief of Army's Military History Conference, Army History Unit, Department of Defence, Canberra, ACT 2600, p. 88.
14 Stockings, *The Battle of Bardia*, p. 29.
15 E. Squires, First Report of Lieutenant General Ernest Squires, CB DSO MC, Inspector-General of the Australian Military Forces, A5954, 1208/15, NAA, 16 December 1938.
16 Ibid.
17 '18th Australian Infantry Brigade, Training instruction number 2, 24 Jan 1940', December 1939–May 1940, AWM 52 8/2/18.
18 Ibid.

19 'Report on Operations 18th Australian Infantry Brigade Operations at Cape Endaiadere, Giropa Point, and Sanananda Area – 14 December 1942 to 20 January 1943', December 1942, AWM 52 8/2/18 [hereafter 'Report on Operations 18th Australian Infantry Brigade'].
20 'Directorate of Military Training, Account of Activities: 3 September 1945–15 August 1945, LHQ Tactical School', AWM 54 881/1/4 part 2.
21 Grey, *The Australian Army*, p. 116.
22 'Order of Battle, 2nd Australian Imperial Forces, 6th Division and Ancillary Troops, 30 November 1939, 6th Australian Division General Staff Branch', October–December 1939, AWM 52 1/5/12.
23 A. Palazzo, *The Australian Army: A History of Its Organisation from 1901 to 2001*, Oxford University Press, Melbourne, 2001, p. 135.
24 P. Dean (ed.), *Australia 1944–45: Victory in the Pacific*, Cambridge University Press, Melbourne, 2016, p. 121.
25 Ibid.
26 'Directorate of Military Training, Account of Activities: 3 September 1945–15 August 1945, LHQ Tactical School', AWM 54 881/1/4 part 2.
27 Ibid.
28 Palazzo, *The Australian Army*, pp. 135–91.
29 Ibid.
30 'Order of Battle, 2nd Australian Imperial Force, 6th Division and Ancillary Troops, 30 November 1939, 6th Australian Division General Staff Branch', October–December 1939', AWM 52 1/5/12.
31 Dennis & Grey, *The Foundations of Victory*, p. 88.
32 '7th Australian Division Operational Instruction Number 1, May 1942', May–July, AWM 52 8/2/18.
33 D. McCarthy, *South-West Pacific Area – First Year, Kokoda to Wau*, Vol. 5, Australia in the War of 1939–1945, Australian War Memorial, Canberra, 1959, p. 1 [hereafter *Kokoda to Wau*], p. 21.
34 'Re-organisation of Infantry Formations in the AMF, Land Force Headquarters, 13 February 1943', AWM 54 422/7/8 [hereafter 'Re-organisation of Infantry Formations', AWM 54 422/7/8].
35 Ibid.
36 'Milne Force Operations Order Number 1', October 1942, AWM 52 8/2/18; '18 Australian Infantry Brigade Instruction No. 17, 20 September 1942', September–October 1942, part 1, AWM 52 8/2/18.
37 'Lessons Learned from 2/10 BN Air Movement, 15 October 1942', October 1942, AWM 52 8/2/18.
38 'Re-organisation of Infantry Formations', AWM 54 422/7/8.
39 'War Tables – Jungle Division, 2nd Australian Corps, 13 March 1943', April–May 1943, AWM 52 8/2/18.
40 'Re-organisation of Infantry Formations', AWM 54 422/7/8.
41 'Organisation of Jungle Formations, Allied Land Force in SWPA, 16 July 1943', AWM 54 422/7/8; 'Re-organisation of Infantry Formations in the AMF, Allied Land Force in SWPA, 16 July 1943', AWM 54 422/7/8.
42 Pratten, *Battalion Commanders*, p. 73.
43 'Re-organisation of Infantry Formations', AWM 54 422/7/8.

44 Dennis & Grey, *The Foundations of Victory*, p. 96.
45 'Re-organisation of Infantry Formations', AWM 54 422/7/8.
46 Ibid.
47 'Review of Composition and Organisation of Jungle Formations, Land Force Headquarters, 25 April 1944', AWM 54 422/7/8.
48 'Subject: Reorganisation of 6 Australian Division, 7 Australian Division, and 9 Australian Division, Headquarters 2 Australian Corps, 14 June 1943', AWM 54 422/7/8.
49 Ibid.
50 Ibid.
51 Ibid.
52 J. Coates, *Bravery Above Blunder: The 9th Australian Division at Finschhafen, Sattelberg, and Sio*, Oxford University Press, Melbourne, 1999, p. 49.
53 'Re-organisation of Infantry Formations', AWM 54 422/7/8.
54 'Field Artillery Jungle Division, Artillery Organisation, Army and Corps Units 1944', AWM 54 422/7/8.
55 'Organisation Jungle Divisions, Deletion of Division Carrier Companies, Australian Military Forces, Chief of the General Staff', AWM 54 422/7/8.
56 'Organisation of Jungle Formations, Allied Land Force in SWPA, 16 July 1943', AWM 54 422/7/8.
57 'Notes on Defence Against Tank Attack, Headquarters 18th Infantry Brigade, 29 March 1942', March–April, AWM 52 8/2/18.
58 Interview, Angus George Suthers, Captain, 2/12th Battalion, 7th Brigade, Keith Murdoch Sound Archive of Australia in the War of 1939–1945, No. 256805, 8 October 1994.
59 'Report on Operations 18th Australian Infantry Brigade'.
60 '18th Infantry Brigade, War Diary', February–March 1943, AWM 54 8/2/18.
61 'Field Artillery Jungle Division, Artillery Organisation, Army and Corps Units 1944', AWM 54 422/7/8.
62 Ibid.
63 'Re-organisation of Infantry Formations', AWM 54 422/7/8.
64 'Field Artillery Jungle Division, Artillery Organisation, Army and Corps Units 1944', AWM 54 422/7/8.
65 A.L. Graeme-Evans, 'The 18th Brigade AIF at Buna, Australia's Pacific Battle of the Somme, January 1943', *Australian Defence Force Journal* 98, January/February 1993, p. 67.
66 'Field Artillery Jungle Division, Artillery Organisation, Army and Corps Units 1944', AWM 54 422/7/8.
67 'Re-organisation of Infantry Formations', AWM 54 422/7/8.
68 'War Establishment – Amendment to WE 11/2/3 Headquarters of an Infantry Brigade', April–May 1943, AWM 52 8/2/18.
69 'Organisation of Jungle Formations, 1 Australian Corps, 22 May 1944', AWM 54 422/7/8.
70 'Review of Composition and Organisation of Jungle Formations, Australian Military Forces, 24 March 1944', AWM 54 422/7/8.
71 'Operations Milne Bay 24 August to 8 September 1942, Lessons from Operations Number 2', Papers of Major General C.A. Clowes, AWM 419/02/10, 3 DRL 4143.

72 'Review of Composition and Organisation of Jungle Formations, Australian Military Forces, 24 March 1944', AWM 54 422/7/8.
73 'Report on Operations 18th Australian Infantry Brigade'.
74 K.R. York, 'Joint operational fires in the offense: The Southwest Pacific campaign to isolate Rabaul', Monograph, US Army Command and General Staff College, Fort Leavenworth, KS, 2014.
75 H. Knight, 'Report of Military Observer in Southwest Pacific Theater of Operations, October 16 to December 30, 1942', Record Group 165 Entry, Military Intelligence Division, 1922–1944, Box 128, file 6140, US National Archives, Washington, DC [hereafter Knight, 'Report of Military Observer'].
76 'Field Artillery Jungle Division, Artillery Organisation, Army and Corps Units 1944', AWM 54 422/7/8.
77 Ibid.
78 Ibid.
79 F. Hartley, *Sanananda Interlude: The 7th Australian Division Cavalry Regiment*, Specialty Press, Melbourne, 1949, pp. 65–6.
80 'Report on Operations 18th Australian Infantry Brigade'.
81 'Composition and Organisation of Jungle Formations, Australian Military Forces, Chief of the General Staff, 4 May 1944', AWM 54 422/7/8.
82 Ibid.
83 'Organisation of an Infantry Brigade', AWM 54 422/7/8.
84 'Composition and Organisation of Jungle Formations, Australian Military Forces, Chief of the General Staff, 4 May 1944', AWM 54 422/7/8.
85 Ibid.
86 '18th Australian Infantry Brigade Intelligence School, Duties of the Brigade and Battalion Intelligence Personnel, December 1943', December 1943, AWM 52 8/2/18.
87 G.F. Pinder, 'The New Guinea campaign, 23 January 1943–31 December 1944', Command and General Staff College, 31 May 1949.
88 M.R. Browning, 'Amphibious warfare and the naval covering force', *Military Review*, Vol. XXV, Command and General Staff College, Kansas, May 1945, p. 57.
89 Another Allied manual for amphibious operations, the British *Combined Operations Staff Notebook* of September 1945, also employed similar verbiage when referring to the lead amphibious element as the 'assault formation'. The UK defined the assault formation as 'formations which are tactically organised and equipped to carry out the initial attack on an enemy coast, and to which separate allocation of landing ships and craft is made'. The second use of the term 'assault' in amphibious warfare is the 'assault scales'. Assault scales quantify the exact numbers of men, vehicles, ammunitions and stores of an assault formation. *Combined Operations Staff Notebook*, Ike Skelton Combined Arms Research Library, US Army Command and General Staff College, Fort Leavenworth, KS.
90 A.V. Arnold, 'Preparation for a division amphibious operation', *Military Review* XXV, May 1945, p. 4.
91 Ibid., p. 4.
92 *Combined Operations: Planning on the Brigade and Unit Levels with Special Reference to Landing Tables and Tonnage Tables*, 1st Australian Corps

Training Instruction Number 10, 12 October 1944, Papers of Lieutenant General F.H. Berryman, AWM PR84/370 419/9/9 [hereafter *Combined Operations: Planning on the Brigade and Unit Levels*].
93 *Field Manual 31-5, Landing Operations on Hostile Shores*, US Army, Government Printing Office, Washington, DC, 2 June 1941.
94 'Combined Operations, Beach Organisation and Maintenance, 1st Australian Corps Training Instruction Number 2/1944', 24 April 1944, Papers of Lieutenant General F.H. Berryman, AWM PR84/370 419/9/9.
95 '18th Australian Infantry Brigade: Report on Operation OBOE TWO', June–August 1945, AWM 52 8/2/18.
96 'Exercise Octopus, Outline Plan of Commander 18th Australian Infantry Brigade', October 1944, AWM 52 8/2/18.
97 '18th Australian Infantry Brigade: Report on Operation OBOE TWO'.
98 Ibid.
99 Ibid.
100 P.R. Mansoor, *The GI Offensive in Europe: The Triumph of American Infantry Divisions, 1941–1945*, University Press of Kansas, Lawrence, KS, 1999, p. 11.
101 'US National Defense Act of June 3, 1916', A1 Entry 5B, Records Group 11, General Records of the US Government, US National Archives, Washington, DC.
102 'Executive Order 8530 Calling Out the National Guard', Army Unit Records 1917–1950, Dwight D. Eisenhower Presidential Library Archives, Abilene, KS.
103 The Louisiana Maneuvers were US Army Chief of Staff George C. Marshall's attempt to avoid a repeat of the overzealous and unrealistic planning he had witnessed as a staff officer in 1918 as part of the American Expeditionary Forces in World War I. A generally unprepared US command at Meuse-Argonne resulted in what Marshall called 'stumbling, blunderings, failures, appeals for help, and hopeless confusion'. The Louisiana Maneuvers were the largest exercises in US history and intended to assist in the reorganisation of the US Army, which had been gutted after World War I. G. Marshall, L.I. Bland, C.N. Wunderlin Jr and S.R. Stevens (eds), *The Papers of George Catlett Marshall: We Cannot Delay, July 1, 1939–December 6, 1941*, Vol. 2, Johns Hopkins University Press, Baltimore, 1986, pp. 280–4.
104 Ibid., pp. 280–4.
105 F.B. Catanzaro, *With the 41st Division in the Southwest Pacific: A Foot Soldier's Story*, Indiana University Press, Indianapolis, 2002, p. 27.
106 R.L. Eichelberger, *Our Jungle Road to Tokyo*, Viking Press, New York, 1950, p. 12.
107 H.A. Gailey, *MacArthur Strikes Back: Decision at Buna: New Guinea 1942–1943*, Presidio Press, Novato, CA, 2000, pp. 102–3.
108 S. Milner, *Victory in Papua: The War in the Pacific, United States Army in World War II*, US Army Center of Military History, Washington, DC, 1957, pp. 132–3.
109 Ibid., p. 133.
110 Eichelberger, *Our Jungle Road*, p. 12.

111 C.E. Heller & W.A. Stofft (eds), *America's First Battles, 1776–1965*, University Press of Kansas, Lawrence, KS, 1986, p. 192.
112 Gailey, *MacArthur Strikes Back*, pp. 104–5.

## Chapter 2: The long road to the SWPA

1 'War Diary, 18th Australian Infantry Brigade, December 1939–May 1940', AWM 52 8/2/18.
2 Ibid.
3 'War Diary, 18th Australian Infantry Brigade, May 1940–November 1940', AWM 52 8/2/18.
4 Ibid.
5 Ibid.
6 Ibid.
7 'War Diary, 18th Australian Infantry Brigade, December 1940 – February 1941', AWM 52 8/2/18.
8 Richardson, 'The siege of Giarabub', p. 3.
9 'War Diary, 18th Australian Infantry Brigade, December 1940 – February 1941', AWM 52 8/2/18.
10 Richardson, 'The siege of Giarabub', p. 9.
11 G. Long, *To Benghazi*, Vol. 1, *Australia in the War of 1939–1945*, Australian War Memorial, Canberra, 1952, p. 294.
12 Richardson, 'The siege of Giarabub', p. 14.
13 'War Diary, 18th Australian Infantry Brigade, March 1941, Appendices', AWM 52 8/2/18.
14 'War Diary, 6th Divisional Cavalry Regiment, March 1941', AWM 52, 2/2/7.
15 Long, *To Benghazi*, p. 297.
16 Manuscript of R.W. Forester, AWM PR01981.
17 Long, *To Benghazi*, p. 298.
18 Calvert, *Stand-to!*; Long, records related to official history, AWM 67 2/17.
19 'War Diary, 18th Australian Infantry Brigade, AWM March 1941, Appendices', AWM 52 8/2/18.
20 Long, *To Benghazi*, p. 302.
21 Ibid., p. 303.
22 Richardson, 'The siege of Giarabub', p. 27.
23 'War Diary, 18th Australian Infantry Brigade, May Appendices', AWM 52 8/2/18.
24 'War Diary, 18th Australian Infantry Brigade, May 1941', AWM 52 8/2/18.
25 B. Maughan, *Tobruk and El Alamein*, Vol. 3, *Australia in the War of 1939–1945*, Australian War Memorial, Canberra, 1966, p. 231.
26 'War Diary, 18th Australian Infantry Brigade, May 1941', AWM 52 8/2/18.
27 '18th Australian Infantry Brigade Training Instruction Number 23, March 1942', March–April, AWM 52 8/2/18.
28 '18th Australian Infantry Brigade, Training Instruction Number 24, March 1942', March–April, AWM 52 8/2/18.
29 'Routine Orders, Headquarters 18th Infantry Brigade, 03 May 1942', May–July, AWM 52 8/2/18.

30 '18th Australian Infantry Brigade, Training Instruction Number 24, March 1942', March–April, AWM 52 8/2/18.
31 'Notes on Defence against Tank Attack, 18th Infantry Brigade, 29 March 1942', March–April, AWM 52 8/2/18.
32 McCarthy, *Kokoda to Wau*, p. 1.
33 'Training in use of Assault and Recce Boats, 18th Infantry Brigade, 29 March 1942', March–April, AWM 52 8/2/18.
34 'War Diary, 18th Australian Infantry Brigade, 16 May 1942', May–July, AWM 52 8/2/18.
35 'Preparation of Exercises, Headquarters 18th Infantry Brigade, 04 April 1942', AWM 52 8/2/18.
36 Ibid.
37 Ibid.
38 Ibid.
39 Ibid.
40 Ibid.
41 'War Diary, 18th Australian Infantry Brigade, 19 May 1942', May–July, AWM 52 8/2/18.
42 '7th Australian Division Operational Instruction Number 1', May 1942, May–July, AWM 52 8/2/18.
43 'Training Syllabus – Road Blocks and Tank Stops, 30 May 1942', May–July, AWM 52 8/2/18.
44 'Headquarters 18th Australian Infantry Brigade Exercise Number 3, 26 May 1942', May–July, AWM 52 8/2/18.
45 'War Diary, 18th Australian Infantry Brigade, 1–15 June 1942', May–July, AWM 52 8/2/18.
46 'Murgon TEWT, Headquarters 18th Australian Infantry Brigade, 16 May 1942', May–July, AWM 52 8/2/18.
47 'War Diary, 18th Australian Infantry Brigade, 15 May 1942', May–July, AWM 52 8/2/18.
48 '7th Infantry Division, Murgon TEWT', June–July, AWM 52 8/2/18.
49 '7th Australian Division Training Notes', May–July, AWM 52 8/2/18.
50 Ibid.
51 Ibid.
52 'War Diary, 18th Australian Infantry Brigade, May 1942', May–July, AWM 52 8/2/18.
53 'War Diary, 18th Australian Infantry Brigade, July 1942', May–July, AWM 52 8/2/18.
54 Ibid.
55 Ibid.
56 'Notes for Commander's Conference, 17 July 1942', May–July 1942, AWM 52 8/2/18.
57 'Training of Liaison Officers, 18 July 1942', May–July 1942, AWM 52/8/2/18.
58 '18th Australian Infantry Brigade Training Memorandum Number 1, 30 July 1942', May–July 1942, AWM 52 8/2/18.
59 Ibid.
60 Ibid.

61 Ibid.
62 'Training Objectives to 31 August 1942, 7 July 1942', May–July 1942, AWM 52/8/2/18.
63 '7th Australian Infantry Division Operational Instruction Number 4, 4 August 1942', May–July 1942, AWM 52 8/2/18.
64 'War Diary, 18th Australian Infantry Brigade, August 1942', May–July 1942, AWM 52 8/2/18.

## Chapter 3: The Battle of Milne Bay

1 E.J. Drea, 'Defending the Driniumor: Covering force operations in New Guinea, 1944', Leavenworth Papers Number 9, Combat Studies Institute, Command and General Staff College, Fort Leavenworth, KS, 1984, p. 3.
2 E.G. Keogh, *The South West Pacific 1941–45*, Grayflower, Melbourne, 1965, p. 185.
3 'Clowes was a regular officer, learned, cautious, and taciturn. He had served through the 1914–18 War as an artillery officer and on the staff and had also commanded at Darwin for three years between the wars. In 1940, he had been chosen as corps artillery commander, and in 1941, led the Anzac Corps artillery in the campaign in Greece.' McCarthy, *Kokoda to Wau*, p. 159.
4 Maroubra Force, which fought a defensive battle to stop the Japanese advance over the Kokoda Track, was a brigade-sized formation; however, Milne Bay is the first battle in the SWPA in which Australian brigades participated as established brigade formations.
5 S. Milner, 'The Battle of Milne Bay', *Military Review*, Vol. XXX, April 1950, p. 18.
6 Ibid., p. 18.
7 Ibid., p. 20.
8 Ibid., p. 20.
9 'War Diary, 18th Australian Infantry Brigade, August 1942', August–September, AWM 52 8/2/18.
10 E.F. Allchin, *Purple and Blue: The History of the 2/10th Battalion, AIF (The Adelaide Rifles) 1939–1945*, 2/10th Battalion Association, Adelaide, 1958, p. 241.
11 Ibid., p. 245.
12 Ibid., p. 245.
13 '7th Infantry Division, Murgon TEWT', June–July, AWM 52 8/2/18.
14 Milner, *Milne Bay*, p. 29.
15 Ibid., p. 29.
16 Keogh, *The South West Pacific 1941–45*, pp. 186–7.
17 A '25-pounder' was the standard artillery piece of the Australian Army at the onset of World War II. The calibre was 3.5 inches with a 7.75-foot barrel. The weight off the shell was roughly 25 pounds, resulting in the name given to the weapon system.
18 Keogh, *The South West Pacific 1941–45*, p. 186.
19 J. Henderson, *Onward, Boy Soldiers: The Battle for Milne Bay 1942*, University of Western Australia Press, Nedlands, WA, 1992, p. 74.

20 Ibid., p. 190.
21 McCarthy, *Kokoda to Wau*, p. 185.
22 Milner, *Milne Bay*, p. 20.
23 G. Long, *The Six Years War: A Concise History of Australia in the 1939–1945 War*, Australian War Memorial, Canberra, 1973, p. 214.
24 Milner, *Milne Bay*, p. 22.
25 'Operations Milne Bay 24 August to 8 September 1942, Lessons from Operations Number 2', 3 DRL 4143 Papers of Major General C.A. Clowes, AWM 419/02/10.
26 Keogh, *The South West Pacific 1941–45*, p. 193.
27 'Notes on Milne Bay Operations, 26 August–8 September 1942', August–September, AWM 52 8/2/18.
28 Keogh, *The South West Pacific 1941–45*, p. 189.
29 Ibid., p. 193.
30 'Notes on Milne Bay Operations, 26 August–8 September 1942', August–September, AWM 52 8/2/18.
31 Long, *The Six Years War*, p. 214.
32 McCarthy, *Kokoda to Wau*, p. 160.
33 Ibid., p. 167.
34 'Intelligence Diary, Fall River, 25–26 August 1942', August–September, AWM 52 8/2/18.
35 'War Diary Notes on Milne Bay Operations, 26 August–8 September 1942', August–September, AWM 52 8/2/18.
36 'Intelligence Diary, Fall River, 26 September 1942, Fall River', August–September, AWM 52 8/2/18.
37 Allchin, *Purple and Blue*, p. 252.
38 Ibid., p. 254.
39 'Intelligence Diary, 27 September 1942, Fall River', August–September, AWM 52 8/2/18.
40 Allchin, *Purple and Blue*, p. 254.
41 'Intelligence Diary, 27 September 1942, Fall River', August–September, AWM 52 8/2/18.
42 Interview, Captain Theo Schmedje, 2/10th Battalion, Keith Murdoch Sound Archive of Australia in the War of 1939–1945, No. 358540, 16 May 1992.
43 Allchin, *Purple and Blue*, p. 260.
44 Ibid., p. 241.
45 'Report on Japanese Tactics – Milne Bay, 2/10 Australian Infantry Battalion, 6 September 1942', September–October, part 1, AWM 52 8/2/18.
46 'Notes on Milne Bay Operations, 26 August–8 September 1942', August–September, AWM 52 8/2/18.
47 Ibid.
48 Interviews, Albert James Wood, Sergeant, D Company, 2/10th Battalion, and Robert Henry Warren, Warrant Officer 2, D Company, 2/10th Battalion, Keith Murdoch Sound Archive of Australia in the War of 1939–45, No. S02405, 17 March 1993.
49 'Intelligence Diary, Fall River, 25–26 August 1942', August–September, AWM 52 8/2/18.

50 Ibid.
51 'Report on Operations – Milne Bay, 2/10 Australian Infantry Battalion', September–October, part 1, AWM 52 8/2/18.
52 Ibid.
53 'Report on Japanese Tactics – Milne Bay, 2/10 Australian Infantry Battalion, 6 September 1942', September–October, part 1, AWM 52 8/2/18.
54 'Report on Operations – Milne Bay, Headquarters 2/10 Australian Infantry Battalion', September–October, part 1, AWM 52 8/2/18.
55 'War Diary Notes on Milne Bay Operations 26 August–8 September', September–October, part 1, AWM 52 8/2/18.
56 'Report on Operations – Milne Bay, Headquarters 2/10 Australian Infantry Battalion', September–October, part 1, AWM 52 8/2/18.
57 'Lessons from Recent Fighting, 7th Australian Infantry Brigade', September 1942, part 1, AWM 52 8/2/18.
58 'Report on Operations of the 18th Australian Infantry Brigade in Milne Bay Area, 26 August–September 42', September–October, part 1, AWM 52 8/2/18.
59 'Report on Japanese Tank', September 1942, Appendices part 1 of 5, AWM 52 8/2/18.
60 McCarthy, *Kokoda to Wau*, p. 171.
61 Milner, *Milne Bay*, p. 29.
62 Keogh, *The South West Pacific 1941–45*, p. 195.
63 Ibid., p. 196.
64 'War Diary Notes on Milne Bay Operations, 26 August–8 September 1942', August–September, AWM 52 8/2/18.
65 Keogh, *The South West Pacific 1941–45*, p. 197.
66 G.M. Hall, *Love, War, and the 96th Engineers (Colored): The World War II New Guinea Diaries of Captain Hyman Samuelson*, University of Illinois Press, Urbana, 1995, p. 135.
67 'War Diary Notes on Milne Bay Operations, 26 August–8 September 1942', August–September, AWM 52 8/2/18.
68 Ibid.
69 Ibid.
70 Ibid.
71 Ibid.
72 Milner, *Victory in Papua*, p. 84.
73 'Operations Diary September 1942, Appendices Part 1', AWM 52 8/2/18.
74 Ibid.
75 Interview, Curtis, p. 70.
76 Allchin, *Purple and Blue*, p. 252.
77 Interview, Curtis, p. 70.
78 'Intelligence Diary, 27 September 1942, Fall River', August–September, p. 43.
79 'Points Noted and Lessons Learnt in Recent Operations, Fall River', August–September, AWM 52 8/2/18.
80 'Intelligence Diary, 27 September 1942, Fall River', August–September, AWM 52 8/2/18.
81 'Points Noted and Lessons Learnt in Recent Operations, Fall River', August–September, AWM 52 8/2/18.

82 McCarthy, *Kokoda to Wau*, p. 169.
83 'Points Noted and Lessons Learnt in Recent Operations, Fall River', August–September, AWM 52 8/2/18.
84 'Operations Milne Bay, 24 August to 8 September 1942, Lessons from Operations Number 2', 3 DRL 4143 Papers of Major General C.A. Clowes, AWM 419/02/10.
85 'Operations Diary September 1942', Appendices Part 1, AWM 52 8/2/18.
86 'Tactical and Other Lessons from Fighting Milne Bay, HQ 2/9 Australian Infantry Battalion, 10 September 1942', September–October, Part 1, AWM 52 8/2/18.
87 Ibid.
88 'Operations Diary September 1942', Appendices Part 1, AWM 52 8/2/18.
89 'Operations Milne Bay, 24 August to 8 September 1942, Lessons from Operations Number 2', 3 DRL 4143 Papers of Major General C.A. Clowes, AWM 419/02/10.
90 Ibid.
91 Ibid.
92 'Intelligence in the Brigade, 18th Infantry Brigade, 24 October 1942', February–March, AWM 52 8/2/18.
93 Ibid.
94 Ibid.
95 Ibid.
96 Ibid.
97 Ibid.
98 'War Diary Notes on Milne Bay Operations, 26 August–8 September', AWM 52 8/2/18.
99 'Intelligence Diary 6 September 1942', Appendices Part 2, AWM 52 8/2/18.
100 Allchin, *Purple and Blue*, p. 259.
101 Keogh, *The South West Pacific 1941–45*, p. 189.

## *Chapter 4: The Battle of Buna*

1 Allchin, *Purple and Blue*, p. 305.
2 A.L. Graeme-Evans, 'The 18th Brigade AIF at Buna, Australia's Pacific Battle of the Somme, January 1943', *Australian Defence Force Journal*, No. 98, January/February 1993, pp. 67–70.
3 *Papuan Campaign: The Buna–Sanananda Operation, 16 November 1942–23 January 1943*, American Forces in Action Series, Military Intelligence Division, War Department, Washington, DC, 1944, p. 81.
4 Ibid., p. 57.
5 Milner, *Victory in Papua*, p. 50.
6 J. Luvaas, *Dear Miss Em: General Eichelberger's War in the Pacific, 1942–1945*, Bloomsbery Academic, New York, 1972, p. 30.
7 L. Mayo, *Bloody Buna*, Doubleday & Company, New York, 1974, p. 180.
8 Ibid., p. 180.
9 Eichelberger, *Our Jungle Road*, p. 41.
10 Ibid., pp. 49–51.

11  Mayo, *Bloody Buna*, p. 106.
12  Eichelberger, *Our Jungle Road*, p. 34.
13  Mayo, *Bloody Buna*, p. 182.
14  Eichelberger, *Our Jungle Road*, p. 18.
15  Interview with Geoffrey Holmes, 2/12th Battalion, Archive Number S546, p. 68.
16  'History of the Buna Campaign, December 1, 1942–January 25, 1943', Office of the Commandant, Fort Leavenworth, KS, 1943 [hereafter 'History of the Buna Campaign'].
17  D. Dexter, *The New Guinea Offensives*, Series I: Army, Vol. VI, *Australia in the War of 1939–1945*, Australian War Memorial, Canberra, 1961, p. 519.
18  *US Army Field Manual 100-5 Operations 1939*, p. 235.
19  *US Army Field Manual FM 31-20 Jungle Warfare 1941*. In 1944, the US War Department changed the field manual code of the Jungle Warfare Manual to FM 72-20. The FM 31-20 was later used by US Special Forces.
20  Milner, *Victory in Papua*, p. 92.
21  Mayo, *Bloody Buna*, p. 103.
22  J. Vader, *New Guinea: The Tide is Stemmed*, Ballantine Books, London, 1971, p. 83.
23  'Nominal Role of British Officers', December 1943, AWM 52 8/2/18.
24  Ibid.
25  Allchin, *Purple and Blue*, p. 265.
26  Ibid., p. 265.
27  'Notes on Air Movement and Enplaning, 14 October 1942', October 1942, AWM 52 8/2/18.
28  Ibid.
29  'Lessons Learned from 2/10 Battalion Air Movement', 15 October 1942, AWM 52 8/2/18.
30  Allchin, *Purple and Blue*, p. 265.
31  Eichelberger, *Our Jungle Road*, p. 35.
32  Milner, *Victory in Papua*, p. 307.
33  Ibid., p. 307.
34  'History of the Buna Campaign', pp. 2–3.
35  Ibid.
36  Ibid.
37  Ibid.
38  'History of the 127th Infantry Regiment, Buna Campaign, 16 November 1943 to 1 February 1943', 127th Infantry, US Army Unit Records 1917–1950, Dwight D. Eisenhower Presidential Library Archives, Abilene, KS.
39  Ibid.
40  Milner, *Victory in Papua*, p. 127.
41  'History of the Buna Campaign'.
42  Milner, *Victory in Papua*, p. 127.
43  Eichelberger, *Our Jungle Road*, p. 23.
44  R. Young, 'They too fought the Japanese: The American Army's war in the Southwest Pacific', PhD thesis, City University of New York, 2003, p. 16.
45  'History of the Buna Campaign'.

46 'Journal of the 1st Battalion of the 128th Infantry Regiment', 126th Infantry, US Army Unit Records 1917–1950, Dwight D. Eisenhower Presidential Library Archives, Abilene, KS.
47 Young, 'They too fought the Japanese', p. 26.
48 L. Anders, *Gentle Knight: The Life and Times of Major General Erwin Forrest Harding*, Kent State University Press, Kent, OH, 1985, p. 255.
49 Ibid., p. 26.
50 Allchin, *Purple and Blue*, p. 313.
51 Anders, *Gentle Knight*, p. 250.
52 'Journal of the 1st Battalion of the 128th Infantry Regiment', 126th Infantry, US Army Unit Records 1917–1950, Dwight D. Eisenhower Presidential Library Archives, Abilene, KS.
53 'History of the Buna Campaign'.
54 Ibid.
55 US Army Field Manual 100-5 Operations, p. 19.
56 Dexter, *The New Guinea Offensives*, p. 488.
57 'History of the Buna Campaign'.
58 'Tactical History of 127th Infantry Combat Team during the Papuan Campaign, Buna Area, New Guinea', 127th Infantry, US Army Unit Records 1917–1950, Dwight D. Eisenhower Presidential Library Archives, Abilene, KS.
59 Ibid.
60 'History of the Buna Campaign'.
61 Dexter, *The New Guinea Offensives*, p. 454.
62 'Report on Operations 18th Australian Infantry Brigade'.
63 Ibid.
64 Ibid.
65 'Report on Operations 18th Australian Infantry Brigade'.
66 Ibid.
67 Ibid.
68 Gailey, *MacArthur Strikes Back*, pp. 201–5.
69 McCarthy, *Kokoda to Wau*, p. 456.
70 Ibid., p. 456.
71 Ibid., p. 456.
72 Milner, *Victory in Papua*, p. 264.
73 Allchin, *Purple and Blue*, p. 282.
74 Ibid., p. 320.
75 The after-action reports of the 3rd Marine Division's operations in Bougainville in 1943 emphasised the necessity of amphibious and long-range reconnaissance in the island operations of the South Pacific. The 3rd Marine Division recommended that mechanised units be reorganised into ground reconnaissance units assigned to headquarters Intelligence Sections. *Operations in the Bougainville Campaign, 1 November–28 December 1943*, 3rd Marine Division, 1943.
76 'History of the Buna Campaign'.
77 'Tactical History of 127th Infantry Combat Team during the Papuan Campaign, Buna Area, New Guinea', 127th Infantry, US Army Unit Records

1917–1950, Dwight D. Eisenhower Presidential Library Archives, Abilene, KS.
78 'History of the Buna Campaign'.
79 Milner, *Victory in Papua*, pp. 278–9.
80 Ibid., pp. 278–9.
81 Ibid., pp. 306–8.
82 Ibid., pp. 306–8.
83 Ibid., p. 309.
84 Ibid., p. 322.
85 Knight, 'Report of Military Observer'.
86 H.F. Handy, 'Report of Military Observer in Southwest Pacific Theater of Operations, September 26 to December 23, 1942', Record Group 165 Entry, Military Intelligence Division, 1922–1944, Box 128, file 6140, US National Archives, Washington, DC.
87 Knight, 'Report of Military Observer'.
88 Milner, *Victory in Papua*, p. 332.
89 Eichelberger, *Our Jungle Road*, pp. 59–60.
90 Dexter, *The New Guinea Offensives*, p. 519.
91 '18th Australian Infantry Brigade Group Operations Order Number 3', December 1942 Appendices, AWM 52 8/2/18.
92 Ibid., p. 515.
93 'Report on the Visit to Headquarters 163rd US Regiment, 12 January 1943', January 1943, AWM 52 8/2/18.
94 Dexter, *The New Guinea Offensives*, p. 514.
95 '18th Australian Infantry Brigade Group Operations Order Number 3', December 1942 Appendices, AWM 52 8/2/18.
96 'Report on the Visit to Headquarters 163rd US Regiment, 12 January 1943', January 1943, AWM 52 8/2/18.
97 Ibid.
98 Milner, *Victory in Papua*, p. 345.
99 Dexter, *The New Guinea Offensives*, p. 514.
100 Milner, *Victory in Papua*, pp. 348–9.
101 F.B. Catanzaro, *With the 41st Division in the Southwest Pacific: A Foot Soldier's Story*, Indiana University Press, Indianapolis, 2002, p. 29.
102 Eichelberger, *Our Jungle Road*, p. 6.
103 Dexter, *The New Guinea Offensives*, p. 526.
104 Eichelberger, *Our Jungle Road*, pp. 59–60.
105 F. Hartley, *Sanananda Interlude: The 7th Australian Division Cavalry Regiment*, Specialty Press, Melbourne, 1949, p. 69.
106 Ibid., p. 69.
107 Interview, Curtis, p. 80.
108 Allchin, *Purple and Blue*, p. 319.
109 '126th US Infantry Regiment Operations Order (Handwritten)', January 1943 AWM 52 8/2/18.
110 Ibid.
111 '126th US Infantry Regiment Intelligence Report January 21, 1942', January 1943, AWM 52 8/2/18.

112 'Diary of Suganuna: Translation of Documents Captured by Warren Force 19 December 1942', December 1942, AWM 52 8/2/18.
113 *Report of the Commanding General Buna Forces on the Buna Campaign*, December 1, 1942–January 25, 1943, Ike Skelton Combined Arms Research Library, US Army Command and General Staff College, Fort Leavenworth, KS.
114 'Report on Operations 18th Australian Infantry Brigade'.
115 Ibid.
116 Ibid.
117 Ibid.
118 Ibid.
119 D. Marston, 'Learning and adapting for jungle warfare, 1942–45: The Australian and British Indian Armies', p. 131, in P. Dean (ed.), *Australia 1944–45: Victory in the Pacific*, Cambridge University Press, Melbourne, 2016.
120 Ibid.
121 Ibid.
122 'Translated extracts from Japanese Diaries captured by 128 Regiment', AWM 52 8/2/18.
123 'Report on Operations 18th Australian Infantry Brigade'.
124 'Diary of Suganuna: Translation of Documents Captured by Warren Force 19 December 1942', December 1942, AWM 52 8/2/18.
125 'Report on Operations 18th Australian Infantry Brigade'.
126 Milner, *Victory in Papua*, p. 346.
127 'Report on Operations 18th Australian Infantry Brigade'.
128 Ibid.
129 Ibid.
130 '18th Infantry Brigade Intelligence Log January 22, 1943', December 1942, AWM 52 8/2/18.
131 Young, 'They too fought the Japanese', p. 13.
132 Allchin, *Purple and Blue*, p. 338.
133 Eichelberger, *Our Jungle Road*, p. 57.
134 Heller and Stofft, *America's First Battles*, p. 225.
135 Eichelberger, *Our Jungle Road*, p. 34.

## Chapter 5: Rebuilding the 18th Infantry Brigade

1 Graeme-Evans, 'Pacific Battle of the Somme', pp. 67–70.
2 Coates, *Bravery Above Blunder*, p. 48.
3 '18th Infantry Brigade, Combat Efficiency Report, 14 April 1943', April–May 1943, AWM 52 8/2/18.
4 '18th Australian Infantry Brigade Training Instruction Number 27, April 1943', April–May 1943, AWM 52 8/2/18.
5 In 1942, the 18th Infantry Brigade conducted a company-sized amphibious raid on Normanby Island and a battalion-sized seizure of Goodenough Island. The term 'combined operations' is often a source of some confusion in Allied records owing to the British use of the term to mean joint naval and army actions and amphibious warfare. The formal Allied definition of 'combined' was a multinational operation, as agreed upon at the Arcadia Conference

1941. '18th Australian Infantry Brigade Training Instruction Number 27, April 1943', April–May 1943, AWM 52 8/2/18.
6   'War Diary, 18th Australian Infantry Brigade, May 1943', April–May 1943, AWM 52 8/2/18.
7   Ibid.
8   The 18th Infantry Brigade sailed from Australia on 5 May 1940. After arriving in England, the soldiers of the 18th Brigade served as courtesy and security patrols in London during the Battle of Britain before departing for service in North Africa.
9   The anniversary barbeque was also attended by the 7th Division Commander, General Vasey, as well as the division's other two brigade commanders, Brigadier Dougherty (21st Brigade) and Brigadier Eather (25th Brigade).
10  'Training Instruction Number 28, 18th Infantry Brigade, 5 May 1942', April–May 1943, AWM 52 2/8/18.
11  'Development of the Training Organisation 1942–1945', LHQ Tactical School, AWM 54 881/1/4 part 2.
12  Ibid.
13  Ibid.
14  Ibid.
15  'War Diary, 18th Australian Infantry Brigade', June–July 1943, AWM 52 8/2/18.
16  Ibid.
17  'Review of Composition and Organisation of Jungle Formations, Australian Military Forces, 24 March 1944', AWM 54 422/7/8.
18  'War Diary, 18th Infantry Brigade, June 1943', June–July 1943, AWM 52 8/2/18.
19  'Report on Operations 18th Australian Infantry Brigade'.
20  'War Diary, 18th Australian Infantry Brigade', June–July 1943, AWM 52 8/2/18.
21  Ibid.
22  '18th Australian Infantry Brigade Training Instruction Number 19, 6 July–28 August 1943', June–July 1943, AWM 52 8/2/18.
23  Weekly training schedules for the 18th Brigade Headquarters, subordinate battalions, and companies are available in '18th Australian Infantry Brigade Training Instruction Number 19, 6 July–28 August 1943', June–July 1943, AWM 52 8/2/18.
24  'War Diary, 18th Australian Infantry Brigade', June–July 1943, AWM 52 8/2/18.
25  Ibid.
26  Ibid.
27  'Training with Tanks, 01 July 1943', June–July 1943, AWM 52 8/2/18.
28  The US M3 medium sized tank was a used throughout the SWPA. 'Grant' was a reference to US President Ulysses S. Grant, and a name given to the British model, which had a different turret design from the US version.
29  'War Diary, 18th Australian Infantry Brigade', June–July 1943, AWM 52 8/2/18.
30  Allchin, *Purple and Blue*, p. 341.
31  'War Diary, 18th Australian Infantry Brigade', June–July 1943, AWM 52 8/2/18.
32  Ibid.

33 Ibid.
34 'History of the Buna Campaign'.
35 Allchin, *Purple and Blue*, p. 265; 'Notes on Air Movement and Enplaning, 14 October 1942', October 1942, AWM 52 8/2/18.
36 'Exercise Battle-Axe, 24 July 1943', June–July 1943, AWM 52 8/2/18.
37 Ibid.
38 'Training Instruction Number 28, 5 May 1942', April–May 1943, AWM 52 2/8/18.
39 'Exercise Battleaxe, Appendix C, 24 July 1943', June–July 1943, AWM 52 8/2/18.
40 Ibid.
41 'American Parachute Platoon Combat Practice', 29 October 1943, October–November 1943, AWM 52 8/2/18.
42 Ibid.
43 'War Diary, 18th Australian Infantry Brigade', August–September 1943, AWM 52 8/2/18.
44 '18th Australian Infantry Brigade Training Instruction Number 19', 6 July–28 August 1943, June–July 1943, AWM 52 8/2/18.
45 For example, the 18th Brigade's stores of 3-inch mortars and Vickers machine guns were largely unserviceable, and 20 per cent of the Bren tripods were damaged or were not the correct adapters for anti-aircraft systems. 'War Diary, 18th Australian Infantry Brigade', August–September 1943, AWM 52 8/2/18.
46 'War Diary, 18th Australian Infantry Brigade', August–September 1943, AWM 52 8/2/18.
47 'War Diary, 18th Australian Infantry Brigade, May 1943', April–May 1943, AWM 52 8/2/18.
48 The brigade major, Major Oliver Jackson, would later serve several tours in Vietnam, including one as commander of the 1st Australian Task Force. 'War Diary, 18th Australian Infantry Brigade April 1943', April–May 1943, AWM 52 8/2/18.
49 'Suggested Scale for Battalion Transport, 02 May 1943', April–May 1943, AWM 52 8/2/18.
50 'Training Instruction Number 28, 5 May 1942', April–May 1943, AWM 52 2/8/18.
51 Ibid.
52 Ibid.
53 'Australian Training Centre, Jungle Warfare, Canungra, Training Syllabus, Precis & Instructions', AWM 419/99/2, 3 DRL 6599, Papers of Lieutenant Colonel P.D.S. Starr.
54 'Jungle Warfare Extracts 1943', AWM 54 923/1/5.
55 'War Diary, 18th Australian Infantry Brigade', June–July 1943, AWM 52 8/2/18.
56 'Subject: Junior Leaders Course, 23 October 1943', October–November 1943, AWM 52 8/2/18.
57 'Staff Course, 18th Infantry Brigade', December 1943, AWM 52 8/2/18.
58 'Report on Operations 18th Australian Infantry Brigade', p. 193.
59 'War Diary, 18th Infantry Brigade, 1 December 1943', December 1943, AWM 52 8/2/18.

60 Ibid.
61 '18th Brigade Intelligence School Syllabi', December 1943, AWM 52 8/2/18.
62 'War Diary, 18th Infantry Brigade, 1 December 1943', December 1943, AWM 52 8/2/18.
63 'War Diary, 18th Australian Infantry Brigade', April–June 1944, AWM 52 8/2/18.
64 '18th Brigade Intelligence School, Nominal Roll of Students, 4 December 1943', December 1943, AWM 52 8/2/18.
65 'War Diary, 18th Australian Infantry Brigade', June–July 1943, AWM 52 8/2/18.
66 Ibid.
67 'War Diary, 18th Australian Infantry Brigade', August–September 1943, AWM 52 8/2/18.

## Chapter 6: The Battle of Shaggy Ridge

1 'War Diary, 18th Australian Infantry Brigade', August–September 1943, AWM 52 8/2/18.
2 P. Dean (ed.), *Australia 1943: The Liberation of New Guinea*, Cambridge University Press, New York, 2014, p. 213.
3 The amphibious landing at Lae is discussed in chapter 7.
4 Dean, *Australia 1943*, pp. 61–2.
5 Ibid., p. 211.
6 Ibid., p. 134.
7 Ibid., p. 248.
8 'War Diary, 18th Australian Infantry Brigade', January–February 1944, AWM 52 8/2/18.
9 P. Bradley, *On Shaggy Ridge: The Australian Seventh Division in the Ramu Valley Campaign: From Kaiapit to the Finisterre Ranges*, Oxford University Press, Melbourne, 2001, p. 187.
10 The 18th Brigade's amphibious seizure of Goodenough Island is discussed in chapter 7.
11 Dexter, *The New Guinea Offensives*, p. 187.
12 Bradley, *On Shaggy Ridge*, p. 10.
13 '18 Australian Infantry Brigade Report on Operations Cutthroat', 28 March 1944, Appendices 1944, Part 1 of 2, AWM 52 8/2/18; Allchin, *Purple and Blue*, p. 343.
14 Allchin, *Purple and Blue*, p. 343.
15 Bradley, *On Shaggy Ridge*, p. 184.
16 Eichelberger, *Our Jungle Road*, p. 35.
17 Dexter, *The New Guinea Offensives*, p. 739.
18 Bradley, *On Shaggy Ridge*, p. 184.
19 '18 Australian Infantry Brigade Report on Operations Cutthroat', 28 March 1944, Appendices 1944, Part 1 of 2, AWM 52 8/2/18.
20 Dean, *Australia 1943*, p. 244.
21 Interview, Frank McLean, Corporal, 2/27th Battalion, Keith Murdoch Sound Archive of Australia in the War of 1939–1945, No. S00905, 8 March 1990.
22 Bradley, *On Shaggy Ridge*, p. 195.
23 Dexter, *The New Guinea Offensives*, p. 743.

24 Interview, Frank McLean, Corporal, 2/27th Battalion.
25 Australian War Memorial & Australian Army, *Jungle Warfare: With the Australian Army in the South-West Pacific*, Australian War Memorial for the Australian Military Forces, Canberra, 1944, p. 115.
26 '18 Australian Infantry Brigade Operational Instruction Number 20', 14 January 1944, Appendices 1944, Part 1 of 2, AWM 52 8/2/18.
27 '18th Australian Infantry Brigade Intelligence Summary Number 12', 15 January 1944, January–February 1944, AWM 52 8/2/18.
28 Milner, *Victory in Papua*, p. 139.
29 'War Diary, 18th Australian Infantry Brigade', January–February 1944, AWM 52 8/2/18.
30 Bradley, *On Shaggy Ridge*, p. 184.
31 Dexter, *The New Guinea Offensives*, p. 742.
32 '18 Australian Infantry Brigade Report on Operations Cutthroat', Annex 4, 28 March 1944, Appendices 1944, Part 1 of 2, AWM 52 8/2/18.
33 Dexter, *The New Guinea Offensives*, p. 742.
34 '18 Australian Infantry Brigade Report on Operations Cutthroat', Annex 4, 28 March 1944, Appendices 1944, Part 1 of 2, AWM 52 8/2/18.
35 'War Diary, 18th Australian Infantry Brigade', January–February 1944, AWM 52 8/2/18.
36 Ibid.
37 '18 Australian Infantry Brigade Operational Instruction Number 21', 14 January 1944, Appendices 1944, Part 1 of 2, AWM 52 8/2/18.
38 '18th Australian Infantry Brigade Intelligence Summary 42', 14 February 1944, January–February 1944, AWM 52 8/2/18.
39 'War Diary, 18th Australian Infantry Brigade', January–February 1944, AWM 52 8/2/18.
40 Ibid.
41 Ibid.
42 Ibid.
43 Ibid.
44 'Lessons Learnt in Cape Edaiadre – Giropa Point and Sanananda Area Operations December 1942 and January 1943, and Recommendations Arising Therefrom', January 1943, AWM 52 8/2/18.
45 Prothero, named after an Australian soldier who had accidently drowned in the Wau operations in July 1943, was one of the primary objectives for Operation Cutthroat. Bradley, *On Shaggy Ridge*, p. 185.
46 'War Diary, 18th Australian Infantry Brigade', January–February 1944, AWM 52 8/2/18.
47 Ibid.
48 'War Diary, 18th Australian Infantry Brigade', January–February 1944, AWM 52 8/2/18.
49 *Reconquest: An Official Record of the Australian Army's Successes in the Offensives Against Lae, Finschhafen, Markham and Ramu Valleys, Huon Peninsula, Finisterre Mountains, Rai Coast, Bogadjim, Madang, Alexishafen, Karkar Islands, Hansa Bay, September 1943–June 1944*, Director General of Public Relations, Melbourne, 1944, p. 133.

50 Bradley, *On Shaggy Ridge*, pp. 206–7.
51 *Reconquest*, p. 118.
52 Gailey, *MacArthur's Victory*, p. 140.
53 'War Diary, 18th Australian Infantry Brigade', January–February 1944, AWM 52 8/2/18.
54 Ibid.
55 '18 Australian Infantry Brigade Operational Instruction Number 21', 14 January 1944, Appendices 1944, Part 1 of 2, AWM 52 8/2/18.
56 Dexter, *The New Guinea Offensives*, p. 743.
57 '18 Australian Infantry Brigade Operational Instruction Number 19', 14 January 1944, Appendices 1944, Part 1 of 2, AWM 52 8/2/18.
58 *Reconquest*, pp. 137–8.
59 Dexter, *The New Guinea Offensives*, p. 744.
60 Ibid., pp. 454–7.
61 '18 Australian Infantry Brigade Report on Operations Cutthroat', 28 March 1944, Appendices 1944, Part 1 of 2, AWM 52 8/2/18.
62 'War Diary, 18th Australian Infantry Brigade', January–February 1944, AWM 52 8/2/18.
63 'War Diary, 18th Australian Infantry Brigade', March 1944, AWM 52 8/2/18.
64 '18 Australian Infantry Brigade Report on Operations Cutthroat', 28 March 1944, Appendices 1944, Part 1 of 2, AWM 52 8/2/18.
65 Ibid.
66 '18 Australian Infantry Brigade Report on Operations Cutthroat', 28 March 1944, Appendices 1944, Part 1 of 2, AWM 52 8/2/18.
67 Ibid.
68 Ibid.
69 'War Diary, 18th Australian Infantry Brigade', June–July 1943, AWM 52 8/2/18.
70 '18 Australian Infantry Brigade Operational Instruction Number 21', 14 January 1944, Appendices 1944, Part 1 of 2, AWM 52 8/2/18.
71 'Appendix C to Report on Operation Cutthroat, Artillery', Appendices 1944, Part 1 of 2, AWM 52 8/2/18.
72 Ibid.
73 Ibid.
74 Ibid.
75 Ibid.
76 *Reconquest*, p. 141.
77 Mansoor, *The GI Offensive in Europe*, p. 135.
78 *US Army Field Manual 1-5 Employment of Aviation of the Army*, United States Government Printing Office, Washington, DC, 15 April 1940.
79 *US Army Field Manual 100-20 Command and Employment of Air Power*, United States Government Printing Office, Washington, DC, 21 July 1943.
80 '18 Australian Infantry Brigade Report on Operations Cutthroat', Annex D, 28 March 1944, Appendices 1944, Part 1 of 2, AWM 52 8/2/18.
81 '18 Australian Infantry Brigade Operational Instruction Number 21', 14 January 1944, Appendices 1944, Part 1 of 2, AWM 52 8/2/18.
82 '18 Australian Infantry Brigade Report on Operations Cutthroat', Annex D, 28 March 1944, Appendices 1944, Part 1 of 2, AWM 52 8/2/18.

NOTES TO PAGES 133-8   239

83 '18 Australian Infantry Brigade Report on Operations Cutthroat', 28 March 1944, Appendices 1944, Part 1 of 2, AWM 52 8/2/18.
84 '18 Australian Infantry Brigade Report on Operations Cutthroat', Annex D, 28 March 1944, Appendices 1944, Part 1 of 2, AWM 52 8/2/18.
85 Ibid.
86 '18 Australian Infantry Brigade Report on Operations Cutthroat', 28 March 1944, Appendices 1944, Part 1 of 2, AWM 52 8/2/18.
87 Ibid.
88 Ibid.
89 'Intelligence Appendix B to Report on Operation Cutthroat', Appendices 1944, Part 1 of 2, AWM 52 8/2/18.
90 '18 Australian Infantry Brigade Report on Operations Cutthroat', 28 March 1944, Appendices 1944, Part 1 of 2, AWM 52 8/2/18.

## Chapter 7: Amphibious warfare doctrine

1 Daniel Barbey, Vice Admiral, US Navy, Commander Seventh Amphibious Force, in US Navy, *Command History, Seventh Amphibious Force, 10 January 1943–23 December 1945*, p. 11.
2 D.E. Painter, 'The army and amphibious warfare', *Military Review*, August 1965, p. 37.
3 Ibid., p. 38.
4 Brunei Bay landing has not been examined as a case study owing to the focus on the 18th Brigade, which was at Balikpapan. The 20th Brigade's landing at Finschhafen was conducted with only two battalions and therefore outside the scope of this study. A 'major' landing is defined in amphibious doctrine as the landing of a US regimental combat team (its equivalent being the Australian infantry brigade group) or larger force on a hostile foreign shore.
5 P. Dean, 'To the jungle shore: Australia and amphibious warfare in the SWPA 1942–45', *Global War Studies*, vol. 11, no. 2, 2014, p. 67.
6 Ibid., p. 74.
7 I. Speller, 'In the shadow of Gallipoli? Amphibious warfare in the inter-war period', Gallipoli – Making History Symposium, Menzies Centre for Australian Studies, London, 2001, p. 4.
8 Ibid., p. 5.
9 Ibid., p. 6.
10 Dean, 'To the jungle shore', p. 71.
11 D.C. Emmel, 'The development of amphibious doctrine', Master of Military Art and Science thesis, US Army Command and General Staff College, Fort Leavenworth, KS, 2010, p. 37.
12 'Training in Use of Assault and Recce Boats, 29 March 1942', 18th Infantry Brigade, AWM 52 8/2/18.
13 Allchin, *Purple and Blue*, p. 263.
14 '18th Australian Infantry Brigade Instruction Number 17, 20 September 1942', September–October 1942, Part 1, AWM 52 8/2/18.
15 Ibid.

16 'Normanby Island Operations, 21–23 September 1942, 18th Infantry Brigade', 27 September 1942, September–October 1942, Part 1, AWM 52 8/2/18.
17 'Air Operations Order, Number 9 Operational Group, RAAF, 21 September 1942', September–October 1942, Part 1, AWM 52 8/2/18.
18 'Normanby Island Operations, 21–23 September 1942, 18th Infantry Brigade', 27 September 1942, September–October 1942, Part 1, AWM 52 8/2/18.
19 'Milne Force Operations Order Number 1, 20 October 1942', October 1942, AWM 52 8/2/18.
20 'Intelligence Diary', 11 September 1942, Appendices Part 2, AWM 52 8/2/18.
21 'Milne Force Operations Order Number 1, 20 October 1942', October 1942, AWM 52 8/2/18.
22 *Possible Aerodrome Sites – Goodenough Island*, Appendix B: 'Milne Force Operation Instruction Number 12, 20 October 1942', October 1942, AWM 52 8/2/18.
23 'Milne Force Operations Order Number 1, 20 October 1942', October 1942, AWM 52 8/2/18.
24 '18 Australian Infantry Brigade Summary Number 10, Annex A', September–October 1942, Part 2 of 2, AWM 8/2/18.
25 C. Field, 'Testing the tenets of manoeuvre: Australia's first amphibious assault since Gallipoli, the 9th Australian Division at Lae, 4–16 September 1943', Land Warfare Studies Centre, Working Paper 139, January 2012, p. 24.
26 Letter, Brigadier Chilton to Gavin Long, 23 October 1957, Papers of Brigadier General F.O. Chilton, AMW 93 50/2/23/322 [hereafter Chilton papers].
27 'Notes on Exercise Coconut', August 1943, AWM 52 8/2/20.
28 'Commander Allied Land Forces, Report on New Guinea Operations, 4 September 1943 to 26 April 1944', AWM 54 519/6/58.
29 Ibid.
30 Coates, *Bravery Above Blunder*, p. 67.
31 'Commander Allied Land Forces, Report on New Guinea Operations, 4 September 1943 to 26 April 1944', AWM 54 519/6/58.
32 'War Diary', 20th Australian Infantry Brigade, August 1943, AWM 52 8/2/20.
33 Ibid.
34 Ibid.
35 Ibid.
36 'Notes on Exercise Coconut', August 1943, AWM 52 8/2/20.
37 'War Diary', 20th Australian Infantry Brigade, August 1943, AWM 52 8/2/20.
38 Ibid.
39 'Notes on Exercise Coconut', August 1943, AWM 52 8/2/20.
40 Ibid.
41 Ibid.
42 '20th Australian Infantry Brigade Group, Operations Order Number 2, 24 August 1943', AWM 52 8/2/20.
43 'Extract of Diary of Captain Harold Hamilton, 2/3rd Pioneer Battalion, AIF World War 1939–45', PR83/168 AWM 419/43/27.
44 '20th Australian Infantry Brigade Group, Operations Order Number 2, 24 August 1943', AWM 52 8/2/20.

45 Ibid.
46 '20th Australian Infantry Brigade Group, Operations Order Number 4, POSTERN', 20th Infantry Brigade, September 1943, AWM 52 8/2/20.
47 Ibid.
48 Dexter, *The New Guinea Offensives*, pp. 326–46.
49 '20th Australian Infantry Brigade Group, Operations Order Number 4, POSTERN', 20th Infantry Brigade, September 1943, AWM 52 8/2/20.
50 Extract of Diary of Captain Harold Hamilton, 2/3rd Pioneer Battalion, AIF World War 1939–45, AWM PR83/168 419/43/27.
51 Ibid.
52 Ibid.
53 'Commander Allied Land Forces, Report on New Guinea Operations, 4 September 1943 to 26 April 1944', AWM 54 519/6/58.
54 Dexter, *The New Guinea Offensives*, p. 390.
55 Ibid., p. 392.
56 D. Horner, 'The military strategy and command aspects of the Australian Army amphibious operations in the South-West Pacific Area', in *Australian Army Amphibious Operations in the South-West Pacific, 1942–45*, Proceedings of the Australian Army History Conference, ed. G. Wahlert, Canberra, 15 November 1994, p. 42.
57 Dexter, *The New Guinea Offensives*, pp. 72–3.
58 Ibid., p. 381.
59 'Notes from Conference, 7th Division Headquarters', 23 June 1944, April–July 1944, AWM 52 8/2/18.
60 'War Diary, 18th Australian Infantry Brigade, July 1944', April–July 1944, AWM 52 8/2/18.
61 Allchin, *Purple and Blue*, p. 356.
62 '18th Australian Infantry Brigade Training Instruction Number 1, Planning and Amphibious Training', October 1944, AWM 52 8/2/18.
63 E.N. Prowd, 'HMAS "ASSAULT" combined operations, Port Stephens, New South Wales', Papers of Major General C.A. Clowes, AWM 419/02/10 3 DRL 4143.
64 Ibid.
65 P. Dean, 'Amphibious warfare: Lessons from the past for ADF's future', *Security Challenges*, Vol. 8, No. 1, 2012, p. 65.
66 Ibid.
67 Ibid.
68 'Notes on Training of an Amphibious Division', Headquarters, 9th Infantry Division, Fort Bragg, NC, 30 October 1942.
69 Arnold, 'Preparation for a Division Amphibious Operation', p. 3.
70 D.L. Bjork, 'Waterborne envelopments', *Military Review*, Vol. XXX, February 1951.
71 Arnold, 'Preparation for a Division Amphibious Operation', p. 4.
72 'Notes on Training of an Amphibious Division', Headquarters, 9th Infantry Division, Fort Bragg, NC, 30 October 1942, Ike Skelton Combined Arms Research Library, US Army Command and General Staff College, Fort Leavenworth, KS.

73 Horner, 'The military strategy and command aspects of the Australian Army amphibious operations in the South-West Pacific Area', p. 35; P. Stanley, 'The Green Hole: Exploring our neglect of the New Guinea campaigns of 1943–44', *Sabretache*, Vol. 34, No. 2, 1993, p. 6.
74 Emmel, 'The development of amphibious doctrine', p. 25.
75 Ibid., p. 25.
76 Landing Force Manual, US Navy, Washington, DC, 1927.
77 V.H. Krulak, *First to Fight: An Inside View of the United States Marine Corps*, Naval Institute Press, Annapolis, MD, 1984, p. 81.
78 *Combined Operations: Planning on the Brigade and Unit Levels*.
79 Ibid.
80 '18th Australian Infantry Brigade Planning Timetable for Amphibious Exercise', October 1944, AWM 52 8/2/18.
81 *Combined Operations: Planning on the Brigade and Unit Levels*.
82 Barbey, *MacArthur's Amphibious Navy*, p. 36.
83 Dean, 'Amphibious warfare', p. 69.
84 *Combined Operations: Planning on the Brigade and Unit Levels*.
85 Ibid.

## Chapter 8: Amphibious exercises and rehearsals

1 'War Diary, 18th Australian Infantry Brigade', October 1944, AWM 52 8/2/18.
2 'Staff and Logistic Tables for Amphibious Training Period', October 1944, AWM 52 8/2/18.
3 'War Diary, 18th Australian Infantry Brigade, November 1944', AWM 52 8/2/18.
4 Emmel, 'The development of amphibious doctrine', p. 44.
5 Ibid., p. 66.
6 Landing Craft, Vehicle, Personnel (LCVP) or Higgins boat.
7 '18th Australian Infantry Brigade Outline Plan – Operation Seagull', March 1945, AWM 52 8/2/18.
8 Emmel, 'The development of amphibious doctrine', p. 77.
9 *Combined Operations: Planning on the Brigade and Unit Levels*.
10 Ibid.
11 '18th Australian Infantry Brigade Planning Timetable for Amphibious Exercise', October 1944, AWM 52 8/2/18.
12 Interview, Alec Arthur Little, Private, 2/27th Battalion, Keith Murdoch Sound Archive of Australia in the War of 1939–1945, No. S00927, 27 March 1990.
13 C. von Clausewitz, trans. M.E. Howard & P. Paret, *On War*, Princeton University Press, Princeton, NJ, 1989, p. 119.
14 'Ship Side Training Program', November 1944, AWM 52 8/2/18.
15 'The LCI (L), Operational Instructions for LCI', Amphibious Training Center, 16 August 1943, Army Unit Records 1917–1950, Dwight D. Eisenhower Presidential Library Archives, Abilene, KS.

16 'History of the 127th Infantry Regiment, Buna Campaign, 16 November 1943 to 1 February 1943', Army Unit Records 1917–1950, Dwight D. Eisenhower Presidential Library Archives, Abilene, KS.
17 'War Diary, 18th Australian Infantry Brigade', January–February 1945, AWM 52 8/2/18.
18 Field, 'Testing the tenets of manoeuvre'.
19 Ibid.
20 '18th Australian Infantry Brigade Training Instruction Number 22', November 1944, AWM 52 8/2/18.
21 'Ship Side Training Program', November 1944, AWM 52 8/2/18.
22 '18 Australian Brigade Embarkation Instruction Number 1', November 1944, AWM 52 8/2/18.
23 '18th Australian Infantry Brigade Training Instruction Number 22', November 1944, AWM 52 8/2/18.
24 'Training Syllabus, Appendix A, 18 Australian Infantry Brigade Training Instruction Number 22', November 1944, AWM 52 8/2/18.
25 '18 Australian Brigade Embarkation Instruction Number 1', November 1944, AWM 52 8/2/18.
26 'Exercise Octopus, Outline Plan of Commander 18th Australian Infantry Brigade', October 1944, AWM 52 8/2/18.
27 '18th Australian Infantry Brigade Training Instruction Number 22', November 1944, AWM 52 8/2/18.
28 Ibid.
29 'Exercise Octopus, Outline Plan of Commander 18th Australian Infantry Brigade', October 1944, AWM 52 8/2/18.
30 Ibid.
31 '18th Australian Infantry Brigade Operations Order Number 1, Exercise Octopus', 7 November 1944, AWM 52 8/2/18.
32 Dexter, *The New Guinea Offensives*, p. 381.
33 '18th Australian Infantry Brigade Operations Order Number 1, Exercise Octopus, November 7, 1944', AWM 52 8/2/18.
34 'War Diary, 18th Australian Infantry Brigade, November 1944', AWM 52 8/2/18.
35 'War Diary, 18th Australian Infantry Brigade', January–February 1945, AWM 52 8/2/18.
36 'War Diary, 18th Australian Infantry Brigade', March 1945, AWM 52 8/2/18.
37 '18 Australian Infantry Brigade Operation Order Number 1, Operation Seagull', March 1945, AWM 52 8/2/18.
38 '18th Australian Infantry Brigade Outline Plan – Operation Seagull', March 1945, AWM 52 8/2/18.
39 Ibid.
40 Ibid.
41 'War Diary, 18th Australian Infantry Brigade', January–February 1945, AWM 52 8/2/18.
42 '18th Australian Infantry Brigade Outline Plan – Operation Seagull', March 1945, AWM 52 8/2/18.
43 '18th Australian Infantry Brigade Operation Order Number 1, Operation Seagull', March 1945, AWM 52 8/2/18.

44 Ibid.
45 Ibid.
46 Ibid.
47 Ibid.
48 Ibid.
49 Letter, Brigadier Chilton to Gavin Long, 23 October 1957.
50 'Embarkation Procedures on the Brigade Level – OBOE Two', April–June 1945, AWM 52 8/2/18.
51 Ibid.
52 'Deficiencies of Warlike Stores on Embarkation for OBOE Two', April–June 1945, AWM 52 8/2/18.
53 'Appendix S, Sequence of Planning Concentration and Embarkation, Operations OBOE TWO', April–June 1945, AWM 52 8/2/18.
54 Ibid.
55 'Appendix X, Subject: Ammunition, Headquarters 7 Australian Division', April–June 1945, AWM 52 8/2/18.
56 'Appendix S, Sequence of Planning Concentration and Embarkation, Operations OBOE TWO', April–June 1945, AWM 52 8/2/18.
57 Ibid.
58 Ibid.
59 Long, *The Final Campaigns*, p. 510.
60 'Appendix S, Sequence of Planning Concentration and Embarkation, Operations OBOE TWO', April–June 1945, AWM 52 8/2/18.
61 Ibid.
62 D. Coombes, *Morshead: Hero of Tobruk and El Alamein*, Oxford University Press, South Melbourne, Vic, 2001, p. 202.
63 'Rehearsal Order, CTG 78.2Operations Plan Number 6-45', 7th Amphibious Force, Commander OBOE Two Attack Group, 20 June 1945, Papers of Lieutenant General F.H. Berryman, PR84/370 AWM 419/9/9.
64 Ibid.
65 Ibid.
66 Ibid.
67 Allchin, *Purple and Blue*, p. 368.
68 Long, *The Final Campaigns*, p. 511.

## Chapter 9: *The assault brigade*

1 F. Chilton, 'Notes on Chapter 21, The Seizure of Balikpapan 1957', Papers of Brigadier General F.O. Chilton, AWM 93 50/2/23/322 [hereafter Chilton papers].
2 Letter, Brigadier Chilton to Gavin Long, 23 October 1957.
3 US Navy, *Command History, Seventh Amphibious Force, 10 January 1943–23 December 1945*, pp. 11–53.
4 Long, *The Final Campaigns*, p. 503.
5 'Appendix S, Sequence of Planning Concentration and Embarkation, Operations OBOE TWO', April–June 1945, AWM 52 8/2/18.
6 Long, *The Final Campaigns*, p. 49.
7 Ibid., p. 49.

8 OBOE ONE, 9 Australian Division Operations Order One, 12 April 1945.
9 Ibid.
10 C. Hunter, interview with James Cronk, 'I didn't think it would be like this', AWM Memorial Articles, 29 January 2020.
11 Coombes, *Morshead*, p. 199.
12 P. Stanley, *Tarakan: An Australian Tragedy*, Allen & Unwin, Sydney, 1997, p. 14.
13 'OBOE Two Operation: Desirability of Cancellation', 21 May 1945, Papers of Lieutenant General Sir F.H. Berryman, AMW PR 84/370 419/9/9.
14 Long, *The Final Campaigns*, p. 507.
15 Ibid., p. 506.
16 'Appendix S, Sequence of Planning Concentration and Embarkation, Operations OBOE TWO', April–June 1945, AWM 52 8/2/18.
17 Chilton, 'Notes on Chapter 21, The Seizure of Balikpapan 1957'.
18 'Appendix S, Sequence of Planning Concentration and Embarkation, Operations OBOE TWO', April–June 1945, AWM 52 8/2/18.
19 Allchin, *Purple and Blue*, pp. 366–7.
20 'Appendix S, Sequence of Planning Concentration and Embarkation, Operations OBOE TWO', April–June 1945, AWM 52 8/2/18.
21 '18th Australian Infantry Brigade: Report on Operation OBOE Two', June–August 1945, AWM 52 8/2/18.
22 Ibid.
23 'Appendix S, Sequence of Planning Concentration and Embarkation, Operations OBOE TWO', April–June 1945, AWM 52 8/2/18.
24 Chilton, 'Notes on Chapter 21, The Seizure of Balikpapan 1957'.
25 'Appendix S, Sequence of Planning Concentration and Embarkation, Operations OBOE TWO', April–June 1945, AWM 52 8/2/18.
26 '18th Australian Infantry Brigade: Report on Operation OBOE Two'.
27 'Appendix S, Sequence of Planning Concentration and Embarkation, Operations OBOE TWO', April–June 1945, AWM 52 8/2/18.
28 Ibid.
29 Ibid.
30 Interview, Raymond Gordon Wilson Baldwin, Private, 2/27th Battalion, Keith Murdoch Sound Archive of Australia in the War of 1939–1945, No. S00926, 23 March 1990.
31 Long, *The Final Campaigns*, p. 507.
32 'War Journal 727th Amphibian Tractor Battalion', US Army Unit Records 1917–1950, Dwight D. Eisenhower Presidential Library Archives, Abilene, KS.
33 Ibid.
34 '18th Australian Infantry Brigade Planning Team', June 1945, Appendices, AWM 52 8/2/18.
35 Long, *The Final Campaigns*, p. 510.
36 '18th Australian Infantry Brigade Planning Team', June 1945, Appendices, AWM 52 8/2/18.
37 Chilton, 'Notes on Chapter 21, The Seizure of Balikpapan 1957'.
38 '18th Australian Infantry Brigade Operations Order – OBOE Two', June Appendices 1945, AWM 52 8/2/18.

39 Ibid.
40 Ibid.
41 Ibid.
42 '18th Australian Infantry Brigade Administrative Order – OBOE Two', June Appendices 1945, AWM 52 8/2/18.
43 Allchin, *Purple and Blue*, p. 370.
44 M. Johnston, *Fighting the Enemy: Australian Soldiers and Their Adversaries in World War II*, Cambridge University Press, Melbourne, reprint, 2009, p. 146.
45 Stockings, *Battle of Bardia*, p. 92.
46 '18th Australian Infantry Brigade Operations Order – OBOE Two', June Appendices 1945, AWM 52 8/2/18.
47 Coombes, *Morshead*, p. 207.
48 Interview with Raymond Gordon Wilson Baldwin, 2/27th Battalion.
49 G. Waters, 'OBOE – Air Operations Over Borneo, 1945', Air Power Studies Centre, RAAF Base Fairbairn, Canberra, 1995.
50 '18th Australian Infantry Brigade Operations Order – OBOE Two', June Appendices 1945, AWM 52 8/2/18.
51 Ibid.
52 Ibid.
53 Ibid.
54 Ibid.
55 Ibid.
56 Ibid.
57 Ibid.
58 Ibid.
59 Ibid.
60 Ibid.
61 Ibid.
62 Ibid.
63 Waters, 'OBOE – Air Operations Over Borneo, 1945'.
64 Long, *The Final Campaigns*, p. 505.
65 US Navy, *Command History, Seventh Amphibious Force, 10 January 1943–23 December 1945*, pp. 11–53.
66 Waters, 'OBOE – Air Operations Over Borneo, 1945'.
67 Allchin, *Purple and Blue*, p. 370.
68 '18th Australian Infantry Brigade: Report on Operation OBOE Two'.
69 Ibid.
70 Ibid.
71 Ibid.
72 Ibid.
73 '18th Australian Infantry Brigade Operations Order – OBOE Two', June Appendices 1945, AWM 52 8/2/18.
74 '18th Australian Infantry Brigade: Report on Operation OBOE Two'.
75 Chilton, 'Notes on Chapter 21, The Seizure of Balikpapan 1957'.
76 Long, *The Final Campaigns*, p. 516.
77 '18th Australian Infantry Brigade: Report on Operation OBOE Two'.

78 Ibid.
79 Ibid.
80 Long, *The Final Campaigns*, p. 545.
81 Ibid.
82 Ibid.
83 Johnston, *Fighting the Enemy*, p. 104.
84 '18th Australian Infantry Brigade: Report on Operation OBOE Two'.
85 Ibid.
86 Ibid.
87 Interview, Victor James Geisler, Sergeant, 39th Battalion, Keith Murdoch Sound Archive of Australia in the War of 1939–45, No. S00505, 3 December 1988.
88 '18th Australian Infantry Brigade: Report on Operation OBOE Two'.
89 Ibid.
90 Ibid.
91 Ibid.
92 Long, *The Final Campaigns*, p. 521.
93 '18th Australian Infantry Brigade: Report on Operation OBOE Two'.
94 Ibid.
95 Ibid.
96 Ibid.
97 Ibid.
98 Long, *The Final Campaigns*, p. 406.
99 Ibid., p. 510.
100 Waters, 'OBOE – Air Operations Over Borneo, 1945'.
101 Long, *The Final Campaigns*, p. 509.
102 'War Diary, 2/9th Battalion', 2 July–4 August 1945, AWM 52 8/3/9/43.
103 Chilton, 'Notes on Chapter 21, The Seizure of Balikpapan 1957'.
104 Waters, 'OBOE – Air Operations Over Borneo, 1945'.
105 Long, *The Final Campaigns*, p. 520.
106 '18th Australian Infantry Brigade: Report on Operation OBOE Two'.
107 Ibid.
108 Letter, Brigadier Chilton to Gavin Long, 23 October 1957.

## *Chapter 10: Conclusion*
1 The 33rd and 34th Brigades were formed after the Japanese surrender to serve as occupation forces in the Dutch East Indies and Japan respectively.
2 '18th Australian Infantry Brigade, Training instruction number 2, 24 Jan 1940, December 1939', May 1940, AWM 52 8/2/18.
3 'Directorate of Military Training, Account of Activities: September 3, 1945–August 15, 1945, LHQ Tactical School', AWM 54 881/1/4 Part 2.
4 'Re-organisation of Infantry Formations in the AMF', AWM 54 422/7/8.
5 Graeme-Evans, 'Pacific Battle of the Somme', pp. 67–70.
6 '18th Infantry Brigade, Combat Efficiency Report, 14 April 1943', April–May 1943, AWM 52 8/2/18.

7 'Australian Training Centre, Jungle Warfare, Canungra, Training Syllabus, Precis & Instructions', Papers of Lieutenant Colonel P.D.S. Starr, AWM 419/99/2, 3 DRL 6599.
8 Ibid.
9 Ibid.
10 Ibid.
11 'War Diary, 18th Infantry Brigade, 1 December 1943', December 1943, AWM 52 8/2/18.
12 Ibid.
13 Stockings, *The Battle of Bardia*, p. 29.
14 Ibid.
15 '18 Australian Infantry Brigade Report on Operations Cutthroat', 28 March 1944, Appendices 1944, Part 1 of 2, AWM 52 8/2/18.
16 Horner, 'The military strategy and command aspects of the Australian Army amphibious operations in the South-West Pacific Area', p. 42.
17 Letter, Brigadier Chilton to Gavin Long, 23 October 1957.
18 'Notes on Exercise Coconut', August 1943, AWM 52 8/2/20.
19 'War Diary, 18th Australian Infantry Brigade', October 1944, AWM 52 8/2/18.
20 Coombes, *Morshead*, p. 202.
21 Allchin, *Purple and Blue*, p. 370.
22 Waters, 'OBOE – Air Operations Over Borneo, 1945'.
23 '18th Australian Infantry Brigade Operations Order – OBOE Two', June Appendices 1945, AWM 52 8/2/18.
24 '18th Australian Infantry Brigade: Report on Operation OBOE Two', June–August 1945, AWM 52 8/2/18.
25 Ibid.
26 'Training Instruction Number 28, 5 May 1942', April–May 1943, AWM 52 2/8/18.
27 Mayo, *Bloody Buna*, p. 182.
28 'War Diary, 18th Australian Infantry Brigade', January–February 1944, AWM 52 8/2/18.
29 '18th Australian Infantry Brigade: Report on Operation OBOE Two'.
30 Ibid.
31 'Staff Course, 18th Infantry Brigade', December 1943, AWM 52 8/2/18.
32 'War Diary, 18th Australian Infantry Brigade', June–July 1943, AWM 52 8/2/18.
33 Ibid.
34 Australian War Memorial & Australian Army, *Jungle Warfare*, p. 115.
35 Long, *The Final Campaigns*, p. 406.
36 Ibid., p. 391.
37 'The first man to get a trip home after the surrender was injured that night by a falling bullet after the 2/10th Battalion launched an assortment of flames and tracer fire into the sky. Probably due to a general celebration with three bottles issued per man.' Allchin, *Purple and Blue*, p. 389.
38 Percival, an original member of 2/10th Infantry Battalion since 20 January 1940, left with much ceremony to join the 34th Infantry Brigade as part of the Australian Occupation Force. Ibid., p. 389.
39 Ibid., p. 394.

# BIBLIOGRAPHY

## AUSTRALIAN WAR MEMORIAL
AWM 50 419/99/2, 3 DRL 6599 Papers of Lieutenant Colonel P.D.S. Starr
AWM 52 AIF unit war diaries (1939–45)
AWM 54 Written Records (1939–45 War)
AWM 67 Gavin Long, papers of the Official Historian
AWM 69 Official Histories, 1939–1945 War Series 2, Navy Papers of G.H. Gill
AWM 93 50/2/23/322 Papers of Brigadier General F.O. Chilton
AWM 172 Official History, 1939–45 War, Series 1 (Army), Volume 6: Records of David Dexter
AWM 419/02/10, 3 DRL 4143 Papers of Major General C.A. Clowes
AWM 419/9/9, PR 84/370 Papers of Lieutenant General F.H. Berryman
PR 00560 Papers of Major General G.F. Wootten
PR 3DRL 2632 Papers of Lieutenant General L.J. Morshead
Keith Murdoch Sound Archive:
    Owen Curtis, 2/12th Battalion, Archive Number S541
    Geoffrey Holmes, 2/12th Battalion, Archive Number S540
    Paul Hope, 2/12th Battalion Archive Number S529

## CUSHING MEMORIAL LIBRARY, TEXAS A&M UNIVERSITY
General Walter Krueger Papers, World War, 1939–45, Amphibious Operations

## DUDLEY KNOX LIBRARY, NAVAL POST GRADUATE SCHOOL, MONTEREY, CA
Papers of Admiral Richmond Kelly Turner (US Navy)

## DWIGHT D. EISENHOWER PRESIDENTIAL LIBRARY ARCHIVES, ABILENE, KS, US ARMY UNIT RECORDS 1917–50
32nd Infantry Division, 1940–46, Boxes 878–885
41st Infantry Division, 1943–45, Boxes 960–984
127th Infantry Regiment, Boxes 1345–1347
128th Infantry Regiment, Boxes 1348–1352
163rd Infantry Regiment, 1940–45, Boxes 1404–1406

## IKE SKELTON COMBINED ARMS RESEARCH LIBRARY, US ARMY COMMAND AND GENERAL STAFF COLLEGE, FORT LEAVENWORTH, KS
General Military History Collection
Obsolete Military Manuals Collection
School of Advanced Military Studies (SAMS) Monographs Collection
World War II Operational Documents Collection

## MACARTHUR MEMORIAL LIBRARY, NORFOLK, VA
RG-3 Records of HQ SWPA
South West Pacific Area, Military Intelligence Section, Daily Communiqués
South West Pacific Area, Military Intelligence Section, Special Bulletins

## NATIONAL ARCHIVES OF AUSTRALIA
NAA: A5954, 1208/15, First Report of Lieutenant General Ernest Squires, CB DSO MC, Inspector-General of the Australian Military Forces, 16 December 1938

## NATIONAL LIBRARY OF AUSTRALIA, CANBERRA
MS 1884 Papers of Sir John Monash

## US ARMY CENTER OF MILITARY HISTORY, FORT MCNAIR, WASHINGTON, DC
The US Army in World War II Series

## US MARINE CORPS UNIVERSITY RESEARCH LIBRARY, QUANTICO, VA
Archives Branch, Marine Corps History Division

## US NATIONAL ARCHIVES AND RECORDS ADMINISTRATION, COLLEGE PARK, MD
RG165, Entry 77, File 6140, Box 138
RG165 Records of the War Department General and Special Staffs, Military Intelligence Davison, Regional File 1922–44, Box 138 File 6140
RG338 Records of US Army Forces in the Far East
RG495 Records of GHQ Southwest Pacific Area
RG496 Records of Army Forces Western Pacific

## DOCTRINE
*Australian Military Doctrine, Canberra*
1st Australian Corps Training Instruction Number 2/1944, Combined Operations, Beach Organisation and Maintenance, Headquarters 1st Australian Corps, 24 April 1944
Australian Military Forces, *Soldiering in the Tropics (SW Pacific Area)*, General Staff LHQ issued under the direction, Commander, Allied Land Forces Headquarters, SWPA, 1943

Australian Military Forces, *The Borneo Book for Servicemen*, General Staff and issued under the direction of the Commander-in-Chief (year UNK)
*Infantry Minor Tactics 1941*, Army Headquarters, Melbourne, December 1941
*Infantry Training (Training and War) 1937* (War Office), Reprinted by Australian Government Publishers
*Soldiering in the Tropics* (SW Pacific Area), Land Headquarters, Melbourne, August 1942

## United Kingdom Military Doctrine, London

*Combined Operations Staff Notebook 1945*, Chief of Combined Operations, (BR1293) United Kingdom, September 1945
*Field Service Regulations*, Volume II, Operations – General, 1935, Great Britain, War Office
*Field Service Regulations*, Volume III, Operations – Higher Formations, 1935, Great Britain, War Office

## United States Military Doctrine, Washington, DC

Field Manual 6-5, Field Artillery Organisation and Drill, US Government Printing Office, Washington, DC, 1939
Field Manual 6-20, Field Artillery Tactics and Techniques, US Government Printing Office, Washington, DC, 1941
Field Manual 31-5, Landing Operations on Hostile Shores, US Government Printing Office, Washington, DC, 1941
Field Manual 31-20, Jungle Warfare, US Government Printing Office, Washington, DC, 1941
Field Manual 55-50: Army Water Transport Operations, Washington, DC, Government Printing Office, 1993
Field Manual 100-5 Field Service Regulations (Operations), US Government Printing Office, Washington, DC, 1941
Field Manual 101-5, Staff Officers' Field Manual: The Staff and Combat Orders, US Government Printing Office, Washington, DC, 1940
Field Training Publication 167, Landing Operations Doctrine, Office of Naval Operations Division of Fleet Training, US Government Printing Office, Washington, DC, 1938
Field Training Publication 211, Ship to Shore Movement, General Instructions, US Government Printing Office, Washington, DC, 1943
*Small Wars Manual*, United States Marine Corps, US Government Printing Office, 1940
*US Combined Staff Notebook*, Combined Chief of Operations, September 1945

## PUBLISHED WORKS

Allchin, E.F., *Purple and Blue: The History of the 2/10th Battalion, AIF (The Adelaide Rifles) 1939–1945*, 2/10th Battalion Association, Adelaide, 1958
Anders, L., *Gentle Knight: The Life and Times of Major General Erwin Forrest Harding*, Kent State University Press, Kent, OH, 1985
Anderson, C.R., *Papua, 23 July 1942–23 January 1943*, US Army Center of Military History, Washington, DC, 1994

——*Western Pacific, 15 June 1944–September 1945*, US Army Center of Military History, Washington, DC, 1994

Anderson, N., *To Kokoda*, Australian Army Campaign Series #14, Big Sky Publishing, Sydney, 2011

Ashurst, W., 'A study of naval gun fire-support for infantry in a landing on a hostile shore', Command and General Staff School, Fort Leavenworth, KS, 1934–35

Aston, G.G., *Letters on Amphibious Wars*, John Murray, London, 1910

Australian War Memorial & Australian Army, *Jungle Warfare: With the Australian Army in the South-West Pacific*, Australian War Memorial for the Australian Military Forces, Canberra, 1944

Baker, C. & Knight, G. (eds), *The Clowes Report: The Battle of Milne Bay 1942*, Australian Military History Publications, Sydney, 1995

Baker, N., *More Than Little Heroes: Australian Army Air Liaison Officers in the Second World War*, Strategic and Defence Studies Centre, Australian National University, Canberra, 1994

Ballendorf, D.A., & Bartlett, M., *Pete Ellis: An Amphibious Warfare Prophet, 1880–1923*, US Naval Institute Press, 1st edn, 1996

Barbey, D.E., *MacArthur's Amphibious Navy: Seventh Amphibious Force Operations 1943–1945*, United States Naval Institute, Annapolis, MD, 1969

Bartlett, M.L. (ed.), *Assault from the Sea: Essays on the History of Amphibious Warfare*, Naval Institute Press, Annapolis, MD, 1983

Bennett, C., *Rough Infantry: Tales of World War II*, Warrnambool Institute Press, Melbourne, 1985

Bergerud, E., *Touched with Fire: The Land War in the South Pacific*, Penguin Books, New York, 1996

Blamey, Thomas, *Great Tasks Ahead*, Commonwealth Government Printer, Canberra, 1944

Bradley, P., *On Shaggy Ridge: The Australian Seventh Division in the Ramu Valley Campaign: From Kaiapit to the Finisterre Ranges*, Oxford University Press, Melbourne, 2001

——*The Battle for Wau: New Guinea's Frontline 1942–1943*, Cambridge University Press, New York, 2008

Brune, P., *Gona's Gone: The Battle for the Beach-head 1942*, Allen & Unwin in association with Headquarters Training Command Australian Army, St Leonards, NSW, 1994

——*A Bastard of a Place: The Australians in Papua*, Allen & Unwin, St Leonards, NSW, 2005

Bullard, S. (trans.), *Japanese Army Operations in the South Pacific Area, New Britain and Papua Campaigns, 1942–43*, Australian War Memorial, Canberra, 2007

Catanzaro, F.B., *With the 41st Division in the Southwest Pacific: A Foot Soldier's Story*, Indiana University Press, Indianapolis, 2002

Chan, G. (ed.), *War on Our Doorstep: Diaries of Australians at the Frontline in 1942*, Hardie Grant Books, South Yarra, Vic, 2003

Chapman, I., *Iven G. Mackay: Citizen and Soldier*, Melway Publishing, Melbourne, 1975

Chwialkowski, P., *In Caesar's Shadow: The Life of General Robert Eichelberger*, Greenwood, Westport, CT, 1993
Clausewitz, C. von, *On War*, ed. & trans. Howard, M. & Paret, P., Princeton University Press, Princeton, NJ, 1976
Clay, S.E., *US Army Order of Battle, 1919–1941, The Arms: Major Commands and Infantry Organisations, 1919–1941*, Combat Studies Institute Press, US Army Combined Arms Center, Fort Leavenworth, KS, 2010
Coates, J., *Bravery Above Blunder: The 9th Australian Division at Finschhafen, Sattelberg, and Sio*, Oxford University Press, Melbourne, 1999
Collie, C. & Marutani, H., *The Path of Infinite Sorrow: The Japanese on the Kokoda Track*, Allen & Unwin, Sydney, 2012
*Command History, Seventh Amphibious Force, 10 January 1943–23 December 1945*, US Navy, 1945
Converse, A., *Armies of Empire: The 9th Australian and 50th British Divisions in Battle 1939–1945*, Cambridge University Press, Cambridge, 2011
Coombes, D., *Morshead: Hero of Tobruk and El Alamein*, Oxford University Press, South Melbourne, Vic, 2001
Crawley, R., 'Our second great (mis)adventure: A critical re-evaluation of the August offensive, Gallipoli, 1915', PhD thesis, University of New South Wales at the Australian Defence Force Academy, Canberra, 2010
Crowel, P.A. *Campaign in the Marianas: The War in the Pacific, United States Army in World War II*, Office of the Chief of Military History, Washington, DC, 1993
Crowel, P.A. & Love, E.G., *Seizure of the Gilbert and Marshalls: The War in the Pacific, United States Army in World War II*, Office of the Chief of Military History, Washington, DC, 1993
Dawes, A., *Soldier Superb: The Australian Fights in New Guinea*, F.H. Johnston Publishing Company, Sydney, 1943
Dean, E.J., *New Guinea: The US Army Campaigns of World War II*, US Army Center of Military History, Washington, DC, 1993
Dean, P. (ed.), *Australia 1943: The Liberation of New Guinea*, Cambridge University Press, New York, 2014
——*Australia 1944–45: Victory in the Pacific*, Cambridge University Press, Melbourne, 2016
Dexter, D., *The New Guinea Offensives: Australia in the War of 1939–1945*, Series I, Army Volume VI, Australian War Memorial, Canberra, 1961
Drea, E.J., 'Defending the Driniumor: Covering force operations in New Guinea, 1944', Leavenworth Papers Number 9, Combat Studies Institute, Command and General Staff College, Fort Leavenworth, KS, 1984
Dunn, J.B. 'Lofty', *Eagles Alighting: A History of the Australian Parachute Battalion*, I Australian Parachute Battalion Association, East Malvern, Vic, 1999
Eather, S., *Desert Sands, Jungle Lands: A Biography of Major General Ken Eather*, Allen & Unwin, Crows Nest, NSW, 2003
Eaton, G., 'From teaching to practice: General Walter Krueger and the development of joint operations, 1921–1945', Naval War College paper, Newport, RI, 1994
Eichelberger, R.L., *Our Jungle Road to Tokyo*, Viking Press, New York, 1950

Emmel, D.C., 'The development of amphibious doctrine', Master of Military Art and Science thesis, US Army Command and General Staff College, Fort Leavenworth, KS, 2010

Erskine, G.B., 'Principles and methods of conducting landing operations as illustrated by the action of Japanese forces in various historical instances', Combined Arms Research Library, Fort Leavenworth, KS, 1934

Evans, M., *Amphibious Operations: The Projection of Sea Power Ashore*, Vol. 4, Wheatons, Exeter, 1990

——*Developing Australia's Maritime Concept of Strategy: Lessons from the Ambon Disaster of 1942*, Air Power Studies Centre, Canberra, 2000

Fath, M.F., 'Intrepidity, iron will, and intellect: General Robert L. Eichelberger and military genius', Master of Military Art and Science, US Army Command and General Staff College, Fort Leavenworth, KS, 2004

Fergusson, B., *The Watery Maze: The Story of Combined Operations*, 1st edn, Collins, London, 1961

Feuer, A.B., *Australian Commandos: Their Secret War Against the Japanese in WWII*, Stackpole, Mechanicsburg, PA, 2006 [c. 1996]

Field, C., 'Testing the tenets of manoeuvre: Australia's first amphibious assault since Gallipoli: The 9th Australian Division at Lae, 4–16 September 1943', Land Warfare Studies Centre, Working Paper 139, 2012

Gabel, C.R., *The US Army GHQ Maneuvers of 1941*, Publication 70-41, Department of Defense, US Army Center of Military History, Washington, DC, 1991

Gailey, H.A., *MacArthur Strikes Back, Decision at Buna: New Guinea 1942–1943*, Presidio Press, Novato, CA, 2000

——*MacArthur's Victory: The War in New Guinea 1943–1944*, Presidio Press, New York, 2004

Gallaway, J., *The Odd Couple: Blamey and MacArthur at War*, University of Queensland Press, St Lucia, 2000

Gamble, B., *Fortress Rabaul: The Battle for the Southwest Pacific, January 1942–April 1943*, Zenith Press, Minneapolis, 2010

Gibson, O., *Incident on Shaggy Ridge*, Calvert Publishing Company, Sydney, 1942

Gill, H.G., *Royal Australian Navy 1939–1942*, Vol. 1, Australia in the War of 1939–1945, Australian War Memorial, Canberra, 1957

——*Royal Australian Navy 1942–1945*, Vol. 2, Australia in the War of 1939–1945, Australian War Memorial, Canberra, 1968

Graeme-Evans, A.L., *Of Storms and Rainbows: The Story of the Men of the 2/12th Battalion AIF*, Vol. 2: March 1942–January 1946, 12th Battalion Association, Hobart, 1991

Graham, G.B., *Moresby Mice: A Souvenir of the Papuan Campaign*, Robertson & Mullens, Melbourne, 1943

Grey, J., *Australian Brass: The Career of Lieutenant General Sir Horace Robertson*, Cambridge University Press, Melbourne, 1992

——*A Military History of Australia*, Cambridge University Press, Cambridge, 1999

——*The Australian Army*, Vol. 1, The Australian Centenary History of Defence, Oxford University Press, Melbourne, 2001

Griess, T.E. (ed.), *Atlas for the Second World War, Asia and the Pacific*, West Point Military History Series, Garden City Park, New York, 1985
Gullet, H., *Not as a Duty Only: An Infantryman's War*, Melbourne University Press, Carlton, 1976
Hall, G.M., *Love, War, and the 96th Engineers (Colored): The World War II New Guinea Diaries of Captain Hyman Samuelson*, University of Illinois Press, Urbana, 1995
Hartley, F., *Sanananda Interlude: The 7th Australian Division Cavalry Regiment*, Speciality Press, Melbourne, 1949
Heller, C.E. & Stofft, W.A. (eds), *America's First Battles, 1776–1965*, University Press of Kansas, Lawrence, KS, 1986
Henderson, J., *Onward, Boy Soldiers: The Battle for Milne Bay 1942*, University of Western Australia, Nedlands, WA, 1992
Hetherington, J., *Blamey: The Biography of Field Marshal Sir Thomas Blamey*, F.W. Cheshire, Melbourne, 1954
Holdsworth, D., *Papua New Guinea Battlefields*, University of Papua New Guinea Press, Port Moresby, 2012
Horner, D., *Crisis of Command: Australian Generalship and the Japanese Threat, 1941–1943*, Australian National University Press, Canberra, 1978
——*High Command: Australia and Allied Strategy 1939–1945*, Allen & Unwin, Sydney, 1982
——(ed.), *The Commanders: Australian Military Leadership in the Twentieth Century*, George Allen & Unwin, Sydney, 1984
——*General Vasey's War*, Melbourne University Press, Melbourne, 1992
——*Blamey: Commander-in-Chief*, Allen & Unwin, St Leonard's, NSW, 1998
Isely, J.A. & Crowl, P.A., *The US Marines and Amphibious War*, 1st edn, Princeton University Press, Princeton, NJ, 1951
Johnston, G.H., *The Toughest Fighting in the World: The Australian and American Campaign for New Guinea in World War II*, Westholme Publishing, Yardley, PA, 2011 [1943]
Johnston, M., *That Magnificent 9th: An Illustrated History of the 9th Australian Division 1940–46*, Allen & Unwin, Sydney, 2002
——*The Silent 7th: An Illustrated History of the 7th Australian Division 1940–46*, Allen & Unwin, Sydney, 2005
——*Fighting the Enemy: Australian Soldiers and Their Adversaries in World War II*, reprint, Cambridge University Press, Melbourne, 2009
*Jungle Victory: An Official Story of the Australian Soldier in the Wau–Salamaua Campaign, January 1943–September 1943*, Director General of Public Relations, Australian Military Forces, Canberra, 1944
Keating, G., *The Right Man for the Right Job: Lieutenant General Sir Stanley Savige as a Military Commander*, Oxford University Press, Melbourne, 2006
Kenney, G.C., *General Kenney Reports: A Personal History of the Pacific War*, Deull, Sloan & Pearce, New York, 1949
Keogh, E.G., *The South West Pacific 1941–45*, Grayflower, Melbourne, 1965
Keyes, R., *Amphibious Warfare and Combined Operations*, Cambridge University Press, London, 1943

Kier, E., *Imagining War: French and British Military Doctrine Between the Wars*, Princeton University Press, Princeton, NJ, 1997

Lieto, A.S., 'Amphibious operations: The operational wild card', School of Advanced Military Studies, United States Army Command and General Staff College, Fort Leavenworth, KS, 1990

Lofgren, S.J., *Northern Solomons, 22 February 1943–21 November 1944*, US Army Center of Military History, Washington, DC, 1994

Long, G., *To Benghazi*, Vol. 1, *Australia in the War of 1939–1945*, Australian War Memorial, Canberra, 1952

——*Greece, Crete and Syria*, Vol. 2, *Australia in the War of 1939–1945*, Australian War Memorial, Canberra, 1953

——*The Final Campaigns*, Vol. 7, *Australia in the War of 1939–1945*, Australian War Memorial, Canberra, 1963

——*The Six Years War: A Concise History of Australia in the 1939–1945 War*, Australian War Memorial, Canberra, 1973

Lorelli, J.A., *To Foreign Shores: US Amphibious Operations in World War II*, Naval Institute Press, Annapolis, MD, 1995

Lunney, B. & Finch, F., *Forgotten Fleet: A History of the Part Played by Australian Men and Ships in the US Army Small Ships Section in New Guinea, 1942–1945*, Forfleet Publishing, Medowie, NSW, 1995

Luvaas, J., *Dear Miss Em: General Eichelberger's War in the Pacific, 1942–1945*, Contributions in Military Studies Series #2, Bloomsbery Academic, New York, 1972

Lynch, R., *Darwin to Borneo: World War II*, Seaview Press, Henley Beach, SA, 2000

Malkasain, C., *Charting the Pathway to OMFTS: A Historical Assessment of Amphibious Operations From 1941 to the Present*, CNA Corporation, Arlington, VA, 2002

Mallett, R.A., 'Australian Army logistics 1943–1945', PhD thesis, School of Humanities and Social Science, University of New South Wales at the Australian Defence Force Academy, Canberra, 2007

Marshall, G., L.I. Bland, C.N. Wunderlin Jr & S. Ritenour Stevens (eds), *The Papers of George Catlett Marshall: We Cannot Delay, July 1, 1939–December 6, 1941*, Vol. 2, Johns Hopkins University Press, Baltimore and London, 1986

Marston, D., 'Learning and adapting for jungle warfare, 1942–45: The Australian and British Indian Armies', pp. 121–45, in Dean, *Australia 1944–45*

Matloff, M., & Snell, E.M., *Strategic Planning for Coalition Warfare 1941–1942: The War Department, United States Army in World War II*, US Army Center of Military History, Washington, DC, 1999

Maughan, B., *Tobruk and El Alamein*, Vol. 3, *Australia in the War of 1939–1945*, Australian War Memorial, Canberra, 1966

Mayo, L., *Bloody Buna*, Doubleday & Company, Garden City, NY, 1974

McAulay, L., *To The Bitter End: The Japanese Defeat at Buna and Gona 1942–43*, Random House Australia, Sydney, 1992

McCarthy, D., *South-West Pacific Area – First Year, Kokoda to Wau*, Vol. 5, *Australia in the War of 1939–1945*, Australian War Memorial, Canberra, 1959

McDonald, N. & Brune, P., *200 Shots: Damien Parer and George Silk with the Australians at War in New Guinea*, Allen & Unwin, Crows Nest, NSW, 2004

McGarth, J.J., *The Brigade: A History in the US Army Its Organisation and Employment*, Combat Studies Institute Press, Fort Leavenworth, KS, 2004

McKernan, M., *All In: Australia During the Second World War*, Thomas Nelson, Melbourne, 1983

Merglen, A. (trans. K. Morgan), *Surprise Warfare: Subversive, Airborne, and Amphibious Operations*, George Allen & Unwin, Birkenhead, 1968

Miller, J. Jr, *Cartwheel: The Reduction of Rabaul, The War in the Pacific, United States Army in World War II*, Publication 5-5, US Army Center of Military History, Washington, DC, 1959

Miller, W.A., 'The 9th Australian Division versus the Africa Corps: An infantry division against tanks – Tobruk, Libya, 1941', US Army Command and General Staff College, Fort Leavenworth, KS, 1986

Milner, S., *Victory in Papua: The War in the Pacific, United States Army in World War II*, US Army Center of Military History, Washington, DC, 1957

Moremon, J., 'A triumph of improvisation: Australian Army operational logistics and the campaign in Papua, July 1942 to January 1943', PhD, School of History, Australian Defence Force Academy, University of New South Wales, Canberra, 2000

——*Battle of the Beachheads 1942–43: Buna, Gona and Sanananda, Papua New Guinea, November 1942–January 1943*, Department of Veterans' Affairs, Canberra, 2002

Morison, S.E., *Breaking the Bismarcks Barrier: 22 July 1942–1 May 1944*, Little, Brown, & Company, Boston, 1950

——*New Guinea and the Marianas, March 1944–August 1944*, Vol. 8, History of the United States Naval Operations in World War II, University of Illinios Press, Chicago, 2002 [1953]

Morton, L., *Strategy and Command: The First Two Years, The War in the Pacific, United States Army in World War II*, US Army Center of Military History, Washington, DC, 2000

Newell, C., *The Framework of Operational Warfare*, Routledge, London, 1991

*On Target: With the American and Australian Anti-Aircraft Brigade in New Guinea*, Written and illustrated by men of the front-line forces, Angus & Robertson, Sydney, 1943

Palazzo, A., *The Australian Army: A History of Its Organisation from 1901 to 2001*, Oxford University Press, Melbourne, 2001

*Papuan Campaign: The Buna-Sanananda Operation, 16 November 1942–23 January 1943*, American Forces in Action Series, Military Intelligence Division, War Department, Washington, DC, 1944

Parkin, R., 'Learning while fighting: The evolution of Australian close air support doctrine 1939–1945', PhD thesis, Australian Defence Force Academy, University of New South Wales, Canberra, 1999

Paull, R., *Retreat from Kokoda: The Australian Campaign in New Guinea 1942*, William Heinemann Australia, Richmond, Vic, 1982 [1958]

Perrett, B., *Armour in Battle: Wavell's Offensive*, Ian Allan, London, 1979

Perversi, F.G., *From Tobruk to Borneo: Memoirs of an Italian-Aussie Volunteer*, Rosenberg Publishing, Kenthurst, NSW, 2002

Pinder, G.F., 'The New Guinea campaign, 23 January 1943–31 December 1944', Command and General Staff College, Fort Leavenworth, KS, 1949

Powell, A., *The Third Force: ANGAU's New Guinea War, 1942–46*, Oxford University Press, Melbourne, 2003

Pratten, G., *Australian Battalion Commanders in the Second World War*, Cambridge University Press, Melbourne, 2009

*Reconquest: An Official Record of the Australian Army's Successes in the Offensives Against Lae, Finschhafen, Markham and Ramu Valleys, Huon Peninsula, Finisterre Mountains, Rai Coast, Bogadjim, Madang, Alexishafen, Karkar Is., Hansa Bay, September 1943–June 1944*, Director General of Public Relations, Melbourne, 1944

Reeson, M., *A Very Long War: The Families Who Waited*, Melbourne University Press, Melbourne, 2000

Reid, R., *Milne Bay 1942: Papua New Guinea: August–September 1942*, Department of Veterans' Affairs, Canberra, 2002

——*Kokoda 1942: Papua New Guinea, July–November 1942*, Department of Veterans' Affairs, Canberra, 2003

*Reports of General Macarthur*, Vol. I, *The Campaigns of Macarthur in the Pacific*, Center of Military History, Publication 13-3, Facsimile Reprint, Washington, DC, 1994

Ricks, T., *The Generals: American Military Command from World War II to Today*, Reprint Edition, Penguin Books, New York, 2013

Riegelman, H., *Caves of Biak: An American Officer's Experience in the Southwest Pacific*, Dial Press, New York, 1955

Robinson, B., *Record of Services*, Macmillan & Company, Melbourne, 1944

Rottman, G., *US World War II Amphibious Tactics, Army and Marine Corps, Pacific Theater*, Osprey Publishing, Oxford, 2004

Ryan, P., *Fear Drive My Feet*, Melbourne University Press, Melbourne, 1974

*Salamaua Siege*, Brochure Number 4, The Australian Army at War, Army Directorate of Public Relations, Department of Information, Sydney, 1944

Sayers, S., *Ned Herring: A Life of Lieutenant General the Honourable Sir Edmund Herring*, Hyland House, Melbourne, 1980

Smurthwaite, D., *The Pacific War Atlas 1941–1945*, Cynthia Parzych Publishing, New York, 1999

Snoke, E.R. (ed.), *The Operational Level of War*, Combat Studies Institute, US Army Command and General Staff College, Fort Leavenworth, KS, 1985

Spencer, W.B., *In the Footsteps of Ghosts: With the 2/9th Battalion in the African Desert and the Jungles of the Pacific*, Allen & Unwin, St Leonards, NSW, 1999

Spiller, R., *Combined Arms in Battle Since 1939*, US Army Command and General Staff College Press, Fort Leavenworth, KS, 1992

Stanley, P., *Tarakan: An Australian Tragedy*, Allen & Unwin, Sydney, 1997

Stevenson, R.C., 'The anatomy of a division: The 1st Australian Division in the Great War, 1914–1919', PhD thesis, Australian Defence Force Academy, University of New South Wales, Canberra, 2010

Stockings, C., *The Battle of Bardia*, Australian Army Campaign Series 9, Big Sky Publishing, Sydney, 2015

Sublet, F., *Kokoda to the Sea: A History of the 1942 Campaign in Papua*, Slouch Hat Publications, McCrae, Vic, 2000

Taaffe, S.R., *MacArthur's Jungle War: The 1944 New Guinea Campaign*, University Press of Kansas, Lawrence, 1998

*The Fifth Air Force in the Huon Peninsula Campaign: January to October 1943*, US Air Force Historical Studies, Headquarters, Army Air Forces, Washington, DC, 1946

*The Jap was Thrashed: An Official Story of the Australian Soldier – First Victor of the 'Invincible' Jap, New Guinea, 1942–43*, Director General of Public Relations, Australian Military Forces, Melbourne, 1944

Threlfall, A., 'The development of Australian Army jungle warfare doctrine and training, 1941–1945', PhD thesis, Faculty of Arts, Education and Human Development, Victoria University, Melbourne, 2008

Tregaskis, R., *Guadalcanal Diary*, Random House, New York, 1943

Vader, J., *New Guinea: The Tide is Stemmed*, Ballantine Books, London, 1971

Vagts, A., *Landing Operations from Grecian Days to 1945*, Military Service Publishing Company, Harrisburg, PA, 1946

Wahlert, G., *Anzac Cove to Afghanistan: The History of the 3rd Brigade*, Big Sky Publishing, Newport, NSW, 2015

——*The Western Desert Campaign 1940–41*, Australian Army Campaign Series 2, Big Sky Publishing, Newport, NSW, 2016

*War in New Guinea: Official War Photographs of the Battle for Australia*, Department of Information, Australia [F.H. Johnston Publishing Company, Sydney], 1943

Waters, G., *OBOE: Air Operations Over Borneo, 1945*, Air Power Studies Centre, RAAF Base Fairbairn, Canberra, 1995

Whitehouse, A., *Amphibious Operation*, 1st edn, Doubleday & Company, New York, 1963

Whitney, C., *MacArthur: His Rendezvous with History*, Alfred A. Knopf, New York, 1955

William, M.H., *Chronology 1941–1945, Special Studies, United States Army in World War II*, US Army Center of Military History, Washington, DC, 1989

Williams, P., *The Kokoda Campaign 1942: Myth and Reality*, Cambridge University Press, Melbourne, 2012

Wilson, J.B., *Maneuver and Firepower: The Evolution of Division and Separate Brigades*, US Army Lineage Series, US Army Center for Military History, Washington, DC, 1998

Winton, H. & Mets, D. (eds), *The Challenge of Change: Military Institutions and New Realities, 1918–1941*, University of Nebraska Press, Lincoln, NE, 2000

York, K.R., 'Joint operational fires in the offense: The Southwest Pacific campaign to isolate Rabaul', Monograph, US Army Command and General Staff College, Fort Leavenworth, KS, 2014

Young, R., 'They too fought the Japanese: The American Army's war in the Southwest Pacific', PhD thesis, City University of New York, New York, 2003

## JOURNAL ARTICLES

Agnew, J.B., 'From where did our amphibious doctrine come from', *Marine Corps Gazette*, Vol. 63, Issue 8, 1979

Anderson, J.B., 'Are we justified in discarding "pre-war" methods of training?', *Field Artillery Journal*, Vol. 9, No. 2, 1919

Arnold, A.V., 'Preparation for a division amphibious operation', *Military Review*, Vol. XXV, May 1945

Babcock, K.J., 'MacArthur small ships, improvising water transport in the Southwest Pacific Area', *Army History*, Winter 2014

Bjork, D.L., 'Waterborne envelopments', *Military Review*, Vol. XXX, February 1951

Bill, D.S., 'The amphibious assault – fast, flexible, and powerful', *Proceedings*, Vol. 88/10/716, October 1962

Browning, M.R., 'Amphibious warfare and the naval covering force', *Military Review*, Vol. XXV, May 1945

Clarke, C., 'Exploring the history of the Australian Army through biography', *Journal of the Australian War Memorial*, Issue 34, June 2001

Cole, R.W., 'Jungle operations', *Military Review*, Vol. XXIV, June 1944

Dean, P., 'The forgotten man: Lieutenant General Sir Frank Berryman', *Journal of the Australian War Memorial*, Issue 37, October 2002

——'Commemoration, memory, and forgotten histories: The complexity and limitations of Australian Army biography', *War and Society*, Vol. 29, Issue 2, 2010

——'Amphibious warfare: Lessons from the past for ADF's future', *Security Challenges*, Vol. 8, No. 1, 2012

——'Amphibious operations and the evolution of Australian defence policy', *Journal of the United States Naval War College*, Vol. 11, No. 1, 2014

——'To the jungle shore: Australia and amphibious warfare in the SWPA 1942–45', *Global War Studies*, Vol. 11, No. 2, 2014

——'Raid on Goodenough Island: Australia's first amphibious operation in the Second World War', *Australian Naval Review*, Vol. 1, No. 1, 2016

Dennis, P. & Grey, J. (eds), *The Foundations of Victory: The Pacific War 1943–1944*, The 2003 Chief of Army's Military History Conference, Army History Unit, Department of Defence, Canberra, 2004

Garland, A., 'Amphibious warfare: Where does the Army stand', *Military Review*, Vol. LXII, September 1982

Graeme-Evans, A.L., 'The 18th Brigade AIF at Buna, Australia's Pacific Battle of the Somme, January 1943', *Australian Defence Force Journal*, No. 98, January/February 1993

Hunter, C., 'I didn't think it would be like this', AWM Memorial Articles, interview with James Cronk, 29 January 2020

Johnson, G., 'Forgotten progress: The development of close air support doctrine before World War II', *Air Power History*, Vol. 46, No. 1, 1999

Lawless, R.E., 'The Biak operation', *Military Review*, Vol. XXXIII, May 1953

Linn, T.C., 'Amphibious warfare: A misunderstood capability', *Armed Forces Journal International*, August 1987

Milner, S., 'The Battle of Milne Bay', *Military Review*, Vol. XXX, April 1950

Moore, R.S., 'Blitzkrieg from the sea', *Naval War College Review*, Vol. XXXVI, No. 6, 1983
Nelson, H., 'Kokoda: The Track from history to politics', *Journal of Pacific History*, Vol. 38, No. 1, 2003
Neufled, J., with Y'Blood, W., and Jefferson, M.L. (eds), 'Pearl to V-J Day: World War II in the Pacific', Air Force History and Museums Program and the Air Force Historical Foundation, Naval Officers Club, Bethesda, Maryland, 20–21 July 1995
Paige, B.L., 'Campaigning in the jungle', *Military Review*, Vol. XXIV, April 1944
Painter, D.E., 'The Army and amphibious warfare', *Military Review*, Vol. XLV, August 1965
Raudzens, G., 'Testing the air power expectations of the Kokoda campaign, July to September 1942', *Journal of the Australian War Memorial*, No. 21, October 1992
Schroeder, H.J., 'Replacement pipelines to battle', *Military Review*, Vol. XXV, May 1945
Shindo, H., 'Japanese air operations over New Guinea during the Second World War', *Journal of the Australian War Memorial*, No. 34, June 2001
Shortal, J.F., 'Hollandia: A training victory', *Military Review*, Vol. LXVI, May 1986
Speller, I., 'In the shadow of Gallipoli? Amphibious warfare in the inter-war period', Gallipoli – Making History Symposium, Menzies Centre for Australian Studies, London, 2001
Stevens, D., 'The naval campaigns for New Guinea', *Journal of the Australian War Memorial*, No. 34, June 2001
Stevenson, R.C., 'Not-so friendly fire: An Australian taxonomy for fratricide', Working Paper No. 128, Land Warfare Studies Centre, Canberra, April 2006
Wahlert, G. (ed.), 'Australian Army amphibious operations in the South-West Pacific: 1942–45', Army Doctrine Centre, Department of Defence, Puckapunyal, Vic, 1995
Williams, P.D. & Nakagawa, N., 'The Japanese 18th Army in New Guinea', *Wartime: Official Magazine of the Australian War Memorial*, No. 36, September 2006

# Index

Entries in **bold** indicate images.

Advanced New Guinea Force, 84
Afrika Korps
   offensive at Tobruk, 35–7
air support
   Battle of Milne Bay, 64
   Buna campaign, 77, 80, 81, 92
   Normanby Island amphibious landing, 138
   Operation Cutthroat, 4, 120, 123–4
   Operation Oboe II, 185, 195, 200–2
   Operation Postern, 144, 145, 146
   role in Battle of Milne Bay, 64
   Sanananda campaign, 92
airlifts
   capacity, 115
   combat airlifts, 72–3
Allied cooperation, 70
amphibious exercises and rehearsals
   Exercise Coconut, 143
   Exercise Octopus, 155, 156, 159–64, 211
   historical overview, 156–8
   implementation, 210
   Operation Seagull, 155, 164–7, 211
   reheasal at Morotai for Operation Oboe II, 170–2, 211
amphibious operations
   18th Brigade, 4, 137
   Australian operations, 136
   Borneo, 155
   classification, 148
   fog of war, 212
   Goodenough Island, 139–40
   Landing Craft Infantry (LCI), 160, 161
   Landing Craft Vehicle Personnel (LCVPs), 157

Landing Ship Infantry (LSI), 160, 161, 163
Landing Ship Tank (LST), 160, 161
Landing Tables, 153, 159
Landing Vehicle Tracked (LVTs), 157, 165, 186
largest considerations, 148
major operations in WWII, 136
night landings, 161
Normanby Island, 137–9
Oboe Operations. See Operation Oboe I; Operation Oboe II
planning for, 156, 158–9
scales for, 150–1
US Army operations, 136
US Marine Corps, 136
US Navy support, 22
amphibious warfare
   challenges, 136, 210
   infantry brigades' responsibility for, 4
   planning for, 150–4
   steps, 136
amphibious warfare doctrine
   Australian doctrine, 136, 137, 151
   birth of SWPA amphibious doctrine, 149–50
   British doctrine, 136–7, 151
   development of, 23–4
   terminology, 24
   traditional philosophy, 149
   US doctrine, 137, 151, 157
amphibious warfare training, 22
   18th Brigade, 161
   Amphibious Training Centre, 149, 155
   first training for 18th Brigade, 42

INDEX  263

following Finisterre campaign, 147–9, 155–6
non-infantry units of 18th Brigade, 161
reconstructed 18th Brigade, 97
Shipside Training Program, 161
small boat training program, 137
Trinity Beach facility, 151, 155, 211
US Army training program, 149
US control, 24
anti-aircraft platoons, 15
Armitage (PTE), **79**
armour
  in jungle warfare, 71
  *See also* tanks
artillery
  Battle of Milne Bay, 62–4
  in jungle warfare, 71, 76
  integration with infantry, 99
  Operation Cutthroat, 130–1
  use during Operation Oboe II, 198–200
assault brigades
  designation of 18th Infantry Brigade Group (Jungle) as, 25, 27, 137, 173, 211
  explained, 23
  first use of term, 25
  responsibilities and capabilities, 23, 25
Australian Army
  division structure in World War I, 4
  promotion within, 7
  reorganisation on eve of World War II, 31–5
  strength at end of interwar period, 7–9
  World War II deployments and service, 1
Australian Army units
  1 Armed Regiment, 25
  1 Armoured Regiment, 182, 186, **196**, 197
  1 Armoured Regiment Signal Troop, 26
  1 Australian Army, 14
  1 Australian Corps, 164
  I Corps, 181
  1 Motorised Regiment, 97, 100, 206
  1 Mountain Battery, 80
  1 Naval Bombardment Group, 26

1 Parachute Battalion, 165
1 Regimental Workshop, 26
2 Australian Imperial Force, 7
II Corps, 100
2 Engineer Signal Section, 26
2 Operations Report Team, 26
2/1 Armour Brigade Reconnaisance Squadron, 186
2/1 Field Artillery Regiment, 89
2/1 Field Regiment, 80
2/1 GD Regiment, 25
2/1 Machine Gun Battalion, 25
2/1 Parachute Battalion, 163
2/1 Pioneer Battalion, 187
2/2 Anti-Tank Regiment, 25, 185, 186, 199
2/2 Pioneer Battalion, 116, 121, 122, 123
2/2 Tank Attack Artillery Battery, 182
2/3 Field Company, 144
2/4 Engineer Company, 80, 167
2/4 Field Artillery Regiment, 99, 107, 121, 122, 123, 125, 126, 130, 131, 134, 167, 182, 185, 186, 198, 209
2/4 Field Company, 25, 42, 50, 137, 165, 182, 193
2/5 Field Ambulance, 26, 80, 111, 182
2/5 Field Regiment, 9 Battery, 50, 80
2/6 Cavalry Regiment, 104
2/6 Dental Unit, 26
2/6 Field Amour Regiment, 79, 80, 86
2/6 Heavy Anti-Aircraft Battery, 50
2/7 Cavalry Regiment, 21, 86, 88, 166
2/8 Field Ambulance, 144
2/8 Transport Platoon, 25
2/9 Battalion, 21, 25, 28, 32, 33–4, 50, 53, 59, 63, 79, 80–2, 86, 89, 91, 100, 101, 102, 113, 116, 121, **122**, 124, 126, 127, **128**, 128, 163, 176, 184, 185, 187, 193, 197, 201
2/9 Field Company, 193
2/9 Light Anti-Aircraft Battery, 50
2/10 Battalion, 13, 21, 25, **29**, 32, 33, 39, **40**, 46, 49, 50, 53, 54–7, 65, 66, 72–3, 80, 83, 86, 100, 102,

116, 125–6, 137–9, 163, 166, 167, 169, 176, 184, 185, 186, 187, **188**, 192, 194, 195, 197, 199, 200, 201
2/10 Field Ambulance, 80
2/11 Battalion, 28
2/12 Battalion, 18, 21, 25, 28, 32, 39, 50, 53, 57, 59, 63, **81**, 83, 86, 89, 91, 100, 101, 114, 116, 123, 126, 127, 139–40, **162**, 163, 166, 169, **171**, 176, 184, 185, 186, 187, 192, 197, **212**
2/12 Field Artillery, 144
2/13 Battalion, 143, 144
2/20 Battalion, 28
2/23 Battalion, 145, 146
2/25 Field PK Company, 26
2/27 Battalion, 176, 192
2/125 Brigade Workshop, 26
4 Armoured Brigade Reconnaissance Squadron, 26
5 Air Liaison Party, 185
5 Air Support Party, 185
5 Division, 12
5 Motorised Regiment, 97, 99, 206
6 Air Liaison Party, 185
6 Division, 12, 174
6 Divisional Cavalry Regiment, B Squadron, 31, 32, 33, 34
7 Air Liaison Party, 185
7 Brigade, 48, 50, 51, 53
7 Division, 2, 12, 13, 14, 31, 37, 44–7, 74, 76, 113, 114, 159, 164, 169, 174, 175, 181, 183, 184, 201, 202
7 Division Protection Company, 26
7 Field Military History Section LHQ, 26
9 Battalion, 50, 51, 96
9 Brigade, 203
9 Division, 28, 31, 35, 141, 145, 146, 174
10 Brigade, 203
11 Division, 12
11 Motorised Regiment, 97, 99, 206
12 Brigade, 203
12 Light Anti-Aircraft Battery, 144
XIII Corps, 32
14 Brigade, 203
16 Brigade, 10, 101, 129
17 Brigade, 10, 80

18 Brigade, 31, 46
19 Brigade, 28, 129
20 Brigade, 145, 211
21 Brigade, 46, 114, 116, 118, 119, 165, 168, 176, 192
22 Brigade, 203
24 Brigade, 142–5, 146
24 Field Company, 48, 50
25 Battalion, 50, 51, 57
25 Brigade, 31, 46, 114, 116, 119, 165, 168
26 Brigade, 142, 143, 146, 174, 175
27 Brigade, 203
28 Brigade, 203
30 Brigade, 203
31 Brigade, 203
32 Brigade, 203
34 Brigade, 216
61 Battalion, 50, 51, 53, 56, 57
62 Battery Field Artillery, 141
101 Anti-Tank Regiment, 4 Battery, 50, 59
209 Light Aid Detachment (Type H), 26
Directorate of Public Affairs, 26
Landing Vehicle Tracked (LVTs), 197–8
Australian Recruit Training Centre, Cowra, 10
Australian Strike Force, 29
Australian Training Centre, Jungle Warfare, Canungra, **105**, 106

Barbey, Daniel (ADM), 140, 141, 147, 201
Bardia, Battle of, 9, 184, 209
Berryman, Frank (MAJGEN), 88, 175
Blamey, Thomas (GEN), 49, 83, 141, 175
Blyth, Alan (LTCOL), 120, 125, 182
Borneo campaign, 4
Bostock, William (AVM), 173, 201
Bourne (LTCOL), 147, 155
brigade commanders
  conferences, 215
  in early World War II, 3
  in latter half of Pacific War, 3
  reliance on brigade staff, 215–16
  role, 213–17
Brigade Intelligence School, 121, 207

INDEX 265

brigade staff
  commanders' reliance upon, 215–16
Britain
  Blitz, 29, 30
  defence from German invasion, 29–31
Britain, Battle of, 29
British Army
  division structure in World War I, 4
British Army units
  4 Regiment, Royal Horse Artillery, 32, 34
  6 Hyderbad, 72
  19 Lancers, 72
  Indian Artillery, 72
  Rajputana Rifles, 72
  Royal Armoured Cars, 72
  Royal Berkshire Regiment, 72
  Welsh Regiment, 2 Battalion, 72
Brocksopp, John (CAPT), 138, 139, 147
Brooks, Norman (LT), 182
Buna campaign, 12
  after-action assessment, 83–4, 90–4
  air support, 77, 80, 81, 92
  armour, 71
  artillery, 71, 81, 82, 93, 95
  casualties, 68, 70, 71, 78, 81, 83, 95, 96
  combined arms operation, 83
  conditions, 71, 76
  failed attacks and stalemates, 77
  final large-scale assault, 83
  first clash with Japanese, 76–7
  friendly fire, 77, 82
  ground reconnaisance, 82, 91
  infantry tactics and manoeuvre, 90–1
  Japanese bunker complexes, 88
  Japanese fortifications, 75
  Japanese landings, 74, 76
  MacArthur's claims about, 70
  maps, 91
  maritime resupply, 74
  operations orders, 75, 80
  patrolling, 91
  siege warfare, 71
  start of campaign, 72
  successful attack by 2/9 Battalion, 80–2
  tanks, 93–4
  unsuccessful assault by by US 127 regiment, 82–3
Buna Village and Government Station
  strategic value, 74

carrier platoons, 15
casualties
  Battle of Buna, 68, 70, 71, 78, 81, 83, 96
  Battle of Kokoda Track, 68
  Battle of Milne Bay, 60
  casualty rates for infantry in SWPA campaigns, 19
  Giarabub, Libya, 34, 35
  Guadalcanal, 70
  Operation Cutthroat, **115**
  Operation Oboe II, 194
  Operation Postern, 146
  Sanananda campaign, 68, 87, 96
  Tobruk, 39
Chilton, Frederick (BRIG)
  amphibious training, 147, **152**
  command of 18 Brigade, 96, 213, 214, 216
  command of Makassar Force, 216
  Exercise Octopus, 160
  Operation Cutthroat, 118, 119, 123, 126, 128, 129, 130, 135, 209, 215
  Operation Exchequer, 113
  Operation Oboe II, 168, 173, 176, 177, 182, 185, 194, 195, 197, 199, 201, 202
  on Operation Postern, 141
  Operation Seagull, 164, 165, 166, 167
  on photo interpretation training, 134
  on principle of war, 214
  training of reconstructed 18 Brigade, 97, 100, 103, 105
Citizen Military Forces
  age of commanding officers, 7–8
  strength at end of interwar period, 7–9
Clowes, Cyril (MAJGEN), 50–1, 53, 57, 59, 63, 64, 67
Colchester Garrison, Exeter, 30
combat airlifts, 76
combat readiness—18th Brigade
  April 1943, 96
  June 1943, 99
  July 1943, 102, 104

combat readiness—18th Brigade (cont.)
August 1943, 112
combined arms operations
Battle Sananada, 86–9
experience of US regimental combat teams, 75
See also Operation Cutthroat
combined arms support
fire support centres, 208–10
combined operations
definition, 218
Connelly (CAPT), 182
Curtis, Owen, 60, 68, 88

Daly, Thomas (LTCOL), 169
Dobbs, James (LTCOL), 54, 55–6
Doe, Jens (COL), 86, 87
Drake Force, 139–40

Eichelberger, Robert (LTGEN), 71
Buna campaign, 70, 71, 82
combined task forces, 79
command of US Army Corps, 70
cooperation with Australian counterparts, 70
firsthand knowledge of Japanese army, 78
Sananada campaign, 70, 88
Warren Force, 77–8, 81
Exercise Octopus, **162**

field artillery regiments
need for, 21
restructure and consolidation, 18–19
Fields, John (BRIG), 50, 53, 57
Finisterre campaign. See Operation Exchequer; Operation Cutthroat
Flaherty, Howard (CAPT), 186
Fletcher (CPL), **81**
friendly fire, 34, 35, 77, 82, 195, 202

Gallipoli campaign, 23, 156
German Army
5 Light Division, 37
15 Panzer Division, 37
Afrika Korps, 35–7
combined arms manoeuvres, 98
Giarabub, Libya, **35**
Goodenough Island
amphibious landing, 13
raid by Milne Force, 139–40

Grose, John (COL), 77
Guadalcanal, 49, 70

Hale, Tracey (COL), 77
Harding, Edwin (GEN), 27, 72, 76, 77, 78
Hartley, Frank, 88
Helgeson, Andrew (MAJ), 182
Herring, Edmund (GEN), 75, **92**, 145
Holmes, Geoffrey, 71

Imperial Japanese Army
20 Infantry Division, 118
78 Infantry Regiment, 113, 114, 116, 118, 126, 127
454 Infantry Battalion, 184
Nakai Force, 114
Imperial Japanese Navy
10 Pioneer Unit, 51
22 Naval Base Force, 184
Kure 5 Special Naval Landing Force, 51
Sasebo 5 Special Naval Landing Force, 51
infantry battalions
age of commanders, 7
size, 19
Infantry Brigade Group (Jungle)
as assault brigade, 137
command and administration, 22
composition, 21
foundation of, 42
in action. See Operation Cutthroat
organic combat and support units, 22
subordinate battalions, 21
infantry brigade groups, 6
infantry brigades
commanders. See brigade commanders
composition, 2
evolution, 3, 95, 203
in North Africa, 2, 3
intelligence. See Intelligence Sections
number before and during WWII, 203
number within divisions, 4
role in Pacific War, 1–5
staff. See Staff Section
subordinate battalions. See subordinate battalions

tactics. See tactics
training. See training
Intelligence Section—18 Brigade, **109**
  Brigade Intelligence School, 111, 207
  Buna campaign, 121
  capabilities, 91, 108, 208
  Finisterre campaigns, 121
  ground reconnaisance, 121
  Operation Oboe II, 181, 182
  personnel, 108
  photographic interpretation, 92, 111, 134–5, 208
  professionalisation, 108–12
  sources of intelligence, 110
  training, 110, 111, 121
Intelligence Sections, **109**
  capabilities, 64, 91, 207
  cross-brigade integration of functions, 65
  equipment, 65
  ground reconnaisance, 84
  intelligence corporal position, 110
  intelligence sergeant position, 110
  maps, 65, 82
  personnel, 65, 66, 91
  primary functions, 110
  recommendations from Milne Bay operation, 65–6
  roles and responsibilities, 3, 108, 110–11
  size, 207
  supervision, 7, 22
  tasks, 64
Italian Army
  27 Division, 37

Jackson, Oliver (MAJ), 104
Japanese Navy. See Imperial Japanese Navy units
joint operations
  definition, 218
Joint Overseas Operational Training School (JOOTS), Port Stephens, 147
jungle units
  basic principles of implementation, 12
  cavalry capability, 21
  consolidation at division level, 15–26
  development of, 11–12
  elimination of non-essentials, 13–15

firepower, 20
flexibile groupings, 12
personnel, 14–15, 19
transportation support, 14
weapons and equipment, 13–14
jungle warfare
  artillery and armour in, 71
  scope, 104
  tactics, 106–7
  use of artillery and armour, 76, 83
  Weapons and Equipment table, 104
jungle warfare doctrine
  development of, 11
  principles of jungle warfare, 91
jungle warfare training
  Australian Training Centre, Canungra, **105**, 106
  Battle Course, 106
  British officers trained by 18th Brigade, 72
  contributions of 18th Brigade, 98, 104–6, 206
  evolution, 205
  lack of training for 7 Division before deployment, 44
  lack of training for US troops, 78, 86
  motorised regiments, 98
  primacy of individual soldier in, 105
  priorities for, 105–6
  required for all Allied formations, 95
  Section Assault Course, 106
  Sneaker Course, 106

Kappa Kappa Trail, 72
Kelly, Hilary (CAPT), 182
Kenny, George (GEN), 71, 74, 184
Kokoda Track, battle of, 2, 12, 68
Kumnick, Paul (LT), 39

Lae
  amphibious landing. See Operation Postern
  operation to seize. See Operation Exchequer
Lopcombe Corner, Salisbury Plain, 29
Louisiana Maneuvers, 26
Lowen, Ian (MAJ), 147

MacArthur, Douglas (GEN), 49, 70, 71, 72, 77, 83, 114, 141, 146, 175
machine-gun platoons, 15, 18

Markham Valley, 113, 114
Marshall, Alec (MAJ), 138, 182
Marshall, George C. (MAJGEN), 70
Martin, Clarence (COL), 78, 79
mechanised infantry manoeuvre, 30
Milford, Edward (MAJGEN), 114, 175–6, 179, 201
Milne Bay
  geography, 48
Milne Bay, Battle of, 12, 48
  after-action assessment, 60–7
  air support, 64
  artillery use, 62–4
  casualties, 60
  confrontation with Japanese at KB Mission, 53–7
  environmental challenges, 49
  fought without jungle training, 18
  holding the line, 57–60
  importance, 66
  intelligence reports, 50, 53, 57, 64–6
  Japanese landing, 51–3
  object of, 48
Milne Bay Force
  arrival in the region, 49
  orders, 50
  raid on Goodenough Island, 139–40
  strength, 48, 50
Morshead, Leslie (GEN), 30, 31, 37, 39, 114, 119, 170, 175
Mott, John (COL), 77

Nadzab
  airborne operation to seize. See Operation Exchequer
  as US Fifth Air Force's primary base, 114
naval surface gunfire, 4
New Guinea Force, 75
Noble, Albert (ADM), 170, 201
Normanby Island
  amphibious raid on, 137–9
  Exercise Coconut, 143
North Africa
  arrival of 18th Brigade in Egypt, 31
  assault against Italian forces at Giarabub, Libya, 31–5, **32**
  counterassault at Tobruk, 37–41
  infantry manoeuvre, 12

O'Connor Richard (GEN), 32
Operation Cutthroat, 113
  after-action assessment, 128–35
  air and ground reconnaisance, 121–3, 131
  air support, 4, 120, 123–4
  airlift of 18th Infantry Brigade to Wangiela, 115
  ammunition supply problems, 117
  artillery, 130–1
  assault on Shaggy Ridge, 125–8
  assault preparations, 121–5
  attack plan, 118–21
  casualties, **115**, 127, 128
  communications, 129–30
  control of Finisterre battlespace, 116
  intelligence collection, 121–3
  Japanese fortifications, 116, 118
  logistic, 123
  plan, 114
  resources, 129
  surprise as essential tactic, 118, 126, 129
  tactics, 11
  terrain, 118, 119, 125
Operation Exchequer
  first brief, 113
  seizure of Lae, 114
  seizure of Nazdab airfield, 114
Operation Michaelmas, 114
Operation Oboe I, 169, 174–5
Operation Oboe II, 26
  18 Brigade as assault brigade, 22, 173, 176, 202, 211
  18 Brigade plan for, 187, 189
  after-action assessment, 194–6
  air support, 185, 195, 200–2
  ammunition shortage, 168–9
  amphibious landing, 191–4
  amphibious planning, 181–2
  armour, 186, 196–8
  artillery, 198–200
  beach clearing, 187, 190, 198
  casualties, 194
  challenges, 175, 195
  combined arms support, 184
  Distribution of Force to Convoys, 179
  embarkation of 18th Brigade, 167–70

flamethrowers, 186
friendly fire, 195, 201–2
indirect fire, 198–200
initial idea for, 174
intelligence support, 181, 182
Japanese air power, 185
Japanese artillery, 184
Japanese fortifications, 173, 176, 190, 194, 195, 198, 200
Japanese ground force strength, 183
justifications for cancelling, 175
landing at Balikpapan, 173
landing craft, **190**
Landing Craft Tables, 176, 181
landing diagram, **178**
Landing Vehicle Tracked (LVTs), 186, **192**
mine-sweeping operations, 190
Morotai rehearsal, 170–2, 211
naval bombardment, 4
naval gunfire support, 187–9, 194, 195
naval support, 184
operations order, 176, 177, 182–9
plan for, 175–81
pre-landing operations, 189–91
relations with locals, 183
resources, 167, 168
sand-table, 169
wave diagrams, 177, 179
Operation Oboe III, 174
Operation Oboe IV, 174
Operation Oboe V, 174
Operation Oboe VI, 174
Operation Postern, **142**
after-action assessment, 145–7
amphibious assault, 140–5
casualties, 146
naval bombardment, 145
operational art
at battalion level, 166
combined arms teams, 75, 89
cooperation between infantry and tank units, 93–4
during Operation Cutthroat, 129
introduction, 68
rapid staff planning, 73
origins of 18th Brigade, 7–9

Pakenham-Walsh, Ridley (MAJGEN), 128

Parbury, Cecil (CAPT), 104, 182
Peters, Leslie (CAPT), 182
Phillipson, Ernest (MAJ), 182
photographic interpretation, 92, 111
pigeon-handlers, 20
pioneer units, 21, 91
Pollard, Reginald (LTCOL), 88
Pullen, Norman (MAJ), 182

Ramu Valley, 114
Reidy, Robert (CAPT), 34
Rommel, Erwin (FM), 31, 35
Royal Australian Air Force
  1 Squadron, 25
  1 Tactical Air Force, 189
  4 Army Cooperation Squadron, 145
  4 Squadron, 121, 132
  5 Air Support Party, 26
  5 Army Cooperation Squadron, 101, 145
  6 Squadron, 138
  10 Group, 121
  24 Squadron, 121, 132
  75 Squadron, 50, 138
  76 Squadron, 50, 138
  78 Squadron, 121
  pre-landing bombardment, 189

Saidor
  US Army's amphibious landing, 114
Salient, Battle of the, 37–41
Sanananda campaign
  after-action assessment, 90–4
  air support, 92
  armour, **86**
  artillery, 93
  casualties, 68, 87, 95, 96
  conditions, 71, 87
  infantry tactics and manoeuvre, 90–1
  intelligence, 84
  Japanese bunker complexes, 88
  maps, 84, 91
  maritime resupply, 74
  orders, 89–90
  patrolling, 91
  plans for, 84–6
  reconnaisance, 84, 88, 91
  siege warfare, 71
  significance, 86
  tanks, 93–4

Schmedje, Theo (CAPT), 55
Searle (PTE), **81**
Shaggy Ridge
  peaks, 116
Shaggy Ridge, Battle of. See Operation Cutthroat
siege warfare, 71, 78, 98
snipers, 94
South West Pacific Area (SWPA)
  Australian contribution to ground forces, 1–5
  environmental challenges, 22
  losses and failures of leadership, 77
  misunderstanding of modern war in jungle terrain, 84
  US Army regiments, 26–7
Staff Sections
  administration, 22
  chiefs, 22
subordinate battalions
  command and control of, 129
  leadership challenges, 4
  number of, 11
supply lines
  air resupply, 74
  maritime resupply, 74
Suthers, George (MAJ), 182

tactics
  at Buna campaign, 90–1
  evolution of brigade tactics, 4
  jungle warfare, 106–7
  Operation Cutthroat, 11
  at Sananada campaign, 90–1
tanks
  at Battle of the Salient, 37, 39
  cooperation with artillery at brigade level, 68
  integration with infantry, 83, 93–4, 100
  Japanese use of, 54, 55–7, 66, 94
  training on defence against, 42
Tarakan, Borneo
  amphibious assault. See Operation Oboe I
Taylor, Raymond (MAJ), 182
technological advances
  incorporation, 4
Tobruk, Libya
  counterassault, 37–41
  German offensive, 35–7

Tomlinson, Clarence (COL), 77
training
  amphibious warfare. See amphibious warfare training
  basic training, 204
  Battle-Axe exercise, 101–3
  brigade and subordinate unit exercises, 42–4
  brigade schools, 107–8
  Brigade Staff Course, 107–8, 214
  combined arms assaults, 98
  cooperation of infantry with other arms, 42
  defence against Japanese attack, 42–4
  forward observer training, 20, 98
  gas warfare, 98
  infantry brigades, 204–7
  infantry manoeuvres, 98
  jungle warfare. See jungle warfare training
  Junior Leaders Course, 107
  live-fire exercises, 103, 130, 206
  miniature ranging exercise, 99
  Mount Garnett exercise, 100–1
  Photographic Interpretation Course, 111
  Platoon Commanders Course, 107, 206
  at point of mobilisation 1939–41, 18
  prior to deployment 1939–41, 11–12
  prior to deployment to New Guinea, 41–7
  program to rebuild 18th Regiment, 97–104, 205–6
  siege warfare, 98
  tank and infantry cooperation, 100
Tsukamoto, Hatsuo (COL), 87

Urbana Task Force, 71, 77, 78, 88
US Army
  division structure in World War I, 4
  regiment size, 5
  regiments of the SWPA, 26–7
US Army Air Force
  5 Army Air Force, 123, 189
  13 Air Force, 163, 189
  345 Group (Air Apaches), 121
US Army units
  I Corps, 27, 70, 77
  1/126 Battlion, 76, 80, 89, 90

INDEX  271

1/128 Battlion, 76, 80, 83
2 Engineer Special Brigade, 145
3 Portable Field Hospital, 75
3/128 Battalion, 76, 80, 83
3/503 Parachute Infantry Regiment, 100, 101, 102
4 Portable Field Hospital, 75
5 Portable Field Hospital, 75
7 Field Artillery Battalion, 157
17 Portable Field Hospital, 75
18 Infantry Regiment, 157
23 Quartermaster Detachment, 75
23 Portable Field Hospital, 75
32 Infantry Division (National Guard), 26, 27, 72, 74, 75, 76, 77, 78, 80, 82, 90
32 Ordinance Detachment, 75
37 Ordinance Detachment, 75
41 Infantry Division (National Guard), 26, 27, 84
43 Engineer Regiment, Company E, 50, 57
46 Engineer Regiment, 50
96 Engineer Regiment, 57
104 Coastal Artillery Anti-Aircraft Battalion, 50
107 Medical Battalion, Company B, 75
114 Engineer Battalion, Company B, 75
126 Field Artillery Battalion, 75
126 Infantry Regiment, 27, 72, 76, 89, 95, 114
127 Infantry Regiment, 75, 78, 82–3, 88
128 Infantry Regiment, 27, 76–7, 80, 83
163 Infantry Regiment, 84, 87
503 Parachute Infantry Regiment, 114
532 Engineer Boat and Shore Regiment, 145
632 Tank Destroyer Battalion, 75
672 Amphibious Tractor Battalion, 186, 197
709 Airborne Anti-Aircraft Battery, 50, 57

727 Amphibious Tractor Battalion, 186
801 Photo Section, 75
Amphibious Tractor Battalions, 181
US Marine Corps, 149, 156
US Navy
   Fleet Landing Exercises, 156–7
US Navy Advanced Landing Craft School, 147
US Navy units
   7 Amphibious Force, 22, 140, 147, 149, 151, 170, 184

Vasey, George (GEN), 76, 88, **92**, 114, 118, 119, 128

Waldron, Albert (BRIGGEN), 77
Wanigela Airfield, 73
Warrant Officer Class 1 position, 19
Warren Task Force, 71, 78, 79, 80, 81, 83, 93
Wootten Force, 32
Wootten, George (BRIG), **92**
   amphibious landing at Lae, 140, 141, 146
   amphibious raid on Normanby Island, 138
   on artillery use, 56, 59, 63
   assault of Giarabub, 32
   clearance operation at Milne Bay, 59
   command of 9 Division, 96, 140
   command of 18 Brigade, 31, 214
   command of Warren Force, 79, 82, 83, 87
   on cooperation between units, 42
   counter attack at Tobruk, 37, 39, 40
   on reconnaissance, 82
   Sananada campaign, 84, 86, 87, 88, 89
World War II
   Australian Army deployments and service, 1
   demobilisation, 216
   *See also South West Pacific Area (SWPA)*
wounded, **115**
Wynter, Henry (MAJGEN), 31

# OTHER TITLES IN THE AUSTRALIAN ARMY HISTORY SERIES

Series editor: Peter Stanley

Phillip Bradley *The Battle for Wau: New Guinea's Front Line 1942–1943*
Mark Johnston *The Proud 6th: An Illustrated History of the 6th Australian Division 1939–1946*
Garth Pratten *Australian Battalion Commanders in the Second World War*
Jean Bou *Light Horse: A History of Australia's Mounted Arm*
Phillip Bradley *To Salamaua*
Peter Dean *The Architect of Victory: The Military Career of Lieutenant-General Sir Frank Horton Berryman*
Allan Converse *Armies of Empire: The 9th Australian and 50th British Divisions in Battle 1939–1945*
John Connor *Anzac and Empire: George Foster Pearce and the Foundations of Australian Defence*
Peter Williams *The Kokoda Campaign 1942: Myth and Reality*
Karl James *The Hard Slog: Australians in the Bougainville Campaign, 1944–45*
Robert Stevenson *To Win the Battle: The 1st Australian Division in the Great War, 1914–1918*
Jeffrey Grey *A Soldier's Soldier: A Biography of Lieutenant-General Sir Thomas Daly*
Mark Johnston *Anzacs in the Middle East: Australian Soldiers, Their Allies and the Local People in World War II*
Mark Johnston *Stretcher-bearers: Saving Australians from Gallipoli to Kokoda*
Christopher Wray *Pozières: Echoes of a Distant Battle*
Craig Stockings *Britannia's Shield: Lieutenant-General Sir Edward Hutton and Late-Victorian Imperial Defence*
Andrew Ross, Robert Hall and Amy Griffin *The Search for Tactical Success in Vietnam: An Analysis of Australian Task Force Combat Operations*
William Westerman *Soldiers and Gentlemen: Australian Battalion Commanders in the Great War, 1914–1918*
Thomas Richardson *Destroy and Build: Pacification in Phuoc Tuy, 1966–72*
Tristan Moss *Guarding the Periphery: The Australian Army in Papua New Guinea, 1951–75*
Kate Ariotti *Captive Anzacs: Australian POWs of the Ottomans during the First World War*
Margaret Hutchison *Painting War: A History of Australia's First World War Art Scheme*
Romain Fathi *Our Corner of the Somme: Australia at Villers-Bretonneux*
Aaron Pegram *Surviving the Great War: Australian Prisoners of War on the Western Front, 1916–18*
Alexia Moncrieff *Expertise, Authority and Control: The Australian Army Medical Corps in the First World War*
David Horner *Strategy and Command: Issues in Australia's Twentieth-century Wars*

For EU product safety concerns, contact us at Calle de José Abascal, 56–1º,
28003 Madrid, Spain or eugpsr@cambridge.org.

www.ingramcontent.com/pod-product-compliance
Lightning Source LLC
LaVergne TN
LVHW011007250326
834688LV00004B/125